THE POETRY OF CONSERVATISM

The Poetry of Conservatism

1600-1745

A Study of Poets and Public Affairs from Jonson to Pope

ISABEL RIVERS

RESEARCH FELLOW OF GIRTON COLLEGE, CAMBRIDGE

RIVERS PRESS · CAMBRIDGE

First published in 1973 by Rivers Press Ltd
235 Chesterton Road, Cambridge

© 1973 by Isabel Rivers

Set, printed and bound in Great Britain by
the University Printing House, Cambridge

217473

Contents

Preface

An earlier version of this book was written as a doctoral dissertation in the Department of English and Comparative Literature, Columbia University, New York. I would like to express my gratitude to Columbia and to the Woodrow Wilson National Fellowship Foundation, Princeton for financial support while I was working on it, and to the Mistress and Fellows of Girton College, Cambridge for electing me to the Research Fellowship that enabled me to revise and expand it. I would also like to thank those of my teachers and colleagues who have encouraged my work. Professors Jeffrey Ford, J. A. Mazzeo, Edward W. Tayler and Howard H. Schless of Columbia gave valuable criticism and advice in the early stages. Professor J. B. Broadbent of East Anglia provided me with the opportunity to devote time to Milton, and Lady Radzinowicz of Girton offered helpful comments on the Milton section. My husband has provided much-needed editorial assistance. The book's shortcomings are my responsibility.

I owe a more general debt to previous studies of literature and its historical context in the seventeenth and early eighteenth centuries. In particular I would like to mention the following authors, whose work, even where I have disagreed with it, I have found provocative and stimulating: Warren L. Chernaik, L. C. Knights, G. de F. Lord, Maynard Mack, Ruth Nevo, John Wallace, and Earl R. Wasserman.

In quoting from sixteenth-, seventeenth-, and early eighteenth-century material I have used where possible standard twentieth-century editions, but throughout I have modernised the spelling and expanded abbreviations, though I have retained the original punctuation. Dates given are old style, but with the year beginning on January 1 not March 25. The first reference to a work given in a note is a full one; subsequent references are shortened.

ISABEL RIVERS

Cambridge 1972

Introduction

This is a study of public poetry, its context, its intentions, its uses, and its limitations. Some explanation and definition are called for. By public poetry I mean poetry written with reference to the public world of order, government, and political events. There is a dynamic relation between such poetry and the public world; the poems are a product of particular social conditions and expectations, but they exist to influence the course of political events, to mould society according to their own pattern; they attempt both to reflect the world and to shape it. Their function is to recreate society, but it is also to create an imaginative world of order in opposition to the actual fragmentation of society. The synthesis of the poem is a reflection of the poet's view of society, or of society as it might be; it is also a myth that satisfies the craving for order as the existing world does not. The question of how to read such poetry is a difficult one. To attempt to extract a political or social philosophy from a body of poetry (even though such a philosophy may be explicit) is to give the poetry the wrong kind of emphasis, to narrow it into a document or a manifesto, to judge it by the wrong criteria. But to read a public poem as an artifact divorced from the conditions and the society which produced it and to which it is directed is to ignore its important intentions and functions, to misdirect and limit its potential meaning.

In reading public poetry one must face the question of the relation of the poem to society and to the poet. If one reads the poem as an autonomous object then the question of the relation of the poem to the poet and his attitudes, its place in his career, is irrelevant. But with public poetry which sets out to record, confront, and influence the external world, one must ask what the structure of society was, where the poet stood in the world of politics, what kinds of language and social definition were open to him, in what way social change affected his position and his poetic response to society. Poems which assert a social synthesis deserve to be tested against historical events; one cannot fully understand the nature of poetic order without relating it to political flux and the career of the poet who derived the one from the other.

The phrase 'poetry of conservatism' also needs some explanation.

This study covers the careers of five public poets, which span almost a hundred and fifty years from the end of the sixteenth century to the middle of the eighteenth. Three of them, Jonson, Dryden, and Pope, I have described as conservative poets; Milton and Marvell in different ways stand in opposition to them, both in their political beliefs and in their poetic techniques. 'Conservatism' is a term currently used with varying degrees of consistency to describe political parties and social attitudes mainly in England and America. By using 'conservatism' to describe the position of certain poets in seventeenth- and early eighteenth-century England I refer to a belief in a divinely-ordained, hierarchical society, in which the place of the individual is determined by mutual obligation and dependence. The social conditions in which the values of this kind of conservatism find their best expression are rural communities in which the relations between men are not simply economic but personal and moral as well. Trade and finance, insofar as they suppose competition not cooperation between men, and insofar as their motive is private profit not public good, are inimical to conservative values, but where they are seen to enrich the nation and increase its power they are included in the framework of the good society. The nation, a federation of rural communities in which individuals have their roots, is united under a monarch who exemplifies both moral virtue and the unity of his kingdom, and whose relation with his subjects is personal and benevolent. The court and the capital city in which the court is located are the centre of public life and establish moral and artistic standards; their wealth and magnificence symbolise the nation's greatness. The place of the poet, though he understands the dependent relationship of court and country and the importance of rural virtues, is at court; he is supported by king and government, and in return he supports them through his poetic realisation and defence of the good society.

Though this scheme is deliberately over-simplified, and not all parts of it always receive equal emphasis, it may be said to underlie and often to be explicit in the work of Jonson, Dryden, and Pope. There is a problem for the reader in trying to extrapolate a coherent system from poems written at different times and in reaction to different situations; it will be apparent that not all parts of the system are equally relevant, and that some of them conflict. The attempt to weld them into a coherent whole may involve the poet in some contradictions and falsifications. But the essential aim of conservative poetry can be said to be the creation of an image of public order, which is seen to have a direct relevance to the state of contemporary society, both mirroring and controlling it.

The difficulty for the conservative poet who saw his function in public and political terms was that this set of attitudes became increasingly irrelevant in the face of social and political developments. During this period the relations of the governing classes were in a constant process of conflict and realignment; by the middle of the eighteenth century an equilibrium which satisfied the majority of the people who mattered (in an eighteenth-century sense) had been achieved. But the society which emerged from over a century of discord was very different from the one that some of the participants would have wished for. The obvious landmarks of this process of struggle and transformation are the civil war, the execution of one king, the exile of another, the end of the Stuart regime and the accession of the Hanoverians. But more important than these dynastic changes and constitutional upheavals were the prolonged and permanent ways in which society as a whole was transformed. The scale of life altered: a predominantly rural and localised society evolved into an increasingly urbanised nation dependent on maritime trade (this change was symbolised by the growth of London, which contemporaries regarded either with horror or pride depending on their social preconceptions); the small court world theoretically centring on a glorified but approachable monarch like Elizabeth, maintaining a careful relationship with the nobility and gentry, gave way to the more impersonal executive developed by Walpole, in which the idea of a paternal monarch ruling over loving and trusting subjects played no part. These changes were not necessarily violent, and in some respects English life remained the same. From 1688 on, surface stability was assured by the oligarchic rule of the great landowning families. But as economic and bureaucratic relations changed, some of the social philosophies supporting them changed as well. One result was that a poet like Pope with an essentially traditional view of society found himself excluded from the political arena and obliged to fall back on an anti-social position, which to some extent undermined his view of the good society and the poet's function in it.

To emphasise the social changes that took place and the way they influenced the position of conservative poets who looked back to a different past is not to imply that this past as it was imagined was anything other than an ideal. The problem of the relation of art to life, of the ideal to the actual, was as acute for the Renaissance poet as it was for the eighteenth-century poet who took the England of Elizabeth or the Rome of Augustus as a model. However, one should distinguish between those difficulties that arise for the poet when there is a discrepancy between a public myth and society's actual way of life, and those that arise when the myth itself is no longer appropriate to the society at large. While one cannot say that the conservative ideal ever existed, in the earlier part of the period under discussion it had a wide appeal. It seems fair to say that the majority of men accepted the ideas, promulgated by the Church and the government, of hierarchy, the moral responsibility entailed in economic and social relationships, the benevolent paternalism of monarchy, even if they paid small attention to them in practice. But during this period the enormous changes in the country's life that I have mentioned meant that the connection between the conservative ideal and the actual structure of society became much more tenuous. The familial and corporeal image of society, the sentimentalisation of rural life, the idealisation of court and monarch as a moral focus, these ceased to be viable myths in a world of party conflict, mercantilism, increasing urbanisation. Ideas of social harmony certainly persisted in the eighteenth century, but they were expressed in mechanical or physical rather than organic terms.

The tension between the old view of society and the new tendencies had various dispiriting effects on conservative poets. If an imaginative synthesis is the product of a mind which is always able to see a purpose or pattern underlying events, then the transformation of the immediate external world will not threaten it; no matter how the sublunary world is disrupted, a poet like Spenser remains confident of the unchanging form or the fixed eternity behind the visible mutability. But for poets like Jonson or Pope the discrepancy between their imaginative apprehension of order and their awareness of social change is of acute significance. Their difficulty lies in their inability to mediate between their poetic image and the actual state of the world. Hence we can deduce the other side of conservatism. An ideal which is set forward as a viable model against which to measure and remould existing society becomes in a hostile climate a weapon of satire or a retreat into nostalgia. If society excludes the conservative poet from its political workings then he must find a new position for himself. There are various possibilities to pursue: the Stoic self-reliance or self-discovery of Jonson and Pope, the self-indulgent escapism of much seventeenth-century retirement poetry, or the compromise with day-to-day politics of Dryden's propagandist period.

But conservative poetry, though it is the dominant mode of public poetry in the seventeenth and early eighteenth centuries, is not the only one. The conservative view of society was challenged twice in this period: in the 1640s and 1650s by radical Puritanism, which, in spite of the social and intellectual upheavals it caused, was largely suppressed; and at the end of the century by the beginnings of Whig liberalism, which was to become the prevailing mode of social thought in eighteenth- and nineteenth-century England. Both these sets of attitudes, though they differ in many ways, assume as their model for society not hierarchy and order but motion and change. On the whole these assumptions were not taken into poetry until the end of the eighteenth century. The exceptions in our period are Milton, who understood the inconsistencies in conservative poetry, was totally opposed to the conservative view of society, and developed an alternative poetic of change; and Marvell, who appreciated the psychological appeal of the conservative image of order and applied it pragmatically to changing political circumstances. My object in writing about Milton and Marvell is to define more clearly the assumptions and limitations of conservative poetry; I have therefore given less space to their work and its intellectual background than to that of Jonson, Dryden, and Pope. The questions I have asked with regard to each poet are what his views of society were, how he thought it to be changing, and in what way these changes affected his social attitudes and the possibilities for his position as a public poet.

Chapter 1

Public poetry and its context

IDEAS OF ORDER

Synthetic views of human society and of man's place in the universe are as old as recorded thought, their appeal to the mind is obvious and their uses are many. The Renaissance world inherited and reworked a large and loosely-connected amalgam of classical and Christian treatments of the problems of evil, sin, flux, change, decay. One solution to these problems is a world-view so comprehensive that conflict is theoretically eliminated through its inclusion in a larger unity. Concepts like those of degree, the chain of being, harmony through discord, or correspondence, provide a means of ordering the external world intellectually and socially without ignoring the visible fragmentation and change which might seem to belie that order. But the assumption of the easy acceptance of such a synthesis by Renaissance minds has perhaps been too readily propagated in this century.[1] While one can admit the aesthetic appeal and the psychological usefulness of a scheme encompassing nature, society, man, and God, one should pay some attention to the viability of the scheme in terms of the society for which it was formulated. The relation of ideology to society is a problem of the chicken and egg variety; it is too simple to see a theory of order and hierarchy merely as a rationalisation of social structure, just as it is too simple to assume that because moralistic views of human relations prevailed, these views were necessarily carried into action or the society was necessarily a good one. It is interesting to know not only what ideas and systems men have formulated to deal with existence, but also the interaction of these ideas with the external world, the uses to which they have been put, the way in which they reflect or are modified by or distort external conditions.

One can study ideas or systems of thought for themselves, for their intrinsic value. And one can study them in their context, investigate their origins, their influence, and the uses men have made of them. When one is dealing with ideas in poetry the question is complicated further. Analysis always distorts a poem. On the one hand a poem is a self-contained consistent fiction with its own rules; on the other hand this fiction is a picture of the world. A poem is already a synthesis of experience; ambivalences or contradictions in ideas can be said to be to some extent resolved by their part in the structure of a poem. But it is questionable whether a poem which sets out deliberately to create a universal synthesis, an interpretation of the world, should be read only in its own terms, even if it were possible for the reader to hold his views and his sense of society and historical connections in abeyance. Post-romantic views of the poem as a sacred object, something inviolable, immutable, and distinct from the shapelessness of experience, are unjust to and limit the potential meaning of poems written under the influence of a different view of the relation of art to life. In neo-classical theory the poem is an imitation, it reflects an objective order. It is worth paying attention to what poets of the Renaissance and post-Renaissance period who worked within this tradition thought that they were doing. For these poets the poem is at the same time a finished object resistant to change and time, an imitation of a universal order which change cannot undermine but in which it has a place, and a pattern of order for society to imitate. To give the fullest reading of this kind of poem one should take account of the poet's preoccupations and his intended effects; and one should look critically at the society for which the poet is writing to see how far his view of the relation between the poem and the world is viable. The questions lying behind this attempted reading, which the following chapters will partly try to answer, are what kinds of uses public poetry has, and what kinds of poetry are possible in a given historical context.

The Renaissance world-view, the idea of hierarchy, embraces all aspects of human life in a universal pattern; Hooker's is perhaps the most convenient formulation, because it is expository. In this divine, natural, and human order the proper functioning of each part and the importance of its relation to the whole are emphasised:

> See we not plainly that obedience of creatures unto the law of nature is the stay of the whole world?...For we see the whole world and each part thereof so compacted, that as long as each thing performeth only that work which is natural unto it, it thereby preserveth both other things and also itself. Contrariwise, let any principal thing, as the sun, the moon, any one of the heavens or elements, but once cease or fail, or swerve, and who doth not easily conceive that the sequel thereof would be ruin both to itself and whatsoever dependeth on it?[2]

Though Hooker has much to say about society and the origin of government, his theory is primarily metaphysical; man may be the noblest part of creation but human law is a subordinate part of a much larger scheme. From the theological perspective, specifically human order is

2

not of supreme importance. Hooker's tendency is to seek out the function, the purpose, the part played in the pattern by each object as it is.

It is easy to see the social and political importance of this kind of view, which elevates existing social gradations and differences into an embodiment of absolute order. From this it is an easy step to see the idea of hierarchy as a rationalisation and justification of the status quo, as propaganda. But to see political theory or synthetic views of society as a rationalisation or concealment of 'real' political aims or underlying structure in the interest of particular groups is not to see very much. Undoubtedly power strengthens itself by myths, and undoubtedly the myths of Tudor England were more appropriate to that society than to others with different political structures. One can properly study ideas in themselves without on the one hand regarding them as self-contained systems free of any context, or on the other hand limiting them as rationalisations of particular social conditions or propaganda on behalf of particular interests. Ideas may be as much the product of other ideas as they are of their social matrix; events follow on ideas as much as the other way round, and ideas often persist in contexts in which they seem irrelevant. In spite of the effort of some modern historians to find the 'real' reasons underlying the civil war, one must recognise that contemporaries thought they were fighting for ideas. There is a delicate problem in dealing with ideas of the past which have lost much of their relevance; one must try to get behind them but one must not demolish them.

These remarks are intended as an introduction to the problem of reading poets committed to a view of public order and to a part in the perpetuation of that order. Here I want only to indicate what was believed to be involved in the role of a public poet in social terms. Various elements made up the idea of the Renaissance poet, but perhaps the most important here is the humanist development of the view (which is ultimately Roman) of the pragmatic use of learning, of the place of the man of letters as counsellor to his prince. This view of the poet's moral function of moulding a ruler underlies attitudes to the writing of poetry at least until Pope though, as we shall see, the theory becomes increasingly remote from political realities. The best known statement of this educational view is probably Spenser's claim in the letter to Raleigh that the end of *The Faerie Queene* was 'to fashion a gentleman or noble person in virtuous and gentle discipline'.[3] Though humanists like More and Erasmus and poets like Sidney or Spenser were well aware that the process was not easy, nevertheless the view of government implied is a simple one. It is the prince (and, by extension, the ruling classes) who shape their country through their actions and their moral example. It is the task of the counsellor and the poet to educate the prince, to inculcate the moral values which will thus permeate society, in

3

the case of the counsellor by advice and government service, in the case of the poet by the more indirect but more striking method of idealised fiction which provides the prince with a pattern for imitation. The prince's immediate entourage, the court, becomes a moral centre, the source of national standards, as well as the seat of executive government; the place of the counsellor and poet is in the court world, forming the just prince and the just society.

According to this simplified scheme, the Renaissance poet and his successors see their function as the creation of images of society which both mirror the fundamental order beneath social flux and provide a pattern by which society can be shaped; the desire to implement this pattern involves the poet in the task of educating the ruler. In the rest of this chapter I shall consider the ways in which the image is complicated by events, and the resulting contradictions and ambivalences that the image must absorb if it is not to break down completely. If the poet writes of and for society, and society does not correspond to his idea, then his own view of his position will be affected as will the kinds of poem that he is able to write.

COURT AND COUNTRY

To the majority of poets writing in the period under discussion such a formulation of the use of poetry in providing an image of social cohesion might have seemed satisfactory, but the period itself, at least until about 1720, is above all one of social disruption, of violent uncertainty about the forms society, especially on a political level, should take. What is the relation between poetic image and social reality in this case? Are poems like Jonson's 'To Penshurst', Davenant's *Salmacida Spolia*, Denham's *Cooper's Hill*, or Pope's *Windsor Forest*, all of which eliminate potential conflict through the assertion of social harmony, hopeful but deceptive fictions? In what way can they be said to mirror the reality of seventeenth- and early eighteenth-century England? It is obviously not possible to answer these questions finally, nor to give in a few pages an adequate summary of the history of the period which would provide a means to answering them. Here I intend to examine briefly some aspects of the relations between court and country, a crucial factor in this period, and some of the meanings implied in these terms. Such an examination should lead to a greater understanding of the problems facing poets who were to a large extent concerned with defining and uniting these ideas, and of the apparently contradictory paths they might take as poets when events proved that unity to be illusory.

An ideal view of social relations or political structure may put the best interpretation on existing society, may point to the perfect operation

4

of clumsily working parts; it may also serve to conceal actual tendencies in political relations, the essential conflict between the parts. Thus the idea of a balanced constitution, of a mixed monarchy of king-in-parliament, which persisted throughout the seventeenth century, did reflect the fact that power was shared. Yet it also concealed through an image of harmony the essential struggle for power between crown and parliament that went on throughout the century and that ended probably by 1688, certainly by the early eighteenth century, with the victory of parliament. Similarly the ideal view of the relations between court and country, central and local government, king and people, as mutually supporting components of the national body, is belied in the early seventeenth century by the growing split between court and country, the disparity in religion, policy, morals, and taste, that contributed to the civil war.[4]

The monarchy as politically and symbolically strengthened by the Tudors nevertheless still suffered from weaknesses, which were aggravated under the early Stuarts. Unlike the strong centralised monarchy that evolved in France in the seventeenth century, the English monarchy did not have complete control of local government, of an army, of the system of distribution of offices. For local administration and the implementation of legislation the monarchy depended on the country gentry who constituted the Justices of the Peace. Influence could be brought to bear from above, for example in Star Chamber, or by dismissing the justice from the Commission, but the justices, natives of the counties they administered, were a powerful force who at times thought of themselves as representatives of their localities against the court. The central government's ultimate lack of control can be gathered from Cromwell's unsuccessful experiment with county rule by major-generals, and from the disastrous effects of James II's interference with the Commission of the Peace.[5] An alliance between country gentry and the crown, not simply in parliament but also in local government, was essential if political harmony among the ruling classes and social order at all levels were to be maintained. In the early seventeenth century the crown feared the possible disintegration of local government, resulting partly from its own policies. Elizabeth had kept her nobility at court to keep them out of mischief. In the early seventeenth century the court and the city swelled to unmanageable proportions as flocks of place-seekers descended on London. James I, who made no serious effort to get at the root of this problem, his and Buckingham's extravagance and the multiplication of offices by sale,[6] nevertheless was aware that the problem existed. Both James and Charles made a large number of ineffectual proclamations directed against the building of houses and the residence of the nobility and gentry in the capital. The object of these proclamations was to curb the growth of London and above all to prevent disorder and mobility in the country by ensuring that the justices carried out their

5

work and that the gentry provided employment and hospitality for the poor. The gentry had vital work to do in their localities and they should not be allowed to become expensive parasites.[7]

The proclamations themselves give a clear indication of the ideal view of social hierarchy under benevolent monarchy. In a speech in Star Chamber in 1616 covering a large range of his grievances James recited the frequently-made objections to the disproportionate growth of London and passionately urged the gentry to live in the country:

> Let us in God's name leave these idle foreign toys, and keep the old fashion of England: For it was wont to be the honour and reputation of the English nobility and gentry, to live in the country, and keep hospitality.

The theory of society James puts forward is that each individual has his particular place and function in the social framework, from which he must not deviate:

> Therefore as every fish lives in his own place, some in the fresh, some in the salt, some in the mud: so let everyone live in his own place, some at court, some in the city, some in the country.[8]

A proclamation of 1632 made by Charles, who was anxious to repair his father's errors and hence tried to ensure the enforcement of this proclamation by prosecuting the nobility and gentry who ignored it,[9] gives perhaps the best summary of the social and moral attitudes at stake, the reliance on 'ancient usage', the view of social relations as benevolent. The proclamation contrasts the ideal of a socially useful nobility and gentry with their current parasitical status, which upsets the proper interaction of the mutually dependent classes in the nation:

> For where[as] by their residence and abiding in the several counties where their means ariseth, they served the king in several places according to their degree and ranks, in aid of the government, whereby, and by their housekeeping in those parts, the realm was defended and the meaner sort of people were guided, directed and relieved; but by their residence in the said cities...they have not employment, but live without doing any service to his Majesty or his people, a great part of their money and substance is drawn from the several counties whence it ariseth, and is spent in the city...even to the wasting of their estates, which is not issued into the parts whence it ariseth, nor are the people of them relieved therewith or by their hospitality, nor yet set on work, as they might and would be were it not for the absence of the principal men out of their counties.[10]

An interesting poetic reinforcement and interpretation of an earlier proclamation is to be found in Sir Richard Fanshawe's 'An Ode, upon

6

occasion of his Majesty's Proclamation in the Year 1630. Commanding the Gentry to reside upon their Estates in the Country.'[11] Fanshawe takes an idealistic view of Stuart policy. England's neutrality in the Thirty Years' War (a source of much shame to Puritan opponents of the crown) makes it a perfect island of peace and good government in the middle of war and discord; country life is the source of moral virtue and contentment. Both individuals and the nation are in harmony through their retirement from unnecessary conflict.

If one were to rely solely on proclamations and poems of the kind cited as evidence of Stuart intentions, one might well conclude that the Stuarts envisaged a benevolent, unified social hierarchy in which king, nobility, and gentry played their appropriate parts in their separate but mutually supporting spheres of court and country, and that it was only the selfish recalcitrance of the gentry that prevented the harmonious realisation of this unity. But these proclamations and the policy of forcing the gentry to fulfil their local functions are in fact evidence of a belated recognition by the crown of its dangerous encouragement of the gentry's parasitic characteristics, though chiefly they reveal the essential contradictions in the crown's attitudes to the relations between court and country. James I disliked London a good deal, and preferred to spend his time in a few favoured country houses (though in fact his rural activities were extremely lavish and wasteful); Charles I, a sober and religious man, disliked the parasitic court that had grown up round his father and Buckingham, and tried to cut down the opportunities for place-holding at court; both kings were aware of the economic dangers of a top-heavy court and city. But prevailing attitudes to kingship and the role of a court, which both kings shared, necessitated that ostentatious extravagance which ultimately undermined the function of the court in its relation to the country as a whole. The king and court must be conspicuous, even if, as James theorised in *Basilikon Doron*, they were to be conspicuous as moral examples. This was the great era of competitive magnificence, when nobles vied with nobles and princes with princes in the deliberately wasteful ostentation of dress, court ceremonial such as the masque, and building.[12] Ideally the court was to be the political and moral guide of society as a whole; expenditure on ostentation was intended to symbolise and underline these roles. In practice, however, this ostentation bled the country and had the unwanted effect of alienating country from court and destroying courtly pretensions. As a modern historian says, their vast expenditure on masques for a limited audience may have been thought magnanimous, but James and Charles 'paid for that magnanimity with the nation'.[13] Court magnificence, though theoretically essential, might be self-defeating in practice.

James's and Charles's attempts at palace-building in the 1620s and 30s illustrate the process of alienation.[14] In 1619 the Whitehall banqueting house, itself a replacement, burned down; in 1619–22 the new banqueting house was built to Inigo Jones's Palladian design. This expensive work was completed at a time of financial crisis, but it was not Jones's only project; he also built the Queen's Chapel at St James's (1623–5), intended originally for the Spanish Infanta but in fact provided for Henrietta Maria, began work on the restoration of St Paul's (a project dear to Laud), and finished the Queen's House at Greenwich in 1635 (begun in 1616) also for Henrietta Maria. All this architectural activity was obviously of immense importance in court circles, but it aroused nothing but hostility in the country. The proposed Spanish match for Prince Charles was regarded with suspicion by the nation; but it has been suggested that the vast expenditure on magnificent building in the 1620s when it could ill be afforded can only be understood in terms of James's hope of the fulfilment of the Spanish match.[15] James's ambitions were dynastic rather than national; he saw himself as an international peacemaker through dynastic alliance with the old enemy Spain, while national sentiment favoured joining the alliance of militant Protestantism in Germany. The royal buildings symbolised not national unity but the divergent ambitions of court and country.

There is some disputed evidence that during the late 1630s Charles intended to rebuild the whole palace of Whitehall to a design by Jones.[16] The scheme to rebuild St Paul's was no more successful. James proposed the rebuilding of the cathedral at the same time as the banqueting house, but there was not enough money. In 1631 Laud revived the idea, but he had difficulty in extorting subscriptions, and the work went on slowly until it finally stopped in 1642.[17] In a sermon of 1621 Laud depicted James, because of these civic and religious enterprises, as Solomon building a new Jerusalem;[18] but to some contemporaries it must have seemed that he was building a new Babylon.

These were by no means the last dreams of a glorious metropolis; the great fire of 1666 gave opportunity for rebuilding on an enormous scale, and hopes for a new Whitehall were alive in Anne's reign. The idea of public works as symbols of national greatness is found in Dryden's *Annus Mirabilis*, Pope's *Windsor Forest*, and much Whig writing of the eighteenth century, including Defoe's *Tour through England and Wales*, though the analogy is more often that of Rome than Jerusalem. In the second half of the seventeenth century a magnificent example close at hand was Louis XIV's Versailles, which spurred princes to imitation; it was considered a triumph for William of Orange that while Louis was obliged to suspend work on Versailles because of war expenses, his enemy was able to continue embellishing his Dutch estate at Loo.[19] Such competitive magnificence was not always self-defeating; Versailles served a vital political function.[20] But attitudes to such symbolic ostentation are often ambivalent; pride in national prosperity coexists with attacks on luxury and waste. Ideally the magnificent metropolis or court represents the summit of national achievement, it is a unifying symbol of political greatness and national wealth; in practice such ostentation is often seen as a drain on the nation's resources, and the court as an excrescence with no vital part in the national life. Throughout the seventeenth and early eighteenth centuries pride in London's wealth and splendour coexisted with fear that it was a morbid growth parasitic on the country.

James I and Charles I were aware of the dangers, they respected the national ideal, but they fell into the trap. The court culture of Charles I, with its French Catholic queen, its Laudian divines, its Palladian architecture (which had few imitations outside London until Burlington's revival), its elaborate masques, must have seemed impossibly alien to the country as a whole.[21] Charles II's court suffered from the same kind of isolation; its association with French fashions in government, religion, and manners in no way endeared it to the country. But to see court poets as involved in a deliberate ritual of self-deception[22] is to ignore the complexities involved in the very idea of a court, and the problems facing poets attempting to create an idealised synthesis of conflicting and contradictory materials. The court, the king's entourage, the summit of the hierarchical pyramid, must be a conspicuous object of admiration; but this view presupposes that the country as a whole is in agreement as to what are worthy objects. If court and country are in conflict over basic issues of government, policy, constitutional and religious belief, then the ostentatious court becomes a symbol only of division.

A further example of the complex relations existing between court and country in the period under discussion can be given through a brief examination of the development of the idea of the country and of country attitudes in the late seventeenth and early eighteenth centuries. Some of this material will be discussed and documented in more detail in relevant chapters; this section will give an indication of some of the problems involved.

'Court' and 'country' as used in a political rather than a regional or symbolic sense came to have the meaning, particularly when applied to members of parliament, of government and opposition, members tied to government by electoral influence or place, and independent members truly representing their localities; 'country' in this sense can be a large heterogeneous coalition, as were the opposition groups that confronted Charles I, Charles II, or Walpole, much of which came from the city. The use of 'country' and 'court' as notations for political divisions was much complicated in the late seventeenth and early eighteenth centuries by the party divisions of Whig and Tory, which often cut across the older terminology. 'Country' will be used here not so much to designate the larger cluster of groups opposing the government at any given period

9

as to cover the attitudes of the country gentry, usually a vital component of any country party, who both defended and opposed Charles I, who opposed Charles II and his court at the beginning of his reign and some of whom joined the Exclusion movement, but who largely rallied to his defence against the threat of renewed civil war, who turned against James II when he interfered too far with their local power, and who under William, Anne, and the first two Georges formed the bulk and prop of the Tory party.[23]

The cluster of country or Tory attitudes which crystallised at about the turn of the century is important here in that it reflects both a general paradox of conservatism and the specific problems facing writers like Pope or Swift who attempted to create idealised political or poetic images of national unity out of an essentially isolated and one-sided position. Since conservatives generally tend to resist change and to regard advocates of change as unrepresentative of the society as a whole, their interpretation of society at historical moments when change is the rule rather than the exception is bound to be inaccurate. Their claim to represent the whole nation and to adhere to principles validly reflecting the existing social order, which is supposedly being undermined by a few dissidents, must make them appear as they see their opponents, selfish defenders of a limited interest.

The image of England as a rural society led by landowners, the most politically significant class, remained, with large qualifications, true well into the nineteenth century. But the extreme presentation of this view, of a self-sufficient economy in which trade was a peripheral activity, was false throughout the seventeenth century. The landowning interest was much wider than it was understood to be by the country gentry who felt their social status to be undermined by the growing importance of trade and finance at the end of the century. The Tory position which evolved in reaction to a complex combination of political and social events and changes, such as the Revolution of 1688, the establishment of the Bank of England, the War of the Spanish Succession, the accession of the Hanoverians, was a mixture of old country attitudes, involving hostility to the court, to central government, patronage, wicked advisers, corruption, with attitudes peculiar to the landed interest at this particular time, hostility to traders, dissenters, financiers, Whigs, and continental involvement (from which these were seen to be profiting). In one sense it was an accident, the change of dynasty, that put the Tories permanently into opposition after the death of Anne, in another their attitudes were inevitably those of the reactionary fringe. The political changes reinforced their nostalgic ideas, and made their interpretations of society steadily more irrelevant.

The Tory ideology as a whole thus consisted of two conflicting sets of attitudes, associated respectively with country and court. Bolingbroke's ideal of the independence and integrity of the country gentleman refusing to be ensnared by the tentacles of court influence has Whig and parliamentarian ancestors; it is essentially an opposition view. But at the same time the court, in idea, not as Walpole was seen to have degraded it, was of supreme importance to Bolingbroke; it was the Renaissance ideal, now hopelessly irrelevant, that he wished to revive, with Elizabeth as model. By Walpole's time the court was a prosaic but efficient machine of executive government; the monarchy was no longer regarded with the old veneration, an inevitable development in circumstances where kings succeeded by invitation or act of parliament. These changes found their ironic reflection in Tory attitudes; the Jacobites among them revered king and court as strongly as ever, but it was an anti-king and an anti-court. Though Bolingbroke came to repudiate Jacobitism his solution was of the same kind. The Tories, in their incorporation of the attitudes of opposition, reflected realistically the changes in social views that had taken place, but in their attempt to define society according to their partisan interpretation of events were hopelessly inaccurate. The paradox of their position is that though partly recognising and fearing that they had been pushed to the fringe of society they nevertheless tried to define society as a whole in terms of this fringe.

In theory the multiple interests that compose the nation are reconciled and find mutual support under the unifying figure of the monarch; in practice much of the history of this period can be seen in terms of the realignment and redefinitions of court and country as competing or conflicting interests. This tension is reflected in the literature; poets who tried to unite the two in an image of social harmony were nevertheless often straddling a gulf between opposing interests and concepts. Adherence either to the court ethos of magnificence or the country ethos of retirement and independence must, given the political antagonism between these sets of attitudes, diminish the possibility for the creation of a poetic unity which has more than an imaginary relation to reality.

POETIC TORYISM

The implications and uses of poetic images of the good society vary largely according to the extent to which the idealisation is seen to be actually realisable or the poet feels his relation to society to be useful or antagonistic. Such a poetic image can be used as an optimistic celebration of existing society, or as a means of achieving its imminent transformation, or as a weapon of unrealisable perfection against an unreformable world; it may imply political conviction, a sense of useful public function, optimism about future social improvement, naive idealisation of the primitive, nostalgia for the past, irresponsible escapism, emphasis on self at the expense of society, or a combination of these. The problem the public poet always faces, whatever his political presuppositions, is the relation between his image of the good society, his sense of the disorder in existing society, and his attempt to mediate between the two. The kinds of emphasis that the image will have depend on the poet's sense of the distance between his ideal order and the actual disorder.

The simplified model of the conservative good society given in the introduction can be seen to contain inconsistencies and to be open to different kinds of emphasis and use. Basically one can say that the conflict is between a positive and escapist use of the image, between what can be called the imperial idea and retirement. Particular poems may conflate what seem in the abstract to be conflicting opinions, and it may be difficult to place them at a particular point on the spectrum, since poems do not state points of view so much as work them out. But one should nevertheless try to isolate the separate tendencies that make up the complete image. In its most optimistic and politically conscious form the conservative image is an attempt to weld the disparate elements of society into a whole through an image of good government. It is an imperial idea in that proper harmony between the parts is seen to create not only a good society but a powerful nation able to maintain its position at the expense of the rest of the world; there is a proper hierarchy of international relations as well as of social order. In poems like Dryden's *Annus Mirabilis* or Pope's *Windsor Forest* harmonious relations between members of society and the interaction of varied activities are seen to result in national wealth and power; in this kind of model of the good society potential conflict is absorbed into an image of regulated motion. There is a perpetual chain of cause and effect in the interaction between peace, trade, wealth, good government, social stability; these poems foreshadow much complacent praise of the English blessings of 'peace, commerce, civic virtue, and public works'[24] in eighteenth-century poetry. But such an optimistic view of the mutual support of society given by different activities, which implies an essentially mercantilist idea of the function of trade in upholding the wealth and power of the state,[25] involves suppressing basic conservative distrust of social activities which are generally seen to be inimical to the achievement of a good society. A poem like *Windsor Forest*, though its tone may be confident, rests precariously on a delicate reconciliation of underlying antagonisms. Though the conservative poet attempts to create an image of social harmony, paradoxically the method he uses is often one of fragmenting society and isolating one fragment as an example of unity. He establishes a series of social and moral antitheses, between trade and agriculture, the merchant and the farmer, city and country, luxury and the simple life, money and unbought produce, foreigner and native, extravagance and use. The effects of this kind of division are various; on the simplest

12

level, at the opposite end of the spectrum from the imperial idea, the country life and the moral attitudes it entails are used deliberately to support an anti-social and self-centred retirement. But the implications of retirement, the relation of country life to the country as a whole, of *rus* to *patria*, are generally not so simple. Just as a confident image of harmonious public order can be seen to involve an underlying sense of potential conflict, so an image of the good society as isolated, rural, and hostile to prevailing values nevertheless implies an influential relationship between the isolated fragment and society as a whole.

Some of these complexities can be illustrated in the poems of Virgil and Horace, which are relevant for this study not only as paradigms of the problems involved but as antecedents of attitudes adopted by seventeenth- and eighteenth-century poets. Virgil was to become the stereotype of the epic poet, the prophet of empire, and Horace of the retired poet, independent and free from public affairs, though the roles of both poets were in fact much less clearly defined and frequently ambiguous. Virgil and Horace began their careers during a period of immense political disorder, much worse than anything known in England in the seventeenth century, and then saw order restored at some cost by Augustus; they both suffered and later benefited at the hands of the new regime. Their interest in seeing order established; their hopes of Augustus; their uncertainties about the future; their recourse to images of ancient rural simplicity, indicating both faith in a source of moral and social revival, and despair at the possibility of its achievement: all are expressed in their poems. The ambiguity involved in the use of poetic images of order is indicated by their constant reworking and reinterpretation of these images.

Virgil's fourth *Eclogue* is the best known example of a prophetic celebration of the fulfilment of history, an optimistic identification of the idealised age of gold, the simpler life of the past and the countryside, with the future; there is the same view of history as rebirth, as the renewal of ancient order, that underlies the *Aeneid*. Yet it is difficult to pinpoint the ultimate tendency or implications of such daring attempts to fuse the poetic image with the political reality. One can, as is often done, try to identify the poem's tone by comparison with the sixteenth *Epode* of Horace; whatever the relative chronology and influence of these poems, the divergence in stated attitudes is clear. While Virgil identifies image and reality by prophesying rebirth, Horace separates existing disorder at Rome from the *arva beata*, the happy fields, the equivalent of Virgil's *Saturnia regna*, both in idea and in space. There is no possible identification of the poetic image with the public political world; to seek the happy fields is to flee reality.

Yet the stages in Virgil's depiction of the rebirth of the golden age show the same kind of disparity between the ideal and the actual which to Horace in the sixteenth *Epode* forms an essential barrier to the fulfilment of hope. The first stage of change is not complete:

Pauca tamen suberunt priscae vestigia fraudis.[26]

yet there will remain a few traces of ancient sin.

Trade, war, and toil persist. In the final fulfilment of the cycle, however, trade and work will cease; the ideal society is a universalised rural community in which the independence of the self-supporting farmer is the model for all men. 'Omnis feret omnia tellus' (*l.* 39); *every land will bear everything.* It will be a rural life not only self-supporting but spontaneously productive; the farmer will enjoy fruits for which he has not toiled. The pattern for the whole of society is the idealisation of one part of it. To achieve future happiness the nation must reduce itself. Virgil's celebration, like Horace's despair, is an escape from the complexities of political life.

In the *Georgics* the use of the rural life as a pattern for the nation is explored more carefully, but here again the problem of tone is evident. Is Virgil more interested in the particular values of a way of life separate from society, or in the renewal of a nation? At the end of *Georgic* II, where the countryman's life is praised, the confusion in feeling is apparent; the rural life is both the antithesis to public life and the source of all that is potentially great in the nation. Compared with the hazards and worthless ambitions of war, politics, or trade, the life of the countryman is simple and undisturbed; he has 'secura quies' (*l.* 467), and is indifferent to public calamity. His way of life is deliberately isolated and self-interested. Yet this is the only way of life that approaches the ideal that society must be brought to imitate:

extrema per illos
Iustitia excedens terris vestigia fecit.   (*ll.* 473–4)

When Justice left the earth she made her last footprints among those men.

At the end of the book Virgil specifically identifies country life as it now exists, the life of ancient simplicity by means of which Rome grew great, and the golden age. He implies that Rome will recover greatness by making a particular way of life the basis of the values of the whole society. The country life is a practical example and a metaphor.

For Virgil the rural idea is essentially a part of an all-encompassing image of the good society; yet his emphasis on isolation, self-reliance, and spontaneous growth, his antagonism to trade, the world of affairs, movement and ambition, show the discrepancy between the ostensibly public aim of the vision of rebirth and the example by which it is illustrated. The same tension between the rural image, which is isolated

14

and personal, and the attempt to translate it into public terms is present in Horace's poems, though here the emphasis is rather different. The existence of a dichotomy between the public and private worlds, the urban and the rural, is central to Horace's attempt to work out through his poetry an individual way of life indifferent to public concerns. Often the public world figures in Horace's poems only as a negative touchstone against which to test his private values. But here again one cannot restrict the implications of the rural image. There are many Horaces besides the retired and independent country gentleman that he was to become for his seventeenth- and eighteenth-century imitators. Certainly in many poems – in some of the epistles, for example, and the more personal of the odes – Horace is concerned with his independence and happiness to the exclusion of all else. In *Epistle* I vi, 'nil admirari', or in the much imitated *Satire* II vi, the town and country mouse, his expressed aim is a semi-Stoic peace of mind undisturbed by the demands and fluctuations of the world as symbolised by the town; only in the country is such peace achievable. The latter poem, indeed, together with *Epode* II, is the ancestor of a whole line of versified wishes for a life secluded, comfortable, and free from public responsibilities, though here the wishes have been fulfilled:

Hoc erat in votis: modus agri non ita magnus...[27]

This was in my prayers: a piece of land not very large...

But Horace's use of rural life is more varied and has more overtones than the story of the town and country mouse suggests. For one thing, Horace is constantly critical (in, for example, *Satire* II vii or *Epistle* I xv) of his own motives and honesty in seeking retirement. And the rural life implies much more than one man's contentment and isolation. In the search for his own way of life Horace discovered values appropriate to the whole society. Horace's attitudes to the effects of the civil wars and the fate of Rome under Augustus went through more fluctuations than Virgil's,[28] but he came to share Virgil's technique of identifying rural life, ancient Roman simplicity, the ideal of the golden age, with Augustus' achievements. The identification is not always complete; in *Odes* III v and vi the ancient virtues are set against contemporary degeneracy. But the image of cyclical renewal, the idea of political rebirth, undercuts the despairing dichotomy between private and public, rural and urban, ancient and modern. In *Ode* III iii Augustus is seen to have achieved the renewal of the past, the identification of the ideal with the actual, though the threat of disorder is present in the warning of Troy's fall; in *Ode* IV v political order, the recovery of ancient virtue, and the contentment of rural life are guaranteed by Augustus' rule. The effect of this series of comparisons of the rural, the primitive, the past, and the hoped-for future is that Horace's search for his own independence and way of life is seen to be not so much antithetical to the values of the public world as a necessary stage in the making of the good society.

The same kind of ambiguities and contradictory tendencies that make the tone and ultimate emphasis of Virgil and Horace so hard to determine are present in English country poems of the seventeenth and early eighteenth centuries, but in these there is a pronounced tendency to fragment the image, to emphasise retirement and self-fulfilment at the expense of society, which is perhaps owing to actual conflict between court and country. Though it involves reading with hindsight, one can find a peculiar irony in poems of the 1630s, the period of Charles I's personal rule, which use the country (*rus*) as an image of the harmony and order of the country as a whole (*patria*). In Carew's 'In answer of an Elegiacal Letter upon the death of the King of Sweden...' England itself is an isolated garden, whose prosperity is assured by peace. Though its happiness is defined through the traditional antitheses, in terms of self-interest and rejection of public responsibility, nevertheless in the nation these antitheses are eliminated through harmony between country and court. Thus the contrast is between English peace and leisure, European war and discord:

> what though the German drum
> Bellow for freedom and revenge, the noise
> Concerns not us, nor should divert our joys;
> Nor ought the thunder of their carabins
> Drown the sweet airs of our tuned violins.[29]

In England this discord is eliminated because the whole society has abdicated from the responsibilities of public life; the court, as symbolised by its pastoral masques, is a shepherd's paradise. But though Carew's ostensible aim is to contrast a harmonious society with a discordant one, his tone is the reverse of Horace's in those poems in which rural virtues are seen to have relevance to the regeneration of society. Instead, Carew sees the court as isolating itself from public concerns, and adopting those rural attitudes characteristic of a society essentially disordered and divided. In Fanshawe's ode mentioned above, which has a similar theme, the attempt to create a poetic unity of court and country is more successful in terms of the control achieved over the tone; he integrates Horace's *Epode* II (the source of many an anti-social retirement poem) into a version of the country life which is in harmony with and not antagonistic to the court. But Fanshawe's ode also depends on the image of the whole country in retirement from the concerns of the outside world. The complex tone of these poems, the ambiguity of an image of harmony which is one half of an antithesis, is further complicated for the modern reader who knows how much this image is a hopeful

16

fiction. Yet men who looked back on the 1630s saw these as years when national harmony was a reality. To Clarendon it seemed that men had thrown away peace and prosperity they had not really valued. To Marvell in 'Upon Appleton House' England was 'the garden of the world ere while';[30] following the civil war a public man like Fairfax could achieve his purpose only within the confines of his own garden.

Another genre of which Carew made use, the country house poem, exhibits the same complications of tone.[31] A detailed examination of one of the best of these, Jonson's 'To Penshurst', will be given in the appropriate place, but here some general remarks can be made. The country house poem is a form which has no real Latin analogues, largely because the way of life it reflects has no real counterpart in Roman society. Poems like 'To Penshurst' and Pope's *Epistle to Burlington* (separated by over a hundred years of social change, but based on very similar views of what constitutes the good society) stress the public ramifications of private lives; the country house, presided over by the responsible landowner, is a microcosm of the whole society. This view of the social function of the country house reflects the theoretically harmonious relations and mutual support of monarchy and nobility, central and local government, court and country. But the tone in these poems is rarely so simple; their harmony is precarious, threatened. Almost always the country house and the values it embodies are set as an ideal against disordered reality, usually exemplified by the court or other houses that are seen to have betrayed their function. In several poems, such as Herrick's 'A Panegyric to Sir Lewis Pemberton', Carew's 'To my Friend G.N. from Wrest', Marvell's 'Upon Appleton House', architecture is used as a symbol of division: traditional functional country-house architecture is contrasted with Inigo Jones's court-centred Palladian innovations. Antagonism to the court can have various implications and uses: an anti-court stance may be satirical, a means of measuring the court as it is against the court as it might be, without damaging the idea of the court as the proper moral centre of society; or an anti-court stance may be absolute, with the country house as the symbol of a way of life opposed to and incompatible with that of the court.

In this last emphasis the country house poem overlaps with a much more widely used genre of the seventeenth and eighteenth centuries, the retirement poem.[32] This genre gave an opportunity for the poetic elaboration of tones and attitudes reflecting the increasingly isolated and politically impotent position of the lesser country gentleman, a type distinct from the great landowner of the country house poems. The ultimate source for the attitudes involved is Horace, but a Horace narrowed and shorn of his public concerns and his sense of a unified order; it is Horace content in his Sabine farm, independent, free of public responsibilities and cares. And seventeenth- and eighteenth-century promulgators of this Horatian image all too often ignore Horace's critical juxtapositions and humorous parody. Translations of *Epode* II sometimes drop the last four lines and thus miss the irony and deliberately confused tone of the original. An exception is Matthew Green's *The Spleen*, which manages to convey something of Horace's complex tone in its use of catalogues of necessities to mock but not destroy the frequently self-indulgent wish for retirement.

Though the idea of retirement from public life or of opposition to the world can be morally strenuous as well as escapist, many retirement poems tend to develop their theme in a self-centred and consciously irresponsible way. The serious complexity of Horace's use of the country is in part due to the fact that both tones are present; the country life involves both a hedonistic withdrawal from the demands of public life and a self-reliant strength capable of resisting the attractive but corrupt town. In the more straightforward and simple minded Horatian imitations there is no complexity in the antithesis; the urban life has nothing of value to offer the individual in search only of his own quiet of mind. Poets such as these seem unaware of the implications of the attitudes they present; though many retirement poems make a conventional obeisance to the idea of universal order the terms in which the retirement is seen frequently suggest a breakdown of that idea.

The attitudes involved in the escapist use of retirement can be clearly deduced from Cowley's *Essays*. Cowley relies heavily on his classical predecessors, including Virgil, Horace, Martial, and Seneca (although he has little in common with the last), while remoulding them to fit his own tone. He is humorously aware of the distinctions between pastoralism and actual retirement to the country:

> I thought when I went first to dwell in the country, that without doubt I should have met there with the simplicity of the old poetical golden age...: but to confess the truth, I perceived quickly, by infallible demonstrations, that I was still in old England, and not in Arcadia.[33]

He stresses the comforts of country life rather than any Stoic firmness it might inspire. He loves best 'a little convenient estate, a little cheerful house, a little company, and a very little feast' ('Of Greatness', *p.* 429). Cowley identifies his personal ideal of private comfort without public responsibility with a particular class of country gentlemen whose mid-way position makes such a way of life possible. He uses 'liberty' to describe this state, though a more frequent eighteenth-century usage is 'independence':

> If you ask me in what condition of life I think the most [liberty] allowed; I should pitch upon that sort of people whom King James

was wont to call the happiest of our nation, the men placed in the country by their fortune above an High-Constable, and yet beneath the trouble of a Justice of Peace, in a moderate plenty.

('Of Liberty', *p.* 386)[34]

John Pomfret's much-read 'The Choice' shows how far the retirement wish can become irresponsible and self-regarding. Pomfret's catalogue belies the idea of simplicity and the elimination of unnecessary wants which is an important element in Horace's idealisation of the country. Most important is the reiteration of Cowley's theme, the desire for wealth without responsibility:

> I'd have a clear, and competent estate,
> That I might live genteely, but not great.[35]

The emphasis has shifted from tranquillity of mind to amenability of circumstances; the key words in this tradition are competency and contentation. Charles Cotton, a much better poet than Pomfret, shows some sense of the social and moral implications of this kind of interpretation of retirement. 'The Angler's Ballad' expresses a superficial generalised Toryism; though 'the angler is free/ From the cares that degree/ Finds itself with so often tormented', he acquiesces in the general order in which he feels himself to have a part:

> Whilst quiet we sit
> We conclude all things fit,
>   Acquiescing with hearty submission;
> For, though simple, we know
> That soft murmurs will grow
>   At the last unto downright sedition.[36]

But elsewhere, in 'Contentation', for example, or the first 'Epistle to John Bradshaw', Cotton shows the isolationism, the antagonism to the idea of a diversely harmonious good society, that is implicit in poetic celebrations of the Tory country squire. Cotton deliberately characterises himself as a 'dull northern clod', from the point of view of the courtier or man of business contemptuous of country values; the point is that there is no overlapping of the attitudes peculiar to country and court. Cotton returns from London

> Just the same sot I was e'er I removed,
> Nor by my travel, nor the court improved;
> The same oldfashioned Squire, no whit refined,
> And shall be wiser when the Devil's blind:
> But find all here too in the self-same state...

This state of rural isolation, of indifference to the standards and concerns of public life, has its perfection in the friendship of individuals, as opposed to the throngs of cities and courts. The day that Cotton is joined by his friend Bradshaw

> will raise me above men
> Greater than crowned monarchs are, and then
> I'll not exchange my cottage for Whitehall,
> Windsor, the Louvre, or the Escurial.   (*ll.* 108–111)

Cotton, Pomfret, and a host of other poets who elaborated this image throughout the eighteenth century were trying to make a moral hero or simply a social model out of the type on whom Macaulay poured such scorn, the Tory country squire.[37] Partisan analyses like Macaulay's are useful in making explicit the prejudices that underlie the conservative idealisation; innocence, integrity, and independence can also be seen as ignorance, isolationism, and xenophobia. The opposition or country Toryism expressed in retirement poems is both implicit in and antithetical to the more generous conservative image of a harmonious society. The good society is often seen as a magnified rural community. When this model, with its partisan emphasis on ownership of land, the self-supporting rural life, its hostility to other ways of life, to trade, money, the city, individuals not fixed in a particular soil, is seen to be too limited to form the basis of a coherent social view, the poet who adheres to it is ultimately undermining his own public function. This is not always indicative of failure; some reorganisation of the conservative myth of order must take place when social circumstances make it obviously unviable. What is important and interesting is not so much the myth in itself denuded of its poetic realisation and exposed to analysis, as the kinds of social and poetic uses made of it, the constant reworking and rebuilding of the diverse tendencies and attitudes involved, so that though one can talk for convenience's sake of the conservative image, no two images are ever the same. In the following chapters the conservative image of public order will be traced in terms of both its historical development and its poetic uses in the careers of particular poets.

Chapter 2
Ben Jonson: the nature of aristocracy

THE STOIC POSE

Jonson's career as a writer reached from the precarious stability of the last years of Elizabeth's reign to the middle of Charles I's unpopular experiment in personal rule. In this period the relative positions of crown and parliament shifted, and the traditional social values fostered by the Tudors of degree, obedience, and deference were weakened enough to make possible the outbreak of civil war five years after Jonson's death and the abolition of public institutions as he had known them. Jonson was strongly conscious of living in a period of social and economic change, and he was hostile to what he saw: aristocratic decadence, corruption at court, subversion of a hierarchical society by selfish ambition and greed, the replacement of customary social relationships by financial ones. Not the least important element in Jonson's picture of social dissolution was his sense of the neglect of the true poet, who should be the upholder of the commonwealth, by royal and aristocratic patrons and the general audience of the theatres. In spite of his frequent dictatorial pronouncements on the subject of poetry and its uses, Jonson must have been at times unsure about the direction of his writing and the world he was writing about. But his gloomy assessment of society did not prevent him from taking part in it in various and profitable ways. He held a place in James's court that Spenser would have envied, while asserting an independence of which Pope would not have been ashamed. He combined a deliberate self-distancing, the result of his uneasiness about society, with a conviction that the traditional forms of society were valid and, with his collaboration, could be made to work. While he never ceased to expose the vanities and pretensions of public life, he was willing to serve and direct the aims of monarchy and court.

Jonson felt free to move in and promote the interests of the court society he distrusted (though there is evidence in the masques of his fear of being compromised by this association) because he developed early in his career a satiric pose and a strong personal creed upholding it. Before Jonson came into the orbit of the court and the great aristocratic

houses he was an outsider, an actor and a playwright. The literary
milieu in which he fitted best was not the public world of *The Faerie
Queene* and *Arcadia*, but the critical world of the malcontent satirists
of the 1590s, Marston and Hall. But while obviously belonging to this
milieu, Jonson was anxious to distinguish himself from it, and the
Bishops' Order of 1599 banning the publication of satire (which did
not extend to the stage) helped him. From 1599 to 1601 he used drama
as the medium for 'comical satire'.[1]

The three comedies of this period, *Every Man out of his Humour*,
Cynthia's Revels, and *Poetaster*, are intended to give a coherent exposition
of Jonson's satiric role. But such an exposition was made more difficult
because at the same time Jonson was squabbling with Marston and
Dekker and the audience as a whole who resented what they took to be
the arrogance of his theoretical pretensions. The immediate object of
Poetaster was to satirise Marston and Dekker, and the purging of
Crispinus is the climax of Act V, but Jonson insists that the personal
attack is of minor importance. At the beginning of the play Envy is
trodden underfoot by the armed Prologue, who defends Jonson's view
of himself as it is to be embodied by Horace in the play. The author
pursues 'with a constant firmness' the mean between arrogance and
dejection: he 'rather pities, than envies' his detractors since 'his mind
it is above their injuries' (IV, 206, *ll.* 21–8). Another distinction is
drawn in the play between the irresponsible Ovid and the true poet,
Horace. So Caesar dismisses Ovid:

> I will prefer for knowledge, none, but such
> As rule their lives by it.   (*p.* 282, *ll.* 74–5)

Horace defends himself from Caesar's imputation that poverty is likely
to breed envy; rather his poverty and his learning guarantee his independence:

> Caesar speaks after common men, in this,
> To make a difference of me, for my poorness:
> As if the filth of poverty sunk as deep
> Into a knowing spirit, as the bane
> Of riches doth, into an ignorant soul.
>
> .   .   .   .
>
> But knowledge is the nectar, that keeps sweet
> A perfect soul, even in this grave of sin;
> And for my soul, it is as free, as Caesar's:
> For, what I know is due, I'll give to all.
>   (*p.* 292, *ll.* 79–83, 88–91)

The characters of Horace and of Crites in *Cynthia's Revels* are deliberate

22

restatements, for the benefit of his unsympathetic audience, of Jonson's view of the proper character of the satirist. Mercury says of Crites:

> Fortune could never break him, nor make him less. He counts it his pleasure, to despise pleasures, and is more delighted with good deeds, than goods. It is a competency to him that he can be virtuous. He doth neither covet, nor fear; he hath too much reason to do either: and that commends all things to him. (IV, 74-5, *ll.* 139-45)

Jonson here identifies the satirist and the poet with the Stoic sage, not an obvious identification, as he was well aware. He had already made his chief attempt to distinguish the true critic from the malcontent in *Every Man out of his Humour*; the distinction is brought out in the Theophrastic characters which precede the play:

ASPER HIS CHARACTER

He is of an ingenious and free spirit, eager and constant in reproof, without fear controlling the world's abuses. One, whom no servile hope of gain, or frosty apprehension of danger, can make to be a parasite, either to time, place, or opinion.

MACILENTE

A man well parted, a sufficient scholar, and travelled; who (wanting that place in the world's account, which he thinks his merit capable of) falls into such an envious apoplexy, with which his judgement is so dazzled, and distasted, that he grows violently impatient of any opposite happiness in another. (III, 423, *ll.* 1-13)

Asper's attitudes are independent of circumstance, while Macilente's are the product of them. Macilente finds useless for him the Stoicism that supports the disinterested satirist:

> There is no taste in this philosophy,
> 'Tis like a potion that a man should drink,
> But turns his stomach with the sight of it.
> (*p.* 442, *ll.* 8-10)

But the closeness of these two apparently irreconcilable roles is brought out by the fact that Asper, the presenter, plays the part of Macilente. One object of the play is to metamorphose the malcontent and backbiter into the true satiric commentator by fusing the two characters. Macilente, by becoming 'empty of all envy' (*p.* 596, *l.* 55), adopts the position described as the author's by the Prologue to *Poetaster*. Jonson was concerned with the problem of tone, and irritated by the fact that his attempt to define the character of an Asper, a Crites, or a Horace simply led his audience to identify him as a Macilente.

This series of redefinitions in reaction to criticism is itself evidence of Jonson's failure to maintain the freedom from the effects of envy

23

characteristic of his mouthpieces. The tone of the 'apologetical dialogue' appended to *Poetaster* and of the first 'An Ode. To himself'[2] (their identical last lines express his contempt for the stage) is of defensive resentment. This hostile rejection of comedy, though it is for the purpose of singing 'high and aloof', in tragedy or perhaps in epic, is to some extent self-defeating, since it involves abandoning the critical position of the satirical commentator.[3] Though in the Roman plays the characters of Arruntius and Cicero assume the positions of moral touchstones they do not manipulate the plot in the same way as the earlier figures.

The problems underlying Jonson's ambiguous attacks on his theatrical audience can be more clearly analysed in relation to the controversy which followed the publication of *The New Inn* in 1631. The title page describes it thus: 'As it was never acted, but most negligently played, by some, the King's servants And more squeamishly beheld, and censured by others, the King's subjects...Now, at last, set at liberty to the readers, his Majesty's servants, and subjects, to be judged' (VI, 395). The second 'Ode to himself' was published with the play. It continues the indictment of public taste, and proclaims Jonson's superiority to his audience and his times. These attacks have been criticised as too personal and self-regarding, as lacking in humility.[4] If the poem is unsuccessful it is not for these reasons, since Jonson is consistently self-regarding: his stark ethic demands self-confidence. Carew's 'To Ben Jonson upon occasion of his Ode of defiance...' is politely explicit about Jonson's failure to meet his own standard:

> Why should the follies then of this dull age
> Draw from thy pen such an immodest rage
> As seems to blast thy (else immortal) bays,
> When thine own tongue proclaims thy itch of praise?
>
> (*Poems, p.* 65, *ll.* 23–6)

It is not that the ethic demands humility but that Jonson has been unable to maintain the impervious stance of the satiric commentator. He has moved from the position of Asper to that of Macilente; he is subject to injury. Other poets besides Carew make the same point, for instance R. Goodwin in 'Vindiciae Jonsonianae':

> Revenge those wrongs with pity; ...
>   He that's moved,
> With such men's censures; granteth it half proved
> That he is guilty; innocence no laws,
> Virtue fears no detraction.   (XI, 341–2, *ll.* 13, 61–4)

Others who joined the controversy were willing to accept at Jonson's own valuation the existence of two publics, the inferior and the elite (the prefaces to *Catiline*, also unpopular on stage, were addressed to 'the reader in ordinary' and 'the reader extraordinary' [v, 432]). The rallying round of Jonson's admirers after the *New Inn* fiasco suggests that he needed the praise and acknowledgement that his critical stand in the plays prevented; the odes were perhaps bids for recognition by this higher audience as well as rejections of the pretensions of the lower. However, Jonson's deliberate isolation as a satirist, together with his hostility towards the theatrical audience when it refused to accept his self-definition, and his withdrawal to an audience of the elite, conflicted with his allegiance to the traditional Renaissance view of the poet's legislative function.

The idea that the good poet must be a good as well as a learned man, that his technique is persuasion and his end the moral reformation of the whole society, was formulated by Jonson partly through reading Quintilian, and is to be found restated throughout his critical writings. Two passages in *Discoveries* are important. In the first, having previously enumerated contemporary excesses in style, Jonson notes the power of the 'true artificer':

> How he doth reign in men's affections; how invade, and break in upon them; and makes their minds like the thing he writes.
>
> (VIII, 588, *ll.* 791–3)

In the second Jonson considers both the scope of poetry and the attributes of the poet:

> I could never think the study of wisdom confined only to the philosopher: or of piety to the divine: or of state to the politic. But that he which can feign a commonwealth (which is the poet) can govern it with counsels, strengthen it with laws, correct it with judgements, inform it with religion, and morals; is all these.
>
> (*p.* 595, *ll.* 1032–8)

The same theory is elaborated in the essay dedicating *Volpone* to the universities, but here there is a further motive; Jonson is continuing the self-defence of the comical satires. His attack on poetasters and the uninformed public appears to undermine the viability of his claims; there is a barrier between his view of his function and public acceptance of it:

> If men will impartially, and not asquint, look toward the offices, and function of a poet, they will easily conclude to themselves, the impossibility of any man's being the good poet, without first being a good man. He that is said to be able to inform young men in all good disciplines, inflame grown men to all great virtues...; that comes forth the interpreter, and arbiter of nature, a teacher of things divine, no less than human, a master in manners; and can

25

alone (or with a few) effect the business of mankind: this, I take him, is no subject for pride, and ignorance to exercise their railing rhetoric upon. (v, 17, *ll.* 20–31)

The difficulties involved in combining the part of satirist (which, as Jonson knew, was dangerously close to that of the railing detractor) with that of the positive moral reformer were well brought out by Chapman in a poem written shortly before his death in 1634 and later called 'An invective of Mr George Chapman against Mr Ben Jonson'. The poem attacks Jonson's arrogant division of his readers into the learned few and the ignorant many. Chapman suggests that the former pursue learning for its own sake, 'never exploring truth or consequence, / Informing any virtue or good life' (xi, 411, *ll.* 177–8), and defends the claims of the unlearned to knowledge of what is important, 'which is to know, and be, one complete man' (*l.* 191). Up to this time relations between Jonson and Chapman had been good. They collaborated on *Eastward Ho!*; Chapman wrote commendatory verses for *Sejanus* and *Volpone*, praising Jonson's ethics; Jonson spoke warmly of Chapman to Drummond.[5] That Chapman was able thus to criticise Jonson's definitions shows not so much the resistance of the audience (Chapman was after all one of the learned few) as Jonson's difficulty in closing the gap between theory and practice, in reconciling his divergent attitudes to the place of the poet and the function of poetry.

The milieu of *Poetaster* is the literary and political world of Rome, where poets like Horace and Virgil, though seen as suffering at the hands of the envious multitude, exist in an ideal relationship with their patron Maecenas and their ruler Augustus. For Jonson in 1601 such a situation was only a dream. In the apologetical dialogue he associates himself with Aristophanes, Persius, and Juvenal; if he is to be a reformer it is not through the feigning of a commonwealth but through the exposure of existing society.[6] In *Volpone* or *The Alchemist*, where there is no satiric commentator or author's mouthpiece to interpret the action, the characters' expressed motives of greed and ambition are clearly seen to be an inversion of a public system of values.[7] In the comical satires, however, though the ostensible purpose of an Asper or a Crites may be to point to the discrepancy between the actual state of society and the poet's ideal commonwealth, in fact Jonson is much more concerned with the personal ethics of these figures than with effecting a public change. The comical satires are interesting not because they foreshadow the achievement of the later comedies, but because Jonson uses them as occasions to develop a Stoic ethic which is not necessarily related to satire, and which he uses with more depth and conviction in the poems. Jonson's attempt to fuse the Stoic sage with the satirist in the drama indicates the social difficulties facing him which he was perhaps not

26

ready to acknowledge: his idea of the poet's public function is not readily reconcilable with his sympathy with the tenets of Stoicism.

Interest in Stoicism grew throughout the sixteenth century, particularly on the continent. One should distinguish the different forms this interest took.[8] The most serious intellectual effort of the Renaissance Stoic revival was the attempt to reconcile Stoicism with Christianity. In this form it is generally known as neo-Stoicism. Its chief exponent, Justus Lipsius, tried to produce a composite system capable of incorporating the Stoic wise man and the ideal Christian. His main difficulty was the Stoic doctrine of fate, heretical from a Christian point of view, which he tried to transmute into divine law, which is the expression of Providence, the divine reason.[9] But this ambitious attempt at synthesis involved a complete metamorphosis or rather an abandonment of Stoic ethics. Joseph Hall, in his dedication of *Heaven upon Earth* (1606), an attempt to identify Stoic tranquillity of mind with Christian peace, seems to recognise this; he says,

> I have followed Seneca, and gone beyond him; followed him as a philosopher, gone beyond him, as a Christian, as a divine.

And Hall admits that tranquillity cannot be achieved simply though the natural temper of the soul; divine power is needed to uphold the mind against afflictions.[10] But this is in effect to deny the whole basis of Stoic ethics. Montaigne saw that it was impossible to assimilate the Stoic sage to the Christian. In his early essays he draws heavily on Plutarch and Seneca, and returns continually to the subjects of resistance to pain and preparation for death; but his interest cannot be said to constitute an adoption of Stoic ethics. Where Montaigne seriously considers the relation of Stoic ideas to the Christian view of man, as in the *Apologie de Raimond Sebond*, he is forced to reject the former; man is not self-sufficient, he cannot raise himself without God's grace:

> C'est à notre foi Chrétienne, non à sa vertu Stoique, de pretendre à cette divine et miraculeuse metamorphose.[11]

> *It is for our Christian faith, not his Stoic virtue, to aspire to this divine and miraculous metamorphosis.*

Montaigne (like Pascal later) objects to the Stoic wise man because he is intellectually arrogant, because he is lacking in humility and humanity: he is a fiction untrue to human nature. Such criticisms might suggest that in a Christian society sympathy with Stoicism could only show itself in an attempted reconciliation with the demands of faith, or in a more superficial moralising use of the less outrageous tenets. But the tradition of secular Stoicism is much stronger than this.[12] To adopt Stoic principles, men of the Renaissance were obliged to reject not only Christian teaching about human frailty but, more significantly, their

27

contemporaries' social and political assumptions. There is no indication in Jonson's case that he was aware of the anomaly of his position theologically, nor that he deliberately excluded the dimension of Christianity from his work.[13] The anomaly of which Jonson is conscious and to which he draws attention is the way the Stoic ethic conflicts with the assumptions of a society which honours degree, which depends on universal reverence for monarchy and nobility, and which expects its members to accept the value of fame, glory, and magnificence. It is in opposition to this public ethic that Jonson, and others like him, concentrate on the peculiarly unchristian aspects of the Stoic sage, his arrogance and his self-sufficiency.[14]

To talk of Jonson as a Stoic (rather than as a Christian neo-Stoic like Lipsius) is not to imply that he accepted or was even interested in the scientific structure of classical Stoicism. His chief source was Seneca; by the time that Stoicism had become the popular ethic of the Roman empire much of its original physical and metaphysical theory had become an appendage to what was essentially a moral creed.[15] It was as a moralist that Jonson read Seneca, copied him out in *Discoveries*, and incorporated him in his poems. Even when not borrowing from him, Jonson deliberately used terms such as 'virtue' and 'injury' in the specific meanings allotted them by Seneca.[16]

If the nature of suffering and the structure of the eternal world are seen as Seneca sees them, as inevitable evils which can only be remedied by ignoring them as inessentials, then the attractiveness of Stoicism as a psychological prop and a moral weapon is evident; the external world is diminished as the individual is aggrandised. Stoicism is one kind of response to the breakdown of a system of public order; it is one way in which the intellectual can confront his sense of social impotence. The popularity of Stoicism among sixteenth-century men of letters is paradoxical. They both over-estimated their social importance and took refuge in an anti-social creed. Poets like Chapman, Daniel, or Drayton were in an uneasy position in their societies. They thought of themselves as makers of commonwealths, but they were for the most part excluded from real influence. It was because Jonson was able to move with some freedom in courtly and aristocratic circles that he was able to make use of the public ideals of the society to which as an individual he was hostile.

The kinds of satisfaction and support that Jonson took from Seneca can be seen by considering some passages in *Discoveries*:

Money never made any man rich, but his mind. He that can order himself to the law of nature, is not only without the sense, but the fear of poverty....We covet superfluous things; when it were more honour for us, if we could contemn necessary.... But we make ourselves slaves to our pleasures; and we serve fame, and ambition, which is an equal slavery.... All that we call happiness, is mere painting, and gilt: and all for money: what a thin membrane of honour that is? and how hath all true reputation fallen, since money began to have any?...A man should study other things, not to covet, not to fear, not to repent him: to make his base such, as no tempest shall shake him: to be secure of all opinion; and pleasing to himself, even for that, wherein he displeaseth others. For the worst opinion gotten for doing well, should delight us: would'st not thou be just, but for fame; thou ought'st to be it with infamy: He that would have his virtue published, is not the servant of virtue, but glory.   (VIII, 605–8, *ll*. 1373–5, 1387–9, 1402–4, 1446–9, 1459–67)

Though this is a series of adaptations from Seneca,[17] it expresses Jonson's most uncompromising reactions to the conditions of his society. Two different kinds of external reward, money and fame, are rejected. Money itself is undermining the value of 'true reputation'. In effect Jonson is attacking both the public values of his world, the pursuit of ambition and glory, and the insidious values that are seen to be subverting these, covetousness, the love of money. In opposition to the public world and its dissolution Jonson places the immovable individual who acts only on his own behalf.

Though Jonson's definition of the satiric commentator in the comical satires owes much to Seneca, particularly the idea that he is impervious to attack, free and immovable, and alone able to distinguish true value, it is in the poems that the self-centred emphasis of Senecan Stoicism is best realised. These poems assume that there is a small circle of good men who deliberately hold themselves aloof from the public demands and values of their society and concentrate on standing firm in the face of changeable fortune. Jonson's part is to define the idea of virtue and to urge his friends to live by it. He rarely uses himself as embodiment of the Stoic ideal or as target for moral precepts. One of the exceptions to this general rule is the first ode to himself (*Und.* xxiii, *p.* 174), in which he consoles himself for his failure as a dramatist with the argument that virtue is its own reward:

> Let this thought quicken thee,
> Minds that are great and free,
>   Should not on fortune pause,
> 'Tis crown enough to virtue still, her own applause.

Another is the poem, 'An Epistle answering to one that asked to be sealed of the Tribe of Ben' (*Und.* xlvii, *p.* 218), in which he shows himself attempting to conform to the ideal of self-sufficiency:

> Live to that point I will, for which I am man,
>   And dwell as in my centre, as I can.

And his choice of a motto, as reported by Drummond, indicates his perpetual struggle for self-perfection: 'His impresa was a compass with one foot in centre, the other broken, the word. Deest quod duceret orbem' (I, 148, *ll.* 578-9). But the usual preoccupation of the poems is the moral improvement of others.

In the poems advocating self-sufficiency and indifference to fortune images of immobility, rootedness, and circular perfection often recur. Jonson urges Ferrabosco 'then stand unto thy self' (*Ep.* cxxxi, *p.* 83); he concludes 'An Epistle answering...' with the exhortation 'now stand'. In 'An Epistle to Sir Edward Sackville' (*Und.* xiii, *p.* 157) virtuous men

> live as fast
> As they are high; are rooted, and will last;

Jonson exhorts Sir Henry Neville (*Ep.* cix, *p.* 70) to strive

> To be the same in root, thou art in height.

The image of the circle expresses the same idea; Jonson tells Sir Thomas Roe (*Ep.* xcviii, p. 63)

> He that is round within himself, and straight,
> Need seek no other strength, no other height;

he advises John Selden (*Und.* xiv, *p.* 159)

> And like a compass keeping one foot still
> Upon your centre, do your circle fill
> Of general knowledge.

There are further elaborations of Stoic attitudes: in 'An Ode to James Earl of Desmond' (*Und.* xxv, *p.* 179) Jonson shows the value of misfortune in identifying the virtuous man:

> he is shot-free
> From injury,
> That is not hurt; not he, that is not hit;

in the epistle to Sackville and the 'Epode' (*For.* xi) he emphasises that a man cannot be good by chance and that the basis of virtue is reason. The distinction between intrinsic value and mere externals is constantly drawn. Jonson advises Thomas Roe (*Ep.* xcviii, *p.* 63) to 'study conscience, more than thou would'st fame'; he will wish of Colby, in 'An Epistle to a friend, to persuade him to the wars' (*Und.* xv, *p.* 168), 'that thou dost all things more for truth, than glory'; he praises Sir Henry Cary (*Ep.* lxvi, *p.* 49) because

> He's valiant'st, that dares fight, and not for pay;
> That virtuous is, when the reward's away.

Jonson's clearest statement of a Stoic reaction to the problem of evil is in 'To the world. A farewell for a gentlewoman, virtuous and noble' (*For.* iv, *p.* 101–2). Whatever the affinities between Stoic and Christian *contemptus mundi*, the theological dimension is missing from this poem:

> No, I do know, that I was born,
> To age, misfortune, sickness, grief:
> But I will bear these, with that scorn,
> As shall not need thy false relief.
> Nor for my peace will I go far,
> As wanderers do, that still do roam,
> But make my strengths, such as they are,
> Here in my bosom, and at home.

This is the Senecan world of apparently incomprehensible evil where good men seem to suffer unwarrantably and from which they learn that self-reliance is the only good. But this is not the world in which the Jonsonian hero usually moves. For Seneca it may make no difference whether the hypothetical wise man of his treatises is a poor man or an emperor (though he suggests in *On the Firmness of the Wise Man* that the more conspicuous a man is by birth or position the better he should bear himself). But Jonson as a poet does not have the independence that his Stoic ethic leads him to commend. In some cases he writes for his friends; more often he addresses his social superiors, his patrons and patronesses, courtiers, and officials, who move in a public world that Jonson knows to have no value by contrast with the constant world of the inner self. Nevertheless, while repeating the distinction between the essential and the inessential, between virtue and fame, between goodness and greatness, between name and 'fact', Jonson remains aware of the status of the people he is addressing. The virtue of public men is not simply its own reward, it permeates their society. Jonson, unlike Seneca, does not write to influence the individual alone. The larger function of the aristocracy who are the main subject and audience of his poems is as pattern to the nation: Jonson, in turn, provides the pattern for them. His task is to present the man with the ideal and to make an imaginative identification of the two.

His pursuit of this task often leads Jonson away from the limiting, self-directed emphasis of Stoic ethics. But it is arguable that without the confidence and moral authority provided by his sympathy with Stoicism Jonson would not have moved so easily nor so usefully in the public world. His interest in great men is provoked first by the extent to which they embody his concept of virtue (his attitude to monarchy is necessarily different). Thus in 'On Lucy Countess of Bedford' (*Ep.* lxxvi, *p.* 52) Jonson postulates for his patroness not so much social virtues as 'a learned, and a manly soul'

> that should, with even powers,
> The rock, the spindle, and the shears control
> Of destiny, and spin her own free hours.

One of the best examples of Jonson's complex use of the commendatory poem, involving no modification of his concept of virtue, but illustrating the important relationship between the poet, the poem, and the subject, is the 'Epistle. To Katherine, Lady Aubigny' (*For.* xiii, *p.* 116). In spite of the conspicuous place and family of the lady addressed, the poem sets up a tension between place and virtue, between public behaviour and her conscious retirement and self-interest. The poem itself is presented as an act of defiance:

> 'Tis grown almost a danger to speake true
> Of any good mind, now: There are so few.

Jonson must set apart his poem, Lady Aubigny, and the values he upholds from the taint of usual flattery. What guarantees his praise is his honesty as satirist, and his imperviousness to attack:

> I, that have suffered this; and, though forsook
> Of Fortune, have not altered yet my look,
> . . . . . .
> I, Madam, am become your praiser.

Jonson's poem, though it recognises the lady's public position, emphasises the qualities that are independent of it:

> My mirror is more subtle, clear, refined,
> And takes, and gives the beauties of the mind.

Jonson sets up an ideal of behaviour, of self-reliance in the face of circumstance, and sees Lady Aubigny as fulfilling this ideal:

> You, Madam, young have learned to shun these shelves,
> Whereon the most of mankind wreck themselves,
> And, keeping a just course, have early put
> Into your harbour, and all passage shut
> 'Gainst storms, or pirates, that might charge your peace.

But the fact of her noble standing makes her an example for other wives; though the essence of virtue is self-isolation the existence of public virtue has social repercussions. And Jonson's poem, though it describes Lady Aubigny as she is, will remain her pattern for conduct:

> as long years do pass,
> Madam, be bold to use this truest glass:
> Wherein, your form, you still the same shall find;
> Because nor it can change, nor such a mind.

This beautiful and controlled poem illustrates particularly well the complex connections between Jonson's Stoic pose, his sense of deliberate isolation as a satirist, his attempt to propagate his idea of virtue, his relations with his patrons, and his acknowledgement and direction of the social function of the aristocracy. Jonson's achievement is to unite in an artistic whole the social antagonisms involved in his Stoic sympathies with the idea of the poet's social usefulness.[18] There were various possible directions open to a poet whose work sprang from a traditional view of the public function of art and from antagonism towards a society that seemed to be breaking out of its traditional mould. Jonson's reaction to social change in his time, to the apparent triumph of a new ethic of gain and motion over the old ethic of stability and degree, was to rest on a Stoicism in theory indifferent to all kinds of public value. But unlike Pope, who was conscious of a growing discrepancy during his lifetime between the conventional descriptions of an ideal society and the actual values by which men lived, Jonson did not end by magnifying himself and his interests. The self-centredness of Stoicism does not imply self-consciousness, an interest in what makes men different from each other. None of Jonson's poetic heroes is distinguished as an individual; rather each is seen to approximate to an unchanging moral norm. The hostile reactions to Jonson's dramatic use of the Stoic wise man as satiric commentator and his identification of himself with this role shows that this identification was thought to be to some extent morally shocking. However, it was during this brief and experimental period in Jonson's career that he developed an ethic which (though he modified it to suit the social purposes of his writing) he was never to abandon. The Stoic Jonson is by no means the whole poet, but the beliefs of the former gave meaning and strength to the public work of the latter.

ARISTOCRACY AND THE NEW ENGLAND

Jonson's idea of the uses of poetry, his acceptance of social hierarchy, and his economic situation all combined to make him dependent on the nobility, the subjects of his poems and the authors of his comfort. Jonson was fortunate among contemporary poets in benefiting greatly from patronage, a system that was becoming at this time increasingly burdensome to patrons and authors alike.[19] The early seventeenth century was an uneasy period for the professional writer; he had to compete with the courtly amateur who moved at the centre of the court world while he hung on its fringes; unlike his eighteenth-century counterpart he could not make a living by publishing his work. As a result he tended to regret nostalgically the passing of a mutually beneficial social relationship.[20] The channels open to the professional Elizabethan or Jacobean writer were print or the stage. Of the two, the stage was more financially rewarding: writers like Drayton who found themselves without other means of support were forced to turn to it. Yet Jonson told Drummond that 'of all his plays he never gained 2 hundred pounds' (I, 148, *l.* 566). Print was even more unsatisfactory. The only hope of the professional writer who published his work was to obtain a fee from the frequently unknown aristocrat to whom he dedicated his book; he had to solicit patronage.

Such a system had its dangers. There were not enough potential patrons to support the writers who sought their help. The writer had to compete, to force the attention of the potential patron with exaggerated compliment. Since patronage became an economic rather than a social relationship, it had no continuity; the author was led into perpetual flattery and the exploitation of new patrons.[21] Some writers, among them Jonson and Drayton, resented the indignity inherent in the relationship between poet and patron. One way for the poet to justify his acceptance of patronage was by assuming a tacit bargain between him and his patron: the patron conferred a livelihood while the poet conferred immortality.[22] The idea of donating eternity through verse implies a certain dissatisfaction with the relationship; it is the supreme compliment, but at the same time it suggests the superiority of the poet to his subject. It is his means of asserting his independence; he surmounts the exigencies of the historical and social situation and joins the company of Pindar, Horace, or Chaucer. In an uneasy epistle, 'To Elizabeth Countess of Rutland' (*For.* xii, *p.* 113), a bid for her patronage and for a renewal of that of the Countess of Bedford, Jonson contrasts the meagre things that gold can buy with the power of verse to confer immortality. The poem is built on a comparison between the present gilt age when money is the only bond and the golden age in which the social function of the poet was understood; the relationship of patronage is seen as a true repayment:

> There like a rich, and golden pyramid,
> Born up by statues, shall I rear your head.

Although Jonson was careful to maintain his independence in his relations with the great, this self-conscious emphasis on the value of poetry was not his usual way of doing it; he wrote relatively few poems on this theme.[23]

The patronage of the aristocracy and the king was for Jonson, as for others, an economic necessity. He made the conventional complaints of its inadequacy; Drummond said of him 'he dissuaded me from poetry, for that she had beggared him' (I, 149, *l.* 615). Jonson's pessimism is recorded in *Discoveries*:

> Poetry, in this latter age, hath proved but a mean mistress, to such as have wholly addicted themselves to her.   (VIII, 583, *ll.* 622-4)

34

It is true that Jonson suffered from inadequate patronage in his later years, when he was partly estranged from the court and bedridden: he was obliged to write begging verses to Charles (*Und.* lxviii, lxxvi) and to Lord Weston (*Und.* lxxi). The most moving document of his neglected poverty is the letter he wrote to Newcastle with the fable of the mole called want and the mole-catcher's advice, 'Master it is not in my power to destroy this vermin; the K[ing] or some good man of a noble nature must help you' (I, 214, *ll.* 32–4). But by contrast with what other authors received and with his own profits from the stage, his rewards from patronage were lavish. He had almost continuous support from various patrons, and pensions from James and Charles. His relationship with his patrons was social as well as economic; the friendship and encouragement he received from the Countess of Bedford, Sir Robert Sidney and the Sidney family, and Lord Aubigny, among others, make him one of the best exponents of the values of this system. His gratitude towards the last (with whom he lived for some time)[24] is expressed in a poem which, though confident about Jonson's own worth, does not try to elevate the poet above the patron:

> call posterity
> Into the debt; and reckon on her head,
>   How full of want, how swallowed up, how dead
> I, and this muse had been, if thou hadst not
>   Lent timely succours, and new life begot:
> So, all reward, or name, that grows to me
>   By her attempt, shall still be owing thee.
>
> <div align="right">(<i>Ep.</i> cxxvii, <i>p.</i> 80)</div>

The epistle to Sackville on benefits shows Jonson's perennial concern with the manners and ethics of giving and receiving:

> You cannot doubt, but I, who freely know
> This good from you, as freely will it owe;
> And though my fortune humble me, to take
> The smallest courtesies with thanks, I make
> Yet choice from whom I take them; and would shame
> To have such do me good, I durst not name:
> They are the noblest benefits, and sink
> Deepest in man, of which when he doth think,
> The memory delights him more, from whom
> Than what he hath received.   (*Und.* xiii, *p.* 153)

Jonson's firmness of mind and the ease of his relationship with his patrons allowed him to exploit this relationship without damage to his own independence or the frequently misused place of the nobility.[25]

In the dedication of the *Epigrams* to the Earl of Pembroke, Jonson, following the manifesto of Martial in Book x, xxxiii, says that in the delineation of vices 'I have avoided all particulars' (VIII, 26, *l.* 28). So in the commendatory poems one solution to the inherent danger of praise is to separate the persons from their virtues. Jonson told Drummond that 'he never esteemed of a man for the name of a lord' (I, 141, *l.* 337). This separation of the place and the man is repeated in several poems. In 'To all, to whom I write' (*Ep.* ix, *p.* 29) he warns, 'I, a poet here, no herald am'; in another poem in praise of Sir Thomas Roe (*Ep.* xcix, *p.* 64) he criticises the confusion of place with deed:

> But much it now avails, what's done, of whom:
> The selfsame deeds, as diversely they come,
> From place, or fortune, are made high, or low,
> And even the praiser's judgement suffers so.
> Well, though thy name less than our great ones be,
> Thy fact is more;

in 'To Sir William Jephson' (*Ep.* cxvi, *p.* 75) he writes,

> Thou wert the first, mad'st merit know her strength,
> And those that lacked it, to suspect at length,
> 'Twas not entailed on title;

in 'An Elegy on the Lady Jane Paulet' (*Und.* lxxxiii, *p.* 269) he distinguishes between 'forms' and 'virtues'; in the eighth part of 'Eupheme' (*Und.* lxxxiv, *p.* 282), 'To Kenelm, John, George', he adds to the aphorism ''Tis virtue alone, is true nobility' (the subject of Juvenal's *Satire* VIII) the idea that virtue is studied, not inherited.

To emphasise this distinction involves some irresponsible skirting of the fact of nobility and its social function, of the economic and social causes that first brought poet and patron together and that resulted in the commendatory poem. Jonson's poems are themselves an acknowledgement of the fact that in Jacobean England it was place, not virtue, that commanded respect. Jonson not only admired men for their virtuous isolation, their indifference to the externals of fortune and place; he knew and respected the social and hierarchical importance of the aristocracy. He partly feared flattery, as a betrayal of his independence and a relinquishing of a self-directed system of value, yet he understood its uses.

The degradation inherent in flattering in the hope of reward is expressed in a bitter epigram 'To My Muse' (*Ep.* lxv, *p.* 48). His muse has betrayed him 'to a worthless lord', has made him 'commit most fierce idolatry'; from now on his new muse must teach him to avoid the indignities of social abasement:

> She shall instruct my after-thoughts to write
> Things manly, and not smelling parasite.

36

Yet Jonson manages to defend himself half-ironically, half-seriously:

> whoe'er is raised,
> For worth he has not, he is taxed, not praised.

Praise is a burden, it sets a standard for the man praised, it exposes him. This attitude is elaborated in 'An Epistle to Master John Selden' (*Und.* xiv, *p.* 159), where the subject is praise of authors rather than of men of great place:

> I confess (as every muse hath erred,
> And mine not least) I have too oft preferred
> Men past their terms, and praised some names too much,
> But 'twas with purpose to have made them such.

This may seem disingenuous: if flattery is praise beyond desert, then Jonson is a flatterer. In *Discoveries* Jonson describes how such praise may corrupt:

> For indeed men could never be taken, in that abundance, with the springes of others' flattery, if they began not there [i.e. in self-deceit]; if they did but remember, how much more profitable the bitterness of truth were, than all the honey distilling from a whorish voice; which is not praise, but poison.... There is as great a vice in praising, and as frequent, as in detracting.
>
> (VIII, 596–7, 613, *ll.* 1078–83, 1634–5)

By his use of the commendatory poem, however, Jonson implies that the tendency of excessive praise is not to corrupt the judgement of the man praised, but to provide him with a superior model for behaviour which he is encouraged to imitate and which will in turn make him a worthy pattern for imitation.

Although in the majority of the poems Jonson's subject is private virtue, the unshaken centre maintained in spite of circumstance, there is an important group of poems, particularly those on the Sidney family, where he develops a view of the good society and the importance of friendship, marriage, and the family, relations existing in time which continue and pass on the traditions of the society. Families like the Sidneys are seen to embody inherited social values, and to diffuse them outwards through society while transmitting them to the future.[26] Jonson's finest poem on the moral value and social function of friendship is the ode 'To the immortal memory, and friendship of that noble pair, Sir Lucius Cary, and Sir H. Morison' (*Und.* lxx, *p.* 242). There is an initial antithesis between isolated virtue and public vice, between the individual act, the short perfect life, and corrupting time:

> For, what is life, if measured by the space,
> Not by the act?
> Or masked man, if valued by his face,
> Above his fact?

But Jonson develops a more complex view of the place of the good man in society and in time. Morison was the ideal citizen, filling a role not in opposition to but in tune with the movement of the world:

> All offices were done
> By him, so ample, full, and round,
> In weight, in measure, number, sound,
> As though his age imperfect might appear,
> His life was of humanity the sphere.

He lives in Jonson's poem and in Cary's life:

> Whilst that in heaven, this light on earth must shine.
> And shine as you exalted are;
> Two names of friendship, but one star.

Through admiration of common values the friends grew to imitate each other, and in turn to become the pattern for society:

> Nothing perfect done,
> But as a Cary, or a Morison.

Thus, through the friendship of good men, the ideal of virtue which seems antithetical to society permeates it; Morison's death cannot prevent the perpetuation through Cary of the virtues he represents.

It is through marriage and the family even more than through friendship that Jonson sees the perpetuation of social values. He uses marriage partly as an image of the restrained, virtuous life. Thus he compliments Sir Robert Sidney's wife in 'To Penshurst' (*For*. ii, *p*. 96):

> Thy lady's noble, fruitful, chaste withal.
> His children thy great lord may call his own:
> A fortune, in this age, but rarely known.

Such an image is the basis of his praise of Lady Aubigny as a wife (*For*. xiii). Yet marriage is also a public fact, a symbol of full membership of society; this point of view is the basis of the two marriage masques, *Hymenaei* and *Haddington*, and of the 'Epithalamion' (*Und*. lxxv, *p*. 252). In the latter, the celebration of marriage involves other kinds of social ritual and tradition. Charles I's elevation of Lord Weston (a patron of

Jonson's old age) parallels the social use of marriage in perpetuating tradition. Children propagate their parents' names,

> And keep their fames
> Alive, which else would die,
> For fame keeps virtue up, and it posterity.

Similarly the king's recognition of good men perpetuates fame and encourages virtue:

> when a noble nature's raised
> It brings friends joy, foes grief, posterity fame;
> In him the times, no less than prince, are praised,
> And by his rise, in active men, his name
> Doth emulation stir;
> To the dull, a spur
> It is: to the envious meant
> A mere upbraiding grief, and torturing punishment.

A slighter poem illustrating the influence of family tradition is the 'Ode. To Sir William Sidney, on his Birthday' (*For.* xiv, *p.* 120). On the one hand Jonson warns, characteristically, that birth does not of itself imply virtue; on the other he reminds William (son of Robert, nephew of Philip) of the family example which should guide him and against which he must measure himself:

> they, that swell
> With dust of ancestors, in graves but dwell.
> 'Twill be exacted of your name, whose son,
> Whose nephew, whose grandchild you are;
> And men
> Will, then,
> Say you have followed far,
> When well begun.

This combination of personal virtue with the fulfilment of the promise of a name will make Sidney doubly conspicuous:

> So may you live in honour, as in name,
> If with this truth you be inspired.

The birthday, like marriage a public ritual, will remain a symbol of these ideals and an incitement to their fulfilment.

In several poems Sir Philip Sidney stands as the representative of civilisation. In two poems to the Countess of Rutland, Sidney's daughter (*Ep.* lxxix and *For.* xii) Sidney is the type of the poet; in 'To Mary Lady Wroth' (*Ep.* ciii, *p.* 66), as in the ode to William Sidney, to name her as a Sidney is to praise her, since the name is 'itself, the imprese of the great'. Jonson feels that he need define her virtue no further: 'My praise is plain'. In 'To Penshurst' the tree planted at Sidney's birth exists as a reminder of his perfect life, which was a meeting of the muses. Like the dead Henry Morison, Sidney and the values he represented live on as an example and through the imitation of his family.

Though Jonson's exposition of the Stoic view of virtue is clear enough, his idea of the good society is more vague. What Sidney stands for in the public world is not stated. To his friend Fulke Greville who tried to define his place as the type of the public servant and his understanding of the relation of ideals to practical morality, Sidney was 'that exact image of quiet, and action'.[27] But Jonson was not like Greville writing a retrospective account of Elizabethan government and society, with Sidney's place in it as a historical example. His poems are a living bond between the poet, his subject, and society, they are part of a chain of influence. Their inexplicitness is a result of Jonson's chosen forms, of his decision not to address a nation or a group but to use epistolary verse as a means of transforming society through his influence on individuals. In 'To Penshurst', however, perhaps his most famous and least characteristic poem, Jonson gives as nowhere else a model of the harmonious society in which all the varieties of life and tendencies of human activity are seen to have their place. Yet although the poem presents a microcosm of society, its very form indicates Jonson's essential pessimism about the possibility of transferring the values of individual life to society as a whole.

'To Penshurst' illustrates, embodied in the country house and its uses, the ideal function of the aristocracy, their position in relation to the king above them and the people below, their social responsibility in country life. Society is seen as a stable hierarchy, a harmonious interaction of parts; its continuity is assured by the institution of the family and the transmission of values from parents to children. Human life is in harmony with nature; Penshurst illustrates a universal as well as a social order. The house is distinguished not by artificial ornamentation but by its natural advantages:

> Thou joyest in better marks, of soil, of air,
> Of wood, of water, therein thou art fair.

The personification of the house associates it with natural objects, just as the produce of the estate is humanised; the natural world is seen in the terms of political society:

> Thou hast thy ponds, that pay thee tribute fish,
> Fat, aged carps, that run into thy net.
> And pikes, now weary their own kind to eat,
> As loth, the second draught, or cast to stay,
> Officiously, at first, themselves betray.

Society is tied by the bond of mutual support, to which even natural things acknowledge their obligation; the pike gives up his predatory instincts and dutifully sacrifices himself. The chief image of this mutual dependence is hospitality. The tenants' services are repaid by their lord; economic relations are personal and social. Thus the tenants' gifts are symbolic of affection rather than economic dependence:

> But what can this (more than express their love)
> Add to thy free provisions, far above
> The need of such? whose liberal board doth flow,
> With all, that hospitality doth know!

This hospitality embraces all levels of society, 'the farmer, and the clown', the poet and the king. The social bond both gives meaning to and loosens the idea of hierarchy; a kind of equality is implicit in the importance attached to each member of society:

> comes no guest, but is allowed to eat,
> Without his fear, and of thy lord's own meat:
> ...all is there
> As if thou, then, wert mine, or I reigned here:
> There's nothing I can wish, for which I stay.

King and peasant are equally welcome: the country people join with their masters in welcoming the king. Though James's visit is unexpected, the house is always prepared to receive him:

> what praise was heaped
> On thy good lady, then! who, therein, reaped
> The just reward of her high housewifery;
> ...not a room, but dressed,
> As if it had expected such a guest!

Hospitality is not forced or artificial but a natural condition of the society; the mutual dependence of the component parts is achieved through spontaneity. Each part's function in relation to the rest is known and fulfilled. This traditional knowledge is preserved through the education of the children, who

> Read, in their virtuous parents' noble parts,
> The mysteries of manners, arms, and arts.

Though the introduction of the king is deliberately casual (and there is no indication of his functions and obligations), the careful inclusion of the natural and social hierarchies, so that the poem moves from the four elements up to the king, indicates that this is intended as a portrait of a whole society, as a microcosm, not just a part that has been isolated. Yet at the same time the society of Penshurst is seen in relation to depressing actuality; the poem begins and ends by setting Penshurst against the standard of 'other edifices', 'proud, ambitious heaps'. This comparison complicates the poem's meaning. It is important to decide what Jonson meant by portraying this idealised society, whether he thought he was describing an existing society, or a society that was threatened and passing, or whether the writing of this poem is symptomatic of his antagonism to society as a whole, and is ultimately self-defeating.[28] In order to find the answers to these questions we must examine some of the social developments in Jacobean England and Jonson's own understanding of them.

Jonson's reactions to the conditions of his society were varied and sometimes inconsistent. He was capable of Stoic withdrawal in some of the poems, the castigation of a money-oriented society in the plays, and support of the magnificent self-justification of monarchy in the masques. The reason for this ambivalence is the combination of what he saw as alarming social developments with his own determined adherence to traditional social views, and the peculiar opportunities presented to him by the patronage of great families and of the king. Had Jonson been, like Drayton, a poet excluded from court influence, the Stoic and anti-court tone in his work might have been much stronger, and there might have been much less sense of the feasibility of traditional institutions. One reason why Jonson seems particularly sensitive as a social critic is that his reactions are not uncompromising; he is prepared to test the ways in which existing institutions can be made to work.

Jonson's idea of the social function of the country house was by no means original. His view of the interconnection of hospitality, patronage, philanthropy, and exemplary virtue is shared by Nicholas Breton, writing of Wilton, the home of Sidney's sister the Countess of Pembroke:

Her house being in a manner a kind of little court...a house richly garnished, honour kindly entertained, virtue highly esteemed, service well rewarded, and the poor blessedly relieved.[29]

A more explicit view of the political function of the country house is given in Sidney's *Arcadia*. Kalander's house (which may be modelled on Penshurst) is described in terms similar to those used by Jonson later; in both, the aesthetic mean reflects the quality of domestic life. Pyrocles and Musidorus reach the house,

about which they might see (with fit consideration both of the air, the prospect, and the nature of the ground) all such necessary additions to a great house, as might well show, Kalander knew that provision is the foundation of hospitality, and thrift the fuel of magnificence. The house itself was built of fair and strong stone, not affecting so much any extraordinary kind of fineness, as an honourable representing of a firm stateliness. The lights, doors and stairs, rather directed to the use of the guest, than to the eye of the artificer...: all more lasting than beautiful, but that the consideration of the exceeding lastingness made the eye believe it was exceeding beautiful.[30]

Kalander's house embodies virtuous living, but it does not signify retirement from wider social concerns. The importance of the country house as a source of political and social virtues is contrasted with the misguided pastoralism of Basilius' retirement from his court, which represents an irresponsible abdication of political responsibility; on these grounds Kalander is strongly critical of his prince. The questions underlying the fable are those of the proper relation of the great noble to the king and how responsibility should be shared between them. The dangers are on the one hand overmighty subjects and on the other arbitrary princes: equilibrium must be maintained. The results of too much power on the side of the subject are described in the social conditions at the time of Euarchus' accession:

The name of a king was grown even odious to the people, his authority having been abused by those great lords, and little kings .... For they having the power of kings, but not the nature of kings, used the authority as men do their farms, of which they see within a year they shall go out: making the king's sword strike whom they hated, the king's purse reward whom they loved: and...making the royal countenance to undermine the royal sovereignty. For the subjects could taste no sweeter fruits of having a king, than grievous taxations to serve vain purposes; laws made rather to find faults, than to prevent faults; the court of a prince rather deemed as a privileged place of unbridled licentiousness, than as a biding of him, who as a father, should give a fatherly example unto his people. Hence grew a very dissolution of all estates, while the great men (by the nature of ambition never satisfied) grew factious among themselves: and the underlings, glad indeed to be underlings to them they hated least, to preserve them from such they hated most.[31]

The achievement of the Tudors in breaking the power of the nobility and in harnessing them to the purposes of the monarchy provides Sidney with this picture of social dissolution; a weak monarchy is seen as the first link in a chain of social decay, resulting in the destructive antagonism of the parts of society that should coexist by mutual support. When Euarchus sets out to restore his kingdom, he does not make the mistake of asserting unlimited power; in addition to setting a standard of conduct himself, he is careful to recognise his own dependence on his people:

43

Where most princes (seduced by flattery to build upon false grounds of government) make themselves (as it were) another thing from the people; and so count it gain what they can get from them: and (as if it were two counter-balances, that their estate goes highest when the people goes lowest) by a fallacy of argument thinking themselves most kings, when the subject is most basely subjected: he contrariwise, virtuously and wisely acknowledging, that he with his people made all but one politic body, whereof himself was the head; even so cared for them, as he would for his own limbs: ...in all his actions showing a delight to their welfare, brought that to pass, that while by force he took nothing, by their love he had all.[32]

The balanced society requires the responsible cooperation of prince and nobility; too much power on either side will destroy the balance. The country house and the court in their true realisation are images of each other; they represent stages of the working of good government in society.[33] One important political lesson of *Arcadia* (which was meant, as Greville saw, to have practical application)[34] is its sense of the precariousness of political stability, the constant effort needed to keep the balance. Writing during the more socially divided period of James's reign, Greville thought that Elizabeth had been successful in maintaining this balance; she had tried to keep the old foundations of government, to preserve her state above the affronts of nobility and people; she had restrained her favourites, watched over her ministers, and kept nobility and gentry in their proper place between the throne and the people.[35]

Though Elizabeth's rule seemed a great achievement to contemporaries, it is questionable whether the apparent stability of Elizabethan society, the cooperation of crown and nobility, local and central government, could have lasted, since methods sometimes thought to assure stability in fact tended to its dissolution. Bacon's later *Essays*, written towards the end of James's reign, provide not a model for a good society but (after the manner of Machiavelli) advice as to the maintenance of power; they mark Bacon's appreciation that different groups and interests constantly pull against each other, that to take action in one direction is to invite disaster in another, that equilibrium constantly needs to be redefined. As Bacon saw it, the factors that had to be balanced were strong central government, military strength, the popular reverence for nobility that comes from their magnificent living, the wealth of the country, and the contentment of the commoners; but these elements of a stable society are, as Bacon understood, not necessarily compatible.[36] Important changes were taking place in the relation of nobility to monarchy at this time, which, while seemingly of advantage to the central authority, ultimately had the effect of undermining it.[37] Jonson notes both a decline

44

in the social function of the aristocracy and a change in the dominant ethic: to him these changes are not so much social and economic (though he does associate the new ethic with particular social groups) as moral.

The decline of the aristocracy's military usefulness and the growing effeminacy of society are described in two poems, 'An epistle to a Friend, to persuade him to the Wars' (*Und.* xv, *p.* 162), and 'A speech according to Horace' (*Und.* xliv, *p.* 213).[38] The first of these satirises ambition for wealth and place, vanity, greed, and lechery, which are presented here as they are in the plays as the prevailing social standard. The tone of fierce denigration precludes any real examination of causes. Jonson simply states

> This hath our ill-used freedom, and soft peace
> Brought on us, and will every hour increase.

But he is not seriously proposing English intervention in the Thirty Years' War as a cure for domestic evils. In contrast to this 'vicious ease' Jonson advocates action, the career of a soldier, but at the end of the poem, where the ideal is set against the actuality, it is clear that war is used mainly as a metaphor for the Stoic fortitude portrayed in such poems as 'To the World'. Jonson's hope for his friend Colby is

> That by commanding first thyself, thou mak'st
> Thy person fit for any charge thou tak'st;
> That fortune never make thee to complain,
> But what she gives, thou dar'st give her again;
> That whatsoever face thy fate puts on,
> Thou shrink or start not, but be always one;
> That thou think nothing great, but what is good,
> And from that thought strive to be understood.

This poem is true to the Juvenalian spirit; the degeneracy of society is accepted as a fact, and the only solution is personal honesty. 'A speech according to Horace', however, though it has a similar railing tone, gives a more considered view of the relation of the aristocracy's decline to the state of society. If 'To Penshurst' shows the aristocracy filling their proper social function, 'A speech' shows their disastrous social irresponsibility. The irony is that an attempted revival of the military function of the aristocracy, which is the subject of this poem, would probably have resulted not in a proliferation of Penshursts, but rather in the kind of disintegration described by Sidney.[39]

Jonson sees that the aristocracy's military function has been usurped by citizens; chivalry has been displaced by the trained-bands. There is in the first part of the poem a skilful and malicious attempt to discredit the citizens' aspirations:

> What a strong fort old Pimlico had been!

45

This manipulation of names implies a set of social attitudes:

> keep the glory of the English name,
> Up among nations. In the stead of bold
> Beauchamps, and Nevilles, Cliffords, Audleys old;
> Insert thy Hodges, and those newer men,
> As Stiles, Dike, Ditchfield, Miller, Cripps, and Fen.

It is not only the citizens who come in for this lashing. But the criticism of the aristocracy is of a different kind: Jonson attacks them for their neglect of the moral virtues which give their status meaning:

> Let poor nobility be virtuous: We,
> Descended in a rope of titles, be
> From Guy, or Bevis, Arthur, or from whom
> The herald will. Our blood is now become
> Past any need of virtue.

This is Jonson's often repeated theme, that there is no necessary connection between virtue and blood, but here treated from the opposite point of view. Jonson is not concerned with moral values irrespective of circumstance, but with trying to make a socially conspicuous class useful. He takes two different stands; he attacks both moral degeneracy in the nobility, and change in society as a whole. He sees social developments in moral terms (it is the moral failure of the old nobility that has allowed 'newer men' to rise) but these changes also seem to him inevitable and uncontrollable.

It is in the plays particularly that Jonson associates moral decay with social change. One can read the plays with different kinds of emphasis: one can see them as portraying a deliberately inverted moral world governed by coherent laws, which is understood as such because of a public system of values shared by author and audience; or as satirising particular social developments which are seen to be threatening inherited values.[40] Both treatments are valid. Jonson's ethical position is confused because he combines moral and social interpretation. The scheme of values exemplified by the play characters is both the moral obverse of Stoic self-sufficiency and the social obverse of the hierarchy and mutual dependence implied in 'To Penshurst'.

It is impossible to give an adequate account here of Jonson's major plays, but a brief examination of certain themes and techniques will help to clarify his attitudes in the poems and the kinds of positive direction that were open to him. For the purposes of his drama Jonson assumes that the incapacity of the Senecan vicious man to distinguish between a good and an advantage is universal. Society as seen in *Sejanus*, *Volpone*, *The Alchemist*, and *Catiline* is activated by the desire for money and for power. Although there are characters in these plays who embody Jonsonian

46

virtue (Arruntius, Celia, Bonario, and Cicero), their values do not form the framework of the plays, and it is not because of these values that the characters succeed or fail.

In *Catiline* the chorus does retain something of the function of the commentator of the early satiric comedies, but it explains rather than directs the action. The interesting chorus at the end of Act I expresses both Jonson's sense of the misdirected scheme of values by which society is destroying itself, and his doubt as to whether any public action can arrest this process. Are fluctuation and decay an inevitable condition of society?

> Can nothing great, and at the height
> Remain so long? but its own weight
> Will ruin it? Or, is't blind chance,
> That still desires new states t'advance,
> And quit the old? Else, why must Rome,
> Be by itself, now, overcome?   (v, 452, *ll.* 531-6)

Jonson may be unsure of the answer to these questions, but he is explicit about the process of destruction. After describing the luxury and effeminacy of the Romans, the chorus continues,

> Hence comes that wild, and vast expense,
> That hath enforced Rome's virtue, thence,
> Which simple poverty first made:
> And, now, ambition doth invade
> Her state, with eating avarice,
> Riot, and every other vice.
> Decrees are bought, and laws are sold,
> Honours, and offices for gold;
> The people's voices: and the free
> Tongues, in the Senate, bribed be.
> Such ruin of her manners Rome
> Doth suffer now, as she's become
> (Without the gods it soon gainsay)
> Both her own spoiler, and own prey. (*p.* 453, *ll.* 573-96)

This theme of the essential self-destructiveness of ambition and greed is central to all the plays. If all men are impelled by the same insatiable desire for power, permanent social conflict is inevitable. There may be temporary victors, like Lovewit and Face at the end of *The Alchemist*, or Macro at the end of *Sejanus*, but we can be certain that the cycle of ambition, collision, and destruction will repeat itself. Not only is conflict between man and man inevitable, man cannot live in harmony with nature. Even at the height of their power, when they have surmounted human opposition, the ambitious characters in this world cannot be

47

satisfied. The tendency of their ambition is not merely moral self-destruction or the servitude involved in the pursuit of unattainable ends, but the more frightening prospect of the exhaustion of material resources: the ambitious man destroys himself and the world which is not adequate to contain him. These kinds of destruction are made explicit by the ambitious characters themselves, though they do not always understand the reason for their dissatisfaction. If they did understand they would have reached the position of the Stoic sage and would logically abandon their activities.

Those pursuing the philosopher's stone in *The Alchemist*, gulled by Face and Subtle, cannot understand the absurdity of their desires; Epicure Mammon's elaborate and foolish dreams are for pleasures scarcely known in nature and for that reason desirable. Since the basis of pleasure for him is novelty, achievement must be self-defeating. Epicure Mammon's imaginings (v, 319–20) are the farcical counterpart to Volpone's speech to Celia (v, 82–3, *ll*. 185–205). Volpone seems to control his ambition in that the objects which give him the promise of pleasure are dispensable; while he (and Celia) will maintain an infinite capacity for enjoying infinite numbers of them. But Volpone will never be satisfied, since his ambition will exhaust his material:

> could we get the phoenix,
> (Though nature lost her kind) she were our dish.
>
> (*ll*. 204–5)

Sejanus faces a similar problem. An early soliloquy (IV, 379–80, *ll*. 139–62) shows him anticipating the course of his 'wicked acts', which will prove his power; towards the end of the play, when his ambitions have been realised, he regrets the absence of opposition, the emptiness of ambition that has nothing to feed on:

> Is there not something more, than to be Caesar?
> Must we rest there? It irks, to have come so far,
> To be so near a stay.
>
> .   .   .   .
>
> Winds lose their strength, when they do empty fly,
> Unmet of woods or buildings; great fires die,
> That want their matter to withstand them; so,
> It is our grief, and will be our loss, to know
> Our power shall want opposites.
>
> (IV, 437, *ll*. 13–15, 17–24)

The conflict between man and nature involved in this limitless ambition should be understood with reference to the idea of the harmonious interdependence of man and nature seen in 'To Penshurst'. The antithesis to the ambitious man whose desires are tied to and thwarted by the exhaustibility of nature is the Stoic hero celebrated so often in the poems who wants and needs nothing, who is indifferent to fortune, and whose strength has been achieved through this indifference. The contrasting images of ceaseless motion and rest, conflict and harmony, presuppose both a private ethical standard and a scheme of social values. Both underlie the plays, and one must decide to what extent the drama is impelled by personal moral energy or a desire to identify with and defend a social structure which is seen to be threatened historically by the kinds of action displayed on the stage.

The context of the comedies, as in the satire of puritans and monopolists, is often deliberately contemporary and immediate. Jonson tends to identify the moral characteristics he dislikes with contemporary social and economic developments. That Jonson believes moral decay goes hand in hand with social disintegration is apparent from 'A speech according to Horace', and the epistle to the Countess of Rutland (*For.* xii, *p.* 114), where the social as well as the moral effects of the pursuit of money are observed: gold gives 'pride fame, and peasants birth'. Jonson's reactions to his society are both those of a moralist who would be uneasy in any age, and of a social critic conscious of a specific change in social and economic relationships during a particular period.

But while Jonson clearly shares the prejudices of his contemporaries, one should avoid making the same social interpretations as he does, and one should be wary of trying to identify him with one section of society because he criticises another.[41] He certainly believed things had been better in the past, but it is doubtful whether 'To Penshurst' is intended as an appeal to that past. The tone of this poem is as much implicitly opposed to the court (in spite of its hierarchical pattern) as it is an attack on the socially disruptive ambitions of 'new men' (whoever they might be), the Volpones or the Epicure Mammons.

Jonson puts forward a view of the proper relations between the landowning nobility, their tenants, and the crown, which is not based on a desire to revive the feudal military status of the nobility (even though this status is a touchstone of social usefulness in 'A speech according to Horace'),[42] and which criticises the wasteful and ostentatious relationship between the crown and the competitive nobility encouraged for different reasons by both Elizabeth and James. This criticism emerges both in the comparison between Penshurst and other ambitious, ostentatious piles, and in the description of James's unobtrusive and welcome visit to the Sidneys.

In speaking of 'proud, ambitious heaps' Jonson is not alluding to building by *nouveaux riches*, with no understanding of the social function of the aristocracy.[43] For it was the aristocracy themselves who were becoming increasingly ostentatious at this time, with the object of preserving their crumbling status.[44] Jonson might have had Salisbury in mind;[45] and if the Cecils were new men, so were the Sidneys. Jonson is not appealing to the feudal past but trying to provide an alternative pattern for the dangerous tendencies of the present. Some of the houses built in this period had no domestic, only a symbolic function; they were built at enormous expense to receive the sovereign on progress.[46] It is against the background of a contemporary relationship between crown and great subjects that threatened to be mutually destructive, rather than with a sense of the subversion of old social values, that we should construe the easy reciprocity of 'To Penshurst'.

In this poem, though criticism of the crown's policies is understood, the anti-court tone is constructive; Jonson, like Sidney, envisions the proper relations that should exist between the country house and the court. But the position is a delicate one: the gap between constructive and anti-social idealism is narrow. 'To Sir Robert Wroth' (*For*. iii, *p*. 96), which can be seen as a darker companion piece to 'To Penshurst', is explicitly anti-court; the object of the satire is not so much to reveal the discrepancy between courtly ideals and realities, nor to advocate a reciprocal relationship between court and country, as to present another, better way of life embodied in the country whose values are incompatible with those of the court.

The poem explicitly condemns magnificence, the symbolic ostentation of the court, particularly as characterised by masquing. It is a ritual of waste, which involves the poet too. Wroth does not throng

> to have a sight
> Of the short bravery of the night;
> To view the jewels, stuffs, the pains, the wit
> There wasted, some not paid for yet!

Though the life led by Wroth is seen in similar terms to that at Penshurst, as exhibiting the mutual dependence of people, nobility, and king (James when hunting 'makes thy house his court'), nevertheless the shape of the poem is a contrast between Wroth's virtues, which are essentially private, and public spheres of advancement. The catalogue of opportunities includes all those areas where ambition and greed are seen to be the norm: the military life, the law, trade, and the court.[47] In contrast, at the end of the poem Wroth is seen to live at peace with himself, unenvious of other ways of life.[48] Though Jonson mentions service to the country, the characteristic of the ethics advocated here is that they are self-directed:

> Thy morning's, and thy evening's vow
> Be thanks to him, and earnest prayer, to find
> A body sound, with sounder mind;
> To do thy country service, thy self right;

That neither want do thee affright,
Nor death; but when thy latest sand is spent,
Thou mayest think life, a thing but lent.

Reliance on classical precedents gives poems like 'To Penshurst' and
'To Sir Robert Wroth' an important part of their tone, even where the
tendency of the original is not fully pursued.[49] The themes of the simple,
virtuous life, of attacks on luxury especially as found in the city, are
characteristic of all the four Latin poets who were Jonson's chief models.[50]
Horace and Martial frequently use their own way of life, their freedom
from circumstances, as a touchstone for judging the extravagance around
them. There is in this respect an interesting difference between Jonson
and his models. Jonson leaves us in no doubt, from his stance in the
plays and his hortatory tone in the poems, that he is an arbiter of
virtue; but, although it is the poet who appraises the quality of life at
Penshurst and Durance, in 'To Penshurst' he plays a subordinate role and
he is absent from 'To Sir Robert Wroth'. There is thus a difference in
intention between Jonson on the one hand and Horace, Martial, and
sometimes Juvenal on the other, which is the result of the social situation.[51] Jonson was a professional, writing for a limited circle of which
he was not a member except in his capacity as poet. Although Maecenas
has become the archetypal patron, for Horace he was the man who gave
him independence. When the Latin poets contrast country and town
they have in mind not so much the differences between a rural and an
urban society as between independence, self-sufficiency, freedom to
practise the good life and sycophancy, the status of a client who is tied
to the circumstances of the patronage system.

The fact that Jonson hardly uses this genre of personal poetry should
not make one ignore his oblique allusions to the personal tone of Horace
and Martial. These allusions imply that to an extent he is concerned in
his country house poems with an attitude of mind, a quality of life
which is in some sense anti-social, rather than with depicting society
as a whole and as it might be. Jonson did not perhaps fully see the self-
defeating tendency of his own poems, whose intention is social rather
than personal. His poetic relation to monarchy and aristocracy prevented
the development of a sense of self-identity. In the case of Pope, who
was cut off from this sphere of public usefulness, the self-direction of
Horace was fully realised; Jonson's attention to the needs and status
of his audience limited the direction of his personal ethics.

His function for the Sidney family thus approaches the importance
of his relation to the king. The Sidneys are for Jonson the ideal nobility,
who unite the trappings of their birth, which makes them conspicuous,
with the private ethics of self-sufficiency and ability to scorn circumstance, which gives them the force of an example. Such a combination

of place and virtue is the ideal implied in 'A speech according to Horace'; Jonson moves from the Senecan view of private virtue to the Aristotelian great man.

THE FUNCTION OF A COURT

Jonson's attitude to the court, its life, its rituals, and its values, was ambivalent. On the one hand the court was the seat of the king, the centre of government, the visible embodiment of the crown's strength and the nation's virtues; on the other hand it was an artificial, extravagant, self-deceptive society, where name, place, status, and empty forms were valued above innate worth and substance. Jonson's temperament, personal ethics, and sense of poetic function pulled him in different directions: as a writer, he could either try to fuse the shadow with the substance, the symbol with what it should signify; or he could expose the sham, point to the discrepancy between the ideal and the reality, insist on the irrelevance of public forms to the practice of virtue. In a number of epigrams he gives vent to his hatred of the parasites and posers attracted by the court; in 'An Elegy' (*Und.* xlii, *p.* 199), part of whose object is to attack idealistic and artificial love poetry, he writes of his own relations with court ladies:

> I who live, and have lived twenty year
> Where I may handle silk, as free, and near,
> As any mercer; or the whale-bone man
> That quilts those bodies, I have leave to span:
> Have eaten with the beauties, and the wits,
> And braveries of court, and felt their fits
> Of love, and hate: and came so nigh to know
> Whether their faces were their own, or no.

His contempt for court society and its pretences is expressed by stripping clothes from bodies; in the dedication to the court of *Cynthia's Revels* (his earliest attempt to influence this society), dress is a metaphor for the surface grandeur of court life which must clothe a worthy object. But here also antagonism between body and mind, form and substance, is seen to be inevitable:

In thee [the court], the whole kingdom dresseth itself, and is ambitious to use thee as her glass. Beware, then, thou render men's figures truly, and teach them no less to hate their deformities, than to love their forms: For, to grace, there should come reverence; and no man can call that lovely, which is not also venerable. It is not powdering, perfuming, and every day smelling of the tailor, that converteth to a beautiful object: but a mind, shining through any suit, which needs no false light either of riches, or honours to help it. (IV, 33, *ll.* 6–17)

52

As a writer of masques, a form whose ephemeral quality he tried hard to combat, Jonson was perpetually faced with this antagonism. Although he dominated the masque for twenty-five years, and it is because of his development of the form that it is more than a chapter in social history, it remains true that to a large extent his hands were tied; his innovations were both in structure and seriousness, but he was obliged to accept the part played by the masque in court life and the ethic underlying it. The fact that he was working in a received form and with a particular social function forced him to modify his style and his moral position.[52]

With regard to the heroic and mythological material of the masques Jonson was in two minds. In 'An Execration upon Vulcan' (*Und.* xliii, *p.* 202) he shows contempt for Arthurian and romance matter; he would be prepared to exchange for his own lost writings

> The whole sum
> Of errant knighthood, with the dames, and dwarfs,
> The charmed boats, and the enchanted wharfs;
> The Tristrams, Lancelots, Turpins, and the Peers,
> All the mad Rolands, and sweet Olivers.

In his comedies he ridicules Ovidian romance in the extravagant fantasies of Volpone and Epicure Mammon; of his efforts in epic we have only the mock-heroic 'On the Famous Voyage' (*Ep.* cxxxiii, *p.* 84). His predilection for the middle style in his poems inhibited the use of mythology. Yet also in 'An Execration' Jonson claims to have lost in the fire

> among
> The rest, my journey into Scotland sung,
> With all the adventures; Three books not afraid
> To speak the fate of the Sicilian maid
> To our own lady's; and in story there
> Of our fifth Henry, eight of his nine year.

Further, Drummond reports 'for a heroic poem he said there was no such ground as King Arthur's fiction' (I, 136, *ll.* 148–9), and

> that he had an intention to perfect an epic poem entitled Heroologia of the worthies of his country, roused by fame, and was to dedicate it to his country.
>   (I, 132, *ll.* 1–4)

Jonson was infected by the Renaissance enthusiasm for epic while often in practice turning his back on its form and assumptions.[53] In the masques he may have found an adequate outlet for these aspirations for a national subject, but although he clearly enjoyed the opportunity they gave for a display of erudition, he may at times have resented the need to work in the figurative style, rather than in the plain and 'truthful' style of satire and epistle. But a greater difficulty for Jonson than the structural demands of the masque was its assumption of a public world with appropriate public values.

Jonson's reliance on Senecan ethics in many of his poems indicates a hostility to the ambitions and values of public life, however superficially attractive. He urges the heroes of his poems to understand that fame and glory are just as unworthy as wealth and power, and just as irrelevant to the independent mind. But as a writer of masques, presenting an idealised image of the court world to itself, Jonson could only express his antagonism to the realities of court life by accepting the underlying idea of the king's exemplary function and the moral as well as social importance of concepts like honour, fame, and magnificence. The high moral tone of Jonson's masques is the result of his attempt to give meaning to these imprecise ideas, while at the same time his theorising about the uses of masque and his quarrels with other workers in the same field, Samuel Daniel and Inigo Jones, are evidence of his basic uneasiness and his doubts about being able to reconcile the showy ephemeral form with the weight of meaning placed on it. It is not the political theory, such as it is, in his masques that embarrasses him; rather it is his acceptance of a system of conduct which always refers to public standards and values.

Though the sixteenth-century humanists sympathised with self-centred ethical systems, in their role as counsellors to princes the ideal of virtue they promulgated was public rather than private; chivalric or Christian were overlaid by Aristotelian ethics.[54] The way in which Aristotle was made to serve the interests of Renaissance moralists can be seen from Spenser's letter to Raleigh, on the design of *The Faerie Queene*; ignoring Aristotle's distinction between intellectual and moral virtues, his elevation of the former, and his preference for the contemplative life, Spenser describes his unfinished epic as embodying the two parts of moral philosophy, ethics and politics, or private and public virtue. Arthur is the personification of magnificence, which supposedly according to Aristotle is the perfection of the other virtues.[55] Magnificence meant more to the Renaissance prince than it does in Aristotle's definition, but in spite of general misinterpretation of the direction of Aristotelian ethics the common use made of his ideas in bolstering the aspirations and values of a particular class is not an unfair distortion.[56]

Jonson's admiration for the Stoic idea of the self-direction of virtue might seem to make accommodation to this social ethic in some sense a betrayal. Yet Jonson's most austere poems are the product of a social relationship; the man praised is to imitate the ideal of the poem. In the masque, whose characters are men of place and birth expecting due deference and reward, the idea of imitation is put to more complex uses. Though Jonson remains consistent about the worthlessness of ambition for its own sake, he understands its value as a tool. In a passage in *Discoveries* (probably addressed to the Earl of Newcastle on the education of his sons)[57] he states:

> It is a good thing to inflame the mind: And though ambition itself be a vice, it is often the cause of great virtue. Give me that wit, whom praise excites, glory puts on, or disgrace grieves; he is to be nourished with ambition, pricked forward with honour; checked with reprehension; and never to be suspected of sloth.
>
> (VIII, 615, *ll.* 1687–92)

There is also in *Discoveries* a number of passages on the rule and nature of the wise prince, the subject's proper attitude to him, and the importance of the poet in guiding him, all indicating Jonson's concern with the essential aim of the masque, to help the prince fulfil his function. He sees the relation between king and people in terms of mutual obligation rather than rights or power. The subject's position is one of filial reverence:

> After God, nothing is to be loved of man like the prince: He violates nature, that doth it not with his whole heart. For when he hath put on the care of the public good, and common safety; I am a wretch, and put off man, if I do not reverence, and honour him: in whose charge all things divine and human are placed.
>
> (VIII, 594, *ll.* 986–91)

But between the prince and the man of letters there is a more profound relationship:

> Learning needs rest: sovereignty gives it. Sovereignty needs counsel: learning affords it. There is such a consociation of offices, between the prince, and whom his favour breeds, that they may help to sustain his power, as he their knowledge.... A prince without letters, is a pilot without eyes. All his government is groping.
>
> (VIII, 565, *ll.* 65–9; 601, *ll.* 1234–5)

In these passages (taken in part from Vives) Jonson puts himself firmly in the tradition of Renaissance humanism, which emphasises the duty of the learned man to counsel his prince. He never steps outside this conventional framework, the view of political problems as moral ones. Even in his last years when, following the new reign, his quarrel with Jones, and his illness, he lost his influence at court (he wrote only two court masques for Charles after his accession), and when his friends included the moderates Falkland and Hyde who were critical of the court circle and its policies, there is no evidence that he was interested in any of the current constitutional or religious controversies. The idea of kingship put forward in the masques and illustrated by the performers, though it shows Jonson's strenuous effort to give life and meaning to a symbol, is not intended as political theory; rather, Jonson learns such thory as is evident from James. Working within a framework of received ideas and social customs, Jonson attempts to exploit these, to force king and courtiers by their performance in the masque out of the social ritual of self-admiration and into identification with their idealised moral selves.

The tone and content of Jonson's statements on kingship probably owe much to James I's disquisitions on his role. James is notorious for his exalted view of his function and powers, usually summarised as the theory of divine right. However, the most extravagant claims in his writings are made not on behalf of his actual working powers in the constitution but with reference to his much vaguer symbolic and moral status. He does not make use of symbolism in the way of Louis XIV to bolster his extensions of power. James was in fact anxious that the extent and nature of royal power should not be defined too closely, since analysis stripped away its mystique and revealed its deficiencies:

> That which concerns the mystery of the king's power, is not lawful to be disputed; for that is to wade into the weakness of princes, and to take away the mystical reverence, that belongs unto them that sit in the throne of God.[58]

James made clear in a defensive speech to the Commons the essential distinction between his symbolic and his legal or constitutional status. The first is seen in the widest possible terms:

> Kings are not only God's lieutenants upon earth, and sit upon God's throne, but even by God himself they are called gods. There be three principal similitudes that illustrates the state of monarchy.... In the scriptures kings are called gods, and so their power after a certain relation compared to the divine power. Kings are also compared to fathers of families.... And lastly, kings are compared to the head of this microcosm of the body of man.[59]

But there is a difference between 'the general power of a king in divinity, and the settled and established state of this crown, and kingdom'. Though in the original state of kingship the king's will is law, in the actual state of civil kingdoms kings are bound within the limits of the law. James asserts

> that never king was in all his time more careful to have his laws duly observed, and himself to govern thereafter, than I.[60]

In constitutional practice it seems that James did not want to step out of line; his interest lay not so much in his legal position and powers as in his exalted symbolic status, his exemplary moral function. So he tells Prince Henry,

This glistering worldly glory of kings, is given them by God, to teach them to press so to glister and shine before their people, in all works of sanctification and righteousness, that their persons as bright lamps of godliness and virtue, may, going in and out before their people, give light to all their steps.[61]

The court, the sphere in which the king shines, is seen to exist more to further the practice of virtue than the business of government. James gives much advice on the proper ordering of court society which conflicts lamentably with his own practice. The success of government depends ultimately on the moral character of the prince: Henry is advised,

Let your own life be a lawbook and a mirror to your people; that therein they may read the practice of their own laws; and therein they may see, by your image, what life they should lead.[62]

James tells parliament with regard to the joining of the kingdoms of England and Scotland,

I am the husband, and all the whole isle is my lawful wife; I am the head, and it is my body; I am the shepherd, and it is my flock.[63]

Thus in James's view the prince both has the force of a moral example because of his conspicuous place, and in himself symbolises the unity and harmony of his country.

Though his interest in political polemic was remarkable, James was not original in emphasising the symbolic and moral importance of the kingly image. Elizabeth had well understood the way in which she could provide a focus for her people's emotions, their fear of Spain, hatred of the Pope, Protestant fervour, ambitions for sea empire. Though Elizabeth manipulated her image for political ends, and though it was an idealised one, nevertheless it was the ideal that was needed at the time.[64] The difficulty for James was that he interpreted the monarchical image differently from his subjects. He did not see the need for endearing himself to them personally; unlike Elizabeth he hated crowds. On important issues of policy – in his friendly attitude to Spain and apparent indifference to the Protestant cause in the Thirty Years' War – he was in total opposition to widespread public feeling. His administrative incompetence, extravagance, and obsession with favourites disgusted many old Elizabethan courtiers. The Elizabethan use of art as propaganda had been largely successful; it was much harder for propaganda on behalf of James to succeed.

The danger for the masque, existing as it did in the exclusive and artificial court world and deliberately contributing to its elevation and artificiality, was that it might serve simply as a tool of self-congratulation, or even, through its ostentatious waste, might undermine rather than enhance the status and meaning of monarchy and nobility. Jonson was perpetually conscious of these dangers; his feeling that he never completely overcame them can be inferred from his inconsistent attempts to fuse form and meaning, soul and body, status and virtue, while at the same time trying to dissociate himself from the ephemerality of his work. All writers of masque must have suffered from this sense of wasted effort while at the same time trying to assert their importance. This problem is expressed by Daniel, who was involved in an indirect debate with Jonson over the question of the poet's part.

In the dedication of *The Vision of the Twelve Goddesses* (1604) to the Countess of Bedford, Daniel is conscious of a conflict in purpose between the oral and visual part of the masque; Sibylla is obliged to describe the goddesses after their presentation,

> that the eyes of the spectators might not beguile their ears, as in such cases it ever happens, whiles pomp and splendour of the sight takes up all the intention without regard what is spoken.[65]

This conflict leads Daniel both to undervalue the potential weight of his own part, and to hope that the masque's meaning will not suffer the fate of its form. The masque is not worth the expense of wit:

> Whosoever strives to show most wit about these punctilios of dreams and shows, are sure sick of a disease they cannot hide, and would fain have the world to think them very deeply learned in all mysteries whatsoever.... And yet in these matters of shows...there needs no such exact sufficiency in this kind. (III, 196, *ll.* 268–72, 278–80)

In the Preface to *Tethys' Festival* (1610), perhaps in answer to Jonson's theorising in his notes to *Hymenaei* (1606), Daniel deliberately subordinates his role to that of the architect:

> In these things wherein the only life consists in show; the art and invention of the architect gives the greatest grace, and is of most importance; ours, the least part and of least note in the time of the performance thereof. (III, 307, *ll.* 74–8)

But within the masques themselves Daniel is less self-effacing and less sure that their only life is in show. He is concerned that the passing form should endure through its influence. Thus in the *Twelve Goddesses* Sibylla prays

> That these fair blessings which we now erect
> In figures left us here, in substance may
> Be those great props of glory and respect.
> (III, 203, *ll.* 181–3)

The thoughtful and delicate song from *Tethys' Festival* sees the peculiar beauty of the masque in its brevity, but also hopes that it can survive through the memories of the spectators:

> Pleasures are not, if they last,
> In their passing, is their best.
> Glory is most bright and gay
> In a flash, and so away.
> Feed apace then greedy eyes
> On the wonder you behold.
>   Take it sudden as it flies
>   Though you take it not to hold:
>   When your eyes have done their part,
>   Thought must length it in the heart.
>
> (III, 320-1, ll. 349-58)

Daniel, while claiming less for himself than Jonson, was aware of the same problems and shared the same hopes; he was irritated by Jonson's claims perhaps because they underlined the incongruity of his own position. Jonson's aim, stated in the preface to a late masque, *Love's Triumph*, is 'To make the spectators understanders'. In the preface to *Hymenaei* he contrasts sense and understanding, body and soul, but it is the poet's part to give lasting life to form,

> Else the glory of all these solemnities had perished like a blaze, and gone out, in the beholders' eyes.   (VII, 209, *ll.* 4-6)

It is the danger of oblivion that

> hath made the most royal princes, and greatest persons...not only studious of riches, and magnificence in the outward celebration, or show; ...but curious after the most high, and hearty inventions, to furnish the inward parts:...which, though their voice be taught to sound to present occasions, their sense, or doth, or should always lay hold on more removed mysteries.   (*ll.* 10-19)

This passage gives Jonson's idea of the political function of magnificence and the moral use of the masque, but his description points to his uncertainty: rather than treat the masque as a unity, he deliberately separates its components of form and meaning, allying himself with the latter, and with immortality. Jones, on the other hand, is made the scapegoat for Jonson's uneasiness; his is the bodily part (*Blackness*, VII, 172, *l.* 90), and presumably oblivion.

Jonson's bitter quarrel with Jones (which resulted after 1625 and again conclusively after 1631 in his own exclusion from the field)[66] is indicative not only of his dislike of Jones's elevation of form at the expense of what seemed the only valuable element of the masque, but also perhaps of his unspoken sense that the physical and social conditions of the masque inevitably doomed his attempts to free himself from them.[67] In 'An Expostulation with Inigo Jones' (*U.V.* xxxiv, *p.* 402) Jones's crime is that his elaborate skills and spectacles have completely eclipsed the soul, to which the body should only be a servant:

> O shows! Shows! Mighty shows!
> The eloquence of masques! What need of prose
> Or verse, or sense to express immortal you?
> You are the spectacles of state! 'Tis true
> Court hieroglyphics! and all arts afford
> In the mere perspective of an inch board!
> You ask no more than certain politic eyes,
> Eyes that can pierce into the mysteries
> Of many colours! read them! and reveal
> Mythology there painted on slit deal!
> Oh, to make boards to speak! There is a task
> Painting and carpentry are the soul of masque.

It is not only Jones who is under attack, but the court world and its pretensions, which are unsupported by serious purpose: masquing becomes an image for all that is impermanent, false, deceptive, without intrinsic value, as it is in 'To Sir Robert Wroth', or in 'An Epistle answering...' (*p.* 220) where Jonson prays that his friendship swill be

> Such as are square, well-tagged, and permanent,
> Not built with canvas, paper, and false lights,
> As are the glorious scenes, at the great sights.

Jonson's feeling of being involved in a not altogether worthy enterprise with purposes and results beyond his control was to some extent justified; to contemporaries the question of most interest relating to the masque, after that of ambassadorial quarrels over precedence, was its outrageous expense. A well-known letter of 1606 by Sir John Harington describes how James squandered most of the money granted him by parliament after the discovery of the Gunpowder Plot on entertaining his brother-in-law the King of Denmark; the abject drunkenness of the performers ruined the masque provided for the two kings at Theobalds.[68] Clarendon was thankful that no one imitated the lavish extravagance of Jonson's *Entertainment at Welbeck* (1633) and *Love's Welcome at Bolsover* (1634) provided by Newcastle for Charles; the latter cost £15,000, far in excess of previous sums.[69] Jonson was clearly mortified at his involvement, through his provision of the *Irish Masque* and the *Challenge at Tilt*, with the notorious Essex–Somerset wedding in the winter of 1613/14, as his exclusion of any biographical detail about the origin of these works in the 1616 folio shows.[70]

Through the masque he was brought in contact with those aspects of court life that he despised. But it was in the context of the masque itself, rather than through theory or satire, that Jonson grappled successfully with the ambivalence of magnificence as a value and the ephemerality of the masque's form.

Frequently in Jonson's anti-masques, whose purpose is to provide a thematic opposition to and thus underline the meaning of the main masque, court extravagance and vanity are attacked. These comic attacks, because they proceed from characters who of their nature are to be scorned, both provide an outlet for justifiable unease and at the same time strengthen the basis of the masque's meaning. In the *Entertainment at Althorp* Nobody, a rustic, criticises the court cycle of ambition, ostentation, and reward as symbolised by the masque form (the criticism is carefully aimed at Elizabeth, not at the new regime). The rustics

> come to see, and to be seen,
> And though they dance afore the Queen,
> There's none of these doth hope to come by
> Wealth, to build another Holmby:[71]
> All those dancing days are done,
> Men must now have more than one
> Grace, to build their fortunes on. (VII, 129, *ll*. 260–6)

But Nobody recognises that he is worth nothing:

> But I am Nobody, and my breath
> (Soon as it is born) hath death. (*ll*. 274–5)

There is a more serious antagonist in *Love Restored*. Masquerado reflects lightly on the court's insolvency, but Plutus makes explicit the connection between the masque and political decay. He addresses Masquerado:

> I tell thee, I will have no more masquing; I will not buy a false, and fleeting delight so dear: The merry madness of one hour shall not cost me the repentance of an age.... I will endure thy prodigality, nor riots no more; they are the ruin of states.... I will no more of these superfluous excesses. (VII, 378, 381, *ll*. 34–6, 148–9, 162–3)

But Plutus himself is exposed as an imposter, 'usurping all those offices in this age of gold, which Love himself performed in the golden age' (382, *ll*. 178–9). Plutus attacks the masque not from the point of view of social justice but from parsimony. Cupid's defeat of Plutus is, as has been pointed out, a justification of the idea of liberality and masquing.[72]

The incorporation of criticism within the framework of the masque is well illustrated in Carew's *Coelum Britannicum* (1634). The late date of this masque makes the question of criticism of the court particularly important. Jupiter is seen to be implementing in heaven the example of Charles's reforms on earth; Charles's rule and particularly his marriage are an image of social harmony. Jupiter proclaims a competition for immortality, the reward of virtue, and both Plutus and Paenia (poverty) claim their right of place. Mercury rejects both: Plutus because he is an enemy to virtue, Paenia because her virtue is of a mediocre and servile kind. Instead

> we advance
> Such virtues only as admit excess,
> Brave bounteous acts, regal magnificence,
> All-seeing prudence, magnanimity
> That knows no bound, and that heroic virtue
> For which antiquity hath left no name,
> But patterns only.[73]

The ultimate victors, after Fortune and Hedone have also been dismissed, are Charles and Henrietta Maria; the other claimants only argue on behalf of virtue while the king and queen themselves embody it:

> your actions plead,
> And with a silent importunity
> Awake the drowsy justice of the gods
> To crown your deeds with immortality.
> The growing titles of your ancestors,
> These nations' glorious acts, joined to the stock
> Of your own royal virtues, and the clear
> Reflex they take from the imitation
> Of your famed court, make honour's story full.
>
> (*p.* 175, *ll.* 844–52)

The dynamic relation between virtue, ancestry, place, and imitation surely owes much to Jonson's formulation of the masque's use. Carew shows the nature of and the solution to the problem; the masque through its own working, and by extension the court world, must confront its critics, show the invalidity of their grounds, and demonstrate itself its complex social function.

Criticism of the masque's destructive extravagance is turned aside by argument as well as action; the problem of praise is dealt with more indirectly. The moral problem of flattery even more than the social consequences of ostentation creates a barrier to the understanding of masque. The theory of flattery is that it makes the flattered man better. If we are to judge Renaissance art by its effects – as its practitioners often implied – then its moral failure in some way involves its artistic value. On the other hand if we concentrate on intentions rather than results, this particular difficulty is sidestepped. For Jonson, praise is the material with which he works; it is the point he starts from, not the end he aims at. Contemporary expectations are important. Bacon says in his essay 'Of Praise':

> To praise a man's self, cannot be decent, except it be in rare cases: But to praise a man's office or profession, he may do it with good grace, and with a kind of magnanimity.[74]

The difference between the office and the man parallels the difference between the idealised standard of praise and the man's shortcomings; on each level the man praised is urged to fit a model of behaviour. Praise of the office is the assumption of the masque.[75] While Jonson seems often to be attempting to free the individual from the weight and distractions of his public role, there is necessarily a difference between the praise of private individuals dissociated from their roles, in the poems, and the praise of the king who 'cannot flattered be' (*Ep.* xxxvi, *p.* 38), in the masque. For Jonson James is both the private man and the public office;[76] he already has a symbolic level of existence apart from the one Jonson provides for him in the masque. The purpose of the masque is to unite these two bodies, to make the man deserve the office; it is not flattery if Jonson does not establish James symbolically within the masque since this symbolic level is implied in the very idea of monarchy.[77] The complex levels of kingship in the masque have been pointed out; James has a role in the story, is an idealised example of kingship, and is James King of England.[78] And, we might add, he is James the natural man. The masque is thus the means to an ideal union; it is both the truth, in that the royal actor portrays himself (though James did not actually dance in the masques, as his wife and sons did), and an example for him to fulfil.

Jonson's early entertainments for James, for his coronation and opening of parliament in 1604, argue the theory of example and incitement to imitation. The Genius of London foretells the golden age to come (VII, 102–3); Electra, who will now no longer weep for Troy, implies that Britain has inherited the mantle of empire that passed from Troy to Rome. The theme of the reign will be harmony:

> All tumult, faction, and harsh discord cease,
> That might perturb the music of thy peace.
>
> (VII, 108, *ll.* 752–3)

A pattern is presented for the reign; in 'A Panegyre' the use of praise as advice is explicit. Themis tells James

> that kings
> Are here on earth the most conspicuous things:
> That they, by heaven, are placed upon his throne,
> To rule like heaven: and have no more, their own,
> As they are men, than men. (VII, 115, *ll.* 77–81)

63

The essence of the advice is

> That kings, by their example, more do sway
> Than by their power;   (p. 116, ll. 125–6)

an idea sympathetic to the writer of *Basilikon Doron*.

Though the themes of these two pieces recur throughout the masques, the reason they appear pedestrian here is that there is no relation between the content of this moral advice and the forms used; they are simply harangues. In the masques the use made of James as a focus of the action, as a power manipulating events, and as the end of the design without whom the intricate spectacle could not support itself, gives life to unrealised and conventional theory. In *Hymenaei*, the masque for the politically important but unsuccessful marriage of Essex and Frances Howard, the underlying theme is of union, from the marriage itself to the union of the two kingdoms and of James with his subjects.[79] In the contest between Truth and Opinion on the claims of marriage and virginity, Truth defers to James:

> This royal judge of our contention
> Will prop, I know, what I have undergone;
> To whose right sacred highness I resign
> Low, at his feet, this starry crown of mine,
> To show, his rule, and judgement is divine.
>   (VII, 240–1, ll. 932–6)

It is the presence of James, the image of union, that gives meaning and resolution to the conflict. In *The Haddington Masque*, also for a wedding, praise of James has less relevance to the structure of the fable. Hymen explains to the confused Venus, who is lost, whose court she has wandered into; there follows a passage identifying James with Aeneas (VII, 256). Elsewhere James's presence influences the movement of the masque. In *Love Freed from Ignorance and Folly* Love, baffled by the Sphinx's riddle, is advised by the Muses to look at James's face; James is the means to unlocking and the subject of the riddle:

> Britain's the world, the world without.
> The king's the eye, as we do call
> The sun the eye of this great all.
>
> .   .   .   .
>
> The contraries which time till now
> Nor fate knew where to join, or how,
> Are majesty, and love; which there,
> And nowhere else, have their true sphere.
>   (VII, 368, ll. 285–7, 292–5)

In the *Irish Masque* James is a sun figure by whose light the participants lose their Irish disguises and are metamorphosed into dancing masquers. Similarly in *News from the New World* the masquers are unfrozen through the heat of the king's beams; his nature provides the pattern for the dance:

> This is that orb so bright,
> Has kept your wonder so awake;
> Whence you as from a mirror take
> The sun's reflected light.
> Read him as you would do the book
> Of all perfection, and but look
> What his proportions be;
> No measure that is thence contrived
> Or any motion thence derived,
> But is pure harmony.   (VII, 523-4, *ll.* 336-45)

In *The Vision of Delight* Fancy's antimasque is succeeded by the Bower of Zephyrus; Wonder is answered,

> Behold a king
> Whose presence maketh this perpetual spring,
> The glories of which spring grow in that bower,
> And are the marks and beauties of his power.
>   (VII, 469, *ll.* 201-4)

James makes real what Fancy tells (*l.* 207). In this masque James's influence is embodied in deliberately lightweight terms. But the contrast between James and Fancy underlines the relation of the masque form to reality. The masque is on one level an artificial game; but it is in the life of James and the court that it assumes its value and its meaning. In *Pleasure Reconciled to Virtue* Jonson is explicit about the way spectator and masquer are united through the action and meaning of dance:

> For dancing is an exercise,
>   not only shows the mover's wit,
> but maketh the beholder wise,
>   as he hath power to rise to it.   (VII, 489, *ll.* 269-72)

The dancing of the nobility, whose movement is directed by James, in a dance which is a reflection of his harmony is an artificial exemplification of the ideal relations between king and society.

The idea of James's influence, of his importance as a historical example, receives elaborate treatment in *Prince Henry's Barriers*, Jonson's only masque with Arthurian material as the framework. Henry took part in only three of Jonson's masques, the Barriers which followed *Hymenaei* (1606), the *Barriers* (1610), and *Oberon* (1611), the *Barriers* of 1610 forming part of the ceremony for his investiture as Prince of Wales. In the dedication to the copy of the *Masque of Queens* which he made at Henry's request, Jonson writes

> Whether it be that a divine soul, being to come into a body, first chooseth a palace fit for itself; or, being come, doth make it so; or that nature be ambitious to have her work equal; I know not: But, what is lawful for me to understand, and speak, that I dare; which is, that both your virtue, and your form did deserve your fortune. The one claimed, that you should be born a prince; the other makes that you do become it.
>
> <div align="right">(VII, 280, <i>ll.</i> 7–14)</div>

In Henry is seen a perfect union between the individual's body, his virtue, and his office. In *Prince Henry's Barriers* Henry becomes Meliadus, the chivalric knight, who is also Miles a Deo: the forms embody the ideal. A particular emphasis is given to the treatment of history and time by the fact that Henry is not the present but the future king. Arthur, who appears as a star, tells the Lady of the Lake to bring forward the knight Meliadus who will restore lost chivalry; at the same time he exhorts her to release the buried Merlin. Merlin gives Meliadus a historical survey (perhaps Jonson is imitating Merlin's prophecy to Britomart in *The Faerie Queene*, Book III, canto iii); the mythical Arthurian and the historical material run parallel, both lines culminating in Henry and his father James. Henry as the chivalric knight Meliadus will be as famous as any legendary hero; James is the epitome of the idea of kingship. The historical material thus has a hortatory and comparative function. Merlin describes his royal heroes as 'spurs to virtue', but the chief spur for Henry is James himself, who embodies all past kings and thus surpasses them:

> But all these spurs to virtue, seeds of praise
> Must yield to this that comes. Here's one will raise
> Your glory more, and so above the rest,
> As if the acts of all mankind were pressed
> In his example. Here are kingdoms mixed
> And nations joined, a strength of empire fixed
> Conterminate with heaven; The golden vein
> Of Saturn's age is here broke out again.
>
> <div align="right">(VII, 333, <i>ll.</i> 335–42)</div>

The living monarch embodies the past, and influences the course of the future; his 'name shall set / A goal for all posterity to sweat' (*ll.* 353–4). Yet the future itself is present, not merely in the example of James, but in the person of Henry who will fulfil that example. The model of the past and the hope of the future are united for the spectator in the living symbols of the prince and his father.

The ideas of fame, reward, incitement, and example are crucial to the attempt to dignify the spectacle of the masque with 'more removed mysteries'; they are also a logical result of the fact that Jonson's business in the masques is not with a private ideal of self-sufficient virtue but with a social fact, the public, ostentatious world of monarchy and aristocracy. In *Pleasure Reconciled to Virtue* the ideal of virtue is austere and deliberately dissociated from the social prominence of the masquers:

> Strive to keep her your own,
> 'tis only she, can make you great,
> though place, here, make you known.
>
> (VII, 491, *ll.* 346–48)

But elsewhere in the masques Jonson constantly refers to the critical relations between virtue and fame. He accepts the Aristotelian emphasis on honour as a reward, and on reputation as an enforcement of the disposition to virtue. His projected epic was to describe 'the worthies of his country, roused by fame'. *News from the New World* concludes with this interchange between the two heralds:

> 1 HER.
>
> See, what is that this music brings,
> And is so carried in the air about?

> 2 HER.
>
> Fame, that doth nourish the renown of kings,
> And keeps that fair, which envy would blot out.
>
> (VII, 525, *ll.* 379–82)

The Masque of Queens is perhaps the best example of Jonson's treatment of the relation between fame and virtue: the Argument is described as 'A celebration of honourable, and true fame, bred out of virtue' (VII, 282, *ll.* 6–7). The antimasque of witches, who in their language, their dress, and their dance are the antithesis to and foil for the main masque of queens, is dispersed by a 'sound of loud music' (*p.* 301, *l.* 355),

> With which, not only the hags themselves, but their hell, into which they ran, quite vanished; and the whole face of the scene altered; scarce suffering the memory of any such thing. (*p.* 301, *ll.* 356–9)

It is important that discord, of its very nature, is effaced from the memory, to be replaced by the lasting knowledge of virtue through fame, embodied in the 'glorious and magnificent' (*ll.* 359–60) House of Fame. This striking antithesis demonstrates a paradox stated in the 'Epithalamion' (*Und.* lxxv):

> The ignoble never lived, they were awhile
> Like swine, or other cattle here on earth:
> Their names are not recorded on the file
> Of life.

In the masque, Heroic Virtue is the father of Fame and its preserver, but for the spectator fame is the approach to virtue. The first song after the procession of masquers concludes 'Sing then good fame, that's out of virtue born, / For, who doth fame neglect, doth virtue scorn' (*p.* 315, *ll.* 729–30). In the last song the antithesis between greatness and goodness found so often in the poems is implied, but here is it between greatness and true fame, the result of goodness:

> Who, virtue, can thy power forget,
> That sees these live, and triumph yet?
>
> .   .   .   .
>
> Force greatness, all the glorious ways
> You can, it soon decays;
> But so good fame shall, never:
> Her triumphs, as their causes, are for ever.
>
> (*p.* 316, *ll.* 764–5, 770–3)

In poems such as the ode on Henry Morison the idea of immortality is annexed to virtuous action; the poet's role is subordinate to that of the actor. But in the masques, especially *The Masque of Queens*, the dynamic relation between virtue and fame is shown: the promise of fame is necessary to the existence of virtue. The poet has an important place in this chain of causes; it is in the masques rather than in his other works that Jonson can claim to be a feigner of commonwealths. Thus the House of Fame in *The Masque of Queens* is supported by columns of 'men-making poets' (*p.* 302, *l.* 386); Arthur urges the Lady of the Lake to free Merlin in *Prince Henry's Barriers* because

> when thou shutst him there,
> Thou buriedst valour too, for letters rear
> The deeds of honour high, and make them live.
>
> (VII, 326, *ll.* 102–4)

Two masques which demonstrate the need for the poet as recorder of fame and preserver of virtue are *The Golden Age Restored* and *Chloridia*. In the first Pallas, after the antimasque of the Iron Age, calls forth Astraea and the Golden Age, who ask her, 'But how without a train / Shall we our state sustain?' (VII, 424, *ll.* 107–8). In answer Pallas calls down Chaucer, Gower, Lydgate, and Spenser, who awaken

68

the masquers to perform their dances. Though James's presence gives meaning to the restoration of the golden age – Astraea says 'I feel the godhead' (p. 429, l. 231) – it is the poets who are the mediators between the ideal and its realisation. As she ascends Pallas commands them:

> Like lights about Astraea's throne
> You here must shine, and all be one,
> In fervour and in flame.
> That by your union she may grow,
> And, you sustaining her, may know
> The age still by her name. (p. 428, ll. 206–11)

The 'hinge' of *Chloridia*, which is similar to that of *The Golden Age Restored*, is the decreee of Jupiter that the goddess Chloris is to be 'stellified on earth' (l. 10). After the antimasque, a tempest, and the main masque, of Chloris and her nymphs, have been danced,

> out of the earth, ariseth a hill, and on the top of it, a globe, on which Fame is seen standing, with her trumpet in her hand; and on the hill, are seated four persons, presenting Poesy, History, Architecture, and Sculpture. (VII, 759, ll. 275–8)

In a dialogue with the chorus, Fame establishes herself as the protector of virtue; in turn the four arts answer:

POESY
We that sustain thee, learned Poesy,

HISTORY
And I, her sister, severe History

ARCHITECTURE
With Architecture, who will raise thee high,

SCULPTURE
And Sculpture, that can keep thee from to die,

CHORUS
All help (to) lift thee to eternity. (p. 760, ll. 306–15)

In this masque, however, the relation of Fame to Chloris is not evident in the way that the role of the poets is crucial to the sustaining of Astraea. Though Jonson provided the rather laboured verse, the invention and design of the rise of Fame was Jones's. We know what Jonson really thought of it. In 'An Expostulation' he sneers at

The majesty of Juno in the clouds,
And peering forth of Iris in the shrouds!
The ascent of Lady Fame which none could spy
Not they that sided her, Dame Poetry,
Dame History, Dame Architecture too,
And Goody Sculpture, brought with much ado
To hold her up.

Chloridia was their last collaborative effort; Jonson's expression of these opinions no doubt led to the final collapse of the partnership. But though the masque lacks unity, and the presentation of the four arts is banal, Jonson's anger is perhaps directed as much at the public ethic underlying the masque form as at Jones's particular conception in *Chloridia*.

One should not insist too much on the fact that Jonson's late words on the subject of his collaboration with Jones are so pessimistic; the collaboration lasted many years and produced the best of the Jacobean court masques. Though Jonson was hesitant about the masque as a form because he was constrained by its demands, nevertheless these demands, the need to entertain and celebrate the king and his court, gave him an unrivalled opportunity to put into practice the traditional Renaissance concept of the poet's reforming and legislating function. In the masque the brazen world shades into the golden. The masque is courtly pastime, but it is also the king's fame, a mirror of himself, the example he may become. It is an inducement, a promise, and a reward, both true and ideal. The poet is the means of fusing office and individual, ideal and actuality; the masque is the image of the fusion.

Jonson's perpetual interest in the idea of the moral influence of an aristocracy, whether an aristocracy of virtue or of the socially conspicuous, allowed him to pursue, perhaps to some extent unconsciously, what may appear in retrospect to be conflicting ends. Jonson saw his function, as in the dedication to *Volpone*, in moral and social terms; in the masques there is an extraordinary union between these purposes, between the poet's intentions and his public usefulness. On the one hand Jonson was involved in the social ritual of publicizing symbols; on the other he undertook to expand the function of king and nobility, to make them moral examples for society. While giving them the fame that they demanded, he recreated them. But this community of interest between the poet and the monarchy and nobility he served does not necessarily make true a statement that there was 'no impassable gap between the world of the poet's vision and Jacobean and Caroline England'.[80] The gap was no smaller for Jonson than for later writers; the Stoic and anti-court tendencies in his work indicate his uneasiness and his attempts to free himself from the pressure of accepted public values. Jonson was by no means happy with the requirement of deference in a hierarchical society. One way of seeing his status and the structure of society in general was expressed by his friend Sir John Roe, after their eviction from court for disturbances during the performance of *The Vision of the Twelve Goddesses*:

> Forget we were thrust out; It is but thus,
> God threatens kings, kings lords, as lords do us.[81]

Jonson was aware of the hollowness of a social hierarchy unsupported by useful moral purpose, and the danger of the monarchy's self-inflation; yet he himself contributed to that aggrandisement of the court which increased political and social tension and helped bring about the collapse of the whole structure. Jonson could not see the logical incompatibility of his various tones and positions; one can trace no chronological development in these attitudes. His consciousness of social upheaval did not make him revise his view of the conventional political framework. This curious amphibiousness of Jonson, his antipathy to and conscious support of his society, is partly attributable to the date of his career. For writers after the civil war the problem was both more complex and more clear-cut. Milton had to rethink the assumptions of humanist poetics. Dryden had a far more acute sense of the working of politics than Jonson; his treatment of monarchy is as much a question of definition as of celebration. In Pope the anti-social tendency of Jonson's work reached its logical conclusion. It was not open to Jonson in the way of more politically conscious writers of later generations to examine, weigh, or reject the political framework of his society; hence his antagonism expressed itself in a negative moral creed which did not prevent him when necessary from giving full support to the acknowledged functions of existing institutions.

Chapter 3

Poets and Revolution

In the period from 1640 to 1660 the conservative idea of order was challenged by the beginnings of a very different way of seeing society and history, and by the overthrow of customary forms of government. This is by no means to suggest that there were two sides in the English revolution, one concerned with maintaining existing order, the other with bringing about revolutionary change. The paradox of the English revolution lies in the way most of its protagonists combined religious radicalism with conservative social attitudes; the illogicality of such a combination is epitomised in the disappointing outcome of Cromwell's career. What began as in many ways a conservative movement to limit the growing authority of Charles I and the Laudian bishops, and to return to the understood forms of the ancient constitution and the reformed church, resulted by stages in the destruction of monarchy and the splintering of church organisation. Only a minority saw the political implications of Puritan religious belief.[1]

In spite of the almost accidental character of the development of the revolution, one can nevertheless define in abstract and simplified terms the radical element in Puritan thought which conflicted with the conservative world view.[2] In place of the celebration of stability, hierarchy, and order in the existing world, radical Puritanism is above all concerned with the process of history. When the conservative criticises the world, it is by means of an idealised, Platonic model; the Puritan, committed to the working out of Christian history, looks to the future, to the glorification of man in Christ and to the new heaven and earth. Though both are aware of the inadequacy of life as it is, the conservative sees the order that underlies disorder, and hopes that the actual may approximate to the ideal; the Puritan expects the reformation of existing order and the perfection of the new order. Where the conservative values tradition, ceremony, and customary social forms, the Puritan emphasises the private man and the inner light. The conservative celebrates society's rulers as the embodiment of its values; the Puritan sees no necessary connection between the political and religious hierarchy, between the ruler and the saint. In practice these ways of seeing political and religious order were not often understood to be incompatible; the Presbyterians, for example, remained royalists. But in its tendencies the Puritan emphasis on reformation and the perfecting of the individual was in strong opposition to the conservative emphasis on social order, even though the political implications of these tendencies were repressed in 1660 and did not reappear till the end of the eighteenth century.

This chapter deals with the effects both of the confrontation of conservative with radical Puritan ideas of the world, and of the constitutional changes from the 1640s to the 1660s, from civil war, commonwealth, and protectorate to restored monarchy, on the careers of two poets, John Milton and Andrew Marvell. By temperament and by religious and political belief they were opposed to the conservative tradition I have defined, but it is worth studying their work in the context of conservative poetry both because it elaborates an alternative view of the relation between poetry, society, and change that conservative poets implicitly rejected, and because Milton and Marvell themselves drew on and contributed to conservative tradition. In the case of Milton this was because of the humanist assumptions on which his understanding of poetry was based, in the case of Marvell because of his recognition of the need to link change to traditional social forms.

JOHN MILTON: REFORMATION AND REGENERATION

Milton spent his youth in training himself for and defining his vocation, until in 1642 at the age of thirty-three he pledged himself to the readers of *The Reason of Church Government* to write within a few years a true poem based on inspiration, learning, experience, and insight. Thus while engaged in polemic on behalf of his Presbyterian friends he finally publicly committed himself to the ambition which he had been tentatively outlining since 1629, and which his education had prepared him for, the unification of the careers of poet and priest in a great work of art.[3] The actual career for which his father had intended him from his childhood with his own agreement was the ministry of the church,[4] but Laud's high-handed interference with church ritual and with Puritan preaching and publication in the 1630s made such a course completely impossible to him. The ambition to be a poet must have coexisted with the ambition to be a priest (Milton started to write before he went to Cambridge), and both these aims in a young man of his humanist and religious educational background were conventional. Twenty years earlier he might have been able to pursue both ambitions together without experiencing any tension between them and without combining them in any original way. It was the particular sequence of political events in the 1630s and 40s which made him first withdraw from one of his vocations to lean more heavily towards the other, and then, as he realised the extraordinary opportunities for action suddenly afforded him, unite the two and reinterpret his humanist ideals in a revolutionary definition of the poet. The humanist antecedents of Milton's thought, his place in Renaissance tradition, his aristocratic leanings, have often been emphasised; but his interpretation of the political moment completely transmuted his inherited assumptions. Unlike Jonson, from whom he learned a great deal about the social role of the poet, he must be read chronologically for an understanding of the process by which his view of poetry was created. Jonson's mind did not develop because he did not think historically; Milton's whole career was an effort to shape history.

It is worth indicating the conventional, inherited element in Milton's thought, and the stages by which he arrived at the definition of his career.[5] The long passages of self-explanation and dedication in *The Reason of Church Government* and *An Apology...(for)...Smectymnuus* were the culmination of twelve years of testing out in poetry of the idea of the poet's public and personal responsibility. Milton's education at St Paul's, based as it was on the theories of Erasmus, emphasised the pragmatic, moral use of learning; at Cambridge Milton was critical of what seemed to him the arid intellectualism of the curriculum.[6] His third prolusion attacked the scholastic emphasis on logic and philosophy, and defended the humanist subjects, poetry, rhetoric, and history. Education was seen to have a social and moral rather than an intellectual end. His seventh, and finest, prolusion gave a portrait of the man of knowledge and virtue as a hero, conquering nature and legislating for society. In the small tractate *Of Education* written in 1644 Milton distilled all that was valuable in the educational experience of his youth, without here indicating his awareness of the revolutionary direction in which a literal interpretation of humanist ideals could lead. The two famous definitions of education both testify to Milton's conventional humanism and imply the significant ways in which it was to be modified. The first places man in relation to God, the second in relation to society:

> The end then of learning is to repair the ruins of our first parents by regaining to know God aright, and out of that knowledge to love him, to imitate him, to be like him, as we may the nearest by possessing our souls of true virtue, which being united to the heavenly grace of faith makes up the highest perfection.   (Columbia, IV, 277)

> I call therefore a complete and generous education that which fits a man to perform justly, skilfully and magnanimously all the offices both private and public of peace and war.   (280)

The immediate end of education, as is made clear by the detailed account of Milton's academy, is the formation of a class for public life, with both a political and a cultural function. The ultimate end of education is to reverse the effects of the fall of man. Here Milton is not concerned with the Baconian attempt to harness external nature, but with the perfecting of human nature. Education provides the means to virtue, which together with grace makes the perfect Christian. The function of education is political and ethical; it is concerned both with order, the maintaining of standards, the dissemination of culture, and with change, the regeneration of the individual.

Just as Milton accepted the pragmatic, ethical emphasis of humanist educational theory, so he accepted the didacticism of humanist poetics. His interpretation of both was to be crucially modified by his Puritan sympathies. During the 1630s, having rejected the priesthood to which he had originally dedicated himself, he continued to train himself for the future, and in the poems of these years, experimenting with different styles and modes and conceptions of poetry, he groped for a definition of the poet that would encompass the priest and be an adequate tool for his sense of purpose. Milton abandoned the idea of the priesthood probably by 1632,[7] the year his Cambridge career ended, when he may also have written the undated letter to a friend critical of his inactivity, enclosing sonnet VII 'How soon hath time the subtle thief of youth'. In both poem and letter Milton defends his apparent idleness as a search for maturity, as a preparation for self dedication and not as self indulgence. The choice was not only his; the 'great taskmaster' had expectations which he must fulfil. He must work with time and the will of heaven to train himself for the future task even though it was not yet clearly defined:

> If the love of learning as it is be the pursuit of something good, it would sooner follow the more excellent and supreme good known and presented and so be quickly diverted from the empty and fantastic chase of shadows and notions to the solid good flowing from due and timely obedience to that command in the gospel set out by the terrible seizing of him that hid the talent. It is more probable therefore that not the endless delight of speculation but this very consideration of that great commandment does not press forward as soon as may be to undergo but keeps off with a sacred reverence, and religious advisement how best to undergo not taking thought of being late so it give advantage to be more fit, for those that were latest lost nothing when the master of the vineyard came to give each one his hire. (Columbia, XII, 324)

Though he is imprecise in this letter, the poems of this period make it clear that he was moving towards the idea that poetry was to be the task. But it must be an adequate conception of poetry. The most immediate example for Milton in the early 1630s was that of Jonson. Jonson had created a social role for the poet, transmuting the economic relationship of patronage into a moral one, providing the existing social order with an idealised other self. In the early 1630s Milton tried not so much to fit himself to as to explore the role created by Jonson.[8] One of Milton's intentions in the writing of poems like the 'Epitaph on the Marchioness of Winchester' or the two masques, *Arcades* and *Comus*, was to establish a circle of patrons and to use these patrons as symbols of moral worth, as a medium for his didactic purpose. His hope of using the relationship of patronage in this way persisted into the period of his Italian journey; *Mansus*, his tribute to the generosity of the one-time patron of Tasso, probably written in 1639, is the last expression of this hope. Such a use of patronage implied an acceptance of social forms, of the poet's celebratory function. The Jonsonian model was too limited for Milton's uses, and as he tested it he broke it.[9] With the Jonsonian conception of the poet as teacher and public figure he wished to combine his thwarted vocation as priest. The basis from which Jonson judged society was a Stoic self-reliance; the poetic self that Milton defined for himself was much more elaborate. Milton could not possibly accept the compromise in Jonson's career between the search for virtue and the celebration of society. *Comus* veers away from the masque tradition; the idea of virtue it puts forward, of chastity, which means the freedom of self-conquest aided by grace, has very little to do with the social and cultural idea of virtue that Jonson's masques inculcate. One has only to compare Comus with Carew's *Coelum Britannicum* of the same year,[10] in which the Egerton boys also took part, to see how far Milton abandons aristocratic ritual.

The view of reality put forward in *Comus* is, as has often been pointed out, Platonic. Virtue is a process of ascent from earthly 'defilement' and 'contagion', the 'sin-worn mould' of the body, to the calmness and serenity to be achieved in the 'palace of eternity'. The Attendant Spirit's opening speech (*ll.* 1–17) establishes the opposition between frenetic and worthless earthly motion and eternal peace; the path from one to the other is a negative divesting of earthly corruption. This impression is modified by the speeches of the Elder Brother (*ll.* 452–74) and the Lady (*ll.* 761–78, in reply to Comus), where the possibility of the virtuous earthly life is defined in more positive terms. Nevertheless it is important (and paradoxical) that the ascetic idea of separation from the world is being tested at the same time as the conception of poetry as social celebration. For a time Milton understood the priestly element in his poetic vocation in the limited terms of purity and chastity, as a mark of preparation for his task.[11] His ideas of chastity were derived, as he explains in the account of his development in the *Apology for Smectymnuus* (Columbia, III i, 303–6), from reading Dante and Petrarch, Arthurian romance, Plato, and St Paul. In several poems he tests the idea of the pure poet-priest against other more social, less serious definitions. In *Elegy VI* to Charles Diodati, written at about the same time as the *Nativity Ode*, the elegiac poet with his social licentious life is contrasted unfavourably with the epic poet and his priestly purity:

His youth must be chaste and free from crime, his morals strict and his hand unstained. He must be like you, priest, when, bathed in holy water and gleaming in your sacred vestment, you rise to go and face the angry gods. ...For the poet is sacred to the gods: he is their priest: his innermost heart and his mouth are both full of Jove.[12]   (*ll.* 63–6, 77–8; trans. in *Poems, pp.* 118–19)

This comparison of the elegiac and the vatic poet is not academic. Milton had written Ovidian verse; *Elegy VI* goes on to describe the writing of the *Nativity Ode*; the autobiographical implication is obvious. Yet again the poem is not a commitment, but an exploration; Milton's experiments with devotional poetry antedate his brief Jonsonian period. In *L'Allegro* and *Il Penseroso* the balance between two conflicting modes of living and of seeing poetry is much more carefully maintained; Milton compares without preferring the happy man's choice of the social forms, masque, comedy, and elegiac verse, to the thoughtful man's choice of tragedy and allegorical epic.

These explanatory poems show that Milton was unwilling to commit himself to the writing of a particular kind of poetry, to poetry as a calling rather than an intermittent activity, until he had trained himself ethically and intellectually. The danger of isolation implicit in this view can be seen in *Ad Patrem*; here the emphasis on retirement overshadows Milton's didactic commitment.[13] The poem, like the letter to his friend, defends his reluctance to pursue a practical career, but here there is no emphasis on time, no waiting on providence; instead, Milton assures his father that all his early education, his continued self-training, is the necessary condition to the creation not of a social being immersed in daily cares but of a poet withdrawn and separate from the world, who exists in the eternal, harmonious, indestructible world of art:

My fiery spirit which whirls round the hurtling spheres is already singing, as it flies among the starry choirs, a deathless melody, an indescribable song.... Therefore I, who already have a place, though a very low one, in the ranks of the learned, shall one day sit among those who wear the ivy and the laurels of victory. Now I shall no longer mix with the brainless mob: my steps will shun the sight of common eyes.[14]   (*ll.* 35–7, 101–4; trans. in *Poems, pp.* 153, 155)

The poet of *Ad Patrem* turns his back on life for the eternal sphere of art; there is no connection between the two. Yet Milton's studies in the years 1632 to 1638, chiefly of ecclesiastical and political history, were obviously intended to supplement the idealist, intellectual education of Cambridge; their end was humanist and pragmatic. And it was during these years that Charles I tried to extend his prerogative powers and Laud to enforce his church policy. The poet-priest of *Elegy VI* and platonist poet of *Ad Patrem* are redefined in *Lycidas*. Through the medium of pastoral the poet whose theme is the disparity between earthly and heavenly value, whose goal is an eternal fame that 'lives and spreads aloft by those pure eyes, / And perfect witness of all-judging Jove' (*ll.* 81–2), is united with the priest defined not in terms of his personal purity but his relationship with his flock. The poet-priest is now constrained by time, he cannot wait for the 'mellowing year'; art is not a separation from life. The pastoral (literary) mode is interrupted by 'the dread voice' which reveals the reality that the convention opposes, and emphasises the pastoral (priestly) responsibility for the state of the church. The poem itself resolves the tensions between the poet and the priest, the obligations to art and to society, in the injunction to 'weep no more', in the mounting of Lycidas

> Where other groves, and other streams along,
> With nectar pure his oozy locks he laves,
> And hears the unexpressive nuptial song,
> In the blest kingdoms meek of joy and love.   (*ll.* 174–7)

The eternal world of art and the heaven which is the culmination of Christian life are identified. The search for the blest kingdoms is not an isolated, personal one.

Thus Milton's Italian journey, in which his object was 'not to learn principles but to enlarge experience, and make wise observation',[15] and which took him away from England at a time when episcopacy and prerogative were beginning to be challenged, gave him the opportunity of assessing from a distance how he might as an individual unite his vocation with that of his country. His reception in Italy among scholars and academicians made clear to him that he might pursue if he wished the career of Latin poet, isolating himself from provincial interests and aiming at a European audience. Instead he convinced himself that his duty was to his country and his native language; his poem was to be a British epic. This was not in itself an original conception. During the last ten years he had tested devotional, platonic, and aristocratic modes of poetry; now he was to aim at a national audience, using the example of ancient and modern epic. He describes this change in emphasis in *The Reason of Church Government*:

> If I were certain to write as men buy leases, for three lives and downward, there ought no regard be sooner had, than to God's glory by the honour and instruction of my country. For which

cause, and not only for that I knew it would be hard to arrive at the second rank among the Latins, I applied myself to that resolution which Ariosto followed against the persuasions of Bembo, to fix all the industry and art I could unite to the adorning of my native tongue; not to make verbal curiosities the end, that were a toilsome vanity, but to be an interpreter and relater of the best and sagest things among mine own citizens throughout this island in the mother dialect. That what the greatest and choicest wits of Athens, Rome, or modern Italy, and those Hebrews of old did for their country, I in my proportion with this over and above of being a Christian, might do for mine.   (Columbia, III i, 236)

This new decision to be a national, patriotic, prophetic poet sent him to British history. In the two Latin poems probably written in 1639, *Mansus* and *Epitaphium Damonis* (his elegy for Diodati), Arthur and other ancient British heroes were offered as the subjects of the new epic. In the latter poem he suggested that he had already started work on it. But this superficial and hastily conceived plan came to nothing. In the course of his historical study Milton soon discovered that the Arthurian material was not British history but literary myth and Tudor and Stuart propaganda; he was to treat it critically in a few years' time in his *History of Britain*.[16] And after his initial feeling of confidence he was not sure that his poem was to be an epic; he began making plans for dramas, both sacred and historical. Milton's literary ambitions at the beginning of the 1640s still seem exploratory and tentative. He had come back from Italy with large scale patriotic plans, but without any positive attitude towards his country on which he could base such plans. He was thinking much more in terms of literary convention than of his own relation to England.[17] There is no sense of society in the poems of the 1630s; Milton had no acknowledged public position on which to base such a sense. The church, which would have provided him with a place, a community, a hierarchy, had thrown him back on himself. The entourage of aristocracy, the patronage relationship, seemed attractive to him but he knew that it was limiting. In 1640 he had no audience and he had no real subject matter for a patriotic poem. He had only an overpowering sense of obligation.

The prospect of political and religious reformation opened by the Long Parliament gave a new meaning to Milton's idea of the poet. In the antiprelatical pamphlets he seized the opportunity of hastening the reformation of the church from whose ministry he had previously dissociated himself. He suddenly had a vision of an England which was not a Christian or a platonic or an artistic ideal, existing in another dimension like the 'celestial consort' of 'At a solemn music', or the 'hurtling spheres' of *Ad Patrem*, or the 'blest kingdoms' of *Lycidas*, but realisable in the present. At the conclusion of *Of Reformation*, the celebrated prayer for the deliverance of England, Milton sees the proper functioning of the poet as consequent on the reformation of church and state: he mediates between this just society and the future kingdom of God, preserving it for the new heaven and earth:

Then amidst the hymns, and halleluiahs of saints some one may perhaps be heard offering at high strains in new and lofty measures to sing and celebrate thy divine mercies, and marvellous judgements in this land throughout all ages; whereby this great and warlike nation instructed and inured to the fervent and continual practice of truth and righteousness, and casting far from her the rags of her old vices may press on hard to that high and happy emulation to be found the soberest, wisest, and most Christian people at that day when thou the eternal and shortly-expected king shalt open the clouds to judge the several kingdoms of the world, and distributing national honours and rewards to religious and just commonwealths, shalt put an end to all earthly tyrannies, proclaiming thy universal and mild monarchy through heaven and earth.

(Columbia, III i, 78–9)

In the long autobiographical preface to Book II of *The Reason of Church Government*, in which Milton covenants with the reader to become such a poet, he considers in greater detail the moral and social function of literature, and makes public his indecision about appropriate form, whether epic, dramatic, or lyric, with examples drawn from classical, Italian, and biblical literature. The account of the poet's status and his public influence is worth quoting at some length:

These abilities, wheresoever they be found, are the inspired gift of God rarely bestowed, but yet to some (though most abuse) in every nation: and are of power beside the office of a pulpit, to inbreed and cherish in a great people the seeds of virtue, and public civility, to allay the perturbations of the mind, and set the affections in right tune, to celebrate in glorious and lofty hymns the throne and equipage of God's almightiness, and what he works, and what he suffers to be wrought with high providence in his church, to sing the victorious agonies of martyrs and saints, the deeds and triumphs of just and pious nations doing valiantly through faith against the enemies of Christ, to deplore the general relapses of kingdoms and states from justice and God's true worship. Lastly, whatsoever in religion is holy and sublime, in virtue amiable, or grave, whatsoever hath passion or admiration in all the changes of that which is called fortune from without, or the wily subtleties and refluxes of man's thoughts from within, all these things with a solid and treatable

81

smoothness to paint out and describe. Teaching over the whole book of sanctity and virtue through all the instances of example with such delight to those especially of soft and delicious temper who will not so much as look upon truth herself, unless they see her elegantly dressed, that whereas the paths of honesty and good life appear now rugged and difficult, though they be indeed easy and pleasant, they would then appear to all men both easy and pleasant though they were rugged and difficult indeed. (III i, 238-9)

After considering ways in which such persuasive art might be made more publicly accessible, Milton returns to himself and his ambitions, and the circumstances in which he would be able to realise them:

The accomplishment of them [his intentions] lies not but in a power above man's to promise; but that none hath by more studious ways endeavoured, and with more unwearied spirit that none shall, that I dare almost aver of myself, as far as life and free leisure will extend, and that the land had once enfranchised herself from this impertinent yoke of prelaty, under whose inquisitorious and tyrannical duncery no free and splendid wit can flourish. (p. 240)

In *An Apology* he restates in active terms his view of the need for personal preparation:

He who would not be frustrate of his hope to write well hereafter in laudable things, ought himself to be a true poem, that is, a composition, and pattern of the best and honourablest things; not presuming to sing high praises of heroic men, or famous cities, unless he have in himself the experience and the practice of all that which is praiseworthy. (Columbia, III i, 303-4)

It is well at this point to summarise the attitudes Milton had so far expressed with regard to poetry in general and his own poetic role, and the way in which they are reinterpreted in these well known statements in relation to his understanding of the historical moment. Milton regarded the life of the poet as a process of dedication and training; the poet must first create himself before he can create a poem and thus recreate his fellows. The poet is thus isolated from mankind, just as the poem, itself embodying and envisaging perfected form, is separate from reality. But the justification for the poet's isolation is that he can change reality. His function is hortatory, magisterial, exemplary. He mediates between ideal and reality. Like a priest, he shows heaven and the path to it. So far, Milton does not depart in theory (though perhaps in emphasis and fervour) from the assumptions of Renaissance poetic. And as long as (because of his disgust with Laudian innovation and repression) the ideal world of art seemed a long way distant from reality, his emphasis was more on the poet's nature than his use, even though tradition and convention taught him that the poet's function was public and his concern was with society. The attack on the bishops at the end of 1640 suddenly suggested to Milton that the reformation of the church in England could now be completed, that the godly society could come into being, and that he as poet could have a valid public function in that society, serving to maintain its godliness until the second coming. The important point is that Milton now sees the reformation of society as a precondition to his assuming his proper position as a poet. Poetry alone cannot reform society, cannot even 'flourish' under the 'impertinent yoke of prelaty'; by temporarily relinquishing poetry for political action, both of which are concerned with the same end, Milton is serving the cause of both society and poetry. It is at this point that he breaks with the conservative interpretation of the relation of art to reality. The conservative poet can only transfigure reality through art, or in his pessimistic moments turn his back on reality for the perfection of art. Milton's commitment to the Puritan view of society and history gave him a new perspective; reality, the existing organisation of church and state, can be changed directly to approximate to the ideals of art and religion.

Milton's interpretation, or misinterpretation, of time is crucial here, and the fact that he misinterpreted it meant that the confident definition of the poet in *Of Reformation* and *The Reason of Church Government* as sustainer of the godly society could not be realised. He obviously expected his pamphleteering career to be a short one, and that reformation would soon be accomplished. He could not possibly foresee nearly twenty years of political involvement and the complete defeat of both political and religious reformation. But it was not long before the concern of the antiprelatical pamphlets for the speedy establishment of the godly society gave way to emphasis on the individual's need for freedom from the pressures of a society struggling to make itself godly. Milton's interest moved from end to process. Perhaps his sense of the separateness of art from life in the formative years of the 1630s was too strong; but certainly Milton never, except in the brief period from 1641 to 1644, had a strong sense of society as a system of relationships, or of his place as a member of it.[18] One can apprehend, for example, Jonson's idea of the good society, but it is much harder to grasp Milton's understanding of it, partly because initially it is described in the symbolic language of religious enthusiasm but also because this enthusiasm is replaced by a change of interest which entails a shadowy vagueness in such ideas as nation or society. Much of Milton's political theory is lifeless because the word 'people' on which so much logically depends has no life for him except in a very limited sense.

In the major poems of the 1660s Milton came to believe that the workings of time and providence are beyond human comprehension, that a closed godly society is not a desirable nor an achievable human ambition, and that the individual search for paradise not paradise itself is the end of action and the subject for poetry. To understand how Milton reached this position we must try to trace a pattern in the development of his political and religious ideas, to detach from his prose the elements that went to the creation of his prophetic poetic self and his major poems. It was his religious interests that led Milton into politics, and although some of his most controversial tracts – *The Tenure of Kings and Magistrates*, *Eikonoklastes*, the *First* and *Second Defences*, *The Ready and Easy Way to Establish a Free Commonwealth* – are concerned solely with political change, it was ultimately for the sake of religion that he wrote them. Forms of government became for him only a means to an end, the pursuit of religious liberty, which was itself only a means to an end, the regeneration and glorification of the individual man which could not be completed in this life. He shared this ordering of priorities with Cromwell, and was therefore able to continue working for his regime when those whose interest was a specific kind of political reform or a specific kind of religious community turned against him.[19] Milton's mainly religious interest is shown by the fact that he did not write his first specifically political tract, *The Tenure of Kings*, until 1649, when he saw the need to associate himself with the Independents against the Presbyterian parliamentarians, and took no part at all in the important political debate of the early 1640s between king and parliament on the issue of the nature of the constitution. Most of the important theorists of the 1640s and 50s – the Levellers, Filmer, Hobbes – were concerned with the problem of sovereignty, of the source of power in the state. Milton dealt with this problem only as a framework to his real concern, the religious liberty of the individual under power.[20]

In the antiprelatical tracts Milton's views on government are superficial and orthodox; for a short time he appears in the guise of a Presbyterian royalist. There are several attitudes expressed in these tracts which are contradictory in their tendencies, and Milton did not hold them in balance for long. The underlying assumption is that monarchy is the proper form of government. We know from the commonplace book that in his course of study of political history in the 1630s and early 1640s he was interested in the problem of the subject's obligation to a tyrant and in the relative merits of commonwealths and monarchies, but this by no means implies that he was a committed republican at this time.[21] One argument against the bishops is that they are undermining the monarchy (this was to be the main charge brought against them by Marvell in the 1670s). Milton uses for the state the familiar corporal image, with the head being threatened by 'a huge and monstrous wen little less than the head itself, growing to it by a narrower excrescency'. The simple solution is to cut off this 'heap of hard, and loathsome

84

uncleanness' (*Of Reformation*, III i, 48–9). Coexisting with this conventional image of the state is the enthusiastic vision already cited of the godly society about to be born, and the final annihilation of earthly government in God's 'universal and mild monarchy' (*p.* 79). A further, and ultimately the most significant, element is the idea that the ministry has nothing to do with ritual, ceremonial, tradition, that it must not be 'grounded in the worldly degrees of authority, honour, temporal jurisdiction' (*Reason of Church Government*, III i, 199), but that 'it is the inward calling of God that makes a minister' (*Animadversions*, III i, 156).

Milton's royalism lasted only as long as he thought that Charles I would accommodate the Puritan reformation; he later argued first against tyranny and then against monarchy itself, and had nothing but contempt for the Presbyterians who would not see the logic of this position.[22] The conventional royalism of the antiprelatical tracts is much less significant than the tension between Milton's hopes for a new reformed England and his sense of religion as a matter for the individual. The problem was that the Presbyterian image of the good society, nourished on Calvinist theology, was exclusive and authoritarian, while the religious habits of mind on which it depended were private and individual.[23] The inevitable political defeat of a total vision of a good society which can only incorporate a fragment of existing society can be illustrated by a quotation from Richard Baxter (who was a moderate Presbyterian), regretting after the Restoration the lost opportunities of the English people. Baxter uses a vocabulary very similar to Milton's in *Of Reformation* and *Areopagitica* to describe the universal implications of his idea, yet his idea is a partisan one threatened by different parties on either side:

> I must add this to the true information of posterity, that God did so wonderfully bless the labours of his unanimous faithful ministers that had it not been for the faction of the prelatists on one side that drew men off, and the factions of the giddy and turbulent sectaries on the other side...England had been like in a quarter of an age to have become a land of saints and a pattern of holiness to all the world, and the unmatchable paradise of the earth. Never were such fair opportunities to sanctify a nation lost and trodden underfoot as have been in this land of late.[24]

The conviction of lost opportunity that Milton stated so strongly just before the Restoration was very different from Baxter's. The difference had its origin in the irony that just as Milton was defining the conditions of the godly society he was attacked by the godly as one of the sectaries who were threatening to destroy it. Milton's divorce pamphlets of 1643–44 disgusted the Presbyterians; since they rejected him he could no longer identify himself with them. But he did not immediately move on from his national idea. In *Areopagitica*, the most optimistic and passionate of his political statements, and the most enduring of his prose works, the rebuff he had received led to a change in emphasis in his idea of the good society. The immediate issue of the Long Parliament's censorship of controversial religious tracts disabused Milton of the simple assumption stated in *Of Reformation* that the excising of prelacy would solve England's problems. He began to consider the process of political change, to concentrate on the necessary means rather than on the hoped-for end. Virtue now seemed to him purification by trial, rather than by separation (as is suggested by some of the early poems). The good society is not achieved by protection from evil, but by exposure to and triumph over it. The process is one of action; Milton moves from the image of peaceful heavenly monarchy to images of toil, effort, awakening, searching, strength:

> The shop of war hath not there [London] more anvils and hammers waking, to fashion out the plates and instruments of armed Justice in defence of beleaguered Truth, than there be pens and heads there, sitting by their studious lamps, musing, searching, revolving new notions and ideas wherewith to present, as with their homage and their fealty the approaching reformation.... What wants there to such a towardly and pregnant soil, but wise and faithful labourers, to make a knowing people, a nation of prophets, of sages, and of worthies.... Methinks I see in my mind a noble and puissant nation rousing herself like a strong man after sleep, and shaking her invincible locks: methinks I see her as an eagle mewing her mighty youth, and kindling her undazzled eyes at the full midday beam.... (Columbia, IV, 341, 344)

In spite of the Presbyterians' movement towards repression and exclusion, the presbyter is not quite yet for Milton 'old priest write large' ('On the new Forcers of Conscience', *c.* 1646). The initial victories of Puritanism made him confident that the nation was chosen by God, that it was in his protection, that he was shaking it 'with strong and healthful commotions to a general reforming' (*p.* 350), and that controversy and experiment must be tolerated because they could only be productive of good.

Milton did not publish another political tract until 1649. The intervening years had seen the emergence of the army as a political force, the defeat of the royalists, the prevarication of Charles about a political settlement, the ranging of the army Independents against the Presbyterian parliament and assembly, the royalists, and Scots, and the final defeat and execution of the king. Instead of the reformation he had envisaged these were years of bitter political and religious conflict, with the initiators of reform, the Presbyterians, as Milton pointed out angrily in the *Tenure of Kings*, turning their backs on the consequences of their movement. From now on he was to be the defender, not of the active, open, parliamentary system envisaged in *Areopagitica*, but of a minority government in no way representative even of the reforming element in the nation, depending for its survival entirely on the support of the army. And yet it was for the sake of liberty that he defended this government. This paradox has outraged some of Milton's modern readers, and it was the basis of sharp attacks by contemporary critics of the commonwealth. Yet one must follow his arguments with sympathy to understand the difficult position in which he found himself.

The repeated assumptions of Milton's political writings in the Interregnum period are of the opportunity for the realisation of liberty afforded by the time, the heavy responsibility placed on men to use it properly, and the dangers likely to result from its abuse. In the late 1640s Milton was working on his *History of Britain*, which he had perhaps begun in the same spirit of patriotic fervour that he showed in his plans for a national epic. Yet now he saw that the opportunity was being misapplied; in the digression to his *History* known as the *Character of the Long Parliament and Assembly of Divines* (first published in 1681 but probably written in 1648) he laments the fruitlessness of the Presbyterian and parliamentarian victories that seem to him to have resulted only in intolerance and greed:

> They who but of late were extolled as great deliverers, and had a people wholly at their devotion, by so discharging their trust as we see, did not only weaken and unfit themselves to be dispensers of what liberty they pretended, but unfitted also the people, now grown worse and more disordinate, to receive or to digest any liberty at all.... For liberty hath a sharp and double edge fit only to be handled by just and virtuous men, to bad and dissolute it becomes a mischief unwieldy in their own hands.
>
> (Columbia, x, 323–4)

He now distrusted the idea of an open society because it did not produce the reformation he hoped for; the destroyers of liberty in Milton's account would force the defenders of liberty into a repressive position to protect the interest of the whole. Thus Milton's interest shifts from the national idea, the good society in itself, to the men on whom (like Fairfax in 'On the Lord General Fairfax at the siege of Colchester') the responsibility devolves to achieve that society. In *The Tenure of Kings* Milton played into the hands of the opponents of the new regime by using the contract theory, stressing the rights of the people as a whole, to justify the removal of a ruler:

> Since the king or magistrate holds his authority of the people, both originally and naturally for their good in the first place, and not his

own, then may the people as oft as they shall judge it for the best, either choose him or reject him, retain him or depose him though no tyrant, merely by the liberty and right of free born men, to be governed as seems to them best. (Columbia, V, 14)

The flaws in this kind of argument were easily seen by Salmasius, the propagandist hired by Charles II to discredit the regime (though he himself misunderstood the nature of the English monarchy, defining it in Filmerian absolutist terms):

The form of government which [the English fanatics] have introduced is quite new and was unheard of in former times. It is not popular, nor kingly, nor aristocratic, but military. Will they deny this? If they do deny it, the fact itself refutes them.... Whom, therefore, will they convince of that which they mouth, that the supreme sovereignty resides with the people, when the leaders of the army are exercising tyranny and are oppressing the people themselves in harsh and intolerable servitude?[25]

In spite of Milton's language on this occasion it is difficult to believe that he was interested in the constitutional and legal aspects of the problem. The king's execution and the government of the Rump were patently illegal. Constitutional or democratic arguments were meaningless for Milton, since he had no respect for tradition in itself, and he did not understand liberty in quantitative terms; he now thought that the majority of the people must be taught how to use liberty. Hence in his subsequent political writings his emphasis is on the few who can understand and profit from their opportunities. In *Eikonoklastes* the minority are set apart by God:

This therefore we may conclude to be a high honour done us from God, and a special mark of his favour, whom he hath selected as the sole remainder, after all these changes and commotions, to stand upright and steadfast in his cause; dignified with the defence of truth and public liberty.... (Columbia, V, 74)

In the government's official answer to Salmasius, *The [First] Defence of the People of England*, with reference to the exclusion of the Presbyterians from parliament (Pride's Purge) he distinguishes the part that 'was for slavery and peace, with sloth and luxury, upon any terms' from the part that 'kept demanding liberty, and no peace but what was sure and honourable' (VII, 511). The legalist objection to this definition is given by Filmer, who makes an acute analysis of Milton's reply to Salmasius from the point of view of the need for an absolute authority in the state:

If the sounder, the better, and the uprighter part have the power of the people, how shall we know, or who shall judge who they be?[26]

But Milton was concerned not with the legal but the moral basis of authority. In the *Second Defence*, written under the newly-established Protectorate, he shows himself conscious of the difficult position of the government, threatened on one side by royalists and Presbyterians, on the other by republicans and religious radicals. In his horror at the prospect of 'victuallers and hucksters from the city-shops, and herdsmen and graziers from the villages, for our senators' (VIII, 247), he shares the social conservatism of Cromwell. Yet he does not see a social fear of the egalitarian elements in the revolution as the basis of his defence of the army-supported Protectorate; he defines 'free' and 'unfree' in moral terms, though including some significant social commentary:

> As to be free is precisely the same thing as to be pious, wise, just and temperate, careful of one's own, abstinent from what is another's, and thence, in fine, magnanimous and brave – so, to be the opposite of these, is the same thing as to be a slave; and by the wonted judgement, and as it were by the just retribution of God, it comes to pass, that the nation, which has been incapable of governing and ordering itself, and has delivered itself up to the slavery of its own lusts, is delivered over, against its will, to other masters – and whether it will or no, is compelled to serve.   (Columbia, VIII, 249, 251)

The Protectorate is thus the temporary but necessary government of the free over those who have shown themselves to be slaves. Milton's stern warning to the people to choose between slavery and liberty, to move on from a state of pupillage, is preceded by a similar warning to Cromwell, in the guise of panegyric, to use his position to create the circumstances for the propagating of liberty. The liberty that Milton hoped would be realised under the Protectorate included liberty of conscience and the proper reforming of the church, which entailed its complete disestablishment and the voluntary election and support of ministers by their congregations.[27] Cromwell made an attempt to extend toleration, with important exceptions, as the relevant clause in the Instrument of Government of 1653 makes clear:

> XXXVII That such as profess faith in God by Jesus Christ (though differing in judgement from the doctrine, worship, or discipline publicly held forth) shall not be restrained from, but shall be protected in, the profession of the faith and exercise of their religion; so as they abuse not this liberty to the civil injury of others and to the actual disturbance of the public peace on their parts: provided this liberty be not extended to popery nor prelacy, nor to such as, under the profession of Christ, hold forth and practice licentiousness.[28]

Cromwell was caught between his political fear of and his religious sympathy with the radical sects, but his parliaments were much less inclined to toleration than he was; and towards disestablishment no move was made. After the death of Cromwell Milton realised that a Protectorate was not the means to the liberty he had defined; he must have been aware how closely Cromwell's rule was moving towards kingship. In the two remaining years before the Restoration he cast about among Richard Cromwell's parliament, the Rump, and finally Monk, in an attempt to persuade each in turn to settle the political problem and concentrate on the religious one. The *Letter to a Friend* of October 1659 states Milton's principles clearly:

> The terms to be stood on are, liberty of conscience to all professing scripture to be the rule of their faith and worship; and the abjuration of a single person. (Columbia, VI, 104)

These desperate appeals to one group after another, often aggressively confident in tone, are disheartening, but they do not imply that Milton was authoritarian or inconsistent in his principles. He was tired of the disagreement over a political settlement, which did not seem to him the real issue; he was afraid that the rift between army and Rump would result in the loss of everything that was important. The suggestion in *The Ready and Easy Way to Establish a Free Commonwealth* for government by a perpetual Grand Council was meant to obviate the need for constitution making on which so much energy had been wasted in the Interregnum period.[29] The political problem must be solved once and for all in order to guarantee religious liberty. The essential argument of *The Ready and Easy Way* is that 'this liberty of conscience which above all other things ought to be to all men dearest and most precious, no government more inclinable not to favour only but to protect, than a free commonwealth' (VI, 142). Although in his emphasis on local government, the role of the gentry in the counties, and the need for the diffusion of education and culture, Milton shows a sense of the structure of national life much more strongly than in the earlier political tracts (he argues the importance of education in a different context in *Considerations Touching the Likeliest Means to Remove Hirelings*), nevertheless the running comparison between commonwealth and monarchy shows how individualist his view of politics had become as his religious ideas had changed. In the antiprelatical tracts and in *Areopagitica* he had imagined religious reformation in social terms; the end of church reform would be the godly society. After his disagreement with the Presbyterians and his experience of supporting an unpopular minority regime, Milton's perspective shifted; political reform, the permanent establishment of an executive, would be the means to individual religious freedom, which is not envisaged in social terms. The comparison between life under a monarchy and a commonwealth in *The Ready and Easy Way* is like the comparison between bishops and true ministers in the antiprelatical tracts. In a monarchy the people are slaves to form, ceremonial, artificial order, symbolism without substance, whereas in a commonwealth they live as free, isolated individuals:

> [In a free commonwealth] they who are greatest, are perpetual servants and drudges to the public at their own cost and charges, neglect their own affairs; yet are not elevated above their brethren; live soberly in their families, walk the streets as other men, may be spoken to freely, friendly, without adoration. Whereas a king must be adored like a demigod, with a dissolute and haughty court about him, of vast expense and luxury, masques and revels, to the debauching of our prime gentry both male and female; not in their pastimes only, but in earnest, by the loose employments of court service, which will be then thought honourable.
>
> (Columbia, VI, 120)

A king is good for nothing

> but to bestow the eating and drinking of excessive dainties, to set a pompous face upon the superficial actings of state, to pageant himself up and down in progress among the perpetual bowings and cringings of an abject people, on either side deifying and adoring him for nothing done that can deserve it. (p. 121)

The same comparison is made in *Paradise Lost* when Adam goes to meet Raphael:

> Mean while our primitive great sire, to meet
> His godlike guest, walks forth, without more train
> Accompanied than with his own complete
> Perfections, in himself was all his state,
> More solemn than the tedious pomp that waits
> On princes, when their rich retinue long
> Of horses led, and grooms besmeared with gold
> Dazzles the crowd, and sets them all agape.
>
> (*Poems, pp.* 696–7; Book V, *ll.* 350–7)

Milton no longer saw politics as a system of order intrinsically valuable but as machinery. He had moved from the idealisation of a godly society, to a definition of virtuous leadership which would constrain the unfree until they knew how to live well, to the pragmatic recognition of the need for a stable system of government that would allow men the civil liberty to be themselves, the religious liberty to regenerate themselves. He would not tolerate prelacy or popery because they implied political and religious servility, the sacrifice of the individual's freedom of conscience to authority. As his view of religion became more private and individual, as he understood the political failure of the Interregnum years, he began to understand that men could not be compelled to be free. Statements in the tracts of 1659 and 1660 indicate that he regretted his support of a military regime. Cromwell's most dictatorial acts had been undertaken in the belief that he was the instrument of providence, but Milton, like many of his contemporaries, was now much less sure that the workings of providence could be known. In the *First* and *Second Defences* he divided the nation into free and unfree and offered the unfree coercion by the free for their own good. Now in *The Ready and Easy Way*, published in two editions at a time when there was a growing belief that a return to the settled forms and mystique of monarchy would solve all political problems, Milton offered the free minority among the English a last choice, setting out the respective advantages and disadvantages as strongly as he could, between the freedom of a commonwealth and the servility of monarchy. The choice for Milton was a rationally obvious one, hence the ironic optimism of the title, yet he knew that the people were 'choosing them a captain back for Egypt' (VI, 149). Within a short time after the publication of the second edition the Convention Parliament voted for the restoration of Charles II.

Two different voices speak in *The Ready and Easy Way*; the rational voice of public persuasion, demonstrating the easy path to liberty, and the isolated prophetic voice, disgusted and ashamed at the English for their neglect of their opportunity, their inability to complete what they have undertaken:

> That a nation should be so valorous and courageous to win their liberty in the field, and when they have won it, should be so heartless and unwise in their counsels, as not to know how to use it, value it, what to do with it or with themselves; but after ten or twelve years' prosperous war and contestation with tyranny, basely and besottedly to run their necks again into the yoke which they have broken, and prostrate all the fruits of their victory for naught at the feet of the vanquished, besides our loss of glory, and such an example as kings or tyrants never yet had the like to boast of, will be an ignominy if it befall us, that never yet befell any nation possessed of their liberty. (Columbia, VI, 123)

The persuasive oratorical voice needs a national audience, who will be moved to act. The isolated prophetic voice testifies to truth regardless of hearers:

> Thus much I should perhaps have said though I were sure I should have spoken only to trees and stones; and had none to cry to, but with the prophet, *o earth, earth, earth!* to tell the very soil itself, what her perverse inhabitants are deaf to. (*p.* 148)

The Restoration finally deprived Milton of the opportunity to address a national audience on a national subject. In the prophetic voice of

Paradise Lost, preserved from evil days by communion with the heavenly muse who will find him a fit audience (Book VII, *ll.* 1–31), Milton's definition of his poetic role may seem to have come full circle from the image of the isolated, purified poet explored in the poems of the 1630s. First Milton trained himself apart from the world, then immersed himself in public life, then withdrew as a prophet. But there is an enormous difference in the isolation of the later years, which can partly be understood by the symbolic mark that separated Milton. In the early years this mark was purity, in the later years it was blindness. Milton associated his blindness with duty and with experience; he finally lost his sight after writing the *First Defence*, and explained in 'To Mr Cyriack Skinner upon his blindness' his complete acceptance of this sacrifice:

> What supports me dost thou ask?
> The conscience, friend, to have lost them overplied
> In liberty's defence, my noble task,
> Of which all Europe talks from side to side.
> This thought might lead me through the world's vain mask
> Content though blind, had I no better guide.   (*Poems, p.* 414)

His blindness was thus a proof of his commitment to public service, to active involvement in reformation. He rebuked the German diplomat Henry Oldenbourg in 1654 for his suggestion that his pamphleteering was preventing him from pursuing more important studies. Milton admitted that he was neglecting other less gruelling interests, but he did not regret it, 'for I am far from thinking that I have spent my toil, as you seem to hint, on matters of inferior consequence' (XII, 65). Far from being a wasted labour, Milton regarded his Latin defences of England in epic terms. He compared them with the *Iliad*, *Odyssey*, and *Aeneid*, in particular in the sense that in the course of the revolution so far he was describing a limited, unified action, and that the implied end of the British epic, the establishment of the new Troy, was yet to come. He had fulfilled his plans of 1639–42 to be a national poet, yet the poem could not be his creation only. He had done his part:

> I have celebrated, as a testimony to [my fellow-citizens], I had almost said, a monument, which will not speedily perish, actions which were glorious, lofty, which were almost above all praise; and if I have done nothing else, I have assuredly discharged my trust.
>
> (VIII, 253)

But the poem begun by the poet-orator must be completed by the people:

> If, after achievements so magnanimous, ye basely fall off from your duty, if ye are guilty of anything unworthy of you, be assured,

posterity will speak, and thus pronounce its judgement: the foundation was strongly laid, the beginning, nay more than the beginning, was excellent; but it will be inquired...who completed the fabric.

(*pp.* 253, 255)

His national conception of poetry required a national response, the creation of a new society.

As Milton came to see that such a society could not come into being without the cooperation of its members, and that most men would choose 'bondage with ease' before 'strenuous liberty' (*Samson Agonistes, l.* 270), his conception of poetry changed again, and his scope became both larger and more particular, from orator addressing a nation, to prophet addressing human history and each individual. Thus his blindness has another, more important meaning. It became to him a symbol of knowledge as well as of action. The knowledge was of two kinds, knowledge through suffering, or understanding of the need for patience, and knowledge through revelation. In the first sonnet on his blindness he provides a very different answer from the confident interpretation he gives Skinner; here he separates patience and endurance from action:

> God doth not need
> Either man's work or his own gifts, who best
> Bear his mild yoke, they serve him best, his state
> Is kingly. Thousands at his bidding speed
> And post o'er land and ocean without rest:
> They also serve who only stand and wait.

(*Poems, p.* 330)

He also saw his blindness as a gift of second sight, of inner light (in contrast to the royalist view that it was a divine judgement for his wickedness in defending regicide); hence in the *Second Defence* he associated himself with blind prophets and sages of antiquity like Teiresias and Isaac, and in *Paradise Lost* (Book III, *l.* 35) with Homer.[30] His blindness was a mark of his experience and his insight.

It is wrong to assume that because Milton's hopes for political reformation were finally defeated in 1660 he therefore became pessimistic about the possibility of changing history or conquering evil, or that he lapsed into authoritarianism.[31] We have only to compare Milton's reactions to political defeat with those of poets of conservative temperament in similar circumstances to see how inappropriate such assumptions are. Milton never became reconciled to disorder as a component of order as Spenser and Pope were, though he emphasised variety in order;[32] he never accepted a separation between the disordered world and the self-reliant individual, as Jonson and Pope did – the fallacies of Stoicism are criticised in both *Paradise Lost* and *Paradise Regained*; he never lost

94

his faith in man as an individual, or became afraid of his destructive tendencies, as Dryden did. In spite of his disappointment with the English for their betrayal of their opportunities he did not turn in on himself. The basis of his view of ethics and of the poet's function remained change; men must change themselves, the poet must show them how to do so.[33] But Milton's sense of the problem of change was now more realistic, based as it was on his political experience. In the early 1640s he had assumed that voluntary change in society as a whole, reformation, was imminent and easy to achieve. Then in the 1650s he believed that specific political changes must be made, by force if necessary, so that freedom for individual change, regeneration, would be possible. It was during this stage of his thought that he wrote *Christian Doctrine*,[34] his system of theology which deals not with society but with the Christian liberty of the individual, the process by which each Christian can pass from regeneration to glorification. In the poems of the 1660s he came to see that servility was a state of mind, and that individual regeneration must precede social reformation, but that the process of reformation would not be completed within human history. Milton now gave the idea of change and time a wholly different emphasis.

In the poems of the last fifteen or so years of his life, Milton explored the problems of change and time on three levels, in terms of the whole process of Christian history (chiefly in *Paradise Lost*), in terms of human society (chiefly in *Samson Agonistes*), and in terms of the lives of individuals (in all three poems, but especially in *Paradise Regained*).[35] Milton's aim in these poems in justifying the ways of God to man is to show what man might be, what prevents him from reaching and how he can be taught to reach his end, how he can unite his will with the working of providence. Though the world-picture of *Paradise Lost* is hierarchic, though God has appeared to many of Milton's readers as an authoritarian despot, the poem's emphasis is not on order, stability, man's fixed place in the universe, but on motion and change. Raphael explains to the unfallen Adam the universal hierarchy in which everything is working upwards:

> One almighty is, from whom
> All things proceed, and up to him return,
> If not depraved from good, created all
> Such to perfection, one first matter all,
> Indued with various forms, various degrees
> Of substance, and in things that live, of life;
> But more refined, more spiritous, and pure,
> As nearer to him placed or nearer tending
> Each in their several active spheres assigned,
> Till body up to spirit work, in bounds
> Proportioned to each kind.   (Book v, *ll.* 469–79)

Unfallen man can expect to reach the angelic state:

> Your bodies may at last turn all to spirit,
> Improved by tract of time, and winged ascent
> Ethereal, as we, or may at choice
> Here or in heavenly paradises dwell.   (*ll.* 497–500)

The direction of man's movement is in his own control. God offers grace; man has the capacity for self-knowledge, he is 'magnanimous to correspond with heaven' (VII, 511); he can either rise or fall. The fall is man's attempt to rise in the wrong way, the rejection of self-knowledge, power over self, for empire, attempted power over nature. The liberty of obedience to God's pattern for man, which can readily be apprehended by the reason, is rejected for servility to appetite, ambition, and dissatisfaction. Milton does not contrast evil motion with good stability, but good and bad motion with each other. There can be no perfect, stable human society. The process of human history, as described by Michael to Adam in Books XI and XII, is one of constant conflict between reason and appetite, knowledge and power, liberty and servility; only a minority of men will understand this process. Men will be afraid of their humanity, of their nakedness, of what they are capable of; society will inflict 'outward rites and specious forms' (XII, 534), 'carnal power' (*l.* 521) and secular authority on individual religious freedom, and because the majority will not choose freedom, this infliction will be just:

> Yet sometimes nations will decline so low
> From virtue, which is reason, that no wrong,
> But justice, and some fatal curse annexed
> Deprives them of their outward liberty,
> Their inward lost.   (Book XII, *ll.* 97–101)

Though the path to virtue is easy, though obedience to God means simply choosing to be fully human, since 'God and nature bid the same' (VI, 176), most men will prefer to cling to the props of fallen earthly society, place, form, tradition, and will not recognise that

> God attributes to place
> No sanctity, if none be thither brought
> By men who there frequent, or therein dwell.
> (Book XI, *ll.* 836–8)

Men cannot seek escape in an idea of paradise, since paradise is action not rest. Yet Adam, faced with this knowledge of the course of human history, will need 'true patience' (XI, 361) to accept that, given choice, the majority of men will not choose to be free. Only when the race of time is over, when time stands fixed, will righteousness and justice be a universal condition; until then the regenerated individual is offered 'a paradise within' (XII, 587) in his own self-knowledge and fortitude.

Paradise Lost shows what is meant by the loss of liberty and how the course of human history will be a struggle, unsuccessful until the end of time, to regain it. *Samson Agonistes*, drawing on one event in human history as an example for all societies, shows how one man's recovery of liberty will provide an example for, but will not itself save, a nation. The chorus, like Adam, have accepted the justice of God's ways, the need for patience in the face of human rejection of liberty. They contrast 'celestial vigour' (*l.* 1280) and fortitude, active and passive virtue; Samson, in the process of his regeneration, in his active cooperation with the opportunity provided by providence, seizes liberty, but he can only act on his own behalf. He is an exemplary hero, but throughout the play he emphasises the Israelites' refusal to cooperate with him. Israel must 'find courage to lay hold on this occasion' (*l.* 1716). If it does not, the blame will be on man, not on providence; the few will rejoice in the free act of Samson and accept with fortitude the servility of the rest.[36]

It is an underlying assumption of *Paradise Lost* and *Samson Agonistes* that humanity is divided into the few who are free and the many who are servile, or, as the chorus of Samson see it, into the common rout and the elected saints (*ll.* 674, 678, 1288). However there is nothing necessary or Calvinist about this division; in *Christian Doctrine* Milton repudiates the idea that God has reprobated or damned any individuals from eternity. Salvation is open to all who will accept it.[37] Milton's own experience made such a division seem probable for the future of mankind, yet this was not a pessimistic conclusion. In spite of the tragic rejection by the English of their revolutionary opportunity, nevertheless 'all is best, though we oft doubt' (*Samson, l.* 1745), because the way to liberty, through God's providence and grace and Christ's example, is open; the choice is man's:

> The world was all before them, where to choose
> Their place of rest, and providence their guide.
>
> (*Paradise Lost*, XII, 646–7)

The duality of this process, the uniting of human choice with divine providence, is exemplified in the dual nature of Christ, human and divine. Christ exists at two levels of meaning for Milton. He is the process of history, the path for humanity through time to timelessness; he will

> bring back
> Through the world's wilderness long wandered man
> Safe to eternal paradise of rest.   (*ll.* 312–14)

He is also everyman, struggling for and achieving the paradise within. He is both the end, in that he providentially leads man through history to eternity; he is also the process, in that he shows man how and what to choose in order to cooperate with providence. It is this second aspect of Christ that *Paradise Regained* is about.

It may seem odd to talk about choice in the context of *Paradise Regained*, since the most striking aspect of the poem is rejection. One reason why Milton has repelled many readers is that he has defined his positive concept of Christian liberty in what are in a worldly sense negative terms: obedience in *Paradise Lost*, rejection of temptation in *Paradise Regained*. When Christ has rejected the temptations of kingly and military power, earthly glory, and human learning, Satan asks

> Since neither wealth, nor honour, arms nor arts,
> Kingdom nor empire pleases thee, nor aught
> By me proposed in life contemplative,
> Or active, tended on by glory, or fame,
> What dost thou in this world?   (Book IV, *ll.* 368–72)

Though Christ is man, his perspective is that of eternity. Milton's concern is to show the process of self-conquest that is open to every individual with God's grace, and the proper understanding of time that is a necessary part of it. Through the rejections made by Christ he is criticising, as in all his work, the human reliance on external irrelevancies – traditions, rewards, honours – for satisfaction, but he is also criticising his own emphasis on forced political solutions, his earlier belief that enlightened leadership might set the English free. Christ refuses to help the Israelites or the Romans, since they will not help themselves:

> What wise and valiant man would seek to free
> These thus degenerate, by themselves enslaved,
> Or could of inward slaves make outward free?
>   (Book IV, *ll.* 143–5)

There will be no perfect human society; there will only be the perfect heavenly monarchy, whose time of coming no human being will foresee:

> All things are best fulfilled in their due time,
> And time there is for all things, Truth hath said:
> If of my reign prophetic writ hath told,
> That it shall never end, so when begin
> The Father in his purpose hath decreed,
> He in whose hand all times and seasons roll.
>   (Book III, *ll.* 182–7)

> Means there shall be to this, but what the means,
> Is not for thee to know, nor me to tell.   (Book IV, *ll.* 152–3)

To support the necessary human trust in God's "due time and providence" (III, 440) Christ teaches patience. Even more important than

Milton's criticism of the idea that political reformation can be achieved without individual regeneration is his emphasis on what exactly self conquest and patience constitute. He strenuously attacks the idea that at a time of political repression and social decadence the individual should turn back on himself as the only fixed point of value. Christ uses language which might seem to imply such an answer:

> He who reigns within himself, and rules
> Passions, desires, and fears, is more a king;
> Which every wise and virtuous man attains.
>
> (Book II, *ll.* 466–8)

But such self conquest is not selfish or proud; it cannot be reached by man through his own strength. Christ rejects Satan's offer of Stoic philosophy (among others) and his suggestion that 'these rules will render thee a king complete / Within thyself' (IV, 283–4):

> Alas what can they teach, and not mislead;
> Ignorant of themselves, of God much more,
> And how the world began, and how man fell
> Degraded by himself, on grace depending?
> Much of the soul they talk, but all awry,
> And in themselves seek virtue, and to themselves
> All glory arrogate, to God give none,
> Rather accuse him under usual names,
> Fortune and Fate, as one regardless quite
> Of mortal things.   (Book IV, *ll.* 309–18)

The Stoic believes that he has no control over external circumstances, only over his own mind. But Milton believes that if men will only change themselves, with God's help they can change the world. Patience and fortitude are the prelude to action:

> Who best
> Can suffer, best can do.   (Book III, *ll.* 194–5)

One can compare the pointless Stoicism of the devils in the first two books of *Paradise Lost*. In their assumption that through strength of will they can steel themselves against the pains of hell, they forget that hell itself is the result of their own degeneracy. But the most dramatic confutation of Stoic self-reliance is in Satan's last temptation of Christ. Satan argues that Christ's rejections so far could have been achieved by merely human strength:

> Opportunity I here have had
> To try thee, sift thee, and confess have found thee
> Proof against all temptation as a rock

> Of adamant, and as a centre, firm
> To the utmost of mere man both wise and good....
>
> <div align="right">(Book IV, <i>ll.</i> 531–5)</div>

He wishes to test Christ's divinity, and urges him with heavy sarcasm to stand on the pinnacle of the temple, a feat impossible to a human:

> There stand, if thou wilt stand; to stand upright
> Will ask thee skill....   (<i>ll.</i> 551–2)

The Jonsonian moral hero is constantly being exhorted to stand, to rely on his own completion and circular perfection, to rest on his own centre.[38] Satan erroneously believes that man is capable of this self-sufficiency, but morally, not where it is physically impossible. He expects Christ either, as a man, to fall and die, or, as God, to be rescued in falling by angels. But neither happens; refusing to tempt, but trusting God, Christ stands, and Satan falls, 'smitten with amazement' (<i>l.</i> 562). The meaning of this episode for man, apart from establishing Christ's divinity, is that with God's grace he can stand, not like the Stoic in opposition to the world, but like the armed Christian,[39] in preparation for action. Though Christ refuses to seize an earthly kingdom for himself, this does not mean that the Christian must retire from the world, or that his virtues are only passive ones. True Christian patience is active:

> They also serve who only stand and wait.

The Christian, assisted by grace, guided by providence, is both active and passive: he acts in the struggle for his own regeneration, and having achieved that, may act in the world to persuade others; yet with patience and fortitude he suffers the knowledge that the world will not be wholly reformed until its final destruction.

In these poems Milton is no longer addressing society but the few who will understand how to be free. His message is bleak but not pessimistic. He no longer believes in the nation as a corporate whole, nor in the aristocratic few who can act on behalf of the rest. The free society is a movement of individuals in process of regeneration. The unfree society is a static form imposed on a people who have knowingly abdicated their individuality. The poet cannot remake society, but he can show individuals how they can remake themselves. Thus though Milton starts with the humanist belief that the poet should shape society, he moves very far from conservative interpretations of that belief. Perhaps the greatest difference is not his early conviction that he should take part in social reformation, but the position he reached after his recognition of political failure. When he saw that men did not wish to cooperate with providence, he did not turn his back on the world; he continued to believe in man's capacity for change.

ANDREW MARVELL: THE LIMITS OF POETRY

Marvell may seem in some ways to be out of place in a study of this kind. He was not a self-conscious man; he left very little in the way of autobiographical explanation of his political opinions (chiefly in letters to his nephew William Popple in the 1670s) and nothing in the way of comment on his poems, except what is contained in the poems themselves. He was not a professional poet, and published few poems in his lifetime. We can only date accurately a handful of his poems, and we cannot be sure that some of the poems attributed to him were written by him. We do not know how he felt about his successive stages of political affiliation, from royalist to Cromwellian to 'country', or if he saw any continuity in his development from lyric to panegyric poet, to satirist and pamphleteer. For a long time after his death there were two Andrew Marvells; the liberal patriot pamphleteer, whose vogue lasted into the nineteenth century, and the lyric poet destroyed by political and scientific revolution, who is largely a discovery of the twentieth century.[40] More recently there have been attempts to find an underlying consistency, political and temperamental, in his changing ideas and poetry, to regard his career as a whole.[41] While such attempts are to be welcomed, the search for consistency can be carried too far. It is a mistake to look in the lyrics for evidence of a particular intellectual commitment, to see them as illustrations of a system of ideas such as neo-Platonism.[42] The development that will be traced here is how a particularly subtle, receptive and intelligent mind reacted to revolution and Restoration, how the course of political events influenced the kind of poet and the kind of man Marvell was able to become. Such an emphasis will admittedly involve neglecting some of Marvell's most characteristic poetic qualities.

Marvell's literary career seems to have gone through three phases. On the whole the change from one phase to another is chronological, since the changes are largely precipitated by external political events, but sometimes these phases overlap, since they also represent different but coexisting states of mind. The stages in Marvell's political affinities and public life can be indicated first. He took no part in the civil war, being abroad at the time; his sympathies in about 1648 and 1649 seem to have been royalist, since his poems have cavalier heroes. In 1650 he veered towards a qualified approval of Cromwell; his sympathies were now Puritan but not republican. His position was ambiguous, however; from about 1650 to 1653 he worked for Fairfax who had broken with Cromwell and was in retirement in Yorkshire. In 1653 he decided to commit himself to the regime. He applied to Milton for a post, which he did not get; instead he moved to Eton, as tutor to Cromwell's ward. In 1657 he obtained the secretaryship with Milton, and in 1659 became a member of parliament. This was to be his chief occupation until his death in 1678. At the beginning of the Restoration period he undertook official diplomatic work, but from about 1666–7 he became increasingly critical of the government, for both political and religious reasons, and finally worked actively against it. Throughout this period his politics were those of a constitutional royalist.

Many of Marvell's poems cannot be associated with specific stages in his career, but internal evidence provides a rough guide to dates of composition, about which there is broad general agreement. In the first phase of his poetic career, that is in the majority of his lyrics, Marvell is a poet writing completely outside the tradition that is discussed in this book. These poems, though serious, are not didactic; they do not attempt to persuade the reader of particular truths, nor to recommend particular acts. They are poems of intellectual exploration and play, in which different languages, ideas, or sets of tensions and opposites are tested. Some of the most important of these opposites are reason and feeling, sensuality and asceticism, love and time, body and soul, nature and art (or civilization), individual and society, retirement and action. Often these opposites are resolved, but only within the terms of the poem itself; the resolution does not imply subsequent action, and the resolution of one poem is often contradicted by the resolution of another. We know that some of these poems were written in the Yorkshire period, and it seems reasonable to assume that the majority were written between the late 1640s and the end of 1653. It may be argued that the religious lyrics are of a later date, but their tone does not seem to imply commitment to action or a rejection of the stance adopted in other poems.[43] In the second phase of his career, coinciding with his commitment to the Cromwellian regime, Marvell wrote a different kind of poetry, assuming a direct relationship between life and art. In 1650 in his first poem on Cromwell he had explored the connection between balance and commitment, poetry and action; between 1653, when he tried to enter public service, and 1658, when Cromwell died, he concentrated on public poetry, attempting to define Cromwell's role, to provide a new set of forms and myths to replace the ones that had been overthrown. These poems were intended both to interpret and in one case to influence public events. In the third stage of his career Marvell came to see literature in more negative terms, as a weapon, an aid to action. This does not mean that his satires were only negative and destructive. On the contrary, he tried to counteract the heroic, courtly royalism that Waller and Dryden were creating by his support for a broader royalism based on the relationship between king and country. The idea of this relationship, with varying degrees of emphasis, underlies the poetic satires and the prose pamphlets. But the creation of an alternative sustaining theory became less important as the problem became one of averting crisis. The chief concern of Marvell's last years was the growing threat of political absolutism and religious intolerance, and his last works were devoted to exposing this threat. In his attack on the court and the conspiracy to separate king from country he clung to the idea of the independence and integrity of the country gentry. In this forced abandonment of a public for a more private social myth Marvell in some ways anticipated, though it may seem paradoxical, the position that his enemy Dryden was to work out for himself at the end of his life.

Readers and critics of Marvell, including those who have a particular interest in the last phase of his career, are in no doubt as to the disastrous effect his commitment to public life and his change in attitude to the function of poetry had on the quality of his poems. But the decision to take active part in political life or to adopt a particular point of view is not necessarily inimical to the writing of good poetry. The best poetry does not necessarily comprise tension, balance, paradox, and irony, as some twentieth-century readers have thought. For Milton there was an intimate connection between poetry and action, and his experience of the processes of political change made him a greater poet. Marvell, however, at first saw poetry and action as opposites. In the decision to take part in public life and to write a different kind of poetry defining Cromwell and the Protectorate he consciously chose to exclude certain aspects of his poetic nature. Like Milton, he had a strong sense of time; the priorities of the moment demanded that he should abandon one kind of life, and one kind of art, for another. 'An Horatian Ode upon Cromwell's Return from Ireland' sets out the need for choice, though Marvell was not to act on it for another three years:

> The forward youth that would appear
> Must now forsake his muses dear,
>   Nor in the shadows sing
>   His numbers languishing.
> 'Tis time to leave the books in dust,
> And oil the unused armour's rust,
>   Removing from the wall
>   The corslet of the hall.[44]

Marvell here assumes that art is a product of leisure, and that the exigencies of the time demand a rejection of art for action. In the next three years Marvell had ample opportunity to weigh these conflicting claims, and his best poems seem to be a result of this period of leisure. He associated the conflict with the careers and choices of two men, Fairfax and Cromwell. He was aware of the onesidedness of both positions; a choice for one way of life or one kind of action excludes other qualities or possibilities.[45] The Cromwell of 'An Horatian Ode' represents a political strength and realism which is appropriate for the time but disregards and destroys inherited civilisation and law. The Fairfax of 'Upon the Hill and Grove at Bilborough' and 'Upon Appleton House' represents a concern for personal integrity and civilised values which at a time of political crisis involves retreat from the world and a rejection of political demands. Cromwell moves from retirement to action, Fairfax from action to retirement. Marvell subjects both to the same half critical, half approving assessment, and makes a different choice in different poems. Whereas Marvell implies that Fairfax and Cromwell are opposites, Milton, who had already decided in favour of action and assessed the political needs of the situation, urged Fairfax in his sonnet of 1648 to assume the position of enlightened leadership that was later to be Cromwell's; in the *Second Defence* when he praised the heroes of the revolution, Fairfax among them, who had broken with Cromwell, it was partly with the purpose of ensuring that Cromwell remained true to its principles. Marvell's praise and comparison is personal and fluctuating; Milton's is public and persuasive.

Fairfax in many ways represented the best of the conservative, country opposition to Charles I. He fought the war to make the king come to terms, to curb his prerogative. His dilemma was created by Charles' refusal to behave in the ways mapped out for him. He refused, unlike Cromwell, to recognise that Charles was the obstacle to any kind of political settlement. He could not accept the implications of his army's success. Though Independent in his religious attitudes, he sympathised with the Presbyterians. He would not associate himself with the king's execution, and he would not lead the army into Scotland against his former allies. His resignation left the position at the top open for Cromwell. Marvell in 1650 recognised that political victory achieved by military means would have to be consolidated in the same way:

> The same arts that did gain
> A power must it maintain. (Macdonald, *p.* 121)

Fairfax recognised no such necessity, and after his resignation he had nothing further to do with the commonwealth.[46]

The Fairfax whom Marvell joined as tutor to his daughter was thus a disappointed man, with no public future open to him; but as a sick man he was grateful to be released from responsibility, and he was certain of the values which had led him to reject his military career. In the poems Marvell wrote in praise of Fairfax's new retired way of life, 'Upon the Hill and Grove at Bilborough' and 'Upon Appleton House', he showed the greatest respect for the qualities of mind that led the general to his decision. Yet the praise he accords him is qualified by its tone and by the introduction of his own questioning and ironic sensibility in the latter poem. He is not advocating retirement, nor accepting the antitheses implied by Fairfax's decision, but starting with the fact of his patron's life and the tradition of the country house and retirement poem he explores, sometimes irreverently, the incompatibilities and ambiguities that can be seen to underlie ostensible moral commitment. His interest is in the way the mind can make its own categories, can move from one to the other without necessarily making a choice. This capacity is particularly exemplified in 'The Garden' (which together with the mower poems may have been written, though there is no way of establishing this, during the Yorkshire period); what may seem a deliberate opposition between ambition and quiet, society and solitude, body and soul, is undercut by the nature of the transitions, by the absurdity that Marvell allows to play around what he praises. Mental and physical pleasures do not exclude each other; the garden is at the same time a place of active sensuality, creative imagination, meditation, and impossible seclusion from the world. Marvell plays with other literary gardens, but not for the purpose of defining a specific garden of his own.

In his two poems on Fairfax Marvell makes use of the tradition of the country house poem which identifies moral virtue with natural and social forms.[47] Thus he emphasises the correspondence between the man, the landscape, the house, and the poem. In 'Upon the Hill and Grove' variety in natural phenomena and changes in poetic tone reflect the general's qualities and the stages of his career:

> Therefore to your obscurer seats
> From his own brightness he retreats:
> Nor he the hills without the groves,
> Nor height but with retirement loves.

(Macdonald, *p.* 79)

'Upon Appleton House' begins by establishing the idea of proportion; nature, the house, the general and his qualities, the poem which encloses them all, are identical in their structure:

> But all things are composed here
> Like nature, orderly and near....   (*ll.* 25–6)

> Humility alone designs
> Those short but admirable lines,
> By which, ungirt and unconstrained,
> Things greater are in less contained.   (*ll.* 41–4)

And Marvell uses traditional stages in space and time: Fairfax, his house, his garden, the fields beyond, the world outside; his ancestry, his actions, his future in his daughter. Yet the system of order and correspondence that is set out at the beginning of the poem is not maintained; Marvell deliberately departs from the social and moral tradition he appears to be working in. He does this in two ways; he looks at the same event from different perspectives, so that Fairfax's retirement is both praised and criticised, and he introduces his own character as poet, fanciful and self-mocking, so that an element of doubt is cast on what appear to be plain moral statements. It may perhaps be argued that Marvell is so sure of his own position and of what he values – 'How safe, methinks, and strong, behind / These trees have I encamped my mind' (*ll.* 601–2) – that he can afford to play with his material, leaving his basic meaning unaffected; but his irony does not work quite in this way.

The different meanings given to retirement all qualify each other. First there is the artificial retirement of the cloister, to which the nuns try to force 'virgin Thwaites'; this retirement is unnatural because it separates men from women, and forcibly excludes the wildness of the world outside:

> Within this holy leisure we
> Live innocently as you see.
> These walls restrain the world without,
> But hedge our liberty about.
> These bars enclose that wider den
> Of those wild creatures, called men.   (*ll.* 97–102)

In the parody battle that follows, the nuns with their religious trappings are easily defeated by the sexuality of Fairfax (the general's ancestor). Marriage is established as a superior state to celibacy; the nuns become an episode in a fairy tale. Secondly there is the retirement of England, separate from the world, but violated by the actions of its inmates so that it is now a wasted Eden. Thirdly there is the retirement of Fairfax himself, who has neglected the garden of England for the sake of the garden of his mind, where

> he did, with his utmost skill,
> Ambition weed, but conscience till.   (*ll.* 353–4)

Yet this cultivation of 'flowers eternal, and divine' is also seen as a slightly absurd floral imitation of 'warlike studies' (*l.* 284). The garden is laid out
> in sport
> In the just figure of a fort.   (*ll.* 285–6)

Fairfax's retirement is a poor parody of his public life, yet his moral superiority to the wasted world outside can only be achieved through retirement. Fourthly there is the retirement of the poet, who moves from formal garden to field to wood to river, from social and moral celebration to allegory and ironic meditation. As an 'easy philosopher', he can interpret nature mystically, sensually, allegorically, selfishly;

with no external obligations, he can laugh at them from his place of safety

> where the world no certain shot
> Can make, or me it toucheth not.
> But I on it securely play,
> And gall its horsemen all the day.   (*ll.* 605-8)

And finally there is the retirement of Maria Fairfax, who resists the ambush of unworthy suitors, but who prepares herself for future marriage; her virtues are the paradigm for natural order which exists only in retirement and no longer in the world outside:

> 'Tis not, what once it was, the world:
> But a rude heap together hurled;
> All negligently overthrown,
> Gulfs, deserts, precipices, stone.
> Your lesser world contains the same.
> But in more decent order tame;
> You heaven's centre, nature's lap.
> And paradise's only map.   (*ll.* 761-8)

Each act of retirement is seen in terms of its opposite; yet paradoxically the military imagery which links each episode can emphasise either the strenuousness of moral choice or the fertility of poetic invention. Retirement can be decision, escape, example, or indulgence.

By emphasising the idea of perspective, by showing that the categories of the poem are not absolutes but created by the mind of the poet, Marvell is putting forward a completely different view of art from that which underlies Jonson's poems of social celebration. In the section on the poet's wandering and withdrawal (XLVII–LXXXI) natural events are seen in terms of artistic conventions and the creations of fancy. The meadows are more changeable than masque machinery – a 'scene that turns with engines strange' (*l.* 385). They are peopled by mowers who are characters in an allegory of the poet's invention, and to oblige him nature will imitate art:

> [She] cries, he called us Israelites;
> But now, to make his saying true,
> Rails rain for quails, for manna dew.   (*ll.* 406-8)

Depending on his shifting perspective nature provides material for political allegory, mystical knowledge, or moral commentary to the easy philosopher, who himself changes his 'mask' at whim from 'inverted tree' (*l.* 568) to 'prelate of the grove' (*l.* 592) to imprisoned lover and martyr (LXXVII) to 'trifling youth' (*l.* 652). The poet here does not imitate nature, nor recreate order lost in nature, but invents; his fancy can manipulate reality, his mind 'creates, transcending these, / Far other worlds, and other seas' ('The Garden'). Reality is changed by his description of it; his interest is not truth but variety of attitude. Thus an artificial and elaborately cultivated garden can be emblematic to Fairfax of his moral choice and to the poet of 'The Garden' of a better order of time, yet to the mower in 'The Mower against Gardens' it can represent vicious human adulteration of nature.

Although there is undoubtedly political subject matter in 'Upon Appleton House', because of this flexibility it is very different from the specifically political poems. Marvell is not persuading or making a choice; he is not saying that Fairfax should have acted differently, or that his own continued retirement on Fairfax's estate would be inappropriate.[48] Yet from the perspective of the world and of action he does imply that Fairfax's motives are too fine, just as from the perspective of his commitment to public service and the political moment he recognises that his poetic skills, his ability to manipulate reality, are too variegated and too artificial. Action is coarser than retirement; the poetry of action, which concentrates on the present moment, is more limited for Marvell than the poetry of invention and play with its freedom of point of view.

In his poems on the Cromwellian regime Marvell did not totally eliminate such characteristics, but he chose to write from a specific perspective. His wit and sense of play, his delight in converting reality to the terms of artistic conventions, were to reappear in the Restoration satires, particularly in *Last Instructions to a Painter*. His intellectual flexibility, the basis of his poetic qualities, was also the basis of his political decision. Unlike the revolutionary Milton or the conservative Dryden Marvell had no commitment to an ideal of political life, whether as an end of history or a model of order, to which reality should be made to approximate. He had a profound sense of the dual nature of time, time as the whole process of history, or providence, and time as the present of political action which each individual faces. The problem for the individual in deciding his allegiance and for the public poet in defining his subject is to understand the relationship between the two. In *The Rehearsal Transprosed* Part I, in a much quoted passage, Marvell argued that political and religious liberty would have come about providentially in the 1640s without men taking arms against the king:

> For men may spare their pains where nature is at work, and the world will not go the faster for our driving. Even as his present Majesty's happy Restoration did itself, so all things else happen in their best and proper time, without any need of our officiousness.[49]

It may be that in 1672 Marvell had come to believe that he had been wrong in associating the events that led to the Interregnum with the workings of providence, but elsewhere in *The Rehearsal Transprosed* he was, naturally enough, not completely honest about his own connections with and sympathy for the Cromwellian regime.[50] *The Rehearsal Transprosed* was directed at meddling Anglican divines who by their officiousness and extremism were threatening to destroy a flexible and workable constitution. Providence at this point was on the side of inaction, of letting things be. In 1650 matters were very different. In 'An Horatian Ode' Marvell shows great feeling and respect for the constitution that has been destroyed, but makes clear his belief that it is too late to adhere to it now. Charles represents the long past of history and tradition, 'the great work of time', 'the kingdom old', 'the ancient rights', but this past has been totally disrupted by a different kind of time, fate, which breaks and remoulds, and whose agent is 'restless Cromwell', who is 'the three forked lightning' and 'angry heaven's flame'. A civilisation has been destroyed by a natural force; while what is lost must be deplored, the political problem is in the future. 'An Horatian Ode' sets out to show that Cromwell's military conquest was necessary, and that the process of destruction and consolidation must continue for the time being. But the poem also looks forward to the creation of the new order, the new mould into which the kingdom is to be cast. Thus Cromwell is not only the elemental force, the agent of destruction, but the man, industrious and self knowing, the servant of the people who is subject to their control:

> So when the falcon high
> Falls heavy from the sky,
> She, having killed, no more does search,
> But on the next green bough to perch;
> Where, when he first does lure,
> The falconer has her sure. (Macdonald, *pp.* 120–1)

In 'An Horatian Ode' Marvell is above all concerned with the present moment, the need to accept the fact of the overthrow of tradition. In 'The First Anniversary of the Government under O. C.' his concern is with making the immediate events of Cromwell's rule fit the patterns of providence, with defining his role in history; his perspective switches from the short to the long view.[51] But Marvell's problem is still an immediate and practical one, the settlement of the constitution. The poem's double emphasis on the movement of time and the building of the state is an attempt to resolve the problems faced by Cromwell in his unwilling metamorphosis from general to protector.

Cromwell habitually regarded himself as an agent of providence, not as an individual acting on his own behalf. His military victories and the overthrow of the Stuarts were proof of God's plan for the English. He continued to believe this in spite of his disappointment successively in the Rump, the Nominated or Barebones Parliament, and the first Protectorate Parliament. Thus he rebuked the last of these in his dissolution speech of 1655:

> The scriptures say, the Rod has a voice, and he will make himself known, and he will make himself known by the judgements which he executeth. And do we not think he will, and does, by the providences of mercy and kindness which he hath for his people, and for their just liberties, whom he loves as the apple of his eye? Doth he not by them manifest himself?[52]

But the ways of providence were not always clear. Cromwell repeatedly found himself forced by events into taking actions which he disliked – the execution of the king in 1649, the dissolution of the Rump and of the Nominated Parliament in 1653. He was embarrassed by the absolute military power he held in part of 1653 and 1655; he wanted parliamentary government but he would not allow the continuation of parliaments that were socially too radical or religiously too conservative. The basis of his rule was always military in spite of trappings invented to conceal this fact. The establishment of the Protectorate was an attempt to give an aura of legality and constitutional form to the regime, a compromise between military dictatorship and monarchy. Cromwell had considered the idea of assuming the crown in 1652, but it was impossible then, as it was in 1657 when he was offered the crown by parliament, because of army opposition. Cromwell had to reconcile his belief in religious liberty, which he shared with the army leaders, with his desire for social stability, which he shared with the conservative elements in the nation who longed for a return to known constitutional forms. The latter were ultimately the more powerful; the Protectorate as redesigned in 1657 was becoming more and more like monarchy (to the disgust of republicans like Mrs Hutchinson) and Cromwell's funeral was a royal one (Evelyn described him as 'lying in effigy in royal robes, and crowned with a crown, sceptre, and mund, like a king').[53] The step to Charles Stuart was a short one.

In 1650 Marvell had seen Cromwell both as an irresistible force and as an individual under parliamentary control. The image of the falconer suggests that Marvell (like Cromwell himself at this point) expected the government of the commonwealth to be ultimately parliamentary even though military power had established it. In 1651 the commonwealth's enemies at home were finally defeated but that did not help its constitutional problems. Cromwell felt driven by divine authority to dissolve the Rump which would not dissolve itself; but the rule of the saints he expected from the Nominated Parliament proved too radical for him and for an important number of its members. The Protectorate under the Instrument of Government of December 1653 was designed to provide both political stability and religious freedom. It was a very unpopular constitution; since it was neither the rule of the saints nor a republic (as it involved the government of a 'single person') it was attacked by fifth monarchists and republicans; it had none of the emotional, historical or legal authority of monarchy. The protector was in need of propaganda that would weld into a symbolic whole the contradictory elements in his rule, that would interpret the theory behind it.[54] The royalist attitude was simple; Cromwell was an ambitious hypocrite who had always aimed at monarchy. The view is put at its crudest in the royalist ballad of 1649 'A coffin for King Charles; a crown for Cromwell; and a pit for the people'. Cromwell is seated on the throne:

> So, so, the deed is done,
>   The royal head is severed,
> As I meant when I first begun
>   and strongly have endeavoured.
> Now Charles the I is tumbled down,
>   the second, I do not fear;
> I grasp the sceptre, wear the crown,
>   nor for Jehovah care.[55]

The office of protector must be differentiated from, and shown to be superior to, that of king; the defined constitution of the Instrument must be shown to be compatible with the millenarian element in Puritan thought, and the elevation of a single person to be compatible with republican egalitarianism. These are some of the aims that Marvell set himself in 'The First Anniversary'.[56]

The nature of Marvell's panegyric of Cromwell can be appreciated by comparing it briefly with that of Milton in the *Second Defence*.[57] Milton published the *Second Defence* in May 1654 after the dissolution of the Nominated Parliament and before the sitting of the first Protectorate Parliament; Marvell presumably wrote 'The First Anniversary' in December 1654 (a month before Cromwell was to dissolve that parliament). Though Milton's concern is partly with directing the career of an individual, and Marvell's is with the symbolic and historical explanation of that career, Marvell's panegyric is ultimately more realistic.

In the *Second Defence* Milton accepts Cromwell's view of the Rump and Nominated Parliaments as respectively self-interested and socially dangerous. Cromwell's elevation seems divinely ordained and just, because the people have given evidence of their innate lack of freedom, while Cromwell through his self-conquest has prepared himself from the beginning for public office:

A commander first over himself, the conqueror of himself, it was over himself he had learnt most to triumph. Hence, he went to encounter with an external enemy as a veteran accomplished in all military duties.... (Columbia, VIII, 215)

Only the ambitious or the envious or the ignorant will disapprove of power being vested in the wise. It is right that Cromwell should govern and that he should be marked out. Milton here takes issue with Cromwell's republican critics, and he seems to approve of the office of protector. At the same time he approves of it only insofar as it does not isolate or elevate Cromwell too far; he insists that the protector must not assume the characteristics of king. The individual is much more important than his office:

> Though it can add nothing to dignity, yet as it is expedient, for virtues even the most exalted to be finished and terminated by a sort of human summit, which is counted honour, you thought it right, and suffered yourself, for the public benefit, to assume something like a title, resembling most that of *pater patriae*, the father of your country; you suffered yourself not to be raised indeed, but to descend so many degrees from on high, and to be forced as it were into the ranks; despising the name of king for majesty far more majestic.
>
> (*pp.* 223, 225)

It is essential that Cromwell should use his position properly, to further the liberty of the people who have misused it, and not to enforce his own authority. Milton warns him:

> Indeed, without our freedom, you yourself cannot be free: for such is the order of nature, that he who forcibly seizes upon the liberty of others, is the first to lose his own, is the first to become a slave.
>
> (*p.* 227)

The Protectorate embodied for Milton the paradox in his political beliefs, and hence he was uneasy about it. He was not a committed republican,[58] and he was prepared to give it his support as the only workable government at the time. Insofar as it represented government by the meritorious few it was good, but insofar as it represented abdication of responsibility by the many it was bad. As an individual Cromwell was the type of the free virtuous man, but as protector he was proof of the reluctance of the English to accept their freedom. The Protectorate was politically expedient, but any form of government would be a failure for Milton until England became a nation of Cromwells.

In the long view Milton hoped that the actions of the English would render Cromwell's position unnecessary. Both Milton and Marvell regard Cromwell from the perspective of the present and of history. But whereas Milton envisages an ultimately free society to which this society is a stepping stone, Marvell is much more concerned with strengthening the Protectorate, with fitting the moment to its context, with calculatedly providing an ideal perspective from which Cromwell's actions and status can be properly valued. The context in which Marvell sets Cromwell is both practical and theoretical. The Protectorate is threatened on the one hand by republican and millenarian and on the other by royalist criticism. Marvell's most obvious technique is contrast. Thus he defends the political expediency of Cromwell's acts in 'growing to thyself a law' (*l.* 263) by emphasising the danger represented by Levellers and Fifth Monarchists – 'ambitious shrubs' (*l.* 264) and 'accursed locusts' (*l.* 311). Throughout the poem Cromwell's rule is compared with that of kings, selfish, irreligious, and incompetent, who are characterised as 'unhappy princes, ignorantly bred, / By malice some, by error more misled' (*ll.* 117–18). Cromwell is thus differentiated from his opponents. But more important than the technique of contrast is that of assimilation. Marvell's aim is to show that far from being their enemy Cromwell embodies the aspirations of millenarians, republicans, and royalists alike. Hence his main technique is to assimilate the vocabularies and values of these disparate traditions to the position of Cromwell, and, paradoxical though it may be, to unite these into a complex whole. Unlike Milton, Marvell is aware of the psychological methods by which power must be maintained. He sees the need to fit wherever possible Cromwell's originality to old patterns of thought.

The poem unites the movement of time and the establishment of order. In his treatment of time Marvell uses millenarian ideas and language, though he is carefully tentative in his statements about the future. Cromwell's movement forward and upward separates him from the 'weak circles' (*l.* 4) of ordinary lives; his contraction of time frees him from the prison of perpetual and useless circularity to which kings are subject:

> 'Tis he the force of scattered time contracts,
> And in one year the work of ages acts:
> While heavy monarchs make a wide return,
> Longer, and more malignant than Saturn:
> And though they all Platonic years should reign
> In the same posture would be found again.   (*ll.* 13–18)

In this motion by which he 'cuts his way still nearer to the skies' (*l.* 46) Cromwell does not act as an individual but is impelled by providence:

> What since he did, an higher force him pushed
> Still from behind, and it before him rushed,
> Though undiscerned among the tumult blind,
> Who think those high decrees by man designed.
>
>   (*ll.* 239–42)

Cromwell seems fit to interpret the signs of the times, to destroy the beast and the whore, to usher in the last days. But the muse hollows 'far behind / Angelic Cromwell who outwings the wind' (*ll.* 125–6), and 'a thick cloud...intercepts the beams of mortal eyes' (*ll.* 141–2). The obstacles to the achievement of the millenuium are abroad the nations who will not join a Protestant alliance, and at home those who will not accept the Protectorate as Cromwell has accepted the will of heaven:

> But men alas, as if they nothing cared,
> Look on, all unconcerned, or unprepared;
> And stars still fall, and still the dragon's tail
> Swinges the volumes of its horrid flail.
>
> . . . .
>
> Hence that blest day still counterpoised wastes,
> The ill delaying, what the elected hastes.
>
> (*ll.* 149–52, 155–6)

Marvell turns millenarianism against the millenarians. 'If these the times, then this must be the man' (*l.* 144); if men understand the present moment in the terms of dynamic change and transformation, then to obtain the desired end it is their duty to cooperate with the government whose work they are hindering.

In his treatment of order Marvell uses ideas and language from royalist tradition, though in such a way as not to exclude republican opinion. The paradox is stated by a foreign prince:

> He seems a king by long succession born,
> And yet the same to be a king does scorn.
> Abroad a king he seems, and something more,
> At home a subject on the equal floor.   (*ll.* 387–90)

Marvell's argument is that the Protectorate embodies all the advantages with none of the disadvantages of kingship. The argument is implied in the imagery of harmony and architecture by which Marvell characterises the constitution of the Protectorate. The instrument with which Cromwell Amphionlike raises the edifice of the state is the Instrument of Government. Without the office of protector the building represented by the commonwealth is composed of contradictory elements that will not hold together:

> None to be sunk in the foundation bends,
> Each in the house the highest place contends. (*ll.* 81–2)

Cromwell as protector harmonises the discord and saves the fabric of the building by pressing down on it. The Protectorate, by the political stability it assures, guarantees the freedom of constructive opposition:

> They, whose nature leads them to divide,
> Uphold, this one, and that the other side;
> But the most equal still sustain the height,
> And they as pillars keep the work upright;

While the resistance of opposed minds,
The fabric as with arches stronger binds,
Which on the basis of a senate free,
Knit by the roof's protecting weight agree.   (*ll.* 91-8)

At home Cromwell paradoxically assures the advantages of republicanism
by uniting the state under an individual; abroad his imperial triumphs
make him more regal than the monarchs, both in his millenarian character
as Protestant Captain and in his assumption of the cosmic influence
attributed to kings. He is a sun and a star, the soul that animates the
body of the nation (*l.* 380); his fall from his coach, implying his death,
presages cosmic disturbances:

It seemed the earth did from the centre tear;
It seemed the sun was fallen out of the sphere....
                                                (*ll.* 205-6)

The originally uncontrollable force of 'An Horatian Ode' shattering
ancient forms is now controlled by as it assumes those forms.

'The First Anniversary' is directed at the opposition to the Protectorate
both in and outside parliament, originating from a variety of points of
view, which threatened the existence of the Protectorate and which
caused Cromwell to dissolve parliament in January 1655. In his assumption that millenarians, republicans, and royalists could be reconciled
Marvell was impossibly optimistic, but this does not mean that the poem
is a naive idealisation of an artificial constitution. It is a serious political
attempt to strengthen a regime, and an imaginative apprehension (of
which Milton was never capable) of the contradictory elements that
went into the making of the revolution. Marvell always had an acute
sense of the times, of what was inevitable or necessary or to be rejected
at a particular historical moment. He appreciated the convergence of
revolutionary with conservative modes of thought; in 'The First Anniversary' he provided an imaginative unification in order to persuade
Cromwell's opponents to recognise the significance of his rule.

Marvell's treatment of Cromwell's fall from his coach ironically foreshadows his perspective and his literary techniques after the Restoration.
His aim here was to invest a slightly ridiculous event, which had been
the occasion for satirical commentary, with symbolic importance, to
indicate the danger for England that Cromwell's death would imply.
A royalist balladeer in 'A Jolt on Michaelmas Day' read a very different
symbolism into the event:

Not a day nor an hour
But we felt his power
  And now he would show us his art;

> His first reproach
> Is a fall from a coach,
> And his last will be from a cart![59]

The royalist prediction of Cromwell's ultimate end proved to be more accurate, and the roles of royalist satirist and puritan propagandist were reversed. Marvell's main task in his satires written after the Restoration, both verse and prose, was to deflate exaggerated symbolism, to draw attention to the reality underlying propaganda, and to point out that royalist emphasis on idealisation and theory was misshaping the practical relations between king and people. The moment required a different perspective; during the Interregnum Marvell wrote from the perspective of history and poetic symbol to invest a period of unrest with continuity; after the Restoration he wrote from the perspective both of political reality and of a particular conception of monarchy to correct dangerous tendencies in practical politics and royalist theory. His poetic technique was now negative rather than creative, but this was because of his sense of the demands of the time; his political position was by no means merely destructive.

Marvell did not join in the barrage of congratulation that greeted Charles II, some of it from praisers of Cromwell like Waller and Dryden, but this does not mean that he completely disapproved of the Restoration. From his attitude to Cromwell and his statements in his attacks on Samuel Parker it is clear that what he valued in a government was flexibility in politics and toleration in religion. The Declaration of Breda made by Charles II might have persuaded him that where the commonwealth and Protectorate had failed, the restored monarchy might succeed. Marvell must have been disappointed at the division between army and civilians which destroyed the constitutional experiment of the 1650s, but he recognised the need for order and a final settlement of the constitution which was indicated by the growing royalist feeling in the country. His elegy on Cromwell's death was much more monarchic in tone than 'The First Anniversary'. Marvell was not committed to republicanism nor opposed to monarchy; his only commitment was to making the best of the existing government provided by providence.[60] He had seen the Protectorate as the means of guaranteeing stability together with the opportunity for change; a parliamentary system needed the control of the 'roof's protecting weight'. Similarly he saw constitutional monarchy as the means of combining order with parliamentary freedom. During the period of the Protectorate he had taken the side of Cromwell against the parliamentary opposition which he saw to be destructive; after the Restoration he took a parliamentarian position against what he saw to be the absolutist tendencies in royalist theory and practice. His clearest statement of the proper functioning of constitutional monarchy is given at the beginning of *An Account of the Growth of Popery, and Arbitrary Government in England* (1677):

> The kings of England rule not upon the same terms with those of our neighbour nations, who, having by force or by address usurped that due share which their people had in the government, are now for some ages in the possession of an arbitrary power...and exercise it over their persons and estates in a most tyrannical manner. But here the subjects retain their proportion in the legislature; the very meanest commoner of England is represented in parliament, and is a party to those laws by which the prince is sworn to govern himself and his people.

After explaining the relationship between prerogative and law, Marvell sums up his view of the constitution:

> A king of England keeping to these measures, may without arrogance, be said to remain the only intelligent ruler over a rational people.... There is nothing that comes nearer in government to the divine perfection, than where the monarch, as with us, enjoys a capacity of doing all the good imaginable to mankind, under a disability to all that is evil. (Grosart, IV, 248-50)

Marvell's view of the proper relation between king and parliament animated the early opposition to Charles I and became commonplace after 1689.[61] But as *The Growth of Popery* was designed to show, this view of the constitution was increasingly threatened in the 1670s. Marvell's aim as a politician and a writer was to make it workable. His criticism was directed at dogmatic royalist theory, at the attempt of High Anglican divines like Samuel Parker to translate monarchy into absolutism, at Anglican intolerance and later at evidence of the attempt to spread Catholicism, and at the day to day handling of politics, at the corruption and incompetence of the government revealed in the second Dutch war, at the French alliance in the third Dutch war, at the extravagance of the court and the venality of the House of Commons. Marvell's opposition was active; he worked as a member of parliament (and in 1674 perhaps as a member of a pro-Dutch conspiracy);[62] his writing was an extension of action, an attempt to achieve the same end by rhetorical persuasion and attack. His methods varied depending on the audience he chose, and as he acquired a sense of his own helplessness in the face of increasing danger. In his private letters to his nephew William Popple written in 1670-1 he reveals a disgust and a loss of hope that he does not allow himself to show, for political and rhetorical reasons, in his public writing:

> It is...my opinion that the king was never since his coming in, nay, all things considered, no king since the conquest, so absolutely

powerful at home, as he is at present. . . . In such a conjuncture, dear Will, what probability is there of my doing anything to the purpose?

We are all venal cowards, except some few.

The court is at the highest pitch of want and luxury, and the people full of discontent.[63]

It has been pointed out how as the situation deteriorated Marvell abandoned serious political satire for doggerel.[64] Nevertheless however witty or apparently light-hearted his treatment he regarded his subjects with the utmost seriousness. He wrote of his work on Part II of *The Rehearsal Transprosed*,

I am (if I may say it with reverence) drawn in, I hope by a good providence, to intermeddle in a noble and high argument which therefore by how much it is above my capacity I shall use the more industry not to disparage it.[65]

As the times made him modify his techniques, so they made him modify the emphasis of his constitutional view. The political idea underlying his most important post-Restoration works, *Last Instructions to a Painter* (1667), *The Rehearsal Transprosed* (1672–3), and *The Growth of Popery* (1677), is that the nation consists of king and country whose open, reciprocal relationship is perverted by the ambition and conspiracies of ministers, courtiers, and divines. In all his satires Marvell sets himself the task of exposing this situation. In the first he holds up king and country to each other; in the second he appeals to the king; but in the third this appeal seems conventional, the sense of conspiracy is over-riding, and hope is placed only in a minority of country members. In the verse satires of the 1670s such as *Further Advice to a Painter* (1671) Marvell's attitude to Charles is entirely critical. As events limited the functioning of the constitution which he favoured so they limited his means of persuasion.

It is easy to see why Marvell, who played with the idea of perspective and distortion in 'Upon Appleton House', was attracted to the convention of the painter poem. In *Instructions to a Painter* (1665) Waller, using as his basis the doubtful English sea victory over the Dutch at Lowestoft, attempted to provide a heroic framework for English imperial ambition. Events are interpreted and heightened through the medium of classical heroism; the underlying image is of the battle of Actium, with Charles as Augustus conquering the treasure of the East, while the Duke of York is Achilles and Mars. In the envoy to the king the navy is seen as the emblem of Charles's power:

> His club Alcides, Phoebus has his bow,
> Jove has his thunder, and your navy you.
>
> (*POAS*, I, 32–3, *ll.* 315–16)

These instructions are not simply an attempt to cast a flattering light on events; it is a persuasion poem on the importance of the navy. The painter depicts what has taken and what should take place; he is told

> Last draw the commons at his royal feet,
> Pouring out treasure to supply his fleet.　　(ll. 305-6)

The numerous answering advices and instructions to a painter turn the convention against Waller, from the perspective both of the unpalatable truth of the events concealed by Waller's overlay of myth and epic simile, and of a rival view of the merits of the war and of the proper relation between king and commons. *The Second Advice to a Painter* (which may be by Marvell)[66] turns the Actium image against the court; the Duchess of York is a lecherous and greedy Cleopatra:

> Never did Roman Mark within the Nile
> So feast the fair Egyptian crocodile.
>
> (*POAS*, 1, 39, ll. 71-2)

Where Waller lauds heroism, the *Second Advice* exposes cowardice. In the *Third Advice* the fire of London is seen as a judgement on attempts by the government to misinterpret naval incompetence as victory in 1666:

> Now joyful fires and the exalted bell
> And court-gazettes our empty triumph tell.
> Alas, the time draws near when overturned
> The lying bells shall through the tongue be burned;
> Paper shall want to print that lie of state,
> And our false fires true fires shall expiate.
>
> (*Ibid.*, p. 74, ll. 163-8)

Far from the navy being emblematic of power, it is the wooden horse to England's Troy (l. 448). The painter instructed by the satirist does not conceal or exaggerate like the courtier:

> What servants will conceal and counsellors spare
> To tell, the painter and the poet dare.　　(ll. 439-40)

The Last Instructions to a Painter (the satire most certainly attributed to Marvell) deliberately draws attention to the artistic techniques of the truth-telling satirist, painting without colours, daubing, looking through a microscope, finishing the picture roughly with art surpassed by anger (*pp*. 99-100, *ll*. 1-28).

But the aim of these satires is not merely to reveal truth, to destroy court myths. The underlying structure of Waller's poem – the appeal to the king, the instructions to the painter to show what the relationship of king and country should be – is maintained throughout. In *Last Instructions* Marvell satirises heroic imagery and the mythology that dresses up court life, with the purpose of showing what true heroism is and how a valid mythology might function. He manipulates two layers of convention, the convention of the true and false painter, and the convention of game and literary artifact. This emphasis on the artificial is part of an attempt to define the true. Thus the fight in the commons over the excise is seen as a game of trick-track, with the members as the pieces; but court are black while country are white. The image becomes military, and the country members burlesque Spenserian knights. This treatment would seem to cast ridicule on the opposition leadership, were it not followed by a passage idolising 'the unknown reserve that still remained':

> A gross of English gentry, nobly born,
> Of clear estates, and to no faction sworn;
> Dear lovers of their king, and death to meet,
> For country's cause, that glorious think and sweet;
> To speak not forward, but in action brave,
> In giving generous, but in counsel grave;
> Candidly credulous for once, nay twice,
> But sure the devil cannot cheat them thrice. (*ll.* 286–94)

De Ruyter's journey up the Medway is seen in terms of sexual seduction and masque triumph, and the destruction of the fleet at Chatham in terms of mock biblical analogy; deserters from the burning ships are Shadrack, Meshack, and Abednego (*l.* 648), and the captive Royal Charles is Samson (*l.* 735). Against such parody is set the death of Douglas, the loyal Scot; here sexual is combined with religious imagery as part of a definition of true heroism:

> Like a glad lover the fierce flame he meets
> And tries his first embraces in their sheets.
>
> .   .   .   .   .   .
>
> Round the transparent fire about him glows,
> As the clear amber on the bee does close,
> And, as on angels' heads their glories shine,
> His burning locks adorn his face divine.
>
> (*ll.* 677–8, 681–4)

Against the portrait of Charles selfishly neglecting business for pleasure, absurdly mistaking a vision of 'England or the peace' (*l.* 906) for one of a potential mistress, is set Charles 'sun of our world' (*l.* 956), who should live in a mutually beneficial relationship with his people:

> Ceres corn, and Flora is the spring,
> Bacchus is wine, the country is the king. (*l.* 973–4)

Against the series of portraits of corrupt courtiers, St Albans, the Duchess of York, Lady Castlemaine, Clarendon, the sun spots who strive 'to isle our monarch from his isle' (*l.* 968), is set the image of the ideal servant. The purpose of the poem is to expose the courtiers for what they are, to show Charles the ideal relationship between king and country, and to induce him to bring it into existence, so that he will become 'himself the painter and the poet too' (*l.* 948):

> Give us this court and rule without a guard.   (*l.* 990)

In *Last Instructions* Marvell opposes a corrupt court which sees itself in falsely ideal terms with another ideal of the relationship between court and country. It is an essential element in Marvell's political poems that the idealising and mythologising of political relations, which he sees as a basic need, must reflect reality, otherwise it can only be destructive and dangerous. This idea is implied in *Last Instructions* where Marvell warns against the courtiers who

> The kingdom from the crown distinct would see
> And peel the bark to burn at last the tree.   (*ll.* 971–2)

If the king is separated from the people, whether by incompetent government, dogmatic theory, or an illegal extension of his powers, the people will turn against the king. This is presumably why Charles I shows his son 'the purple thread about his neck' (*l.* 922). In *The Rehearsal Transprosed* the warning is made explicit. Samuel Parker, Marvell's opponent, originally a Puritan but now a career High Churchman, had argued that Charles should exercise a Hobbesian sovereignty (Marvell points out the closeness of his principles to 'the territories of Malmesbury'),[67] with complete control of the church, so as to crush nonconformity. Marvell's answer is an argument from history and from common sense. Parker's obsession with the idea of legislating for complete order and conformity in church and state, as an answer to the anarchy imagined to result from toleration, is not only cruel, malicious, and bigoted, it is also disastrous to the church and state that it is his professed aim to uphold. The High Anglican clergy have learned nothing from history; they appear determined to mislead Charles II as their Laudian predecessors misled his father. Whereas Parker blames the civil war on rebellious parliamentarians, Marvell blames it on ambitious divines who taught Charles I to mistake the nature of his power,

> and having made the whole business of state their Arminian jangles and the persecution for ceremonies, did for recompense assign him that imaginary absolute government, upon which rock we all ruined.
> (Grosart, III, Part I, *pp.* 211–12)

Now the whole process is being repeated. Marvell's purpose in attacking Parker, as he explains in Part II, is to expose this fact:

> My greatest incentive was…the perniciousness of the whole design of his books, tending, in my opinion, to the disturbance of all

government, the misrepresenting of the generous and prudent counsels of his Majesty, and raising a misintelligence betwixt him and his people.... (*pp.* 265–6)

In order to prevent this 'misintelligence' from occurring, Marvell appeals directly to Charles. But the nature of the appeal is very different from that in *Last Instructions*, where he emphasises the symbolic relation between king and people. Whereas Parker's concern is with an absolutist theory of kingship and a particular definition of order, Marvell carefully avoids defining his own religious stand or presenting an alternative theory of government such as constitutional royalism to counter Parker's Erastianism and absolutism. Instead he appeals to Charles as an individual, to his political good sense, to his clemency, and not least to his love of wit. (Marvell made a just calculation of the importance of this last element, since Charles, delighted with the book, ensured that it was licensed.)[68] Of course the portrait of Charles that emerges is not meant to be entirely realistic; the clement, prudent, indulgent king is a rhetorical model. Marvell may well have disapproved of the Declaration of Indulgence from a constitutional view (he was to attack it in *The Growth of Popery* on the grounds that it extended the prerogative),[69] but he defends it in Part I of *The Rehearsal Transprosed* because as an act of toleration it is embarrassing to Parker. Instead of dealing with political theory in abstract, Marvell is concerned with the practical consequences of theory. The consequences of Anglican dogmatism he sees to be either, as he argues in *Mr Smirke; or the Divine in Mode*, the debasing of 'the reason and spirit of the nation, to make them fit for ignorance and bondage',[70] or, as he argues in *The Rehearsal Transprosed*, though not in those words, another civil war. When pressed by Parker he cautiously gives some indication of his personal beliefs in Part II, but again emphasising that practice is more important than theory:

> I most certainly do believe that the supreme magistrate hath some power, but not all power, in matters of religion.... The power of the magistrate does most certainly issue from the divine authority.... But the modester question...would be, how far it is advisable for a prince to exert and push the rigour of that power which no man can deny him.... [Princes] are responsible to him that gave them their commission for the happiness or infelicity of their subjects during the term of their government. It is within their power, depends upon their counsels, and they cannot fail of a prosperous reign, but by a mistaken choice betwixt rigour or moderation.
>
> (Grosart, III, 304, 370–2)

Like Milton Marvell believed that church and state should be separate, that the concern of the clergy should be the gospel and not politics, and that men are rational and should follow their consciences. Unlike Milton he believed that men need the regulating framework of conventional constitutional forms within which to exercise their political and religious liberty, that they must trust their ruler, that the symbolic languages they devise for defining the relationship between ruler and ruled are not harmful but necessary for trust to operate. *The Rehearsal Transprosed* was a calculated attempt to persuade Charles to understand this relationship between liberty, order, and the mystique of power. But Marvell ceased to believe that Charles could be persuaded. *The Rehearsal Transprosed*, while exposing the dangerous tendencies of High Anglican thought to the country at large, is specifically a warning and an appeal to the king to dissociate himself from it. *The Growth of Popery*, however, while retaining the constitutional convention of distinguishing the king from his evil advisers, in this case referred to throughout as 'the conspiracy', is not directed at the king but at the country. Marvell ends the pamphlet with a plea to the king, with the assumption that only he can put the situation right:

> This book, though of an extraordinary nature...was written with no other intent than of mere fidelity and service to his Majesty, and God forbid that it should have any other effect, than that...his Majesty, having discerned the disease, may with his healing touch apply the remedy. (IV, 414)

But the warning of danger, of the design 'to change the lawful government of England into an absolute tyranny, and to convert the established Protestant religion into downright popery' (*p.* 248), is made not to him (and Marvell may by now have come to regard him in fact though not in constitutional theory as its origin) but to the people as a whole. The source of anxiety is now not an incompetent court, as in the painter poems, nor the intolerance of Anglican divines, but the implications of the French alliance for political and religious liberty. Marvell's aim is to create an informed and united opposition in the House of Commons, and the heroes of his book are the independent country members:

> There is an handful of salt, a sparkle of soul, that hath hitherto preserved this gross body from putrefaction, some gentlemen that are constant, invariable, indeed Englishmen; such as are above hopes, or fears, or dissimulation, that can neither flatter, nor betray their king or country: but being conscious of their own loyalty and integrity, proceed through good and bad report, to acquit themselves in their duty to God, their prince, and their nation.... (IV, 329)

He does not envisage, as in *Last Instructions*, the unity of king and country. His theoretical belief in the balanced constitution is undermined by his emphasis on the isolation of these men; his concluding appeal to the king by his deliberate attempt to create an opposition to his policies.

There are thus three versions of Charles that Marvell uses in his post-Restoration political writing. There is the theoretical constitutional monarch exercising his prerogative under the law and respecting the legal rights of his subjects; there is the idealised flexible and good natured individual who is assumed to be open to persuasion of the superiority and practicality of such a view of monarchy; and there is the irresponsible, selfish delinquent of the last verse satires and of the mock speech from the throne of 1675.[71] These three versions are not inconsistent; Marvell is determined to make the restored monarchy politically viable, a benefit to and not an imposition on the nation, and with this end in view he can use theoretical statement, personal panegyric, or satirical exposure, depending on his view of the demands of the immediate situation and of the audience he needs to address at a particular moment. His literary techniques are the tools of his political aims.[72]

It was thus inevitable that as the political situation deteriorated Marvell lost his interest in literature as such. He abandoned poetic panegyric partly because royalist myth was in the hands of the opposite party who did not share his view of human nature; he could not destroy that myth simply by presenting a rival one, he had to expose its practical consequences. His definition of the country point of view, with a conspiracy of ministers subverting the constitution and separating the king from the people, was not, as it was to become in the eighteenth century, a romantic fiction opposed to practical politics, but an acute assessment of immediate dangers.[73] The nature of Marvell's choice, his ultimately political rather than poetic aim, can be clarified by comparing him with Dryden. Marvell obviously disliked Dryden as an individual as well as for his poetry and politics; by calling Samuel Parker Mr Bays (Dryden in Buckingham's *Rehearsal*) he attributed to Parker Dryden's bombastic heroics and to Dryden Parker's dogmatism and absolutism.[74] But it should not be assumed that their poetic problems and their political principles were totally opposed.[75] Both were drawn to the theory of the balanced constitution; both used different images of the king depending on circumstances, as abstract figurehead or as benign individual. Yet their motives for writing, their reactions to political events, and their solutions to problems were very different. Marvell was always flexible and detached in his attitude to ideas; he recognised the usefulness of traditional accounts of political relations, but he knew when they must be discarded; the society he valued needed order not for its own sake but to guarantee tolerance and openness. He believed in men's rationality, their ability to adapt themselves to circumstances and to devise elastic political systems. Dryden's attitude to politics, though flexible, was not pragmatic in this way. He was an idealist, who hoped to shape political life to a preconceived pattern, but he did not share Marvell's faith in human nature, so that when his pattern was threatened he became authoritarian. He was first and last a poet, so that when there was no longer a public function for his poetry he devised a new one, based partly on the country myth that Marvell had helped create. But Marvell used this myth for political not poetic purposes. When one considers the time Marvell spent with Fairfax and the retirement poems he wrote in the early 1650s one can imagine what he might have made of his own idealisation of the country gentry in the 1670s, if his purpose had been, like that of Dryden and Pope later, the creation of his own poetic identity. The possibilities for Marvell as a poet after the Restoration were limited by the events which he saw threatening a workable constitution and an open society, and by his own practical attempts to achieve it; but ironically he provided some of the vocabulary and ideas for later conservative poets who did not share his faith in political action.

Chapter 4
John Dryden: the recreation of monarchy

THE MUSES' EMPIRE

Dryden is a poet who demands peculiar sympathy and attention from his reader. Because he was caught up as a poet in the confusion of contemporary politics, because his career followed so closely the procession of political events, his poems cannot be understood fully without constant reference to their context. It is difficult for the reader to separate Dryden's beliefs and attitudes as a whole from his response as a poet to particular events. The order expressed in his poetry was not merely an idealisation; his poetry was partly history, it described what was as well as what should be. Thus we find that Dryden's ideas and style are constantly being modified and confused by events. Many of his literary difficulties and the question of his stature as a poet are related to his feeling for the needs of the time; his career as a writer can be seen as an unresolved search for a public mode that could both shape and reflect his society.

There are perhaps two main ways of reading Dryden's poems. One can read them thematically, in order to isolate the coherent attitudes that constitute his ideal view of the good society; and one can read them chronologically, as products of particular political developments and as attempts to influence their immediate course. This flexibility on the reader's part is necessary if one is adequately to account for Dryden's own difficulties and his apparent inconsistencies.[1]

One of his central ideas is that there is a necessary connection between good government, the flow of trade, social stability, and great art. These topics are often described in terms of each other. Dryden appears, that is, to have a fixed idea of the structure of social and universal order and of its relation to an appropriate symbolic language. But in practice his shifts in 'kind', in style and technique, alternating between heroic, panegyric, pindaric, blank verse, satire, couplet, rhyme, his varying poses of extravagance, heroic abandon, moderation, or scepticism, indicate his uneasiness and his difficulty in establishing a successful public mode for his subject matter. Dryden's sense of the order depending on monarchy implies a relation between monarch and society that is publicly understood.

But in post-Restoration England there was no universal political agreement conforming to Dryden's ideal; unfortunately Charles seemed to his subjects actually or potentially a Bourbon absolutist, a constitutional monarch, or a Doge of Venice. In the face of such political conflict Dryden's own attitude to monarchy wavered. Before examining the ways in which the pressure of events modified Dryden's ideas and his sense of his political usefulness, I shall establish the ideal view of the function of poetry that underlies all of Dryden's work.

Though Dryden must have felt the conflict in political definitions, the real possibility of another civil war, as a threat both to his view of order and to his position as a poet, nevertheless, even after the Revolution of 1688 that involved the deflation of his most sacred public symbols, he retained an elaborate and optimistic view of the muses' empire, of the place of poetry in society. It is a commonplace of his writing throughout his career that only the good society produces good art. This is put forward partly as the simplest of deductions from history; as Lisideius says in *An Essay of Dramatic Poesy* (1668), 'We have been so long together bad Englishmen, that we had not leisure to be good poets.... The Muses...ever follow peace.'[2] Thus the preeminence of French writers under the patronage of Richelieu is explained. The corollary to this historical view is stated by Neander, the spokesman of the moderns:

> And though the fury of a civil war, and power for twenty years together abandoned to a barbarous race of men, enemies of all good learning, had buried the Muses under the ruins of monarchy; yet, with the restoration of our happiness, we see revived poesy lifting up its head, and already shaking off the rubbish which lay so heavy on it. (Watson, I, 76)

The obvious benefits that accrue (or should) to poets under sympathetic monarchy are emphasised; in *Threnodia Augustalis* (1685) and 'To my Dear Friend Mr Congreve' (1694) Charles appears in retrospect as the husbandman tilling the hard and thorny soil, and reaping the harvest of art and science (though Dryden must admit that Charles was not very earnest in this role; for the poets 'little was their hire, and light their gain').[3] In the Epilogue to the Second Part of *The Conquest of Granada* (1672) Dryden points out (though apparently too brazenly for his contemporaries) the court's refining influence on wit, language, and conversation.

The idea of the empire of wit is thus, at its simplest, a belief that war and social upheaval do not contribute to the flourishing of art, while peace, wealth, and stable government under monarchy do. But the idea is much richer and more complex than this. In *Annus Mirabilis* (1667), a poem inspired by sectarian prophecies of disaster, the Dutch War, plague, and fire, events tending to the destruction of the promise of the

Restoration, the idea and its implications have their widest and most ambitious though not their most poetically successful expression. Dryden is not here concerned with poetry or the arts in particular, but with the idea of the development of learning, with the complex relationships that constitute civilisation.

The good society in *Annus Mirabilis* moves perpetually in two different ways, circular and progressive. On the one hand civilisation is the culmination of effort and of change: the development of navigation is seen as the result of the gradual amassing of knowledge, the new London will rise phoenix-like from the ashes of the old. Civilisation constantly builds on the valuable but limited achievements of the past. On the other hand it consists of an interaction of mutually dependent parts. Almost the first analogy Dryden uses in the poem is the old comparison of the physical with the political body, a comparison given added weight by his use of new seventeenth-century science: 'Trade,...like blood should circularly flow.'[4] The proper motion of trade and wealth in society is paralleled by the mutual relation of king and people, which reflects that of God with the creation ('God's anointed God's own place supplied'), a father with his children (Charles's pity, care, tenderness, and suffering are repeatedly mentioned), a physician with his patient, curing political disease (Charles has worked 'To bind the bruises of a Civil War, / And stop the issues of their wasting blood'), and encompasses the divided functions of the English constitution ('peaceful Kings o'er martial people set, / each others poise and counter-balance are').[5] The tone of *Annus Mirabilis* is partly prophetic, and implies a progressive view of civilisation; in place of war, destruction, the wasting of blood, the misdirection of wealth, the mistrust of king and people, Dryden has a vision of English victory, peace, free trade, wealth, and empire. But the underlying idea is of the mutual dependence of the several components of civilisation. Monarchy achieves the health of the body politic, stopping wasted blood, supporting trade which circulates like blood. In turn the development of learning, which is assured by the political stability of the monarchy, adds to the growth of trade; the implication is that the wealth resulting from trade strengthens monarchy. This benevolent circle entails the two ideas of growth (the spread of wealth) and of stability (the maintaining of political institutions and trade in their regulated channels). Trade, government, and health are constantly seen in terms of each other.

The particular role of the poet and the arts in this process is elaborated elsewhere. The system of analogies recurs easily and perhaps in some cases unconsciously throughout Dryden's writing.[6] In 'To my Honoured Friend, Dr Charleton' (1663) the mutual relation of political and scholastic tyranny is implied; the restored monarchy allows the growth of unfettered learning and free trade. In 'A Discourse concerning Satire' (1693) good writing is seen partly in terms of monetary wealth; Dryden tells Dorset, the type of the true poet and judge,

> you are empowered, when you please, to give the final decision of wit; to put your stamp on all that ought to pass for current; and set a brand of reprobation on clipped poetry, and false coin. A shilling dipped in the bath may go for gold amongst the ignorant, but the sceptres on the guineas show the difference.   (Watson, II, 79)

In the same essay Boileau's imitation of the ancients is seen as usury, repayment with good coin; its value is assured by Louis XIV's proper use of his monarchical role, for 'the stamp of a Louis, the patron of all arts, is not much inferior to the medal of an Augustus Caesar'. Economic and poetic wealth grow in the same way:

> Mutual borrowing, and commerce, makes the common riches of learning, as it does of the civil government.   (p. 81)

And Dryden's inability to find enough variety of language for his translation of Virgil is seen in terms of bankruptcy, the breaking of banks and exchequers, and payment 'in hammered money, for want of milled'.[7] These statements are not intended simply as witty analogies, though Dryden obviously enjoys pursuing the metaphorical possibilities. The seriousness underlying the wit is evident in some of the prologues and epilogues presented at Oxford and in the epistles to Dryden's fellow poets Roscommon and Congreve.

'To the Earl of Roscommon, on his Excellent Essay on Translated Verse' (1684) expresses the codevelopment of empire and poetry (as of monarchy and learning in 'To Charleton'):

> The muses' empire is restored again,
> In Charles his reign, and by Roscommon's pen.
> (Kinsley, I, 387, ll. 28–9)

Roscommon's art, in complimentary reference to his career in 'court and camps', is seen in military terms; and Dryden celebrates the advent of a new empire of art in terms of trial by combat and subjugation:

> Now let the few beloved by Jove, and they,
> Whom infused Titan formed of better clay,
> On equal terms with ancient wit engage,
> Nor mighty Homer fear, nor sacred Virgil's page:
> Our English palace opens wide in state;
> And without stooping they may pass the gate.
> (ll. 73–8)

As has been pointed out, Dryden gave conventional analogy wit and depth by making use of specific political events.[8] In 'To Roscommon' the assimilation of monarchical, military, and poetic empire is made easier and more appropriate through reference to Roscommon's career and the contentious relations of England and Ireland (Roscommon was Irish by birth). In the case of 'To my Dear Friend Mr Congreve, On His Comedy, called *The Double-Dealer*' the related ideas and metaphors of the empire of wit, the conquest of the ancients, the cultivation of learning, and the reconstruction of the temple of art are made more vivid by placing Congreve not only in a symbolic and idealised history but in the hard present, in the England of James's deposition from the throne and Dryden's deposition from the laureateship. The empire of wit is asserted but also threatened. In Dryden's poem Congreve is metaphorically enthroned, but political involves poetic revolution; James gives way to William, and Dryden and Congreve to Shadwell and Rymer:

> Oh that your brows my laurel had sustained,
> Well had I been deposed, if you had reigned!
> The father had descended for the son;
> For only you are lineal to the throne.
>
> . . . .
>
> But now, not I, but poetry is cursed;
> For Tom the second reigns like Tom the first.
>
> (Kinsley, II, 853, *ll.* 41–4, 47–8)

The idea of civilisation set out in *Annus Mirabilis*, of monarchy, political health, trade, wealth, and learning, can no longer function when one of its component parts is damaged. The danger for Dryden is that his system of analogies is not a historical description of the functioning of society but an idealised abstraction, while in reality Macflecknoe is seated on the throne of wit.

The fear that political differences are threatening the whole system is implied in the contrast between Oxford and London used in the Oxford prologues and epilogues. Oxford is the ideal society – 'crowded Oxford represents mankind' – where jarring parts are tuned, where antitheses between body and mind, pleasure and care, prerogative and might, are reconciled.[9] Oxford is the seat of peace and arts, to which poets return to learn its precepts as ambassadors do the instructions of princes;[10] it symbolises just rule in government and poetry. In contrast, as monarchy is threatened in London so is poetry; Dryden as upholder of the order embodied by Oxford can get no recognition there:

> He owns no crown from those Praetorian bands,
> But knows that right is in this senate's hands.[11]

The disordered political sense of Londoners is corrupting their taste. The triumph of Whiggism would mean that 'religion, learning, wit, would be suppressed'.[12] In prologues and epilogues addressed to his

London audience Dryden furiously elaborates this theme, explicitly connecting corruption in art with revolution in government:

> The plays that take on our corrupted stage.
> Methinks resemble the distracted age;
> Noise, madness, all unreasonable things,
> That strike at sense, as rebels do at kings!
> The style of Forty one our poets write,
> And you are grown to judge like Forty eight.
> (Prologue to *The Loyal General*, Kinsley, I, 205, *ll.* 12–17)

The true poet is a lawful monarch whom critics, like Whigs under the guise of reform, are attempting to destroy.[13] There are numerous other examples where Dryden plays on this image, making the fullest possible use of contemporary political allusion and cant. The level of seriousness is of course not always the same. Attacks on the politics and literary judgements of the London audience do not carry the considered view of the relation of monarchy and art expressed in 'To Congreve'. But Dryden seems always to have borne in mind a sense of the interacting levels of society, so that simply to take up a subject whether with humour or seriousness might entail an appropriate reference to an analogous subject on another plane.

What may seem a relentless hammering on the relation of faction to bad art may be explained by examining the implications of Dryden's complex view of society for his position as a poet. Dryden holds onto his system of analogies even when, as after the Revolution, the state of political society must seem in some way to deny its validity. The system threatens to become merely an idealisation in terms of which the actual state of society can be criticised. But Dryden did not think in these terms. Unlike Pope, he did not thrive poetically on the discrepancy between the ideal and the actual. And in the poems of his last years he did not make use of his opposition to the existing government in this way, though his ideas were modified. For Dryden the enthronement of Shadwell did not seem the way of the world as the enthronement of Theobald or Cibber did for Pope. Dryden's relation to his material and his public was more difficult. His public poems are written to persuade king and people of the value and truth of his description of society, to mould them into his system. His difficulties arise as reality slips out of his pattern and as he in turn modifies his pattern in reaction to fluctuating events. His problem is one of politics, of juggling with the system, and of style, of knowing how to persuade.

Discussions of Dryden's use of panegyric have too often assumed that the nature of what was to be said was necessarily obvious in its content and agreeable to the addressee, and that it was the amplification and embellishment of the agreed subject matter that was open to Dryden's ingenuity. To Scott, Dryden's panegyrics were simply the fashion of the day – rendering unto Caesar the things that were Caesar's.[14] Johnson, who was utterly unsympathetic to this part of Dryden's work, tended to see him as a self-abasing praise-making machine, which could turn out infinite variations on what was essentially the same subject:

> I know not whether, since the days in which the Roman emperors were deified, he has been ever equalled.... When once he has undertaken the task of praise, he no longer retains shame in himself, nor supposes it in his patron.... He considers the great as entitled to encomiastic homage, and brings praise rather as a tribute than a gift.... It is indeed not certain that on these occasions his judgement much rebelled against his interest.[15]

The oratorical view of Dryden has been expanded by later critics; one suggests that poetry was for him 'how you ornamented and gilded the bare statement', while another points to wit as the essence of the panegyrical style (while insisting that the chief function of panegyric is the perfecting of an imperfect world through idealising art).[16]

Such separations of the style of panegyric from its content and purpose imply that Dryden's function was as publicist and embellisher of official attitudes. To some extent he was performing the expected: as laureate he was a crown servant working for his fee. Charles's place as king certainly invited praise (as his actions invited the attacks that began to appear in the middle of his reign). But there was nothing obvious about the direction such praise should take. In Dryden's case there was a perpetual conflict between his view of the ideal ordering of society and his commitment to the Stuart monarchy with all its failings. The system that animates much of Dryden's poetry, the hierarchy of analogous relationships between God, king, people (and poet), was by no means an acceptable model for all of post-Restoration society, nor even always for Dryden himself. Until the Revolution of 1688 settled some of the vexed constitutional questions of the seventeenth century (and even after this William's full use of his prerogative gave cause for alarm) the respective roles of king and parliament in government were loosely defined and open to all kinds of pressure and interpretation. The central theme of Charles's reign has been described as the attempt to establish a clear relationship between crown and parliament.[17] Some of Dryden's best work in political panegyric and satire is directed towards this attempt, but this was not necessarily of immediate help to the monarchy which he saw it as his role to support. The difficulty is caused by the dual role of his political poetry; it serves both as admonition and propaganda. Some of the ideas worked out in *Absalom and Achitophel* make it evident that Charles and his laureate and historiographer were sometimes at cross purposes. Dryden's attempt to establish himself as a political moderate and to make monarchy conform to such a position marks a flaw in his ideal system, since Charles and James both had as their model not so much the constitutional royalism of men like Clarendon and Halifax (to which Dryden leans) as the exemplary rule of Louis XIV. This political problem is reflected in the confused variety in Dryden's style and critical pronouncements, and in his changes in political position which have allowed later readers to see him as a Hobbesian or a Trimmer.

Thus it is impossible for the reader of Dryden to separate the question of his style from his politics. Because of the uncertainty in the nation and consequently in Dryden's own mind about the proper relationship between crown and parliament, king and people, Dryden's role as supporter of the Stuarts was confused. One must decide what kind of monarchy Dryden thought he was defending, and the effectiveness of the poetic weapons he used. Since it is difficult to give a single answer to the political question, the question of style becomes correspondingly more complicated. In this section I shall try to relate Dryden's use of the heroic grand style, his interest in epic, heroic drama, and pindarics, to his occasional covert sympathy with royal absolutism of the kind that was being established in France by Louis XIV. The connection between absolutist theory and the grand style was made explicit by a Whig critic (though inappropriately with reference to *Absalom and Achitophel*):

> Write on, and more than winds or frenzy range,
> Keep still thy old prerogative to change;
> 'Tis poor humanity that's kept in bound
> Whilst power unlimited is godlike found.
> Then thy great self, thou wondrous poet, show:
> Honour and principles disdain, for know
> Thy mercury's too proud to fix so low.
> All laws and bounds let thy wild muse despise,
> And reign the prince o' th' air in which it flies.[18]

Dryden's attacker has in mind particularly the apparent opportunism of the praiser of Cromwell and Charles. As an assessment of Dryden's politics at the time of the Exclusion Crisis it is as much a travesty as Dryden's representation of the Whigs often was. Since royal absolutism in England was for various reasons impossible, and since Dryden's attitudes to it were ambiguous and sometimes hostile, it is untrue to the political situation and to the complexity of Dryden's mind to see him as in any way a propagandist for Stuart absolutism.

The straightforwardness of Louis XIV's political aims, and of the propaganda used in support of them, contrasts markedly with the indecision of the Stuarts and the resulting inconsistencies and hesitancies in the attitudes of men like Dryden who defended them. The function of the artist as defined by Louis was to celebrate, interpret, and reinforce the power of centralised monarchy, to ensure its public acceptance and the peaceful incorporation of the dissident elements in the nation whose power had been subverted.[19] Charles II has been criticised by J. H. Plumb for his failure to strengthen the monarchy, following the example of Louis XIV, by the exploitation of intellectual and artistic propaganda. Charles's attempt to guide the monarchy towards French absolutism was accompanied (perhaps inevitably) by deceit. There was no official rationalisation of the absolutist position; such propaganda as Hobbes provided was damaging. Plumb argues that materials existed for monarchical ideology and aggrandisement, and that Charles and James hurt their cause by neglecting to use them.[20]

The reasons for the weakness of the monarchy, as analysed by Plumb, explain both the failure of Charles and James to push constitutional monarchy into absolutism, and the non-existence of a covering propaganda and ideology to further the attempt. Though by the end of Charles's reign it might appear that England was about to succumb to the new European pattern of strong centralised monarchy together with the destruction of local or feudal power, nevertheless certain basic ingredients for success were lacking. The monarchy was not wealthy enough to exist without parliament, nor was it supported by a standing army (though control of the militia was ceded to the king by the Militia Act of 1661).[21] The religion that was basic to the intellectualisation of Louis' authority was hated and feared by the subjects of Charles and James (Danby's attempt to dissuade the crown from a pro-French policy and to base monarchy on the support of the Anglican church was not effective, though it gave shape to the Tory party). Attempts to destroy the structure of local government were disastrous; Charles's interference with the borough charters and ignoring of the Triennial Act at the end of his reign were tolerated because they broke the power of the Whigs, but James's remodelling of county government resulted in his downfall. These underlying tensions, the basic divergence in the political aims of the king and a large part of the nation, indicate that a necessary propaganda would have had to be built on deceit, on concealment of unpopular aims and of public disagreements. It would have been a hollow propaganda, unsupported by real power and hence unable to help effect the achievement of the desired aims.

135

While Charles seems to have admired Louis and his form of government, he was not inspired by the same motives. James was certainly interested (as Charles was not) in abstract questions of kingship, but neither had Louis' feeling of public identification with the fortunes of the nation. Charles was less concerned with his country's greatness and his *gloire* than with security; he was much less committed to the restoration of Catholicism than James. He wanted to rule without the interference of parliament, which had after all caused his father's death and his own exile. Louis provided both the model for such rule and the financial subsidies that could help make it possible. For Charles absolutism meant personal independence rather than national power or prestige.[22]

There is no evidence that Dryden knew of or would have acquiesced in all the ambitions of Charles and James insofar as each king appealed to the financial support and the political model of Louis XIV. In his working out of the idea of the relation of prerogative, privilege, and law Dryden set forward a view of monarchy which, though he may not have fully understood this, did not coincide with Charles's own. Nevertheless for a variety of reasons, including the prospect of another civil war and his Hobbesian obsession with social stability, Dryden must have been tempted by absolutist theory.[23] His lifelong concern with the idea of heroic epic, his experimentation with heroic drama, panegyric in the grand style, and pindarics, all indicate his wish for an unshakeable public authority and for escape from the responsible freedom implied in the political theory of a balanced constitution and in the idea of art as an instrument of reason and persuasion. It is not necessary (and it is untrue to Dryden's temperament and the circumstances in which he worked) to claim too much consistency for him, but it is worth examining the causes that underlie his uncertainties and changes of direction.

With none of Boileau's caution about epic,[24] Dryden announced his willingness to be Virgil to Charles's Augustus. But it had to be a reciprocal relationship: Dryden's ambition was inevitably dampened by Charles's niggardliness and lack of interest. In the dedication of *Aureng-Zebe* to Mulgrave he set out his conditions and his intentions. Through Mulgrave's good offices he had already suggested the subject to the king and duke, but there had been no response. As a result

> the unsettledness of my condition has hitherto put a stop to my thoughts concerning it. As I am no successor to Homer in his wit, so neither do I desire to be in his poverty.

Mulgrave is asked to jog the royal memory. Interestingly enough Dryden's ambivalence about the whole project is explicitly stated:

> For my own part, I am satisfied to have offered the design; and it may be to the advantage of my reputation to have it refused me.
>
> (Watson, I, 191)

In 'A Discourse concerning Satire' (published in 1693 when he was no longer laureate) he elaborates on the proposed theme, which earlier had been stated simply to be English history with Charles and James as its heroes; the possible subjects are Arthur or the Black Prince. The technique of panegyric can be deduced from Dryden's view of Spenser, whom he reads as readily identifiable historical allegory. He indicates clearly his historical and political intention:

> After Virgil and Spenser, I would have taken occasion to represent my living friends and patrons of the noblest families, and also shadowed the events of future ages, in the succession of our imperial line. (Watson, II, 92)

Dryden's few ventures into historical allegory may perhaps make one grateful that he was 'encouraged only with fair words' by Charles. *King Arthur*, which would have been performed with *Albion and Albanius* preceding it in 1685, as a celebration of Charles's triumph over Whiggism at the period of his life when he can most justly be seen as exercising absolute rule, was cancelled because of his death;[25] the refurbished version performed in 1691 was much altered 'not to offend the present times, nor a government which has hitherto protected me' (S-S, VIII, 135). As it stands the opera is devoid of political significance and is memorable only for Purcell's music. *Albion and Albanius*, enlarged and changed to include Charles's death, was performed later in 1685. In form it is one of the last of the court masques, a ritualistic celebration of James's ascendancy over his opponents, and a further expression, essentially unsuited to the medium, of Dryden's considered view of the nature of lawful monarchy and the arbitrary tyranny implied in popular rule. Whatever the cause, it was not a success. It has always seemed a good joke that this celebration of the triumph of monarchy over democracy was interrupted by news of Monmouth's rebellion.[26]

There were insuperable obstacles facing Dryden in his attempt to establish the role that Virgil had for Augustus or the Academies and pensioners had for Louis. It was only in the panegyric or the heroic play that he was able to approach this role. But the burden imposed on the heroic play doomed it: it was at once a reflection of the taste of the court, and at the same time, on the model of the Renaissance epic, meant as didactic exhortation. At different times Dryden's comments on the heroic play and the theatre expressed both points of view: during the period when he was mainly involved in the composition of heroic drama, in the late 1660s and 1670s, he tried in dedications and criticism to give an idea of what the heroic play might be, but he was later anxious to insist that his interest in the theatre was largely commercial, and that 'I never writ anything for myself but *Antony and Cleopatra*' (Watson, II, 207).

Dryden's main exposition of his view of the nature of the heroic play and its relation to courtly society is to be found in 'Of Heroic Plays: An Essay', prefixed to *The Conquest of Granada*, and in the dedication of the same play to the Duke of York. In the adulatory dedication of *The Indian Emperor* to the Duchess of Monmouth in 1667, Dryden had attributed the success of the heroic play to the approbation of the court, but he had not explored the relationship with the audience further.[27] In the case of the later *Conquest of Granada* (published in 1672) Dryden sees the situation as more complex.

The origin of the heroic play (which Dryden recognises as a pheno-menon of the Restoration stage) is seen as Davenant's amalgamation of Italian opera and Corneille; Dryden has developed the form in accordance with his own axiom 'that an heroic play ought to be an imitation, in little, of an heroic poem'. Consequently his roaring hero Almanzor is said to be modelled on Achilles and Rinaldo.[28] His estimate of his hero is extremely defensive, and he may have come to regret this critical judgement as he did his bombast. But Almanzor is seen to be more important than this. Almanzor may be modelled on the heroes of Homer and Tasso, but Charles and James themselves are like Agamemnon and Achilles; Dryden makes a laboured attempt to establish a dynamic relationship between the example of past epic, its embodiment in the lives of the king and duke (James's life is 'a continued series of heroic actions'), and the further incitement provided by contemporary art ('the feigned hero inflames the true').[29] This elaborate combination of theory, compliment, and self-justification is certainly evidence of Dryden's view of the use of epic, but we must question whether it is an accurate description of his actual practice in the heroic play.

The problem of the form and assumptions of heroic drama is outside the scope of this study, but some general remarks can be made about Dryden's ambiguous handling of the idea of heroism. Dryden seems unable or unwilling to control the moral emphasis of his plays. Heroism and honour in Dryden's plays are worked out in the face of a collapsing social order, rather than upholding or reflecting an existing order. The plays are peopled by despotic usurpers who mouth debased Hobbesian theory and wield lawless might – Maximin in *Tyrannic Love*, Boabdelin in *The Conquest of Granada*, Morat in *Aureng-Zebe*. Some of Dryden's heroes follow the Cornelian pattern of seeking personal *gloire* through conflicts of choice: thus the repeated reversals in political order and their confused effect on individual allegiances allow Almanzor or Aureng-Zebe the opportunity to exhibit their transcendent honour in the face of overwhelming odds. Although Dryden usually regulates events to bring disordered society in line with his views of lawful government,[30] and although he attempts, notably in the case of *Aureng-Zebe* and *Don Sebastian*, to present a Cornelian sense of the complexity of responsible heroism, nevertheless he finds it difficult to separate the inconsistent attitudes of his superheroes, to draw a line between physical strength and heroic virtue. His villains and his heroes are often presented in similar terms. In *Aureng-Zebe* Dryden acknowledges this moral confusion in his earlier plays by sharply distinguishing his hero, who has qualities of humility and piety unknown to the other superheroes, from the villain Morat. But with this play Dryden was abandoning many of the characteristics of the short-lived Restoration heroic drama.

In *Cleomenes* and *Don Sebastian*, the product of the post-Revolution period when Dryden was obliged for financial reasons to turn his hand to plays once more, one can see a deliberate attempt, perhaps inspired by his dislike of the principles underlying the Revolution, to portray responsible kingship, to elaborate the idea of the proper relation of monarch to subjects put forward in the poems. But the heroic plays dating from the earlier part of Charles's reign cannot be said to have such a relation to political reality. The obsession with force, arbitrary rule, and sheer physical strength seems to indicate an irresponsible escapism in Dryden and his court audience. The moral ambivalence of the superhero is explicitly satirised in *The Rehearsal*; Bays says

> I prefer that one quality of singly beating of whole armies, above all your moral virtues put together, 'egad.[31]

Here the superhero is epitomised by the conqueror Drawcansir. If one were to concentrate on certain features it might be as easy to parody Corneille as Dryden; but Dryden himself appeared willing later to admit the justness of some of Buckingham's charges. In the dedication to Lord Haughton of *The Spanish Friar* (which was tragicomedy rather than heroic tragedy) Dryden regrets his excesses:

> I remember some verses of my own Maximin and Almanzor which cry vengeance upon me for their extravagance.   (Watson, I, 276)

He is not turning his back on the heroic style:

> Neither do I discommend the lofty style in tragedy, which is naturally pompous and magnificent; but nothing is truly sublime that is not just and proper.   (*p.* 277)

He insists rather:

> As in a room contrived for state, the height of the roof should bear a proportion to the area; so, in the heightenings of poetry, the strength and vehemence of figures should be suited to the occasion, the subject, and the persons. All beyond this is monstrous: 'tis out of nature, 'tis an excrescence, and not a living part of poetry.
> (*p.* 278)

The heroic play was essentially a form of release and gratification: release for the poet from the restrictions of neo-classical theory and social responsibility; gratification for Charles of his leanings towards absolutism which his own realism and the state of the country would not allow him to pursue.[32] In Dryden's use of panegyric, the problem of an appropriate style, of a public mode, was still pressing. The problem of style was acutely related to the question of Dryden's political position and the rhetorical function of his political poems.

The image of his mode of composition given in the defensive Prologue to *Tyrannic Love* echoes and anticipates a problem perennially explored in his critical prose:

> Poets like lovers should be bold and dare,
> They spoil their business with an overcare.
> And he who servilely creeps after sense,
> Is safe, but ne'er will reach an excellence.
> Hence 'tis our poet in his conjuring,
> Allowed his fancy the full scope and swing.
> But when a tyrant for his theme he had,
> He loosed the reins, and bid his muse run mad:
> And though he stumbles in a full career;
> Yet rashness is a better fault than fear.
> (Kinsley, I, 118, *ll.* 12–21)

This apology was pounced on by Buckingham; Johnson says 'he is too proud a man to creep servilely after sense, I assure you' (IV, ii). Buckingham is not unfair; many of the critical contrasts made in *The Rehearsal* between fancy, elevation, forced conceits on the one hand, and nature and sense on the other, reflect Dryden's own indecisions about the origin and uses of poetry.

His uneasiness about the various sorts of manipulation possible in poetry, its ability to induce either reasoned or emotional agreement, is brought out in his explanation of the style of *Religio Laici*:

> The expressions of a poem, designed purely for instruction, ought to be plain and natural, and yet majestic: for here the poet is presumed to be a kind of lawgiver, and those three qualities which I have named are proper to the legislative style. The florid, elevated and figurative way is for the passions; for love and hatred, fear and anger, are begotten in the soul by showing their objects out of their true proportion; either greater than the life, or less; but instruction is to be given by showing them what they naturally are. A man is to be cheated into passion, but to be reasoned into truth.
> (Kinsley, I, 311, *ll.* 346–55)

The language used suggests that Dryden is dissatisfied with both the technique and the aims of the high style. *Religio Laici* appeared in 1682 after Dryden had abandoned the high style of the immediately post-Restoration panegyrics for the complex persuasion of *Absalom and Achitophel*. But this was not an irreversible development. It is too simple to see Restoration panegyric as existing in an idealistic vacuum and as necessarily being destroyed by confrontation with the actual relations of court and country.[33] For Dryden returned to heroic panegyric in James's reign. *Threnodia Augustalis* (1685), Dryden's funeral ode for Charles, and *Britannia Rediviva* (1688), celebrating the birth of the prince who precipitated the Glorious Revolution, though written within a few years of each other, were produced in very different circumstances. The rout of the Whigs after 1682 and Charles's rule without parliament and in financial security meant that at his death he left James in a very strong position; and James started his reign with twice Charles's income.[34] By 1688, because of fear of his ambitions caused by his tactical blunders, reverence for James's monarchical authority was dissipated. Of the two poems, *Britannia Rediviva*, therefore, presented Dryden with a far more difficult task. It is in *Threnodia Augustalis*, a poem not often read or praised, that we can best see the intentions and the pitfalls of the heroic panegyric, its political uses, and its reflection of a tendency in Dryden's mind. His aim here is not persuasion, but the creation of enthusiasm in the reader. The distinction made by Longinus (whose influence on Dryden was ambiguous) between persuasion and ecstasy is relevant.[35]

Threnodia Augustalis is a 'Funeral-Pindaric'. It is the longest of his panegyrics, and the only one of his public poems to use this curious seventeenth-century genre. Dryden's acknowledged master in the Pindaric ode was Cowley, who described it as 'The noblest and highest kind of writing in verse'.[36] Cowley was deliberately free in his translations from Pindar and in his technical adaptations; he ignored the triad of strophe, antistrophe and epode, and his odes consist of stanzas of irregular lengths and metre. Dryden followed him in this structural looseness. Although he felt that Cowley's language and 'numbers' might be improved, he stated that 'as for the soul of it, which consists in the warmth and vigour of fancy, the masterly figures, and the copiousness of imagination, he has excelled all others in this kind' (Preface to *Sylvae*, Watson, II, 32).

The connection between this definition of Pindaric and Dryden's view of the heroic poem is evident. In 'The Author's Apology for Heroic Poetry and Poetic Licence' Dryden, drawing on Longinus, states that 'imaging is, in itself, the very height and life of poetry' (Watson, I, 203); he goes on to say that 'all reasonable men will conclude it necessary that sublime subjects ought to be adorned with the sublimest, and (consequently often) with the most figurative expressions' (*p.* 207). We are given a further view of the nature of the Pindaric in the preface to *Eleonora* addressed to the Earl of Abingdon. Although *Eleonora*, like the majority of his panegyrics, is written in couplets, Dryden describes it as 'of the Pindaric nature, as well as in the thought as the expression' (Kinsley, II, 583, *l.* 30). What is particularly interesting is the description of his state of mind while writing it (which can be compared with that in the Prologue to *Tyrannic Love*). Although there is an obvious element of irony – Dryden is apologising for his delay in producing the poem – his description of the composition enlarges the position taken in the 'Apology for Heroic Poetry'. He claims to be inspired by a fury, to write in a fit; he remarks that

> the reader will easily observe, that I was transported, by the multitude and variety of my similitudes; which are generally the product of a luxuriant fancy; and the wantonness of wit. (*pp.* 582–3, *ll.* 24–6)

But Dryden is purposely deprecatory. His images are 'beautiful faults'; he writes without the help of judgement. The habit of drawing attention to Pindaric excesses did not originate with Dryden. Cowley abruptly halts his ode on 'The Resurrection' with this irritatingly self-conscious stanza:

> Stop, stop, my muse, allay thy vigorous heat,
>   Kindled at a hint so great.
> Hold thy Pindaric Pegasus closely in,
>   Which does to rage begin,
> And this steep hill would gallop up with violent course,
> 'Tis an unruly, and a hard-mouthed horse,
>   Fierce, and unbroken yet,
>   Impatient of the spur or bit;
> Now prances stately, and anon flies o'er the place,
> Disdains the servile law of any settled pace,
> Conscious and proud of his own natural force.
>   'Twill no unskilful touch endure,
> But flings writer and reader too that sits not sure.
>   (Waller, *p.* 183)

Dryden's constant use of the words 'sublime' and 'bold' in reference to the heroic, with their implications of enthusiasm and rashness, and Cowley's view of the Pindaric as an unbroken horse which may throw the poet, suggest their suspicions of this form. Successful handling of the Pindaric is obviously considered partly a question of taste. There seems to be a connection between the bold figures which are the 'soul' of this form and the metaphysical conceit. And *Eleonora*, which seemed to Dryden to be Pindaric in nature, is the poem that owes most to the example of Donne.

It is a mistake to see Dryden as neglecting the metaphysical conceit in the period between the early elegy on Hastings (1649) and *Eleonora* (1692). Although Johnson saw Dryden as the man who effected the revolt against the metaphysicals, which Waller and Denham would not have been able to accomplish alone, he was perhaps thinking chiefly of metre. Johnson says elsewhere of Dryden (with particular reference to the plays):

> Next to argument, his delight was in wild and daring sallies of sentiment, in the irregular and eccentric violence of wit. He delighted to tread upon the brink of meaning, where light and darkness begin to mingle; to approach the precipice of absurdity, and hover over the abyss of unideal vacancy.[37]

There is a similar poetic impulse behind the heroic plays and the heroic poems. And it seems that for Dryden the Pindaric ode, demanding the exercise of unrestricted fancy, requiring bold, enthusiastic images, replaced the metaphysical conceit in satisfying his taste for bravura. The intellectual shock of the metaphysical conceit becomes a kind of emotional shock. The Pindaric supposes a conspiracy between author and reader to disregard certain norms; it is self-consciously daring.

It is unfair to Dryden to suggest that the use of the Pindaric implies a single, rapturous tone. *Threnodia Augustalis* exhibits various layers of metaphor, allusion, and language, this variety forming part of the tribute to the dead Charles, yet also indicating Dryden's varied intentions in writing the poem. Dryden probably had his eye more on Pindar himself than on the Pindar digested by Cowley. The scenes of the poem are Charles's death bed, the town, the nation; the time is the period of Charles's death, the past of his reign, and the future of James's; the characters are Charles as brother, as friend, as gentleman, as civilising influence, as monarch, as type of God, and James as brother, as classical hero, as military leader, as future monarch. Dryden recreates the events leading up to Charles's death, and the mood of the nation; he reviews the history of the king's reign, he estimates his character, his political skill, his cultivation of art and science; he shows how adversity has tempered James for government, he prays and expects that the new reign will repeat the pattern of, and surpass, the past. These various subjects are expressed in carefully alternated levels of style and tone, yet the whole poem is encompassed in the deliberate creation and transformation of emotion: Dryden attempts to evoke grief, to spur it on, then to control it and substitute for it a carefully elaborated sense of confidence. It is because of the inadequate treatment of the central idea of the poem, the transformation of emotion, that we are not moved in the way that Dryden intends.

The first part of the poem leading up to the moment of Charles's death is a calculated attempt, by the retracing of the narrative of events, to manufacture grief in the reader, and not only grief but the pleasing anguish of false hope. The fact of Charles's death gives an added bite to Dryden's lingering over the news of his brief recovery. Dryden begins with a mighty, petrifying woe, but he does not continue on this monumental level. Instead, he repeatedly takes us to a height of emotion only to retreat from it. The king's false recovery provides a contrast between 'short intervals of joy, and long returns of grief' (Kinsley, I, 446, *l.* 159); the sorrow of James and of the nation is seen in terms of the ebbing and flowing of tides. Dryden twice draws back from a conscious pursuit of excess; referring to James's grief he commands

> forbear audacious muse,
> No terms thy feeble art can use
> Are able to adorn so vast a woe.   (*ll.* 71–3)

From this position he veers in the direction of temporary rejoicing. Again, in the second part of the poem, after describing the glories of Charles's reign Dryden stops at the moment of asking why Charles had to die at the height of his achievement:

> Forgive me Heaven that impious thought,
> 'Twas grief for Charles, to madness wrought,
> That questioned thy supreme decree!   (*ll.* 415–17)

And a similar movement in emotion occurs as Dryden retreats from his 'madness' and begins to manipulate rejoicing for James.

In the second part of the poem after the death of Charles the mood changes from an evocation of grief to a hymn of thanks for his achievements; repetition is used in stanzas 10 and 13 to create the effect of a litany. Dryden then moves from the description of Charles's cultivation of the arts of peace, through his own impious questioning of heaven, to James the military monarch, who will rule the sea as Charles has tilled the land. Again Dryden in stanza 18 invokes heaven, this time to ask that the country may see James with his eyes. He prays on behalf of parliament,

> Let them not still be obstinately blind,
> Still to divert the good thou hast designed,
> Or with malignant penury,
> To starve the royal virtues of his mind.
> Faith is a Christian's and a subject's test,
> Oh give them to believe, and they are surely blest!

And with a daring leap Dryden continues,

> They do; and, with a distant view, I see
> The amended vows of English loyalty.   (*ll.* 498–505)

Prayer has been converted into prophecy. One can say that the whole object of the poem has been to prepare us for this moment so that we will not question the conversion; we can understand why Dryden chose to make his funeral poem a Pindaric when we reach this point and see the emotional change he is trying to effect. Dryden works to create a 'vast' woe that only a vast hope can justify. It is the self consciousness of his attempt at emotional manipulation that makes the reader resist. And if he does resist, he cannot agree to the conspiracy of the poem's conclusion.

Threnodia Augustalis is an ambitious poem, and a complex panegyric; Dryden is doing much more than praising his protagonists. He assumes that his audience needs to be tuned to the level at which they will feel that the praise is appropriate. His ultimate aim is to place James and the country in the proper relation to one another; they both comprise the audience for the poem. Both must be impelled, partly by example but more by the creation of emotional receptiveness, to fulfil their respective roles. James can only be the heroic, magnified monarch if the nation is sympathetic to such a conception of monarchy, if they will reward him with a heroic response. The question is whether a relationship between monarch and subjects on such a level is achievable or indeed appropriate.

Johnson's criticism of *Threnodia Augustalis* – 'there is throughout the composition a desire of splendour without wealth' – is sharp and apt:[38] it draws attention to the faults of taste, to Dryden's ambitious attempt to regulate the rise and fall of emotion, to the disparity between subject and style which Dryden himself underlined as a danger in the dedication to *The Spanish Friar*. Dryden might have argued in his own defence that the heroic style and the Pindaric were appropriate to the subject of monarchy and the emotions it should inspire in the people. One cannot separate the problem of taste from that of politics. Dryden was writing at the moment when the restored Stuart monarchy was at its strongest; 1685 was perhaps the best time in which to celebrate monarchy in heroic panegyric, but Dryden failed to write a great funeral poem for Charles. Although it is always difficult to say why a particular poem is bad, perhaps one can relate the failures of *Threnodia Augustalis* to Dryden's general uneasiness about the grand style and the idea of heroism, and to the political inappropriateness of such attempts to magnify the monarchy. Dryden's experiments with heroism and pindarics express his desire both for release and for a known and fixed social system. But if one sets *Threnodia Augustalis* against Dryden's other public poems one can see that here he only expressed a limited part of his nature. Elsewhere Dryden's sensitivity to the complex evolution of the English constitution and to the perpetual changes in political balance meant that his position was more difficult. In his best political poems his problem was to persuade the king as much as the people.

Dryden's political poems can be seen as a constant attempt in the context of particular events to define the proper role of monarchy, the proper relation of king to people, and to persuade both of the importance of conforming to the definition. This aim is complicated by the extraordinary confusion in political thought in seventeenth-century England, and by the fact that Dryden remained loyal to the Stuarts even at the cost of his most cherished political ideas. This section will trace the varying images of political society which Dryden created in his poems, and the way in which he modified or abandoned them as particular circumstances made them seem more or less appropriate and viable.

Astraea Redux, Dryden's contribution to the flood of panegyric at the Restoration, is his first large-scale use of the public style of heroic analogy.[39] In addition it sets forward a legalist view of government and society which represents his most basic political belief, though this view coexists with others and loses its appeal for Dryden as its relevance becomes doubtful.

In *Astraea Redux* Dryden establishes the method of historical and religious analogy, the juxtaposition of classical and biblical elements, which is repeated throughout his work and which has its most complex expression in *Britannia Rediviva*. One of the effects at which Dryden labours in *Astraea Redux* is the Virgilian epic simile, and one of the poem's main faults is the way in which this style obtrudes, giving rise to the fact that analogies can be divorced from the chief subject matter. But more interesting here than the forging of a public style is the poem's political aim, the lesson it addresses to king and people. It aims at a definition of liberty and law, a reconciliation of monarch and subjects within this definition, and a prophecy (similar to the more elaborate and desperate one at the conclusion of *Annus Mirabilis*) of the kind of society that will emerge as a result of this proper relationship. The poem contrasts faction, division, savagery, war, on the one hand, and reconciliation, peace, united interest and empire on the other.

This antithesis is contained in the historical succession of the Restoration to the years of civil war. Dryden scarcely touches on the events of the last twenty years; it is the ideological implications of these events that matter. The freedom achieved in the Interregnum as a result of the triumph of faction is like Hobbes's state of nature, it is self-destructive:

> The rabble now such freedom did enjoy,
> As winds at sea that use it to destroy:
> Blind as the Cyclops, and as wild as he,
> They owned a lawless salvage liberty,

> Like that our painted ancestors so prized
> Ere empire's arts their breasts had civilised.
>
> <div align="right">(Kinsley, I, 17, <i>ll</i>. 43-8)</div>

False freedom imposes real bonds (<i>l.</i> 152). This experience of tyranny leads the English to an understanding of true freedom. Through its pattern the poem illustrates the parallel sufferings of the separated king and kingdom, and the resulting wisdom that brings them together. Charles is 'at his own cost like Adam wise' (<i>l.</i> 114); the people have achieved a similar knowledge through affliction:

> But since reformed by what we did amiss,
> We by our sufferings learn to prize our bliss. (<i>ll.</i> 209-10)

The poem moves to the moment of reconciliation, Charles's landing at Dover:

> Behold th'approaching cliffs of Albion;
> It is no longer motion cheats your view,
> As you meet it, the land approacheth you. (<i>ll.</i> 251-3)

King and people come together, impelled by a common understanding of liberty and law. Charles is not an arbitrary ruler, 'tied to rules of policy' (<i>l.</i> 260), but a limited monarch bound, like his people, by the law to which he owes his power:

> Your power to justice doth submit your cause,
> Your goodness only is above the laws. (<i>ll.</i> 266-7)

That the relation of mercy to legality can be differently understood is made clear by Waller's contemporary poem on the same subject, 'To the King':[40]

> While to yourself severe, to others kind,
> With power unbounded, and a will confined,
> Of this vast empire you possess the care,
> The softer part falls to the people's share.
> Safety, and equal government, are things
> Which subjects make as happy as their kings.

Dryden tends to see the responsibility as much more evenly divided: king and people are united by their mutual position under the law. However, the vision of empire to which the prospect of this 'united interest' leads (and which is implied in the Virgilian emphasis of the poem, with its motto from the fourth <i>Eclogue</i>) involves a temporary abandonment of the emphasis on limit and balance:

> Our nation with united interest blest
> Not now content to poise, shall sway the rest.
> Abroad your empire shall no limits know
> But like the sea in boundless circles flow. (<i>ll.</i> 296-9)

But this proposal for English mercantile expansion at Europe's expense does not imply any modification of Dryden's theory of internal politics. Such modifications as are to be found in later poems are the result of the strain imposed on the theory by the refusal of both king and people to conform to its specifications.

Astraea Redux, inasfar as it embodies Dryden's views of the constitution, is aimed at Charles as much as at the repentant and lately rebellious English. The images of poise and balance, the ideas of law and limit, the analogies with the English climate, with the balance of sea and land, with the containing of a river by its banks, all of which we find often repeated in Dryden's works, are not original to him but owe their popularity to attempts to define the relationship of king and parliament before the civil war. The problem for royalist supporters of both Charles I and his son was that the constraining theory of a mixed constitution appealed much more to the subjects than to their royal masters. Both kings were prepared when it suited them to claim to be acting within the limits of an agreed constitution against the encroachment on legitimate prerogative of parliaments seeking arbitrary power.[41] In fact both kings, and later James II, saw their prerogative in much less circumscribed terms. Holders of the theory of a mixed constitution could as easily be opponents as supporters of their kings;[42] thus we find, confusingly enough, that parliamentarians and royalists before the civil war, as Dryden and his Whig opponents at the time of the Exclusion Crisis, often speak the same language. And royalists were necessarily obliged to modify their moderate constitutionalism in the direction of the absolutist leanings of their masters. The difficulty is increased by the fact that the need for exact definition of vaguely understood ideas like sovereignty, divine right, prerogative, and privilege only arose when political equilibrium was destroyed and one side or another was pressing for more power. The state of definition at any moment in the century was extremely fluid and was necessarily affected by current political events.

Perhaps in reaction to Macaulay's sharp attack on Dryden as a time server, there have been too many zealous attempts recently to emphasise his political consistency. Guided by his realism and sense of audience, and influenced by external pressure, Dryden modified his attitudes to suit political developments. To clarify the question of his consistency or changeableness, it will be helpful to consider the views that were open to him, and the way these views evolved from particular circumstances. The political theories of which Dryden made use in his poems include constitutional royalism, absolute sovereignty (though this is a new and unorthodox idea), and divine right. Drawing on the wide range of contemporary speculation, Dryden sees monarchy variously in legalist, authoritarian, moral, or symbolic terms. While we may be able to identify his essential preferences, his variations in emphasis are important;

Dryden is torn between proposing a sometimes inappropriate theory, and supporting monarchy, whatever its tendencies, under the auspices of a different theory; between his personal opinions, and his sense of his social responsibility.

The widely-held idea of a balanced constitution in the early seventeenth century involved practical political difficulties. The balance of government was seen in terms of law, not of power; when the partners in mixed monarchy disagreed there was no legal answer to the question of supremacy. The king's authority was legally limited, but when he abused it he could not be coerced by legal means. In spite of this insoluble problem, which was essentially one of power, most royalists and parliamentarians at the beginning of the civil war continued to see government in terms of divided responsibilities under the law and not in terms of sovereignty.[43] The confusion resulting when a theory is strained by circumstances which it is inadequate to account for can be illustrated by the career of Clarendon. Clarendon is perhaps the chief exponent of constitutional royalism, the idea that the king's prerogative, like parliamentary privilege, is a part of the law.[44] Clarendon defined his own view of the English constitution in the early 1640s as follows:

He had a most zealous esteem and reverence for the constitution of the government; and believed it so equally poised, that if the least branch of the prerogative was torn off, or parted with, the subject suffered by it, and that his right was impaired: and he was as much troubled when the crown exceeded its just limits, and thought its prerogative hurt by it.[45]

He was repeatedly critical of Charles I's excessive use of his prerogative, in his frequent dissolutions of parliament and especially in his manipulation of the law in the case of ship-money. But the increasing radicalism of the parliamentary opposition, particularly with relation to ecclesiastical reform, drove Clarendon, in spite of his attempt to maintain a moderate position, to side with the king. Clarendon believed that parliament's far-reaching reforms in the name of the balanced constitution he believed in were making the survival of that constitution impossible; the opposition's appeal to such a theory was deceptive, and concealed their lawlessness and wish to arrogate arbitrary power:

The poor people, under the pretence of zeal to religion, law, liberty, and parliaments, (words of precious esteem in their just signification,) are furiously hurried into actions introducing atheism, and dissolving all the elements of Christian religion; cancelling all obligations, and destroying all foundations of law and liberty; and rendering, not only the privileges, but very being, of parliaments desperate and impossible.[46]

6-2

Like Dryden in reaction to the Exclusionist Whigs, Clarendon insisted, though with a clearer sense of the divergent uses to which the same theory and political language may be put, that managers of the Long Parliament like Pym were guilty of just that illegality and breaking of the bounds of the constitution of which they accused the king.

Denham's *Cooper's Hill* (1642) is perhaps the locus classicus for the literary use of the idea of balance and control, and its concomitant metaphors. The famous image of the Thames indicates not only a theory of balance in style but in politics and social structure as well. Denham's view of English history is that shared by the more extreme parliamentary opposition and the moderate constitutional royalists; Magna Carta represents the sovereignty of law under which king and people have their allotted roles:

> Here was that Charter sealed, wherein the crown
> All marks of arbitrary power lays down:
> Tyrant and slave, those names of hate and fear,
> The happier style of king and subject bear:
> Happy, when both to the same centre move,
> When kings give liberty, and subjects love.[47]

Denham shows that any attempt from either side to break out of the mould will destroy the purpose for which the structure exists:

> Thus kings, by grasping more than they could hold,
> First made their subjects by oppression bold:
> And popular sway, by forcing kings to give
> More than was fit for subjects to receive,
> Ran to the same extremes; and one excess
> Made both, by striving to be greater, less.　*(ll.* 343-8)

In a passage found in the version of 1642 but cancelled from the version of 1655 Denham makes use of the metaphor that recurs in so much Restoration writing, Whig, Tory, or Trimmer:

> Therefore their boundless power tell princes draw
> Within the channel, and the shores of law,
> And may that law, which teaches kings to sway
> Their sceptres, teach their subjects to obey.
>
> (1642 version, *p.* 88)

The first line of this passage may seem to allot to kings that absolute sovereignty that was to be the subject of so much discussion during the Interregnum. But it approximates more closely to the elaborate but not unconstitutional view of James I that in theory (and on a theological level) the king has absolute power while in practice he is bound by the law in the same way as his subjects. For the king to act as though he were outside the law would destroy the system in which the law has meaning.

In spite of the great gulf existing under the restored monarchy between the ambitions of king and parliament, and in spite of royalist reliance on divine right theory to defend the monarchy's tendencies, the theory of the balanced constitution continued to underly much popular examination, both royalist and Whig, of the relation of king and parliament.[48] This mode of thought obviously appealed strongly to Dryden, even though it coexisted with others that were inconsistent and that sometimes succeeded in suppressing this one. The description of the nature of man in *The Hind and the Panther* in constitutional terms, head and heart, reason and mercy, suggesting law and prerogative (Kinsley, II, 476, Part I, *ll.* 259–62), indicates that Dryden saw the poised antitheses of the constitution both as analogous to and as actually reflecting the essential reconciliation of opposites in human nature. The famous passage in *The Medal* likens the constitution to the climate:

> Our temperate isle will no extremes sustain,
> Of popular sway, or arbitrary reign:
> But slides between them both into the best;
> Secure in freedom, in a Monarch blest.
>
> (Kinsley, I, 260, *ll.* 248–51)

But the tension underlying this vision of control is brought out in a different use of the climatic metaphor in the Prologue to *The Unhappy Favourite*:

> Must England still the scene of changes be,
> Tossed and tempestuous like our ambient sea?
> Must still our weather and our wills agree?
>
> (Kinsley, I, 244, *ll.* 18–20)

The increasing separation and mutual distrust of king and parliament as evidenced by the Exclusion Crisis strained the theory of the balanced constitution unbearably so that it became, for a time at least, politically inapplicable.

This unhappy discrepancy between theory and actuality can be illustrated by looking at Dryden's dedication of *All for Love* in 1678 to the Earl of Danby. The dedication is a vigorous expression of the theory of moderate constitutionalism, and the first indication of Dryden's sense of how dangerous to the crown the opposition led by Shaftesbury might be. Dryden sees the English government as a well-poised mean between anarchy and absolutism, commonwealth and tyranny; it suits the situation of the country and the temper of the inhabitants. Whig attempts to alter this equilibrium are subversive, not reformatory, since 'we have already all the liberty which freeborn subjects can enjoy, and all beyond it is but licence' (S-S, v, 322). The constitutional theory is a graceful compliment to Danby, whom Dryden regards as maintaining the necessary poise; Dryden recommends moderation and steadiness of temper as the necessary qualities for a minister, 'that he may stand like an isthmus betwixt the two encroaching seas of arbitrary power, and lawless anarchy' (*p.* 320).

However Danby, one of the more well-meaning and less fortunate of Charles's ministers, represented a policy that pleased nobody. He was unwillingly involved in Charles's French intrigues (and the discovery of this caused his downfall), while at the same time opposing Charles's relations with Louis, furthering the interests of the Prince of Orange by achieving his marriage with James's daughter Mary, and promoting the idea of war with France. He wanted a powerful anti-French monarchy supported by exclusive Anglicanism;[49] this satisfied neither the king's Catholic policy (even though this policy was in abeyance after 1673) nor the opposition's antagonism to a strong prerogative. His attempt at compromise was impossible in the circumstances. It is thus understandable that Dryden gives to the idea of a balanced constitution, of which he sees Danby as an exemplifier, a somewhat vacillating allegiance. It would have taken a braver, more sceptical, and more original man than Dryden, someone like Halifax (of whose trimming views he showed some suspicion), to maintain an equal distance from king and parliament at a time of great political tension. And while the aesthetic appeal of the idea is clear, moderate constitutionalism did not give Dryden the same kinds of satisfaction it gave Clarendon. Dryden does not seem to have had the same nostalgic sense of history and custom that gives the theory its life. Both the pressure of circumstances and his predispositions (which involved, as we have seen, some confusion in his critical opinions) led him to rely on the different idea of divine right.

A vague sense of benevolent paternalism and divine right was the conventionally accepted background to the rule of James I and Charles I, but it coexisted with reverence for the common law and the ancient constitution.[50] What was important was the linking of these imprecise and emotional attitudes with the new clear-cut theory of absolute sovereignty.[51] The practical consequences of the connection are more evident in France; Catholicism, as is made clear by Louis XIV's attempt to stamp out the Huguenots, was an important support of the mystique of his rule. In England, because of the Catholic ambitions of Charles II and his brother, the Tory attempt to make Anglicanism the support of absolutism was doomed; the petition of the seven bishops against James's Declaration of Indulgence made it clear that they were unable to accept passive obedience as the practical conclusion of their inconsistent theory.[52] The intellectual confusion of the Tories is reflected in Dryden's apparently illogical amalgamation of conflicting ideas (though he avoided some of their difficulties by his conversion to Catholicism).[53] But if one considers the political situation in which these different ideas had their origin, one can see how they might coexist in the mind of one man.

In addition to maintaining a strong respect for the idea of a balanced constitution, Dryden, whether moved by hope as a result of the Restoration, or by fear in reaction to the apparent Whig subversion of monarchy, was able at different times to run the gamut from sentimental paternalism to uncompromising absolutism, without giving any indication that he was conscious of inconsistency. Thus he attacks the Trimmers without acknowledging the resemblance of his views to theirs; he insists on the importance of trusting a monarch, James II, whose views on the function of parliament differed completely from his own. But Dryden's reliance on divine right by no means implies a view of the nature of sovereignty like that of Filmer. His particular concern was not with a clearly stated theory: in the passage in *Absalom and Achitophel* (Kinsley, I, 236–8, *ll.* 759–810) in which contemporary views on contract, law, and monarchy are examined, Dryden is sure not so much of his theoretical position as of his practical responses to a specific situation. In addition, constitutional royalism was not a sufficiently personal, animated theory to suit Dryden's strong imaginative sense of hierarchy and correspondence; this place was filled by his constant elaboration of the view of the proper mutual relationship of monarch and subject.

Thus we find in his work repeated definitions of the appropriate virtues of the monarch, mildness and mercy, and the corresponding virtue in the subject, trust. Writing of the trials of war, plague, and fire, Dryden tells the city of London in the dedication to *Annus Mirabilis* (1667),

> Never had prince or people more mutual reason to love each other, if suffering for each other can endear affection.
>
> (Kinsley, I, 43, ll. 15–16)

In the dedication of *Troilus and Cressida* to Sunderland (1679) Dryden sees as the immediately pressing problem that the quiet of the nation must be secured and the mutual trust between prince and people renewed (S-S, VI, 250). The Whigs are assured in the Prologue 'To His Royal Highness' (1682) that

> Kings can forgive if rebels can but sue:
> A tyrant's power in rigour is expressed:
> The father yearns in the true prince's breast.
>
> (Kinsley, I, 262, ll. 27–9)

In *Threnodia Augustalis* (1685) Dryden sees the future success of James's reign depending on parliament's assumption of the responsibility of faith. In the Epilogue to *Albion and Albanius* (1685) the same idea is extended; the people are asked to reward James's truth with trust, and

Dryden suggests that conflict between a king and parliament has meaning only in this benevolent contest:

> To excel in truth, we loyally may strive;
> Set privilege against prerogative:
> He plights his faith; and we believe him just;
> His honour is to promise, ours to trust.

The king's role parallels and embraces both the paternal and the divine; so Dryden goes on to show that the political equilibrium achieved by this mutual relationship is like the creation:

> Thus Britain's basis on a word is laid,
> As by a word the world itself was made.
> (Kinsley, I, 458, ll. 29–34)

Dryden's most elaborate poetic expression of the idea of divine right and of the proper relation of monarch to people is in *Britannia Rediviva* (1688), his last attempt at panegyric and definition on behalf of Stuart monarchy. The use of biblical, classical, and natural analogy carries to a new pitch the heroic style first used in *Astraea Redux*. The delight and the seriousness evident in these prolonged comparisons indicate why the divine and patriarchal interpretations of monarchy were important to Dryden. Most interesting in this respect is the poem's conclusion, where he turns from the implications of the child's birth to the nature of James's rule, and draws an extended parallel between the divine and regal attributes, which itself implies a rejection of the legalistic sovereignty of Hobbes for the moral absolutism of Bossuet. Dryden distinguishes the tyrant from the just king:

> Some kings the name of conquerors have assumed,
> Some to be great, some to be gods presumed;
> But boundless power, and arbitrary lust
> Made tyrants still abhor the name of just.
> (Kinsley, II, 550, ll. 339–42)

This distinction is given meaning by an appeal to the nature of God. Here Dryden takes up an old theological problem with a political purpose.[54] God is omnipotent and immortal, but these are not attributes peculiar to him nor is it these that make him divine. Without the attribute of justice the first two are meaningless:

> Resistless force and immortality
> Make but a lame, imperfect deity:
> Tempests have force unbounded to destroy,
> And deathless being even the damned enjoy,

.   .   .   .

But justice is heaven's self, so strictly he,
That could it fail, the Godhead could not be.

(ll. 349–52, 355–6)

So it is with kings. Dryden ends with a vision of James as the epitome
of justice, reflecting in his control of the kingdom England's imperial
role:

Equal to all, you justly frown or smile,
Nor hopes, nor fears your steady hand beguile;
Your self our balance hold, the world's, our isle.

(ll. 359–61)

Though the licence of panegyric allows Dryden to see James as the
embodiment of divine justice, nevertheless the form the definition takes,
of the distinction between God's attributes, between the tyrant and the
just king, is intended as a salutary lesson. There is some evidence in
The Hind and the Panther and the letters to show that Dryden (like most
moderate Catholics) was alarmed at James's policies; he had no sympathy
with James's attempt to establish himself as an absolute ruler like Louis,
by force if necessary; in his view the proper relationship between king
and people was one of mutual trust.

He conceived this relationship above all as moral and personal, not
legalistic; it is very different, for instance, from Locke's development of
the idea of fiduciary trust which is revocable when broken:

For all power given with trust for the attaining an end, being limited
by that end, whenever that end is manifestly neglected, or opposed,
the trust must necessarily be forfeited.[55]

For Dryden as for Bossuet there is no recourse for the subject whose
monarch has destroyed the proper relationship. And yet there is evidence
in Dryden's changing attitudes to Charles and James, occasioned by the
characters of the respective kings and the strains of the political situation,
of his falling back on the legalistic rather than the moral conception of
absolutism. Throughout his panegyrics on Charles II Dryden draws
attention to his characteristic mercy and mildness. These virtues are
seen partly as the appropriate reflection in a king of paternal and divine
attributes, and partly as a charitable heightening of what seem to have
been Charles's actual characteristics, an easygoing but calculating nature,
an indifference to conflicts of principle, and a willingness to yield. In
Threnodia Augustalis Dryden draws attention both to the divine origin
and the political usefulness of these virtues; Charles is

That all forgiving king,
The type of him above,
That inexhausted spring
Of clemency and love;

(ll. 257–60)

he is also a Fabius, delaying wisely, opposing art to rage (*ll.* 388–93), so that his enemies are deceived:

> So much thy foes thy manly mind mistook,
> Who judged it by the mildness of thy look:
> Like a well tempered sword, it bent at will;
> But kept the native toughness of the steel.   (*ll.* 324–7)

Halifax makes the same observation in less complimentary form:

> His pliantness broke the blow of a present mischief much better than a more immediate resistance would perhaps have done.[56]

Charles's caution does seem to have saved him his throne; he was willing in 1673 to withdraw the Declaration of Indulgence, thus abandoning his and Louis' Grand Design for the conversion of England to Catholicism; in 1680 he was prepared to accept limitations on the future power of his brother though not exclusion, thus making his own position much less intransigent than that of his opponents. James was utterly opposed to these stands; he was against temporising with the Exclusionists, and he advised adhering to the Declaration of Indulgence even at the risk of civil war[57] (with well known results in the case of his own declarations of 1687 and 88). Though Charles's caution won him great power at the end of his reign, and James's obstinacy only brought him exile, Dryden in some cases found more to admire in the latter. He obviously felt uneasy about Charles's devious methods of government; while Charles feinted and temporised, James was blunt and open in his pursuit of the same policy. Dryden's preference is clear from his reference to James's character; the fable of the plain good man in *The Hind and the Panther* (1687) (Part III, *ll.* 907 ff.) reinforces the picture in the Epilogue to *Albion and Albanius*:

> Plain dealing for a jewel has been known;
> But ne'er till now the jewel of a crown.   (*ll.* 5–6)

In one sense this preference is a logical result of Dryden's view of the nature of good government; trust cannot exist in a relationship based on concealment. It also indicates the extent to which Dryden's political attitudes were conditioned not only by his imaginative sense of universal correspondences, his need for a personal and animated ideology, but also by the pressure of the immediate, by fear. Thus in the extraordinarily hysterical appeal 'To the King' prefaced to his translation of Maimbourg's *The History of the League* (a task performed at Charles's request) Dryden, spurred by a morbid desire for revenge on the Whigs, asks the king to abandon his excessive mercy since it is now inappropriate and dangerous:

> It is time, at length, for self-preservation to cry out for justice, and to lay by mildness, when it ceases to be a virtue.   (S-S, XVII, 85)

The appeal to danger in 1684 was absurd; the demand for revenge was simply a reflection of the policy of the king who was now, since the disintegration of the Whigs, able to show his hand. For Dryden thus to follow the royal fortunes shows the incongruity of his position: he is the spokesman for monarchy, whatever its tendencies, even when these involve a betrayal of his own sense of monarchy's proper function.

Absalom and Achitophel, Dryden's best political poem, owes its peculiar tone to this complex combination of purposes and functions; it is both a definition and a defence of monarchy; it deals with the proper role of the people and it attempts to persuade them of the appropriateness of a particular course of action; it is about Israel and England. As a public poet Dryden necessarily wrote of and to the contemporary situation. It is one of the ironies of his role that his identification with the existing government and the status quo meant that he was unable to see that the Whigs were to a large extent impelled by the same prejudices and ideals as himself. Thus Settle's *Absalom Senior*, one of the replies to *Absalom and Achitophel* appearing in 1682, uses Dryden's fiction and his arguments to turn his poem back on itself. Dryden saw this technique as evidence simply of lack of invention; as he says in the 'Epistle to the Whigs' prefixed to *The Medal*:

> Let your verses run upon my feet: and for the utmost refuge of notorious blockheads, reduced to the last extremity of sense, turn my own lines upon me, and in utter despair of your own satire, make me satirise myself. (Kinsley, 1, 252, *ll.* 101–4)

But the point is more important than this. By using the same characters to represent different historical personages, by substituting James for Monmouth as Absalom, Halifax for Shaftesbury as Achitophel (though to make Halifax James's confidant and adviser is a grotesque distortion) Settle shows that even while using the same ideological criteria a completely different interpretation of the same political situation can be given. Thus his analysis of the constitution echoes that of Clarendon, of Denham, and of Dryden himself; its limitations correspond to the nature of the physical universe, to the proper balance of human ambitions, to the trinity. Parliament represents

> That Godlike balance of imperial might,
> Where subjects are from tyrant-lords set free
> From that wild thing unbounded man would be,
> Where power and clemency are poised so even,
> A constitution that resembles Heaven.

The constitution is
> so divinely mixed
> Not Nature's bounded elements more fixed.
> Thus earth's vast frame, with firm and solid ground,

> Stands in a foaming ocean circled round;
> Yet this not overflowing, that not drowned.[58]

And Settle sees Dryden as acting from self-interest just as Dryden saw his Whig opponents. They speak the same language without being able to reach each other.[59] Each side appeals to law, and each accuses the other of attempting to subvert it.

Much Whig verse before and at the time of the Exclusion Crisis (though some of it is outright republican) uses this constitutional argument; in *Popish Politics Unmasked* James is the evil adviser promoting arbitrary power, while Shaftesbury argues the reciprocal relationship of prerogative and privilege:

> Set that aside, and make the law a sham,
> No sovereign you, nor I a subject am;
> For that same law that gives you dignity,
> Gives me my life, fortune and liberty.[60]

The Exclusionists, like the parliamentarians, included a number of conservatives, men protesting against the administration and the corruption at court, independent country members representing local government and the established constitution as they understood it.[61] For these men the Popish Plot provided a focus and outlet for their beliefs and fears. They were afraid of novelty and change, of the crown's abuse of the prerogative. Dryden resolutely refused to believe that men or motives of this kind gave the Exclusion movement its support. He thought, and it is a view deserving as much consideration as the Whigs' (or the parliamentarians') view of themselves, that the Whig ideology was simply rhetoric concealing a revolutionary movement and a real bid for power. Thus his immediate task as public poet at this time was to convince the large body of Whigs of their erroneous assumptions and the subversive designs of their leaders.

The poetic position that Dryden achieved at the time of the Exclusion Crisis and the Tory reaction that followed was different from any that was open to him before or afterwards. His biographer says it is as though in 1680 he left the poet for the historiographer.[62] This is to make a distinction that Dryden would not have accepted, but the emphasis on the historical moment is correct. His other works were of course written with reference to a particular context, but his intention was different. *Annus Mirabilis* was written following a period of national crisis, and to counteract false interpretations of that crisis, but here as in *Britannia Rediviva* the manipulation of rhetoric is not intended for any specific group of people nor to achieve a particular practical result. A rhetorical purpose certainly underlies these poems, but it is less clearly defined; Dryden wants to achieve in the reader an emotional acquiescence in the idea of the mutual support of king and people. The political situation in the late 1670s and early 1680s made such an aim and tone inappropriate and inadequate. The political nation was split into two opposing camps, a living travesty of the idea of a balanced constitution; the renewal of civil war seemed a probability. In reaction to the variations in the situation, to the fortunes and popularity of Shaftesbury and the Whigs and Charles and the Tories, Dryden varied his audience, his tone, his weapons, and his ideas. Between mid 1681, the time of the incipient disintegration of the Whig movement, and 1684, when the Whigs were destroyed as an influence and a party and Charles was able to assert himself completely, Dryden produced two long poems (and part of a third), a play, and three prose tracts, together with such additional commentary as was made possible by theatrical prologues and epilogues. These works were dedicated to healing the rift in society, to bringing the Whigs if malleable back into the normal processes of government, if intransigeant to destroying them, and to supporting throughout the at first cautious and conciliatory and later firm and revengeful attitude of the king.

Charles, having dissolved the three Exclusion parliaments (the one at Oxford in March 1681 was to be the last of his reign), needed to defend himself against comparisons with the unparliamentary rule of his father; hence the influential *His Majesty's Declaration*, presenting the situation as a struggle between law and faction and asserting Charles's respect for parliamentary government, was read in churches. A Whig attack provoked two anonymous replies, one of which, *His Majesties Declaration Defended*, is now attributed to Dryden. At this point Charles's position was still uncertain, and the *Declaration Defended* continues the appeal to moderation and law. By June Charles felt that he could pass to the attack: in July Shaftesbury was arrested. *Absalom and Achitophel* (published in November) reflects a new policy with regard to the Whigs. The difference of tone between the main body of the poem and David's speech has been attributed to the dual purpose of hounding the Whig leaders and of placating the moderates who were opposed to revenge and who had been won by the tone of the *Declaration*.[63]

Such changes in tone are owing to the immediate policies of Charles; more complex changes and ambiguities result from Dryden's sense of his purpose. Throughout these works Dryden maintains the image of himself as a moderate attempting to persuade the moderate members of the other party to realise their mistake and abandon their false position; he appeals to common sense, to the desire for peace and the fear of social disorder. This image of moderation, though useful, is not always accurate. The imaginary addressee of the *Declaration Defended* is a 'lover of the peace and quietness of your country'; the conflict is seen in strictly Clarendonian terms as caused by a faction misleading the people with 'the specious names of religion and liberty', and keeping up an artificial fear of popery and arbitrary power in order to undermine the royal prerogative, destroy the constitution, and substitute the absolute power of the people for the rule of law grounded on reason.[64] The whole process is an inevitable result of any attempt to tamper with the natural balance of the constitution, for ''tis as certain in politics, as in nature; that where the sea prevails the land loses'.[65] *Absalom and Achitophel* supposes an audience of 'the more moderate sort' whose preferences have blunted what might be too sharp satire; Dryden deliberately avoids appealing to extremists of either side: 'they are not the violent, whom I desire to please' (Kinsley, I, 215, *l.* 16; 216, *l.* 34). This is essentially a just description of the poem's intention, though the view of Shaftesbury's role is much exaggerated. But in the later works there is a growing discrepancy between Dryden's claims and his actual tone, a hardening in his practical proposals and in his political ideas.

Though the arguments of *The Medal* (March 1682) are the same as those used hitherto – that the Whigs under pretence of zeal for law seek arbitrary power, that there is no danger of this from the king, that the existing constitution represents a proper balance – the structure of the poem indicates that Dryden had no desire to convince the unconverted of the truth of his arguments.[66] The poem consists of a violent attack on Shaftesbury, London, and the crowd; in other words, on the bulk of the Whig party as Dryden saw it. The aim of *The Duke of Guise* (performed December 1682) is clearly not to convert the Whigs but to frighten the Tories; Dryden's historical analogy, the parallel between the Catholic League, the Covenanters, and the Whigs, is designed to plant in the audience's mind a conviction of the inevitability of civil war unless the Whigs are crushed. The play illustrates the specious arguments by which Dryden sees the Whigs defending their subversive designs; thus the Curate states,

> Rebellion is an insurrection against the government; but they that have the power are actually the government; therefore, if the people have the power, the rebellion is in the king.   (S-S, VII, 25)

Dryden sees the Whigs' aim as the undermining of the king's part in the constitution; as Henry III says, the exclusion of Navarre will benefit the States General at his own expense:

> Five hundred popular figures on a row,[67]
> And, I myself, that am, or should be king,
> An o'ergrown cypher set before the sum.   (*p.* 106)

Dryden's hardening tone is illustrated by his emphasis on social as well as constitutional and political upheaval; in the Prologue the Whigs'

pursuit of their aims is seen to divide the nation and destroy the social
hierarchy:

> Make London independent of the crown:
> A realm apart; the kingdom of the town.
>
> . . . .
>
> Do, what in coffeehouses you began;
> Pull down the master, and set up the man.
>
> (Kinsley, I, 327, 41–2, 46–7)

Dryden's *Vindication of the Duke of Guise* (1683) reasserts the conventional view of the constitution, but this now appears undermined by his interpretation of the situation and his practical proposals. Dryden maintains that Charles is not an absolutist, that the people are not the king's chattels (a view that recalls Bossuet's distinction between absolute and arbitrary government), but his contention that all necessary liberties are secured by the existing laws means that any railing against the administration or any attempt to interfere with the succession constitutes treason (S-S, VII, 172, 215). In the Postscript to *The History of the League* (1684), his last work of specifically anti-Whig propaganda, Dryden claims, rather inconsistently, since he also advocates persecution of the Whigs, that the book's object is

> to make the well-meaning men of the other party sensible of their
> past errors, the worst of them ashamed, and prevent posterity from
> the like unlawful and impious design.   (S-S, XVII, 185)

His political theory is here much more of the divine right than the moderate constitutionalist school; thus though he says that Charles governs by explicit laws, he claims that his authority is divine, that the subject irrevocably gives up his power, and that the king's failure is only punishable by God (*pp.* 153–4). When he sees the Whigs threatening to violate the constitution, Dryden reacts with remonstrance and fear, and finally seeks revenge; if the king does the same, he has no answer. This inconsistency results inevitably from his anomalous position as defender of a regime which does not share his views of the structure and function of government.[68]

The changes in Dryden's tone and attitudes are exemplified by his references to the Trimmers. In November 1682, just after the appearance of *Absalom and Achitophel II*, Sir Roger L'Estrange changed the debaters in his Tory journal *The Observator* from Whig and Tory to Trimmer and Tory. The change is indicative of the reactionary movement of the country as a whole; as the Whigs ceased to be a serious threat the Tories turned their attention to the moderates.[69] The classic defence of the moderate position was made in *The Character of a Trimmer* by Halifax, the epitome of the Trimming policy and hence distrusted at the time of the Exclusion Crisis by Shaftesbury and James, the extremists of

161

either side. Halifax's tract is both a restatement of the idea of a balanced constitution, and a criticism of Charles's policies in the light of these principles. The emphasis is on law, balance, reconciliation, mutual support; trimming principles are seen to underlie not only the English constitution but the climate, the church, the practice of virtue, and the divine attributes of justice and mercy. The Trimmer bases his political attitudes on 'nature, religion, liberty, prudence, humanity and common sense'.[70] He thinks (and these attitudes reflect more on Charles than on the Whigs) that the penal laws against dissenters should in fairness be enforced only to the same extent as those against the papists; he distrusts Louis and the Anglo-French alliance.[71] In principle Halifax was strongly opposed to the absolutist, pro-French leanings of Charles and James, but in practice he gave them a good deal of support. He opposed the Whig mythology of an ancient constitution and fundamental law, and instead asserted the existence of an absolute sovereignty in the constitution.[72] The defeat of the second Exclusion Bill in the Lords is generally ascribed to the opposition of Halifax, Shaftesbury's one-time ally,[73] and this is acknowledged by Dryden in his portrait of Jotham

> who but only tried
> The worse awhile, then chose the better side;
> Nor chose alone, but turned the balance too.
> (Kinsley, I, 239, *ll.* 884–6)

But after having helped defeat the Whigs Halifax opposed their persecution; he did not want Shaftesbury to be tried and he attempted to save Russell after his false conviction for his connection with the Rye House plot.[74] In 1683 and 84, after the discovery of the Whig plots and when retribution was in full swing, Trimming was associated in the minds of men like Dryden and L'Estrange with a policy of leniency towards the Whigs.

Although Dryden shared Halifax's constitutional views including his fear of Louis XIV and French intrigue, and although he seems to have admired him personally (*King Arthur* [1691] is dedicated to him), his attitude to the Whigs was quite different. His close identification with the crown's fortunes resulted in a whole-hearted acceptance of its policies, and a modification of his own constitutional views. In *Absalom and Achitophel* concessions are seen to be dangerous: the worthy few advise Charles

> That no concessions from the throne would please,
> But lenitives fomented the disease.   (*ll.* 925–6)

Dryden seems to have become infected with that exaggerated fear and hysteria of which he accused the Whigs. In the Epilogue to *The Duke of Guise* and the dedication 'To the King' of *The History of the League* his heavy jokes about hanging are frightening; though Macaulay is almost always unjust to Dryden, one must for once agree when he depicts the fiendishness of Dryden's anti-Whiggism.[75] As Halifax was to complain, the Trimmers were the object of more vituperation than the Whigs. In the Epilogue to *The Duke of Guise*, which consists of a dialogue between a Trimmer and a Tory, the idea of a middle balanced policy is ridiculed. The metaphor of a hanging balance is given bite by previous references to hanging by the neck:

> We Trimmers are for holding all things even:
> Yes – just like him that hung 'twixt hell and heaven.
> Have we not had men's lives enough already?
> Yes sure: – but you're for holding all things steady:
> Now since the weight hangs all on one side, brother,
> You Trimmers should, to poise it, hang on t'other.
>
> (Kinsley, I, 328, *ll.* 33–8)

The theory of a balanced constitution which fills a large part of Dryden's imagination is here dismissed with the characterisation of the Trimmers as 'damned neuters' (*l.* 39).

Much of the work that Dryden produced in reaction to the Exclusion Crisis is only of historical interest; but it is important to realise the extent to which his role as a public poet, and his conflicting aims of setting forward his imaginative view of social structure and of influencing political developments, are constantly reassessed in relation to particular events and immediate needs. There is a perpetual cycle of involvement; Dryden writes with an ideal of the true relation of king and subject, the true society, with the intention of making existing society conform to it; at the same time the state of actual political events limits the extent to which the ideal is realisable or relevant, and thus in turn it is the ideal that is modified by events. *Absalom and Achitophel* remains a remarkable achievement because, although we can dissect the levels of theory, political interpretation, policy, personal commitment, and rhetorical persuasion, although it also reflects the immediate moment and is proof of Dryden's poetic dilemma, the inconsistencies and difficulties of the political world are resolved into a whole which is not a travesty of the real situation or Dryden's beliefs.

The main political error of *Absalom and Achitophel*, but one which allows its flexible style, its combination of satire and heroism, and its confident sense of the possibility of restoring society to its customary forms, lies in its misestimation of the kind and extent of the opposition to the crown. One should not insist too much on the motive of fear.[76] This motive and the concomitant desire for revenge play a larger part in the later works where the king's position and hence Dryden's is more straightforward and more rigid. The crowd, for example, is seen as a more important and dangerous segment of society in *The Medal* than in *Absalom and Achitophel*. Dryden like Clarendon thought that the framework of the existing constitution adequately contained religion, liberty, and law; therefore any belief that these could only find their realisation by a change in the balance of the constitution must result from the fact that the people had been deceived as to their interests by men who used the language of these ideas to cloak their destructive and revolutionary intentions. Thus the Jews, though humorous, moody, and headstrong, would merely have remained such had it not been for manipulation of the Popish Plot by Achitophel, who makes use of the plot's 'wished occasion' (*l.* 208). The Jews and Absalom are simply dupes in Achitophel's pursuit of his personal interest. Dryden's catalogue of Shaftesbury's followers differs significantly from a modern analysis of the Whigs as a cross-section of society.[77] Dryden is prepared to admit an element with honourable motives:

> Mistaken men, and patriots in their hearts;
> Not wicked, but seduced by impious arts.   (*ll.* 497–8)

But the majority are either impelled by self-interest, treasonable designs (all dissenters are included in this group) or instinct; all are seen as Achitophel's tools. There is no room in Dryden's theory for the view that a large segment of society might legitimately object to the crown's straining of the constitution. It is in seizing on Shaftesbury as leader, tempter, deceiver, as the embodiment of discord and disaffection, that Dryden indicates his temperamental affinity with much of the conservative reaction to the policies of the crown throughout the century. Achitophel is the inverse of the evil adviser, the powerful magnate, the machinating minister who fills opposition literature. Just as in the early part of Charles's reign there is widespread public feeling that the removal of Clarendon, who comes to embody all that is unpopular in Charles's court or policies, whatever his actual responsibility, will result in a re-establishment of proper relations between king and country, in the same way Dryden feels that Shaftesbury is responsible for the rift in the nation and that his destruction will automatically resolve the conflict.

The poem's chief object is thus to expose Shaftesbury, and its mock-epic style partly follows from this. The technique is the same as in *Macflecknoe*; Shaftesbury is deflated by the heroic stature allowed him as Achitophel. The echoes of *Paradise Lost* reinforce this defeat. The two heroic antagonists are Achitophel and David, but the contest is necessarily unequal.[78] David does not make his appearance until towards the end of the poem, but this in no way belittles him, since he is the standard against which Achitophel's revolt is understood. Though David has but few friends, 'a small but faithful band / of worthies' (*ll.* 914–15), who stand against 'the united fury of the land' (*l.* 917), he is supported by the whole system of order, the proper hierarchy of relationships under the law, from which Achitophel and his faction however numerous are only a temporary deviation. Achitophel must suffer by comparison, by his portrayal as an excrescence from the natural order. He is supported by no rival system of order; his glib manipulation of political theory in his long second speech to Absalom (*ll.* 376–476) appears simply as specious rhetoric. His heroic posture is hollow, he is 'the false Achitophel' (*l.* 150) just as the king is 'the godlike David' (*l.* 937) and just as his son is 'deluded Absalom' (*l.* 683). Dryden must make the people understand this; from knowledge acceptance of existing order will inevitably follow:

> Once more the godlike David was restored,
> And willing nations knew their lawful lord. (*ll.* 1030–1)

Dryden's interpretation of the political moment in *Absalom and Achitophel* allowed him to do two things: by placing Shaftesbury in a magnificent fiction to create and destroy him at one stroke; and, by using the example before him, to illustrate and help bring into being the harmonious society, the ideal relation of king and people. His interpolation (*ll.* 753–810) on political theory and the danger of changing the foundations of society is, because of his underlying confidence, remarkable for its tone of reasoned discourse, for its logical progression. Dryden sees here no tension between theory and fact. It appears in retrospect that his analysis of the motives of Shaftesbury and the Whigs in general and, more important, of the ambitions of Charles with respect to the power of the crown is inaccurate; either out of ignorance or tact he accuses Shaftesbury of policies for which Charles was responsible.[79] But the conflict between interpretation and commitment is not crippling; Dryden maintains the necessary distance from both king and country. *Absalom and Achitophel* is a splendid justification of his perpetual and not always successfully realised struggle as a poet, to describe and influence society, to praise, support, and direct the existing government, while remaining faithful to himself and his beliefs.

BETWIXT THE PRINCE AND PARLIAMENT

In November 1688, five months after the publication of *Britannia Rediviva*, William of Orange landed at Torbay; in February 1689 he accepted the crown jointly with Mary; by March, Dryden was deprived of his offices of Poet Laureate and Historiographer Royal. He was now without a public position or an income. Though he was almost sixty years old at the time of the Revolution, a large proportion of his work was yet to come. Financial necessity meant that he had to continue to write; political necessity meant that he could no longer write in the old way. He was no longer the interpreter, defender and apostrophiser of the government. The two most obvious sources of income were translation and the stage; Dryden wrote three new plays, refurbished his opera, and continued to provide prologues and epilogues for revivals (including *The Secular Masque*), but it is clear that attacks like those of Collier (which appeared in 1698) and his own tangles with censorship (his prologue to *The Prophetess*, which reflected on William's Irish campaign, was banned, and *Cleomenes* was held up at Mary's request) made him reluctant to renew the old unrewarding relationship with the theatrical audience. It was from his translations that Dryden gained in these years his patronage, his living, and, particularly in the case of his Virgil, much of his reputation. But he must have felt that his work as translator of Virgil, supported by subscription and the patronage of his dedicatees, was a decline from his old vision of himself as epic poet supported by the crown and in turn supporting it by his portrayal of the heroic deeds of Charles and James.

Dryden's poverty and his isolation, caused by his office under the previous government and his religion, inevitably resulted in the expression of some bitterness. One possible path open to him was to satirise the new regime; but this was both dangerous and, for a man of Dryden's temperament, a limitation of the uses of poetry.[80] In some cases his reaction did not show itself so much in satire (which presupposes in the satirist a sense of order against which the actual is tested) as in outright cynicism, complete exhaustion with the processes of government and history. Thus in the dedication of *Examen Poeticum* to Lord Radcliffe in 1693 he writes, reflecting on his inability ever to obtain solid preferment and his determination to assert his honesty,

> No government has ever been, or ever can be, wherein timeservers and blockheads will not be uppermost. The persons are only changed, but the same jugglings in state, the same hypocrisy in religion, the same self-interest and mismanagement, will remain for ever. Blood and money will be lavished in all ages, only for the preferment of new faces with old consciences. (Watson, II, 157)

Dryden is criticising not only William's administration (and the re-appearance in it of ministers who were once pillars of the Stuarts) but the nature of all government. In *The Secular Masque* (which has achieved an exaggerated importance as Dryden's considered view of politics by virtue of the fact that it is one of the last pieces he wrote) the inverted progress of history implies not so much a profound pessimism, a restate-ment of the classical version of original sin, as a sense of the absurd, of the ultimate meaninglessness of events. Momus, the god of ridicule, dismisses all the courts and conflicts of the century:

> All, all of a piece throughout
> Thy chase had a beast in view;[81]

Thy wars brought nothing about;
Thy lovers were all untrue.
'Tis well an old age is out,
And time to begin a new.

(Kinsley, IV, 1764–5, *ll*. 86–91)

But the new age, we are sure, will simply repeat the same cycle of absurdity.

One reason why *The Secular Masque* is so startling, apart from its intrinsic wit and daring, is that it is so untrue to the laureate Dryden who believed in the order and purpose of history, or indeed to the later Dryden who tried to find a place in the post-Revolution world. He himself was dissatisfied with his own negative, critical, and complaining reactions. *The Secular Masque* is beyond despair; but Dryden was apparently unable to find in satire an adequate tool to express his position. He frequently approaches it and then veers away. Perhaps the nearest realisation of the use Pope would have made of this situation, of the setting of absolute order against its actual inversion, is to be found in Dryden's miniature *Dunciad*, the poem to Congreve; but his sense of his own losses is too negative and complaining:

Already I am worn with cares and age;
And just abandoning the ungrateful stage:
Unprofitably kept at heaven's expense,
I live a rent-charge on his providence.

(Kinsley, II, 853, *ll*. 66–9)

In *Eleonora* there is a much stronger assertion of himself in the face of the age. He asks the dead Countess of Abingdon to accept

This humble tribute of no vulgar muse:
Who, not by cares, or wants, or age depressed,
Stems a wild deluge with a dauntless breast:
And dares to sing thy praises, in a clime
Where vice triumphs, and virtue is a crime:
Where even to draw the picture of thy mind,
Is satire on the most of human kind.

(Kinsley, II, 594, *ll*. 360–6)

Dryden here verges on the position of Pope, the claim that his isolation is by choice and not by circumstance. But in the poem's preface he deliberately renounces satire.

It is clear that Dryden did not wish to set himself up in opposition to government and society, though, from his actual excursions into political attack, this cannot be attributed to a wish for safety and convenience. As the 'Postscript to the Reader' at the end of the *Aeneid* shows, Dryden

167

did not want to trade on his misfortunes; he still thought of himself as the national poet. He writes that he has encouraged Virgil to speak English; his translation 'will be judged in after-ages, and possibly in the present, to be no dishonour to my native country' (Watson, II, 258). With regard to the regime his principles prevent him from supporting, ''tis enough for me, if the government will let me pass unquestioned' (*p.* 259). In the Prologue to *Don Sebastian* he urges that party conflict is irrelevant to his poetry. The best statement of his maintenance of neutrality as a poet, though not as a man, is found in a letter of 1699; Dryden is explaining that he will not make concessions in order to get patronage:

> If they will consider me as a man, who have done my best to improve the language, and especially the poetry, and will be content with my acquiescence under the present government, and forbearing satire on it, that I can promise, because I can perform it: but I can neither take the oaths, nor forsake my religion.   (*Letters, p.* 123)

But for Dryden to continue to speak as a public poet to the nation some modification of his political principles must take place. That this could be achieved without betrayal of his work up to that point, without evidence of that changeableness that hostile readers like Macaulay were always willing to discover in him, can be seen by examining the fine panegyric and epistle 'To my Honoured Kinsman, John Driden, of Chesterton'.

Some critics have professed to see in the epistle to John Driden a restatement and confirmation of principles maintained by the poet throughout his work.[82] Support is lent to this view by Dryden's own interpretation of the poem as a kind of manifesto:

> In the description which I have made of a parliament man, I think I have not only drawn the features of my worthy kinsman, but have also given my own opinion, of what an Englishman in parliament ought to be; and deliver it as a memorial of my own principles to all posterity.   (*Letters, p.* 120)

But Dryden would not have written in this way of independent country members at the time of the Exclusion Crisis. To see him maintaining unchanged through changing circumstances a certain set of principles is to ignore the extent to which Dryden's ideology is, rather than a fixed structure, a flexible expression of his sense of the pressures and needs of the moment and his ability to influence events. And the problem of modification of principle to accommodate the Revolution was not Dryden's alone, but was faced by men of both parties whose sense of political structure and appropriate solutions had been overturned.

The epistle to John Driden was published in 1700, in the short interval between two wars that were fought chiefly for the purpose of containing the territorial ambitions of Louis XIV, and that were to have a profound effect on the internal economic and political life of England.[83] The restored Stuart monarchy had done its best to model itself on French absolutism, or, where unsuccessful, at least to live under its shadow and with its financial support. William III made it his life's work to control the growing power of France. In spite of some agitation for war with France in the late 1670s, the opposition to Charles's French alliance had no constructive foreign policy to offer. William's involvement of England in continental war completely changed the terms in which the nation's international position was seen. The means by which the king had come to the throne, the nature of his support, his method of ruling, his foreign policy, the influence of his wars on financial institutions and class structure, all these new conditions changed the basis of political issues and party divisions and made the England of 1700 totally different from that of 1685. The Whigs of Charles's reign had been distinguished by their zeal for personal liberties, parliamentary reform, and opposition to the prerogative; the Tories by their support of the prerogative, their reliance on the ideas of divine right and non-resistance. These divisions were thrown into confusion by the Revolution: Whigs nurtured on the idea of opposition were now the supporters of a monarch; the Tory ideology which had arisen in reaction to attacks on the hereditary rights of James collapsed with the flight of the man whose presence made it meaningful, and who, by pressing too hard, had revealed its inconsistencies. It seems that in the early years of William's reign men had difficulty in identifying each other by party. People were forced to talk about new and old, or court and country Whigs, or new (or country) and old (or Jacobite) Tories, or simply court and country. By the 1690s a process of redefinition was taking place.[84] A new Toryism emerged, under the leadership of Robert Harley (who metamorphosed in an active political career from dissenter and Whig to churchman and Tory), consisting of a fusion of Tory and Whig country interests, opposed both to old high-prerogative Tories and to new ministerial Whigs. At the same time as the new Tories became associated with old Whig ideas such as opposition to prerogative, the executive, and placemen in parliament, the new Whigs were disburdening themselves of their old radical connections and were now supporters of strong centralised government. The essential conservatism of the country party, the new Tories, found expression in antagonism to the new taxes, the Whig-supported financial innovations, the standing army, and the continental war. The divisions are not as clear cut as they were to be in the reign of Anne. The new country party had its Jacobite wing, and embraced the country Whigs who had once supported Shaftesbury. But what is involved is not just a changeover of positions, a change in the composition of court and country. Because of the development of political events Toryism as a set of principles had to develop.

Partly because of the date of Dryden's death, the full implications of the new Toryism are not relevant to nor explored in his work. For a sense of the potentialities and the frustrations of early eighteenth-century Toryism as a political and poetic creed we must turn to Pope. But an examination of the reformation of party after the Revolution explains why it was possible for the non-juring Dryden, a Catholic and divine-right Tory, to modify the principles implied by these epithets so as to be able to use his cousin Driden, a Williamite and country Whig, as the mouthpiece for his principles. Dryden's sense of political society, of the public role of the individual, is certainly very different in this poem from that expressed in the Stuart panegyrics. But if it is true that he was now disburdened of the public world, that in the last decade of his life the king as an idea meant nothing to him,[85] if he had inevitably lost one imaginative dimension, yet he had gained another. Dryden's close connection (although not a personal one) with the Stuart court as a political and moral centre meant, in spite of his insistence on the importance of the relationship between crown and parliament, monarch and subject, that he had little sympathy for the country point of view, for opposition to the innovations of the crown based on a conservative adherence to traditional society. Dryden seems to have had none of Jonson's sense of the customary society, of the far-reaching network of social relationships; his idea of the relationship of subject to king is familial and psychological rather than historical or geographical. The fact that by force of circumstances he ceased to be a supporter of the court meant that he was brought into contact with a complex of country attitudes from which he had been alienated not so much by temperament as by necessity.

His turning to the idea of the independent country gentleman as a source of political stability and moral worth reflects the principles underlying the country opposition to Charles in the early part of his reign, before criticism had been deflected from his evil advisers to the king himself. Dryden now became aware of the importance of the qualities that Marvell celebrated in *Last Instructions*: independence, loyalty, honesty, and (if necessary) obstinacy.[86] But what is interesting in 'To My Honoured Kinsman' is the fact that in spite of his new association with country principles Dryden still retained his sense of society as built on a system of correspondences and analogies; in his opposition role he still saw unity. It was a position that anticipated that of Pope; but without Pope's awareness of the anomalies inherent in it.[87]

The epistle to John Driden is another addition to the seventeenth-century development of the Horatian retirement poem, a tradition that Dryden amplifies and also undercuts. We might expect him in political opposition and without an official function to set up a simple antithesis between court and country, between public vices and private virtues, between luxury and utility. But Dryden rejects both the ethical and political implications of such an antithesis. After so many years as a public spokesman, he would have seen it as a kind of defeat to restrict his literary and moral universe to the sphere of private conduct. And the way he sees his heroes as actors both in the present and in history, as self-explaining and symbolic figures, suggests that he did not believe that the individual can be limited to a private sphere of action. For Dryden the private is subsumed in, not antithetical to, the public.[88]

Thus his cousin John Driden is a man who exists in both spheres: he steers 'betwixt the country and the court' (Kinsley, IV, 1533, *l.* 128); he is politically independent and uncommitted to ethical extremes. It is not apparent from the first half of the poem (to *l.* 116) that the retirement theme will be modified in this way. Driden is presented as the rural squire who displays the traditional virtues of justice, charity, and hospitality, who enjoys the traditional pleasures of hunting (tasting, not devouring them [*l.* 61]); his way of life is embodied in the idea of health. But this way of life is not restricted; Driden is both country squire and member of parliament. Hence Dryden says

> You hoard not health, for your own private use;
> But on the public spend the rich produce. (*ll.* 117–18)

With this transition we find a correspondingly development in style; the plain style of the first 16 lines, which are a straightforward adaptation of Horace, gives way gradually to the figurative style of ascending analogy appropriate to great subjects. The rural squire among his neighbours grows into the member of parliament exercising his public office who in turn is symbolic of England's relation with Europe. Although the poem does fall into two halves, its shape is not an opposition but rather consists of the parts of a conceit or a series of interlocking analogies.

At the centre of the poem is his cousin's quality of mind; its nature is established in the first paragraph:

> How blessed is he, who leads a country life,
> Unvexed with anxious cares, and void of strife!
> Who studying peace, and shunning civil rage,
> Enjoyed his youth, and now enjoys his age. (*ll.* 1–4)

The way in which this quality is to be the central point of reference throughout the poem is early made clear by the description of the peace effected through Driden's legal judgements; it is

> Like your own soul, serene; a pattern of your mind.
> (*l.* 16)

The cycle of Driden's life is emblematic of the national life, just as the hare he hunts is emblematic of his:

> The hare, in pastures or in plains is found,
> Emblem of human life, who runs the round;
> And, after all his wandering ways are done,
> His circle fills, and ends where he begun,
> Just as the setting meets the rising sun.　　(*ll.* 62–6)

This cyclical image should indicate to us that the simple opposition between country and court, the enjoyment of hunting by Driden and by princes (probably James II), will not be maintained. In the second half of the poem, where Driden's public activities are introduced, his significance as an emblem becomes apparent. His peace of mind, the peace of his rural life, imply peace between the parties and England's peace with Europe. Driden's rural retreat suggests England's retreat from European affairs:

> Enough for Europe has our Albion fought:
> Let us enjoy the peace our blood has bought.　　(*ll.* 158–9)

England is described in terms of the Stoic, self-sufficient individual who is characteristically the subject of the retirement poem:

> Safe in our selves, while on our selves we stand,
> The sea is ours, and that defends the land.　　(*ll.* 146–7)

Thus the idea of peace is explored at the individual, social, political, and national levels. Driden's halfway position between country and court is similarly developed. His division of his time between rural and city occupations becomes a definition of patriotism: the patriot, who is neither Tory nor Whig, serves both king and country (*l.* 171). His balanced allegiances typify the balanced constitution. The image of Driden as a bachelor living without marital strife in his rural Eden before the fall is taken up again to indicate how the exercise of reasonable government free from faction will make England also an Eden:

> Betwixt the prince and parliament we stand;
> The barriers of the state on either hand:
> May neither overflow, for then they drown the land.
> When both are full, they feed our blessed abode;
> Like those, that watered once, the paradise of God.
> 　　　　　　　　　　　　　　　　　　(*ll.* 175–9)

This passage, both in its ideas and in its characteristic imagery, is a restatement of the theory found often in Dryden's writings, the moderate constitutionalist view that king and parliament have distinct and mutually supporting functions under the law. But Dryden's theories are not to be read out of the context of the poems that give them life. The similarity between this passage and, for example, that in *The Medal* quoted earlier should not conceal the different use to which theory is put in different situations. One cannot really isolate the theory of constitutional royalism, any more than absolute sovereignty and divine right, and say that the positions involved constitute Dryden's ultimate beliefs.[89] Although Dryden's interpretation of the situation in *Absalom and Achitophel* was partly in terms of support or disruption of law, nevertheless under pressure his allegiance was to monarchy, whether working within or without law, since decision on this matter was not seen to be within the purview of the subject. Dryden cannot be said to have been independent in his support of Charles. But his antagonism to the Revolution Settlement meant that he would not tolerate in William abuses of the prerogative he would pass over or defend in Charles. Thus in the epistle to John Driden we find an interesting distinction between king and law verging on the distinction between the king's natural and political body made by the parliamentarians to justify their actions in the civil war; one cannot imagine that Dryden would have countenanced such a distinction in his period as Stuart apologist.

The demands of war and peace are seen to alter the balance of power in favour of king and parliament respectively. The current period of peace after the Treaty of Ryswick thus implies an assertion of privilege against prerogative. As a type of the independent country gentleman who realises these principles in action, Dryden takes his and his cousin's mutual grandfather Sir Erasmus Dryden, who was imprisoned under Charles I for his refusal to pay a forced loan.[90] The whole passage is worth quoting because of its heavy reliance on parliamentarian and Whiggish phraseology and attitudes:

> Patriots, in peace, assert the people's right;
> With noble stubbornness resisting might:
> No lawless mandates from the court receive,
> Nor lend by force; but in a body give.
> Such was your generous grandsire; free to grant
> In parliaments, that weighed their prince's want:
> But so tenacious of the common cause,
> As not to lend the king against his laws.
> And, in a loathsome dungeon doomed to lie,
> In bonds retained his birthright liberty,
> And shamed oppression, till it set him free. (*ll.* 184–94)

Patriot, right, common cause, liberty – these are words and ideas we associate with the parties of Pym and Shaftesbury. The poem is a clear indication of the metamorphosis of Toryism in the years after the Revolution. The contemporary significance of the lines on Erasmus

Dryden seems to be a defence of parliament's right to refuse supplies for a standing army in peace. Dryden voices the cluster of Tory attitudes that were to be more clearly defined in the next decade in reaction to the second war against France: dislike of continental involvement, isolationism, preference of naval to land war, opposition to extensions of the prerogative, reliance on the influence of independent country members. Dryden's poem enables us to see the inner logic of this metamorphosis.

In structure and tone, in its use of an individual as model for society, 'To my Honoured Kinsman' differs greatly from the panegyrics and political poems where Dryden's preoccupation is with public modes of action. Dryden's deliberate remoulding of the retirement theme, his contrasting of the general and specific meanings of court, country, and peace, give the poem its idiosyncratic tone of wit and seriousness. The absence of urgency makes it possible for him to proceed carefully outwards from the state of one man's mind to that of the nation. Our admiration of the character established at the beginning of the poem is intended to lead logically to agreement with Dryden's view of the stable society.

Yet the tone and structure, the associations of the Horatian epistle, the idea of public life as an extension of private virtue, these can be seen to have been forced on Dryden by political events. The place of the public poet had gone with the court, the idea of kingship, the combination of emotional and political attitudes that supported it. Under the Stuarts the conservative mind had been able to find satisfaction as much in defence of as in opposition to the crown. With the political and, more important, the institutional and economic changes at the end of the century, the central government came to seem like a powerful and threatening machine run by a self-perpetuating group of men who ignored the needs and interests of the rest of the country. A conservative sense of order and proper social relationships could now only be expressed as a reaction against what existed. To see how the paradox of a vision of order for a world that seems to have rejected it can be resolved poetically we must turn to the poetry of Pope.

Chapter 5

Alexander Pope: the decline of
a public myth

DISCORDIA CONCORS

Like Dryden, Pope found his idealised view of his poetic function challenged by events, but in a more important and permanent way. Pope inherited the Renaissance idea that the poet should act as legislator and reformer, that his position should be at the centre of society, supported by and supporting government, but political developments placed him after 1714 on the fringes of society and in opposition to those in power. His poetic dilemma reflected the political dilemma of the Tories; while considering themselves representatives of the nation at large they found themselves excluded from power and influence and condemned to impotent opposition. As a result of this political paradox Pope was forced to redefine his poetic role. His view of poetry as the making of a viable myth of order gave way to a poetic vision in which disorder was the norm; instead of synthesizing experience his poetry grew out of the disjunction between ideal and actual, in the opposition of the isolated poet to society as a whole.

In his first important public poem, *Windsor Forest*, published in 1713, the year of the Treaty of Utrecht, the year that was to vindicate Tory propaganda, Pope envisaged the effects of peace: British imperialism would triumph, liberty and concord would spread through the world, persecution, faction, and rebellion would be extinguished. Thirty years later, after the practical intentions of the Tory peace had to some extent been carried out by Walpole, the only empire that Pope found himself able to celebrate in his last great work, *The Dunciad* of 1743, was the restoration of dulness and chaos. In his last defence of his satiric methods of the 1730s, the *Epilogue to the Satires* of 1738, Pope indicated that he had lost his faith in the regenerative power of a national poetic myth; Waller and Boileau could not vindicate Cromwell and Louis XIV, nor would Pope make a god of George II. Flattery simply conceals, distorts, spins 'cobwebs o'er the eye of day';[1] a lie in verse is the same as a lie in prose.[2] In his late satires, the *Epistle to Dr Arbuthnot* and the *Imitations of Horace*, Pope rejects the creative means of myth for the stripping, revealing power of ridicule. Against the falsifications of flattery and the self-betrayal of the poet who perpetuates myths, Pope sets truth as the goal and the vindication of the proud poet who confronts society.

Yet Pope tried to avoid the implications of reinterpreting his role in this way; it did not seem to him that the change in technique involved any change in his outlook. Satire can legitimately be seen as the obverse of panegyric, with the same ethical principles underlying both. Thus in *Windsor Forest* the barbaric actuality of William the Conqueror's England is the inversion of the promise of Queen Anne's peace. The triumph of dulness in *The Dunciad* is the consequence of the destruction of the chain of order which is the subject of the *Essay on Man*. Pope would not have considered that a portrayal of the collapse of contemporary society implied a collapse of the metaphysical structure against which society is measured. His obsessive attempt to find unity and correspondence on the political, social, and metaphysical levels, to synthesise reality, is reflected in the ambitious ethical system which occupied him for five years, and of which the *Essay on Man* and the *Epistles to Several Persons* are only weighty fragments. The last detailed exposition of this scheme appeared in the 'death-bed' *Epistles to Several Persons* of 1744, long after Pope had ceased attempting to make the published form of his work conform to it; but he was still able to indicate where his existing works would fit in the superimposed design of the vast *Essay on Man*.[3] The structure of the projected *Essay* shows that Pope tried to see man and society as a whole; every aspect of human behaviour has its place in the pattern. The scheme falls into four parts. The first consists of the existing *Essay on Man*; the second covers mainly the working of the human mind and its effects: reason, arts and sciences, and the use of learning; the third, politics; and the last, private ethics. Although the last work that Pope published as an acknowledged part of the ethical scheme was *Of the Characters of Women* in 1735, the *Imitations of Horace* can be seen to touch on the last category, and Pope pointed out that *The Dunciad* and the projected epic on Brutus fitted into the second and third categories respectively.

Although Pope clung to this ambitious scheme to the end, it is important to realise that his neat analysis is essentially inaccurate. He abandoned the structure after about 1735 not so much because he was tired of it[4] but because it did not represent his final views of the disordered state of man and society. He no longer saw human life as a harmony of balanced parts but as a conflict of contradictions. The rationalised prose plan shows that he did not voluntarily accept the implications of his poems. Like his predecessor Dryden, Pope wanted to write a national epic. Although his projected epic on Brutus seems to have been worked out in some detail, he never wrote more than a few lines;[5] and it seems unlikely, given that his last work was the revised

176

Dunciad, that if he had lived he would have added much to it. Pope believed that only the poet with the moral capacity to distinguish and exemplify the 'perfect form of civil government'[6] was entitled to attack existing society. *Windsor Forest* clearly embodies such a view of the poet's function; in this poem the threat of reality is balanced by the promise of the ideal. But Pope came to distrust the role of the national poet, which seemed to him ultimately partisan. He told Spence that 'the *Aeneid* was evidently a party piece, as much as *Absalom and Achitophel*'.[7] Pope ultimately had no public ideal to offer as the counterpart to the progress of vice of the *Epilogue to the Satires* or the empire of dulness of *The Dunciad*. His answer is not the ideal society, the unified concept of man of the ethical scheme, but the virtuous few who withdraw from society, who act in spite of it. Pope's ethics are finally private, and his concern is how one man can live.[8]

The breakdown of Pope's unified view of the world, his own limitation of his role as a poet to that of an outsider, and his opposition of the private ethics of benevolence to a hostile economic and political system can be attributed to many things: to his isolation as a Catholic, his financial independence after the success of his Homer, his freedom from the demands of court and political patronage, but mostly to his interpretation of the state of political society. Paradoxically the Toryism that was the basis of the cosmic synthesis of the *Essay on Man* led at the same time to the view that the England of the 1730s was hopelessly disrupted and that the only answer was in personal retreat. Before turning to the causes of Pope's adoption of this view, I shall consider those poems in which he makes out of visible fragmentation an ideal synthesis on the political and metaphysical levels, *Windsor Forest* and the *Essay on Man*.

Windsor Forest, Pope's most serious attempt at a partisan and programmatic public exhortation, was in its final version the product of a period in his life when he was trying hard to resist party conflict. It was difficult for a man at any time in Anne's reign to avoid declaring himself either a Whig or a Tory, but men of both parties were unhappy that this was true. In *The Spectator* Addison and Steele deplored the fierce antagonism felt at all levels of society, and in several letters to his friend Caryll in 1713 and 1714 Pope repeated their unconvincing claim of the irrelevance of party disagreement. The mere lip service paid to the idea of being above party by men of all sides is indicated by the fact that to Pope Steele seemed one of the most factious offenders.[9] Pope tried to keep himself non-partisan by writing in the year of the Treaty of Utrecht both his Tory *Windsor Forest* and a prologue to the Whig *Cato*, but this dalliance with both parties did not last long; although courted by both Addison and Swift, the opposing propagandists, he was shortly to leave his Whig friends.[10] Pope's claim to be above party (a claim he repeated throughout his life) can at this stage of his career be understood in terms of the nature of his Toryism. *Windsor Forest* is as much Tory propaganda as Swift's *Conduct of the Allies*; its anti-Williamite, even Jacobite tendencies (tendencies not in the least shared by Swift) have been pointed out.[11] The resurrection of Tory hopes in Anne's last years allowed Pope to see unity and continuity in political life in a way never again possible to him. The central political idea of the poem, expressed in the symbol of Windsor Forest, is that under Anne court and country are united. This reflects the Tory view that the Harley–St John ministry of 1710–14 (even though it seems to have been a shaky coalition of extremists and moderates) was truly representative of the nation as no Whig ministry could hope to be. The *Essay on Man* and the ethical scheme have as their theoretical basis the idea of harmony, of *discordia concors*, which underlies the view of nature and society in *Windsor Forest*.[12] With the Tory defeat of 1714 and the relegation of his friends to opposition, Pope was forced to abandon the political implication of this idea, his vision of a pax Britannica, with the imperial city of London as the centre and the controlling influence of universal wealth and freedom. But Pope only achieves his vision of the future in *Windsor Forest* by boldly reconciling those tensions and antagonisms in political society which form a central part of his indictment of the England of the 1730s in the *Epistles to Several Persons* and the *Imitations of Horace*. In *Windsor Forest*, appropriately enough, a poem written to celebrate peace, discord is sentenced to 'brazen bonds' and concord triumphs.[13]

The main theme of the poem is that conflicting elements in human nature and in political society may be creatively balanced and controlled to produce, instead of discord and destruction, their opposites, peace and plenty. Although *Windsor Forest* does not include the metaphysical sphere of the *Essay on Man*, Pope indicates the universality of this dialectical pattern by beginning his poem with a description of the physical forest, whose diverse characteristics imitate the world,

> Not chaos-like together crushed and bruised,
> But as the world, harmoniously confused:
> Where order in variety we see,
> And where, though all things differ, all agree.
>
> (1, 149–50, *ll.* 13–16)

The ordered variety of the countryside allows its profitable exploitation; the forest oaks promise the import of luxuries and colonial expansion, and the fields harvest. The divergent profits of land and trade are summed up as 'peace and plenty' (*l.* 42). The phrase 'Ceres' gifts' (*l.* 39) anticipates Pope's later warning to Timon in the *Epistle to Burlington*:

Another age shall see the golden ear
Imbrown the slope, and nod on the parterre,
Deep harvests bury all his pride has planned,
And laughing Ceres re-assume the land.

(III ii, 154, *ll.* 173–6)

To be justified every person and thing should stand in a potentially useful relationship to everything else, and the hierarchy of these relationships should be clearly maintained. Thus rural Windsor reflects the harmonious pattern of the universe, and its component elements of trees and fields have values and uses outside the rural sphere. The disastrous effect of the inversion of such relationships is illustrated in the next section of the poem, the description of William I's misused New Forest, and the state of England under him.

In contrasting Windsor Forest with the New Forest, and the reign of the Stuart Anne with that of the Conqueror William, Pope is implicitly condemning the government of William III and his policy of military containment of France. Tory antipathy to the involvement of an English army in continental affairs is reflected in the emphasis throughout the poem on the importance of the navy and colonial trade. William I's ravaged New Forest implies Tory fears, expressed so often by Swift in his political pamphlets, that England's resources were being wasted in the War of the Spanish Succession; Anne's peace would divert English energies from wasteful continental war to profitable colonial empire.[14] Regardless of its historical accuracy, the contrast between William and Anne is essential to the poem in showing the ideal relation of the monarch to his subjects and the proper balance and exploitation of resources in political society.

The devastated England of William I results from neglect of the hierarchy of use and value. The New Forest replaces populated country; cultivated land gives way to 'a dreary desert and a gloomy waste' (*l.* 44); in order that the king may hunt the farmer relinquishes his land 'and famished dies amidst his ripened fields' (*l.* 56), and in his place the beast is fed. The example of the forest implies the state of society as a whole:

The fields are ravished from the industrious swains,
From men their cities, and from gods their fanes:
The levelled towns with weeds lie covered o'er,
The hollow winds through naked temples roar.   (*ll.* 65–8)

The scale of values by which civilisation is maintained is abandoned: hunting replaces industry, beasts are valued before men, towns and fields turn into deserts, destruction overcomes prosperity. This national disintegration is the work of a tyrant 'furious and severe' (*l.* 46).

Against this threat of destruction is set the hope of order and prosperity under Queen Anne's peace. The difference between the government of the two monarchs is reflected in the contrast between the two forests. The Conqueror's New Forest is imposed upon the people at their expense, it violates order in nature and society; Windsor Forest mirrors the various harmony of the world not only in its physical nature but also in the fact that it encompasses both rural England and the seat of government. The New Forest expresses the antagonism of monarch to subject; Windsor Forest is both court and country. Hence in the Virgilian passage on the happiness of country life (*ll.* 237–58) Pope (here departing from *Georgic* II) finds no antagonism between this way of life and that of courtier and politician. In the *discordia concors* of national life everyone has his place without any resulting tension between the several roles. Anne's peace resolves the previous conflicts of English history, the

> dreadful series of intestine wars,
> Inglorious triumphs, and dishonest scars.   (*ll.* 325–6)

Father Thames predicts the consequence of the new confidence and unity in court and country. Men who would have been wasted in foreign war will 'tend the flocks, or reap the bearded grain' (*l.* 370); warlike propensities will be satisfied with the peaceful hunt. The nation's wealth will be reflected in private and public building; villas will fill the Thames valley, while London will be covered with 'glittering spires, ...the beauteous works of peace' (*ll.* 377–8). Chief of all, a new Whitehall will stand between the cities of London and Westminster. London will inherit the fame and role of Rome; it will dominate the world not through military conquest but through free trade:

> The time shall come, when free as seas or wind
> Unbounded Thames shall flow for all mankind,
> Whole nations enter with each swelling tide,
> And seas but join the regions they divide. (*ll.* 397–400)

And one of the final effects of peace, it is hoped, will be the universal achievement of English prosperity and stability, until

> Peru once more a race of kings behold,
> And other Mexicos be roofed with gold.   (*ll.* 411–12)

The ultimate effect of such balanced harmony in political life, then, is not merely prosperity for Anne's subjects, but the development of a national ethos, symbolised in new public works and especially in the Whitehall where

> mighty nations shall inquire their doom,
> The world's great oracle in times to come.   (*ll.* 381–2)

Pope's political vision is here not isolationist, though there is some confusion in his idea of the complex role England is to play. England's prosperity is to result partly from the extension of colonial trade brought about by the peace, and her wealth supporting her political power is to make her dominate the world; yet at the same time by this influence she is to provide both example and means for other states to achieve comparable prosperity. This idea is a peaceful echo of the view of England's role in world politics found in Addison's *A Letter from Italy* (1701):[15]

> 'Tis Britain's care to watch o'er Europe's fate,
> And hold in balance each contending state,
> To threaten bold presumptuous kings with war,
> And answer her afflicted neighbours' prayer.

In the face of Whig insistence on continental involvement, Pope offers a far more daring and extended imperial vision. But he seems not to see that the exploitation involved in England's colonial expansion prohibits the regeneration of states such as Peru and Mexico; a dominant England is incompatible with the idea of a multiplicity of prosperous and free nations. Yet England's dominance is essential to his view of the hierarchical structure of political life.

It is Anne, with the omnipotence of God in the *Essay on Man*, who surmounts the hierarchy and unites the contraries of political life in harmony. Although Virgil's *Georgics* are the prototype of the moral, topographical genre in which Pope is working, he ignores the implications of Virgil's movement from the countryside to the court. Virgil's farmer embodies the virtues which made Rome great; civil war can be averted by a return to the ancient foundations on which Roman society was built. In *Windsor Forest* the Tory country ideal is implied, but Pope's retired man does not only serve this function; he exemplifies rather the diversity of life possible in the ideally balanced political society. *Windsor Forest* is in some ways Pope's most public political poem. Harmony is not disrupted by individual vice, but by the monarch who, like William I, ignores the proper scale of social values. Pope indicates the monarch's role in controlling and directing the quality of political life; government is the chain binding human beings together sociably.

Windsor Forest is confidently hopeful yet not absurdly so, for the destruction of society in William's England is a recurrent historical possibility. But the faith in the constructive effect of government imposed on society which underlay the writing of this poem was not to last Pope long. After 1714 Pope was at first indifferent and later hostile to the successive Whig governments, and outside court influence; his view of the antitheses inherent in political society became more complex; Walpole's years of peace and prosperity did not satisfy the prophecy of *Windsor Forest*. But Pope did not easily give up his early vision of concord. In the 1730s, shortly before he came to depict the incurable antagonisms in political society in the *Imitations of Horace*, Pope planned his 'ethic scheme' and in the *Essay on Man* set out the universal pattern on the principle of harmony in discord which underlies *Windsor Forest*.

In the *Essay on Man* Pope attempted to give a coherent view of man, society, and the universe, based essentially on traditional theology. In scope it is his most intellectually ambitious poem, but in the problems it raises and the solutions it offers it is largely conventional. Some of the poem's failures of cohesion and persuasion are intrinsic in the subject matter; they can also be attributed to the fact that the poem appeared on the eve of the Enlightenment. In writing the *Essay on Man* Pope had to deal with the lack of a controlling mythology.[16] It may seem odd that he should have undertaken so abstract a work when we consider that in writing satire he was so conscious of the need for the specific image, the living example which would lend focus and meaning to his general ideas. But for my purposes it is more useful to see the poem's difficulties in terms of the relation of Pope's philosophical attitudes to his political position. On the one hand Pope, who remained intellectually committed to the position of 'cosmic toryism',[17] felt the need to provide a poetic statement of the underlying consistency of his religious and political view of the world; yet on the other hand the very failings and tendencies of the poem itself indicate his inability to transfer the universal pattern to the state of the world around him and his own place in it. These failures can be related not only, as is sometimes done, to the question of the irrelevancy of traditional Christian harmony to the eighteenth-century world, but to the irrelevancy of such harmony to Pope's concurrent view of the nature of political society.[18]

The *Essay on Man* was to be only a 'general map of man', which was to be filled out in detail in the later epistles of the ethic scheme.[19] The map is an explanation, *sub specie aeternitatis*, of the pattern inherent in three planes, the universe, society, and man, a pattern expressed both by harmony through discord and by a chain of order. These planes are the subjects of the first three epistles, though Pope does not follow the pattern inwards; he proceeds from the universe to man, and then outwards to society, since his psychological theories are necessary to his explanation of social structure. In the last epistle, whose subject is happiness, the point of view changes from the divine to the human, and it is here that the dazzling efficiency of Pope's all-encompassing structure begins to give way. The theme on which Pope insists throughout is the relation of the parts to the whole, of man to his fellows; but he is finally unable to create a bridge from the universal to the individual.

The interdependence of the component parts of the universe, the 'vast chain of being' (*Ep.* I, *l.* 237), is reflected by the interdependence of creatures within society, the 'chain of love' (*Ep.* III, *l.* 7). This phrase is used metaphorically to describe the attraction of atoms but literally to describe the relations of men. Society works by a system of the mutual fulfilment of needs, so that the man whose place in the structure is restricted is not denied importance nor happiness:

> God, in the nature of each being, founds
> Its proper bliss, and sets its proper bounds:
> But as he framed a whole, the whole to bless,
> On mutual wants built mutual happiness.
>
> (*Ep.* III, *ll.* 109–12)

Thus the difference in the conditions of men, which might be thought to make for tension and misery in society, is seen to have rather the opposite effect:

> Heaven to mankind impartial we confess,
> If all are equal in their happiness:
> But mutual wants this happiness increase,
> All nature's difference keeps all nature's peace.
>
> (*Ep.* IV, *ll.* 53–6)

Social harmony thus imitates both in order and in apparent tension the universal structure:

> Such is the world's great harmony, that springs
> From order, union, full consent of things!
> Where small and great, where weak and mighty, made
> To serve, not suffer, strengthen, not invade,
> More powerful each as needful to the rest,
> And, in proportion as it blesses, blest,
> Draw to one point, and to one centre bring
> Beast, man, or angel, servant, lord, or king.
>
> (*Ep.* III, *ll.* 295–302)

This harmony also has its parallel in man's psychological consistency. The moving principles of human nature, reason and self-love (*Ep.* II, *l.* 54), are apparently but not actually self-contradictory; in fact

> Self-love and reason to one end aspire. (*Ep.* II, *l.* 87)

Seeming inconsistencies of character are controlled by one ruling passion (*Ep.* II, *l.* 123 ff.). Although such a passion, since it may tend either to vice or virtue (*Ep.* II, *ll.* 195–202), may appear to be potentially anti-social, the very diversity of these passions, in keeping with the general theme of order in variety, has beneficial social implications:

> Whate'er the passion, knowledge, fame, or pelf,
> Not one will change his neighbour with himself.
> The learned is happy nature to explore,
> The fool is happy that he knows no more;

The rich is happy in the plenty given,
The poor contents him with the care of heaven.

(*Ep.* II, *ll.* 261–6)

Pope has other devices for insisting on the naturalness of government
and man's reconciliation to the inequities of the social structure. He
uses both Hobbesian and anti-Hobbesian arguments in his effort to
show that government is desirable and profitable to all. Thus on the
one hand he states a pessimistic view of society:

The same self-love, in all, becomes the cause
Of what restrains him, government and laws.

(*Ep.* III, *ll.* 271–2)

But he can also argue for the benevolent origin of government:

The state of nature was the reign of God:
Self-love and social at her birth began,
Union the bond of all things, and of man.

(*Ep.* III, *ll.* 148–50)

Thus God and nature linked the general frame,
And bade self-love and social be the same.

(*Ep.* III, *ll.* 317–18)

Pope thus tries to show that his universal scheme encompasses not only
the relative positions of men in society but also their apparently conflicting
but mutually interacting desires and actions. The scheme is both a
static model and a process.

But here the question arises of how this scheme is related to the
individual life. The human problem can be solved by relating it to
a universal structure, by looking at it from the point of view of the
creator:

He, who through vast immensity can pierce,
See worlds on worlds compose one universe,
Observe how system into system runs,
What other planets circle other suns,
What varied being peoples every star,
May tell why heaven has made us as we are.

(*Ep.* I, *ll.* 23–8)

Evil is reduced by insisting on its relativity; God sees 'with equal eye'

A hero perish, or a sparrow fall,
Atoms or systems into ruin hurled,
And now a bubble burst, and now a world.

(*Ep.* I, *ll.* 88–90)

Nevertheless human life must be lived; and Pope, although he tries hard, having established his pattern, to work outwards again from the individual, cannot really show that his solution for individual life is necessarily related to the universal structure.

From God's point of view, the scheme is a statement of what is; and whatever is, is right. For Pope to state this is both pessimistic and complacent; pessimistic in that it is a reproof to human aspiration, complacent, in that it involves acceptance of and satisfaction with the existing social structure. But from the human point of view the scheme is essentially a statement of what might be; it exists as an ideal to which human behaviour should conform, and as Pope is only too anxious to show, much behaviour threatens to disrupt it. The moral and social problem for Pope seems to be whether one should take order or disorder as the norm against which to measure the tendencies of individual action. Seen with the eye of God, all human contradictions should work finally to eliminate themselves, so that they are easily encompassed by universal order; seen with the eye of man, these contradictions threaten to destroy the scheme of which they should form a part.

The emotion which threatens the whole foundation is pride. Pride is the negation of the idea of order:

> In pride, in reasoning pride, our error lies;
> All quit their sphere, and rush into the skies.
>
> *(Ep.* i, *ll.* 123–4)

Pope sees the structure as being particularly vulnerable; the whole comes crashing down as a result of the slightest attempt to break outside its restrictions:

> On superior powers
> Were we to press, inferior might on ours:
> Or in the full creation leave a void,
> Where, one step broken, the great scale's destroyed:
> From nature's chain whatever link you strike,
> Tenth or ten thousandth, breaks the chain alike.
>
> *(Ep.* i, *ll.* 241–6)

In the fourth epistle, where the problem is one of individual action, of the achievement of human happiness, Pope assumes that the scheme, at least on the social and individual levels, has failed. In the intellectual sphere the answer to pride is submission, acceptance of the pattern imposed by God; but in the social and moral spheres the answer is more complex. What is required in the last is that the individual should recreate in his own life the pattern that has ceased to be evident in society.

In *Epistle* ii Pope argued that the ruling passion helped to make men satisfied with their relative situations. In *Epistle* iv he approaches the

185

idea of happiness from various angles, not all of them consistent. Happiness is open to all, regardless of place, though 'health, peace, and competence' (*Ep.* IV, *l.* 80) are later seen as prerequisites; further on, Pope leaves this Aristotelian position for the Stoic view that 'virtue alone is happiness below' (*Ep.* IV, *l.* 310). There is a real antagonism between the pattern according to which the individual should live and the pattern by which society does live. The virtuous man must attempt to live by the universal scale which God sees, and to set this against the false scale of happiness of wealth, honour, fame, and greatness (*Ep.* IV, *ll.* 287-8) by which society lives. We have here the essence of the antagonism between the individual and society which results in Pope's idealisation of himself and his virtuous friends in the *Epistles to Several Persons* and the *Imitations of Horace*.

However in the *Essay on Man* Pope does not admit the inevitability of the antagonism, although the solutions he recommends imply such an inevitability. It is only the virtuous man who is able to detect the universal chain, yet somehow the 'close system of benevolence' (*Ep.* IV, *l.* 358) which is to be his pattern of behaviour must extend throughout society. The regeneration of society is to come not from the imposition of order from without (as Anne created peace in *Windsor Forest*), but from the development of order outwards from the individual to society, as he comes to detect each link in the chain:

> God loves from whole to parts: but human soul
> Must rise from individual to the whole.
> Self-love but serves the virtuous mind to wake,
> As the small pebble stirs the peaceful lake;
> The centre moved, a circle straight succeeds,
> Another still, and still another spreads,
> Friend, parent, neighbour, first it will embrace,
> His country next, and next all human race,
> Wide and more wide, the o'erflowings of the mind
> Take every creature in, of every kind;
> Earth smiles around, with boundless bounty blessed
> And heaven beholds its image in his breast.
>
> (*Ep.* IV, *ll.* 361-72)

As expressed in this simile, each man's self-love should lead to an appreciation of the chain and should naturally make him fulfil his place in it. From the point of view of God, he does. But Pope knows that the social chain has broken down, that the system of benevolence encompasses few members, and that benevolence is, at best, a limited, private tool. There is no way to reconcile God's and man's view of the system.

THE TORY DILEMMA

In *Windsor Forest* and the *Essay on Man* Pope attempts, while recognising the contradictions between the ideal and the actual, between God's view and man's, to synthesise these opposites by means of the ideas of harmony in discord and reconciled extremes. In the *Imitations of Horace* and *The Dunciad*, however, this attempt at synthesis breaks down; these poems assume an impassable gulf between society's actual corruption and its ideal fulfilment, between society's indifference to truth and the poet's attempts at persuasion. This change in Pope's technique and outlook, from celebration to satire, from public myth to self-reliance, can best be understood in terms of the nature of Toryism and its development. Pope's attitudes to his role as a poet in society, to monarchy, land, money, the relations of the members of the political nation, were all strongly influenced by the political and social events that changed Toryism from a national to an opposition ideology.

One of the main differences between *Windsor Forest* and the *Essay on Man* lies in the fact that in the later work Pope has very little to say about the nature and power of government. Although the *Essay on Man* is based on the traditional concept of the frame of order which was often used in the sixteenth and seventeenth centuries for the political support of monarchy, Pope excludes the significant relation of God in the universe to the king in society. The ideal king of the *Essay on Man* is benevolent and just, but there is no sense that he can either undo or create social order as William I and Anne respectively are seen to do in *Windsor Forest*. Pope's reluctance to attribute a larger role to monarchy in the 1730s should be related to the inevitable antagonism of a Tory sympathiser and friend of displaced Tories towards the Hanoverian dynasty, and to his lack of a court role or voice. But this partisan attitude to monarchy rendered impossible the fulfilment of his hope for a regeneration of national life to be symbolised and effected by the building of public works and the development of public poetry. By the time that Bolingbroke attempted to counteract this sense of Tory alienation through his theory of the patriot king, Pope's own displacement had led him to turn his back on large political solutions.

Pope strongly regretted what he saw as the collapse of a valid symbolism to express and direct the relation of monarchy to people, of court to country, and hence he attacked bitterly, in the *Imitations of Horace* and *The Dunciad*, the perversion of such symbolism in the flatteries of the court and party hacks. But at the same time as he withdrew from the position of public poet and began to concentrate on living an honourable private life in a disrupted society, Pope continued to berate George II for his inadequate fulfilment of his duties and to advocate the programme

187

of public building which had formed an integral part of the development of England's imperial role in *Windsor Forest*. At the end of the *Epistle to Burlington* Pope gives his last and finest statement of the vision of *Windsor Forest*; he asks Burlington to proceed with his architectural successes

> Till kings call forth the ideas of your mind,
> Proud to accomplish what such hands designed,
> Bid harbours open, public ways extend,
> Bid temples, worthier of the God, ascend;
> Bid the broad arch the dangerous flood contain,
> The mole projected break the roaring main;
> Back to his bounds their subject sea command,
> And roll obedient rivers through the land;
> These honours, peace to happy Britain brings,
> These are imperial works, and worthy kings.
>
> (III ii, *pp.* 155–6, *ll.* 195–204)

But the unpublished *Master Key to Popery* indicates ironically that Pope had no real hope that George II would be persuaded in this way:

> There is something at the end of his epistle which looks like a compliment to the king: but sure 'tis a very strange one! just to single out the only good and great things which his Majesty has *not* done for his subjects. His Majesty may do them yet; but so much as I wish the public good, I can hardly desire it should be just at the time, when an impertinent poet prescribes it.[20]

Pope was not expressing a feeling peculiar to the enemies of the Hanoverian dynasty. Lord Hervey, Queen Caroline's confidant, pointed out the diminished national sense of reverence for monarchy as an institution and for George as its representative:

> The enlightened state of the nation with respect to any reverence due to the Crown further than the merit of the head that wore it might claim made very little come to his Majesty's share.[21]

The *Epistle to Augustus* (*Imitations of Horace, Ep.* II i) is a lengthy denigration of George II as a public figure, and criticises him for neglecting poetry as public support, by setting him against the standard of Augustus who 'prohibited all but the best writers to name him'.[22] The court's adoption of the city's commerical values described in *The Dunciad* precludes the realisation in Hanoverian England of the imperial vision Pope had put forward in Windsor Forest. Pope could not remake George II singlehanded; he told Spence in 1744 that 'kings now...[are] the worst things upon earth, they are turned mere tradesmen'.[23] He was appalled at the spectacle George I and the Prince of Wales made of themselves by their quarrel in 1717–18:

> Of late the great have been the shining examples of folly, public and private; and the best translation at this time of *O tempora! O mores!* would be O kings! O princes![24]

The political and social situation allowed Pope nothing but a private voice; as 'Lines to King George II' make clear, public recognition, the playing of Horace to George's Augustus, would involve him in the destructive flatteries of the dunces:

> O all-accomplished Caesar! on thy shelf
> If room for all Pope's works – and Pope himself:
>
> 'Tis true great bard, thou on my shelf shall lie
> With Oxford, Cowper, noble Strafford by:
> But for thy Windsor, a new fabric raise
> And there triumphant sing thy sovereign's praise. (VI, 392)

A *Windsor Forest* written for George II would have required Pope to repudiate the essential features of his conception of the good society; George the tradesman, whose court was dominated by commercial values, was not in Pope's view a national but a partisan monarch, a ruler who, although he did not effect it himself, was representative of the fragmentation of the political nation. Pope saw the Hanoverian court not as the pattern for nor the guide of the nation, but rather a reflection of the ambitions and values of one half of society; it was not the king who ruled, but his chief minister. Given such a situation, the only answer for a poet who hoped to be the spokesman of a unified, integrated society was to stand outside and attempt by satiric exposure to overthrow this unbalanced system. Unhappily for Pope, it was his own system, the cosmic synthesis of the *Essay on Man*, that lost the battle with capitalism and the development of party government.

Pope always liked to claim that he was an eclectic in philosophy and an independent in politics; it was a claim that was repeated several times in the *Imitations of Horace*:

> Sworn to no master, of no sect am I, (IV, *Ep.* I i, *l.* 24)

and,

> In moderation placing all my glory,
> While Tories call me Whig, and Whigs a Tory.
> (IV, *Sat.* II i, *ll.* 67–8)

This posture later on in his life differs from his attempt to be non-partisan during the perpetual party rancour of Anne's reign. By 1728, when Pope, after a long period of absorption in the apolitical work of translating Homer and editing Shakespeare (which involved much public controversy,

189

but mostly of a literary kind) emerged as a satirist, the political climate had changed a great deal. The opposition of parties in Anne's reign, which, though decried on all sides, had been based on real issues, had now virtually broken down, and partly labels had become confused; in spite of Bolingbroke's attempt to organise a coalition, the large and loosely connected group of Walpole's opponents lacked any unifying ideology until Bolingbroke formulated his largely unsuccessful idea of patriotism in the late 1730s. The fact that after the Hanoverian succession Pope had no political allegiance nor public role led him for a time to sentimentalise the idea of retirement from political life;[25] in 1718 he moved to Twickenham, while the year before he had written a letter to Atterbury defining his religious and political positions:

> In my politics, I think no further than how to preserve the peace of my life, in any government under which I live.... If I was born under an absolute prince, I would be a quiet subject.[26]

This pose of retirement in the years immediately following the Hanoverian succession was superficial and shortlived. Pope's political attitudes after 1714 passed through three distinct phases. Partly under the influence of Bolingbroke and Swift (whom he met again respectively in 1725 and 1726) Pope abandoned his political indifference and attempted to re-invigorate Tory ideology as a poetic myth in the *Essay on Man* and the *Epistles to Several Persons*. But the tensions and hesitancies in these poems foreshadow Pope's ultimate recognition that it was impossible to apply an idealised system to a society which had rejected it and to which it had ceased to be relevant. His political optimism gave way in the final *Dunciad* and the *Imitations of Horace* to considered antagonism to society and deliberate self-discovery. Pope, Swift, and Bolingbroke were all in some sense men conscious of outliving an era and a political situation in which they might have served a useful public function, and all were forced in some way to come to terms with this problem.

Before Pope's attitudes can be further clarified it is necessary to pay some attention to the assumptions of Toryism and its metamorphosis.[27] After the Revolution of 1688 the Toryism of those who had backed the Duke of York against the Exclusionists, with its cluster of attitudes such as divine right, insistence on the royal prerogative, passive obedience, and the supremacy of Anglicanism, became largely meaningless and irrelevant. The prerogative ceased to be a major issue;[28] divine right and passive obedience were undermined by those Tories who acquiesced in the accession of William. Party demarcation in the early part of William's reign was inevitably confused. In 1692-4 a realignment of party forces took place; the Whig and Tory country interests fused under Harley as the new country party, while the court Whigs began to abandon their radical constitutional principles and to occupy themselves with the processes and not the principles of government.[29] The tendency to identify Whigs with the court and Tories with the country might seem to anticipate the development in the mid-eighteenth century when the court Whigs had absorbed the Tory aristocracy, when the Tories consisted only of minor gentry, and when the designation 'Tory' gave way to that of 'Country gentlemen'.[30] But in the 1690s new issues arose, of relations with the continent, the question of the war and how to pay for it, which involved party differences based on policy. After 1702 and the accession of Anne the confused party demarcation of William's reign became clear; the war was the most significant factor in distinguishing Whig from Tory attitudes.[31] It was in relation to the war that Swift, Harley's spokesman, defined his sense of the Tory interest.

Swift's writings provide the clearest and most consistent Tory image, partly because Swift, unlike Bolingbroke, did not modify his ideas to accommodate the Tory fall from power in 1714; *Gulliver's Travels* (published in 1726) continues the position of *The Examiner* (1710-11). Swift was not in all respects a typical Tory, if indeed there was such a thing, since the ideological gap between high-flying and moderate Tories was great. As an Anglo-Irishman he was inevitably a Williamite (and had started out as a Whig), while his High Churchmanship and his hatred of dissent made him in that respect an extremist. It is his general definition of the Tory interest that is important.[32]

Swift thought that the real wealth of the country was in land, and that the important and the representative people of England were the landowners, the 'landed interest'. Government should consist of a parliament and ministry representative of the landed interest, and therefore truly national. When parliament and ministry are so constituted (as the Tory Land Qualification Bill of 1711 was intended to ensure, and as Swift rather imaginatively saw the Oxford–Bolingbroke ministry), there is no need for rival political parties, since any group opposed to a nationally representative government, a united court and country, can only be a minority faction. Since the country's wealth is in its land, and it is sufficiently developed to be self-supporting, trade is at most a peripheral activity, irrelevant to the nation's economic survival, and potentially inimical to it (though a reluctant consciousness of the importance of trade was at times forced on Swift, as on all Tories, partly because of the constituency of the Tory party). When the people and their government are in agreement, the practice of politics is uncomplicated, and is a matter chiefly of common sense. There is therefore no need either for abstract speculations as to the nature of politics, nor for an extended central executive. In order that government may work according to this pattern, the education of the aristocracy (who as landowners are the natural rulers of the country) should be practical and moral rather than theoretical.

However Swift, in his period as government spokesman as well as in his far longer period in opposition, thought that current social tendencies were largely antagonistic to the structure of the political nation as he saw it. His immediate function in working for Harley was to persuade the public in favour of a peace to end the war of the Spanish Succession. The length and expense of the wars against Louis XIV meant that money had to be raised by extraordinary means. Since an income tax (which would have affected merchants) was considered too difficult to administer, the war was largely paid for by a land tax.[33] In addition, money was raised by the sale of government bonds, the institution of the national debt. Swift was entirely unable to understand the idea that government could borrow money from its own people. In his view the means of financing the war were having the disastrous effect of transforming what was in a true state of affairs a minority in the nation, the financiers, or 'moneyed interest', into a serious political force. Through taxation and the prolonging of the war (and of the loans and funds), wealth and its concomitant, political power, were passing from the landed to the moneyed interest. The stability of society was being upset; the national interest was being discarded in favour of the interest of the moneyed few.

At the bottom of Swift's view of the divisions in society was a sense of the difference between true and false value, between usefulness and waste. He favoured the Land Qualification Bill, 'the greatest security that ever was contrived for preserving the constitution', because it protected the real wealth of the nation from the encroachments of those who had none, 'or at least only what is transient or imaginary'.[34] The King of Brobdingnag epitomised Swift's view of the function of government and of the relation of value and use:

Whoever could make two ears of corn, or two blades of grass to grow upon a spot of ground where only one grew before; would deserve better of mankind, and do more essential service to his country, than the whole race of politicians put together.[35]

Swift's views, and particularly the techniques he used to set them forward, are an interesting foretaste of Pope's antitheses between such mythologised figures as Balaam and the Man of Ross. In the Tory propaganda during the Spanish war the figure of Marlborough assumed the same dimensions and symbolic overtones as Walpole did for the opposition of the 1720s and 1730s. Marlborough embodied for Swift a complex of tendencies he detested: the concentration of luxury instead of the proper distribution of wealth, the exploitation of the people by government, the upheaval of society for the benefit of the few at the expense of the many, the abandonment of the appropriate English policy of isolated self-interest for intervention in continental affairs.[36]

Swift's understanding of the war and Marlborough's place in it is elaborated in Arbuthnot's *The History of John Bull* (1712). The witty transformation of the war into a law suit over land inheritance is a clear indication of Tory interests and piejudices. Marlborough is Humphrey Hocus the lawyer, the middleman who enriches himself at his clients' expense. The building of Blenheim, the focus of much Tory resentment at Marlborough's rise, is well used by Arbuthnot as an example of the encroachment on land by new men:

A good swinging sum of John's readiest cash, went towards building of Hocus's country-house.[37]

The role played in the war by the Dutch, who were the inevitable victims of Tory xenophobia, particularly in relation to the Tory view of their unnatural alliance with Whigs, trade, and dissent, is seen entirely in terms of the enriched tradesman's movement to the land, of the unhealthy rise of the *nouveaux riches*:

From a plain tradesman, with a shop, wharehouse, and a country-hut, with a dirty fish-pond at the end of it, he [Nick Frog the Dutchman] is now grown a very rich country gentleman, with a noble-landed estate, noble palaces, manors, parks, gardens, and farms, finer than any we were ever master of.[38]

Swift's antipathy to trade amounted to an obsession; in *Gulliver's Travels*, written when the conflict of interests as understood in the war years was much less relevant, he argued both through the example of Brobdingnag and the suggestions of the Houyhnhnms that England should be entirely self-supporting.[39] However, Swift, Bolingbroke, and the Tories in general, both in their theoretical attitudes and in their admission that the parliamentary party was not homogeneous, were ready when necessary to abandon the extreme thesis that the party represented strictly the landed interest. When he was official propagandist Swift was well aware that many Tories expected the Treaty of Utrecht to provide trading benefits to England. They felt it was their turn to make a profit in place of the financiers who were parasitically living off the national debt. In *The Conduct of the Allies*, therefore, Swift accused the Whigs both of beggaring the gentry and of ruining trade while in *Windsor Forest* Pope voiced Tory hopes of free trade as a means to national regeneration.[40]

It was the Whig writers who had a real sense that the long-term national interest was more flexible than was indicated by Tory propaganda (which concentrated on the immediate effects of the war). In *The Spectator* Addison depicted the rival interests of land and trade in Sir Roger de Coverley the Tory squire and Sir Andrew Freeport the city Whig, but he joined them in a club, and throughout his paper tried to show how the landed and moneyed interests might be united. Thus he deplores the fact that William Wimble, the younger son of a country gentleman, is not put to a trade because the gentry think it beneath them;[41] trade seems to Addison the binding force of society:

There are not more useful members in a commonwealth than merchants. They knit mankind together in a mutual intercourse of good offices, distribute the gifts of nature, find work for the poor, add wealth to the rich, and magnificence to the great.[42]

He shows Andrew Freeport in his old age retiring to the country to assume the duties of a patriarchical landowner:

As the greatest part of my estate has been hitherto of an unsteady and volatile nature, either tossed upon seas or fluctuating in funds; it is now fixed and settled in substantial acres and tenements. I have removed it from the uncertainty of stocks, winds, and waves, and disposed of it in a considerable purchase. This will give me great opportunity of being charitable in my way, that is in setting my poor neighbours to work, and giving them a comfortable subsistence out of their own industry.[43]

Fifteen years later Defoe also observed the interdependency of the old nobility and new merchants, the circular motion of trade. In *A Tour through England and Wales* (1724–6) he noted how London's wealth spread into the surrounding countryside, and how tradesmen established themselves in landed estates. At the same time he was anxious that the benefits of trade, the wealth accruing to the nation, should be evenly spread. To Defoe it appeared that in spite of the flow of wealth from London outwards the reverse tendency was stronger. Defoe's sympathies were always with the enterprising small tradesman, and he regarded the large finance companies with Tory disapproval. He thought the institution of the national debt as pernicious as Swift, but he observed its social effects differently: he saw that the status of large landowners was changing because they took advantage of this new field for investment. At the same time as wealth from trade was going into land, wealth from land was going into funds, causing the nobility and gentry to leave the country for a large part of the year to converge on the capital. The resulting overextension of London was causing it to be parasitic, to drain the resources of the country. Defoe voiced the hope Swift had expressed earlier: that if the peace continued, the public debts would be paid off, the funds would cease to exist, the gentry would disperse to their proper sphere, the country, and London would shrink to its natural size:

Then, I say, will be a time to expect the vast concourse of people to London, will separate again and disperse as naturally, as they have now crowded hither.[44]

During the war years Swift's analysis was relevant enough to form a useful ideology and weapon. After 1714 Toryism, as a practical programme and as a general ideology, changed radically. The Tory Treaty of Utrecht, since it was against Hanoverian interests, alienated the Elector George; as George I he became a Whig king. With the imprisonment and flight of the Tory leaders the party was without a focus, and the hopeless cause of Jacobitism did not provide it. The Toryism of church and king could not survive the death of Anne; the inadequacy of the Pretender meant that the issue of divine right, the problem of a king *de jure* versus a king *de facto*, ceased to be vital after 1720.[45] Toryism merged with the opposition country ideology, Whig in origin, which had crystallised during the reign of Charles II. The attitudes of this opposition or country Toryism during Walpole's ministry can be summarised as follows: in relation to specific issues, antagonism to the land tax and the national debt, belief that parliament should consist of landowners and that placemen should be excluded, opposition to the growth of the executive and the curtailment of the powers of local government, dislike of a standing army and of English involvement in continental affairs, suspicion of the growth of London and the monopoly and finance companies; and in a more general and emotional sense, xenophobia, isolationism, dislike of any extension of the machinery of politics, belief in the basic simplicity and practicality of good government, hatred of luxury, ostentation, or any interference with the traditional balance of society. By the 1730s the more extreme of these views were relevant only to the minor gentry; they were not all voiced by Walpole's opponents, since much of that opposition was war-mongering and expansionist. These attitudes were no longer held together by a coherent national aim, nor did they have a real parliamentary base.

In his propaganda for peace, Swift had expressed the central paradox of Toryism, that society is divided, but that somehow the more powerful section is only a splinter interest, while the rest is the true interest of the people, the integral nation. This paradox is basic to Pope's difficulties in his attempt to reconcile his imaginative sense of universal order with his recognition of actual fragmentation. In Swift's case the antithesis was between money and land, but in the 1720s and 30s Bolingbroke found it more appropriate to see it as between court and country, the executive government and the rest of the political nation. Bolingbroke managed to avoid some Tory difficulties by changing the basis of his political manifesto. In his extreme Tory period, as he explained in *A Letter to Sir William Wyndham*, he held views similar to Swift's: that the Tories, the landowners, represented the true national interest, while the Whigs bolstered their limited interest by an alliance with dissenters, the Bank of England, and the Dutch.[46] In his patriot phase he said less about this transfer of power; he concentrated his attack on Walpole on the corruption and over-extension of the central executive. But he was still involved in the anomalous position of using opposition to advocate the end of party government. Pope absorbed all the complexities and paradoxes of Toryism, but he did not accept the patriot solution for the main dilemma of the anti-Walpole opposition, their alienation from power. In the *Epistle to Burlington* (1731) and the *Epistle to Bathurst* (1733) Pope tried to resolve the contradictions between the Tory ideal of representing a unified society and their fear of being in fact only a powerless fragment of society. Finally, in the *Imitations of Horace*, he ceased to fight for any political reunification of society or any political solutions for fragmentation.

The ideal hero of the *Epistle to Burlington* is the patriarchal land-owner, whose rural role does not conflict with but rather complements his wider public function:[47]

> His father's acres who enjoys in peace,
> Or makes his neighbours glad, if he increase;
> Whose cheerful tenants bless their yearly toil,
> Yet to their lord owe more than to the soil;
> Whose ample lawns are not ashamed to feed
> The milky heifer and deserving steed;
> Whose rising forests, not for pride or show,
> But future buildings, future navies grow:
> Let his plantations stretch from down to down,
> First shade a country, and then raise a town.
>
> (III ii, *pp.* 154–5, *ll.* 182–90)

This is the Tory ideal of the unified society, the society of Penshurst, where each member in the hierarchy supports and is supported by the others. Thus Burlington's Palladian scheme, which is to be the physical embodiment of the ideal of private life, should stimulate George II to the fulfilment of the imperial works worthy of kings; the monarchical role is summit, pattern, and in itself contains the other roles of social life. This is the ideal presented in *Windsor Forest*, of the related usefulness of all things; it is a recreation of the pattern of the *Essay on Man*, the system of benevolence whereby the individual comes by stages to understand his relation to society in the way that the stone causes widening circles on the lake.

However, one of the many paradoxes in Pope's lifelong attempt to mediate between an ideal of private conduct and an unideal world lies in his use of Burlington's revival of Palladianism as a means to a hoped-for regeneration of national life. In opposing the Palladian ideal to Timon's baroque extravaganza, Pope thought that he was distinguishing between the true and the false view of the function of the great house and the great man in society. In the first half of the seventeenth century Inigo Jones's court-centred innovations, which were felt to emphasise a barrier between court and country, were decried in favour of traditional Elizabethan and Jacobean architecture, which was seen to symbolise the proper local and national function of gentry and nobility. But the antithesis that Pope makes between the Wren–Vanbrugh baroque school and the Burlington Palladian school is not capable of the same kind of interpretation. The ultimate effect of an antithesis between these schools is not so much an opposition of the old view of the proportioned, harmonious house, reflecting its proper social function, to the luxurious, ostentatious house of the *nouveau riche* who is bursting the bounds of society or of the decadent aristocrat who is neglecting his proper role; rather it is an opposition of the villa, which is the embodiment of the private, self-centred life, to the great house and the whole idea of the political and social meaning of magnificence.[48] In attacking Timon, Pope is to some extent making the traditional criticism of the misuse of a house by a political or financial magnate to enhance his prestige; Timon is the Salisbury-Clarendon-Marlborough-Walpole type.[49] However, the development of the Palladian villa and the loss of interest in the building of the great house after about 1760 indicate that Pope is not so much harking back to the traditional view of the patriarchal house (although this is the ideal that he sets against Timon) as foreshadowing the new view of the country house, reflecting private values and existing for leisured retirement.[50] Ultimately, as appears in the *Imitations of Horace*, Pope was more interested in his own private role as an individual at his Twickenham villa than in the social, patriarchal role of his aristocratic friends, such as Bathurst at Riskins or Cobham at Stowe. This is not to say that the tendency to isolated individualism is explicit in the *Epistle to Burlington*; on the contrary, the poem is another of Pope's attempts to assert the possibility of synthesis, of a unified society. Nor was Burlington's Palladianism initially antithetic to the public idea of a house; his Chiswick villa, the prototype of the new suburban villa of retreat, was not intended to be lived in but was built to house his art collection.[51] However, the spread of Palladianism ultimately meant a rejection of both the ostentatious, baroque style of building and the old patriarchal ideal. Though in the *Epistle to Burlington* Pope's interest was in the public uses of Palladianism, in the *Imitations of Horace* the tendencies of the new architecture were exemplified in his own way of life.

Both the *Epistle to Burlington* and the *Epistle to Bathurst* attempt to continue the scheme of the *Essay on Man*. The basic metaphysical problem of *To Burlington* is how a man like Timon can fit into the cosmic order, when his actions, his way of life, his house, are all seen to disrupt that order. The grandeur of the house is completely disproportionate to its owner:[52]

> Greatness, with Timon, dwells in such a draught
> As brings all Brobdingnag before your thought.

> To compass this, his building is a town,
> His pond an ocean, his parterre a down:
> Who but must laugh, the master when he sees,
> A puny insect, shivering at a breeze! (*ll.* 103–8)

In the garden the roles of nature and art are exchanged:

> The suffering eye inverted nature sees,
> Trees cut to statues, statues thick as trees. (*ll.* 119–20)

In the house the forms and meanings of social rituals have become confused; the chapel has assumed a secular and the feast a religious function, thus depriving both of value:

> And now the chapel's silver bell you hear,
> That summons you to all the pride of prayer:
> Light quirks of music, broken and uneven,
> Make the soul dance upon a jig to heaven. (*ll.* 141–4)

> Is this a dinner? this a genial room?
> No, 'tis a temple, and a hecatomb. (*ll.* 155–6)

All the poem's examples of false taste violate the basic principles of use and sense by which art can be judged to fit the universal scheme of things. Timon's prodigality represents a complete negation of the kind of society that Pope would like to see, and he deliberately concludes his poem with a re-statement of the ideal, unified society of *Windsor Forest*. But at the same time Timon is seen to have his place, even his usefulness, in the structure of society:

> Yet hence the poor are clothed, the hungry fed;
> Health to himself, and to his infants bread
> The labourer bears: What his hard heart denies,
> His charitable vanity supplies. (*ll.* 169–72)

The problem is essentially the same one that Pope failed to solve in the *Essay on Man*. Seen with the eye of God, all human actions though extreme in their tendencies are reconciled within the universal pattern; seen with the eye of man, society has surely disrupted the universal pattern, and it must therefore be recreated.

The problem is more acutely stated in the *Epistle to Bathurst*. There is a basic contradiction between the two methods Pope uses in these epistles to account for and oppose the fragmented nature of society as he sees it. The prophecy or hope of an idealised, unified society to set against the grotesque world of Timon does not play its part in *To Bathurst*, where Pope is far more concerned in some way to justify existing society. The central vindication of God's ways and man's is found in the following lines, which develop the argument of the usefulness of Timon's prodigality:

> Hear then the truth: ''Tis heaven each passion sends,
> 'And different men directs to different ends.
> 'Extremes in nature equal good produce,
> 'Extremes in man concur to general use.'
> Ask we what makes one keep, and one bestow?
> That power who bids the ocean ebb and flow,
> Bids seed-time, harvest, equal course maintain,
> Through reconciled extremes of drought and rain,
> Builds life on death, on change duration founds,
> And gives the eternal wheels to know their rounds.
>
> (III ii, *pp.* 106–7, *ll.* 161–70)

There is a great difference between setting up an idealised unity as a model, and asserting an existing unity of universally reconciled opposites.

While in *To Bathurst* Pope does not apply the first of these methods, he is inevitably uncomfortable with his use of the second. For this poem is his strongest portrayal, before the *Epilogue to the Satires* and the last book of *The Dunciad*, of the conquest of society by the new financial order, of the triumph of Swift's moneyed interest, of the new insubstantial world of paper credit, banks, bubbles, fraud, and Sir Balaam. The villains of *To Bathurst*, the forgers, gamblers, bankers, Charitable Corporation swindlers, and projectors, all overturn society by their abuse of the proper function of money; in this world wealth is 'given to the fool, the mad, the vain, the evil' (*l.* 19). The poem's main question is how the individual should confront this society:

> Since then, my lord, on such a world we fall,
> What say you?
>
> (*ll.* 79–80)

But the poem's chief intellectual solution, the theory of reconciled opposites quoted above, is inappropriate, and Pope really knows this. The new uses of wealth concentrate power in the hands of the few, who can buy and sell society and reorder the hierarchy of value. What should have value, the proper distribution of wealth, the proper ordering of society, is completely subverted by what ostensibly has no value:

> Blessed paper-credit! last and best supply!
> That lends corruption lighter wings to fly!
> Gold imped by thee, can compass hardest things,
> Can pocket states, can fetch or carry kings;
> A single leaf shall waft an army o'er,
> Or ship off senates to a distant shore;
> A leaf, like Sibyl's, scatter to and fro
> Our fates and fortunes, as the winds shall blow;

Pregnant with thousands flits the scrap unseen,
And silent sells a king, or buys a queen.   (*ll.* 69–78)

This sense of the inversion of value, of the basing of value on something inherently valueless, is a central aspect of Tory unease and confusion in a capitalist society they did not understand. Swift's feeling that money, as opposed to the real value of land, was essentially imaginary wealth, has already been mentioned; Gay, who suffered losses in the South Sea Bubble, contrasted the diminishing power of poetic imagination in contemporary society to the new extraordinary power of paper wealth; the poet, the perceiver of real value, must give way to the jobber, whose power is based on something that is the negation of value.[53]

The bubble was ample proof for the Tory wits that the new world had arrived. Pope cannot solve the problem by trying to make Cotta and his son cancel each other out, nor by presenting Sir Balaam as the unhappy and ridiculous antithesis to the Man of Ross. The point that comes across strongly in *To Bathurst* is that the new moneyed order is irresistible; as the wizard (Walpole?) prophesies to Blunt, a director of the South Sea Company:

> 'At length corruption, like a general flood,
> '(So long by watchful ministers withstood)
> 'Shall deluge all; and avarice creeping on,
> 'Spread like a low-born mist, and blot the sun;
> 'Statesman and patriot ply alike the stocks,
> 'Peeress and butler share alike the box,
> 'And judges job, and bishops bite the town,
> 'And mighty dukes pack cards for half a crown.
> 'See Britain sunk in lucre's sordid charms,
> 'And France revenged of Anne's and Edward's arms!'
>
> (*ll.* 137–46)

We are half way to the establishment of the empire of Chaos.

In the inexplicit world of the *Essay on Man* the theory of the ultimate reconciliation of extremes (which is there applied mainly to conflicting passions in the individual) may have seemed feasible to Pope; but the Mandevillian paradox of private vices, public benefits, which is the social form this theory takes, is irrelevant to Pope's view of the development of society in the *Epistle to Bathurst*. Mandeville's paradox is designed to show that an expanding, ambitious, wealthy society cannot exist by the virtues appropriate only to a primitivistic, limited one:

> Bare virtue can't make nations live
> In splendour: they, that would revive
> A golden age, must be as free,
> For acorns, as for honesty.[54]

Mandeville accepts the facts of the financial revolution; his attempt is mainly to reconcile others to it, to point out the irrelevance of old-fashioned ethical schemes to the new world. He approves of prodigality, luxury, and pride because they support trade and the economic well-being of society.[55] But Pope is trying to stretch this paradox for a purpose to which it cannot be fitted. He asserts that under the hand of God human vices work for and not against the universal scheme; the prodigal and the miser cancel each other out. At the same time he sees that these vices (which for him are real vices, not just apparent ones, as they are for Mandeville) have the effect of destroying social order, of making impossible any proper distribution of wealth. Pope cannot approve the economic boom which it is Mandeville's aim to promote; he judges society by the primitivistic ethics which Mandeville regards as outmoded.

Pope's final answer to the question 'since then, my lord,...What say you?' differs both from the political ideal of a unified society of *To Burlington* and from the intellectual accommodation attempted here and in the *Essay on Man*. The proper distribution of wealth in society is more effectively achieved by the individual who himself encompasses the mean than by the ultimate universal reconciliation of extremes. Bathurst is made to exemplify this mean, the joining of economy and magnificence, splendour and charity, plenty and health; he moves between the extremes 'of mad good-nature, and of mean self-love' (*l.* 228).

The charity of the individual is thus the chief weapon against the inequities of society. The figure symbolising the successful opposition of a private ethic to the encroaching public one is the Man of Ross. In several ways the Man of Ross repeats the pattern of the ideal patriarchal landowner; his charities extend to public works. But he does not have the aristocrat's necessary public role; his private sphere of virtuous activity is antithetic to the idea of fame:

> Who builds a church to God, and not to fame,
> Will never mark the marble with his name.   (*ll.* 285–6)

And in a letter to Tonson Pope emphasised the fact that the image of the Man of Ross was intended as a deliberate contrast to the conventional idea of the magnificent aristocrat:

> My motive for singling out this man, was twofold: first to distinguish real and solid worth from showish or plausible expense, and virtue from vanity: and secondly, to humble the pride of greater men, by an opposition of one so obscure and so distant from the sphere of public glory, this proud town.[56]

The Man of Ross embodies the system of benevolence of the *Essay on Man*, the individual's means of recreating the chain of love within the framework of his own life. But the impression that Pope cannot help creating in this poem is of the powerlessness of the benevolent individual against the tendencies of the new acquisitive society.

Of the various solutions open to the early eighteenth-century Tories, of the various means of avoiding the consequences of what was seen to be a disrupted society, Pope took the path that eventually led him to turn his back on politics, on myths, and on the attempt to impose harmony. Swift and Bolingbroke in the earlier part of the period tried to suggest that the section of society with which they were in sympathy was in fact the real unified political world; Bolingbroke attempted a recreation of this view on a broader scale in his theory of patriotism. Pope tried to avoid the implications of the disruptions he saw by asserting an intellectual synthesis into which all human aberrations fitted; order should not be named imperfection. Ultimately, the contradictions in this view made Pope fall back on a private ethic as the only weapon against an incurable world. In the *Imitations of Horace* Pope's interests centred more on the maintaining of his own integrity and less on the recreation of a unified and hierarchical society. And in the process he passed from the nostalgic, mythological Toryism of Swift and Bolingbroke to something like the sceptical Toryism of Samuel Johnson.

PATRIOTISM AND INDEPENDENCE

The *Imitations of Horace*, particularly the *Epilogue to the Satires* of 1738, and the four-book *Dunciad* of 1743 are sometimes thought of as being Pope's most political poems. They were certainly written at a time when Pope's friendship with many of the 'patriot' opponents of Walpole brought him in contact with the attempt to formulate a new ideology to counteract the tendencies of Walpole's powerful bureaucracy, and with the practical techniques used in the struggle to oust the chief minister. Pope's knowledge of politics and of political machinery, as his absorption of contemporary patriot cant phrases shows, was much more direct between about 1733 and 1743 than at any earlier period of his life.[57] Bolingbroke was no doubt his 'guide, philosopher, and friend' in the political as well as the philosophical sphere. But it is a mistake to think of Pope's relationship with Bolingbroke in these years as analogous to that of Swift with Harley in 1710-14. Bolingbroke's attempt to coordinate the opposition failed to give him any real authority; and after a rebuff by the opposition Whigs he retired to France from 1735 to 1738. Pope was not really the opposition laureate,[58] the spokesman for patriotism as Swift had been the spokesman for the Tories. Although Pope was moved to outrage by the same conditions in contemporary society as Bolingbroke, although he shared the same conservative sympathies, this does not mean that Bolingbroke's theory of patriotism was acceptable or even relevant to him. Pope's continued admiration for Bolingbroke the man, whom he thought 'something superior to anything I have seen in human nature',[59] his pride in their friendship, only serve to accentuate the difference in their political outlooks. Pope came to think, like Swift, that society could be changed only by the efforts of a handful of good men; Bolingbroke, writing to Swift of the ineffectiveness of moral writers in reforming society, maintained that 'national corruption must be purged by national calamities'.[60] Bolingbroke's is the wide political view, of reform by the upheaval of institutions; Pope's view is limited, pessimistic, and opposes the individual to the institution.

Bolingbroke's theory of patriotism was to some extent a reworking and a bringing up to date of the Toryism for which Swift was spokesman. There were important strategic differences; the Toryism shared by Bolingbroke and Swift in 1710–14 (as admitted by Bolingbroke in *A Letter to Sir William Wyndham*) was deliberately partisan and exclusive, and in some ways anticipated the narrow-bottomed government that Walpole in fact achieved. After his fall from power and his abortive flight to the Pretender, Bolingbroke realised that Jacobitism was a cul-de-sac and that the Tories were doomed unless they abandoned their extremism and were brought into the main stream of political life. Apart from providing an apology for his life, one of the main objects of the *Letter to Wyndham* was to warn the Tories against Jacobitism.[61] The separation of Toryism from Jacobitism was at first hard to achieve, since Walpole kept himself in power and the Tories down by identifying them with the Pretender's cause and exploiting public fear of revolution.[62] The exclusiveness of Walpole's government provided Bolingbroke with the opportunity he needed. In the late 1720s and 1730s there existed a heterogeneous group of opposition Whigs, Hanoverian Tories, Jacobite Tories, prospective placemen, traders, and squires who were frustrated by Walpole's administrative and economic policies. Bolingbroke was concerned to find a theme that could bring together the disparate elements of the opposition, even though he realised that dissident out-of-office Whigs could not be welded to country Tories. Patriotism was not cynically intended simply as a rallying-cry for all who were out, but Bolingbroke certainly abandoned his more rigorous Tory tenets. He was now anxious to drop the party designations of Whig and Tory and to revert to the older distinction between court and country, which allowed him to hold out a hand to potential allies like the dissenters whom he had previously spurned.[63] The problem was that the opposition were agreed on few issues except the excise;[64] patriotism never became the general creed that Bolingbroke hoped. Its failure lies in its nature; patriotism was an attempt to build a new national ideology out of opposition principles.

The declared object of *A Dissertation upon Parties* (published in *The Craftsman*, Bolingbroke's journalistic weapon against Walpole, in 1733-4) was to fix public attention on the danger of corruption in contemporary society.[65] By corruption Bolingbroke meant chiefly the destruction of the independence of parliament and the growth of a powerful bureaucracy (which he thought was increased by new systems of taxation). This tendency, he thought, was undermining the constitution. He evolved a new version of the Tory claim to represent the national interest in relation to this view of the danger to the constitution: his party divisions consist of those against the government but for the constitution (i.e. Bolingbroke and his friends); those against both government and constitution (perhaps the Jacobites); and those in the government, but against the constitution (Walpole).[66] It is the familiar Tory paradox, that those in power are unrepresentative while those in opposition are the real supporters of government. Bolingbroke discusses at some length the nature of the constitution and the question as to which party can be said really to support the Revolution Settlement. But by the constitution Bolingbroke seems ultimately to mean the preservation of the power and independence of the private member (essentially the country gentleman) which is being inevitably eroded by the establishment of modern executive control.[67] At the bottom of this is the feeling so dear to Swift that government is really a simple and practical matter.

Bolingbroke's answer to this tendency in contemporary government is idealistically nostalgic and unworkable. The proper balance of the constitution can be restored by the patriot king, who is non-partisan, controls faction, purges the court, and reverses the trend to ministerial government.[68] The unlikely candidate for this role was Frederick Prince of Wales, to whom the official version of the *Idea of a Patriot King* was dedicated in 1749 (although it was written ten years earlier). Bolingbroke was playing the well-known political game of the eighteenth century in attaching himself and his political ambitions to the heir. But the *Patriot King* looks much more to the past than the future. As a man who had been in power and who hoped to return to it, Bolingbroke needed a platform and a helping hand. But when the book was published the old coalition had collapsed, the fall of Walpole had changed nothing, and Bolingbroke was almost in his grave. *The Idea of a Patriot King* suggests not so much his own disappointments, as his disappointment with the whole of society. Its ideal is a portrait of the society he thought had existed in the past; somehow, by the coming to the throne of patriot Frederick, the developments of government in the last hundred years were to be arrested and reversed. The new society was to be one in which everyone had his place, where there was no party conflict, and of which the court was the moral and administrative centre. The hero of the *Patriot King* is Elizabeth, who represents for Bolingbroke personal rule able to control faction and powerful courtiers. This is a curious idealisation of a court for the sake of advocating limitation of the powers of central government.

This idealisation of the past is central to Bolingbroke's theory of patriotism. The reverse of the myth of contemporary corruption is the myth of the ancient perfect constitution. In the face of an alien society Bolingbroke found a means of reasserting the Tory consciousness of representing the true nation, of understanding the true nature of government. Because its ideal existence is set in the past rather than in a romanticised present, Bolingbroke's patriotism is perhaps more desperate (it certainly seems more unrealistic) than Swift's Toryism. Bolingbroke has been accused of confusion in his attempt to join a realistic analysis of the social and economic causes of corruption and change in political society with an anachronistic appeal to a humanist prince to avert that change and restore the old order.[69] But it was essential to Bolingbroke's political cause to find a mythology that would replace lost and irrelevant Tory dreams of divine right and a Stuart succession, and that would control and direct their amorphous opposition to the government. The failure of patriotism was inevitable, but it remained an attempt to put forward a positive solution to contemporary problems, to impose change from above rather than simply to hope for subversion from within.

Given the importance that Pope attached to the monarch's personal power to shape society in *Windsor Forest*, it is remarkable the extent to which he remained unmoved by the idea of the patriot king. Perhaps Brutus would have been his patriot king, but the epic was never written. His suppression of the unpublished *1740* (though this may be due to the poem's outspokenness) indicates his lack of interest in a new rejuvenating myth. And *1740*, the only poem where Pope explicitly advocates Bolingbroke's idea, hoping that 'one man's honesty [might] redeem the land',[70] is devoted mainly to an attack on all parties in the opposition coalition. Reform through political means is hopeless:

> The plague is on thee, Britain, and who tries
> To save thee in the infectious office dies.
> (IV, *p.* 336, *ll.* 75–6)

The appeal to the Prince of Wales seems rather a desperate abandonment of politics than a serious proposal of a new solution.[71]

Pope shows small interest in the appeal to history essential to patriotism. It is perhaps more appropriate to see James Thomson as the laureate of the patriots, even though his orientation was far more Whig than Pope's. In Thomson's *Liberty* (1735–6), also dedicated to the Prince of Wales, the high points of English history are the reigns of Alfred and

Elizabeth, Magna Carta and the Revolution Settlement. Thomson's ideal virtues are independence and integrity, the antitheses of luxury and corruption. These words are to be understood in the political sense that Bolingbroke gives them, rather than with Pope's moral and personal emphasis. Thomson's liberty is a political not a personal aim; it should be sustained by

> independent life;
> Integrity in office; and o'er all
> Supreme, a passion for the commonweal.[72]

Thomson shares Bolingbroke's concern for the voice of the independent propertied man in government.

He also shares Bolingbroke's potential political optimism; in *The Seasons* he attempts to establish a synthesis like that of *Windsor Forest*, a world bound by the golden chain of commerce but peopled by retired men of virtue. This optimism is inherent in the sense Bolingbroke and Thomson have of the cyclical movement of history, in their romantic view of the past. Pope was certainly also capable of romanticising the past: Rome, as a standard against which to measure contemporary society, meant to him what the England of Elizabeth did to Bolingbroke. But he saw the present, particularly in *The Dunciad*, not so much as a decline from the past, nor as the end of a cycle, but as a complete inversion of the ideals of civilisation, a final uncreation of the good society. This attitude meant that he was unable to see any prospect of reversing this trend, any political means that would avert decay. The independence that is the basis of his poetic role in the *Imitations of Horace* is not the independence prized by Bolingbroke. It does not signify the wealth of the free land-owner who is able to resist the inveiglements of corrupt bureaucracy, but an anti-social position that is to some extent forced on him by the state of society and his inability to find a place in it.

Pope can easily be identified with the patriots by the grievances he lists; he voices opposition warmongering and expansionist views in the *Epistle to Augustus* (*Ep.* ii i, *ll.* 394–403), and complaints of Walpole's extensive system of bribery and patronage in Donne's *Fourth Satire* (*ll.* 130–65), to give only two examples. But although his indictment of society can, like Bolingbroke's, be contained in the idea of the spread of corruption, there is no compensating political ideal to set against it, no theory of the perfect constitution from which the current government is an aberration. The problem of living in such a society for Pope was not the same as it was for Bolingbroke. As a poet, a private man, who by religion and health as well as by political affiliation was barred from public life and a public voice, Pope had to decide who he could speak to, what his own position was. In the *Imitations of Horace* his concern became increasingly private, with the living of his own life on the terms he could maintain in spite of society, rather than with the re-establishment of a society in which the poet's proper public role could be fulfilled.

In the *Epilogue to the Satires* virtue, though it can 'choose the high or low degree' (Dia. I ,*l.* 137), is seen to exist in a private sphere, and it is effective almost by accident:

> Let humble Allen,[73] with an awkward shame,
> Do good by stealth, and blush to find it fame. (*ll.* 135–6)

In contrast, vice has come to be accepted as the public norm:

> In golden chains the willing world she draws,
> And hers the gospel is, and hers the laws; (*ll.* 147–8)

> See thronging millions to the pagod run,
> And offer country, parent, wife, or son!
> Hear her black trumpet through the land proclaim,
> That 'Not to be corrupted is the shame.' (*ll.* 157–60)

This sense of the triumph of inverted values to which there can be only limited and private resistance is the subject of *The Dunciad*. The portrayal of general corruption can only be understood in terms of the ideal that has been corrupted; but though an ideal society is implied, it is seen to be unattainable. The new world of Settle's vision in Book III is 'to nature's laws unknown' (*l.* 241);[74] the empire of chaos is moulded of 'dull and venal', it is an ironic fulfilment of the cyclic return of the golden age, the 'Saturnian days of lead and gold' (Bk. IV, *ll.* 15–16). It is a world controlled by a mechanical theology (Bk. IV, *ll.* 471–91), the complete opposite of the animated scheme of the *Essay on Man*; of arbitrary government, the enemy to learning; a world peopled by hostile individuals with no consciousness of their relation to the whole, to whom the Goddess's advice is 'be proud, be selfish, and be dull' (Bk. IV, *l.* 582). More specifically, it is a world in which the poet, because he is ignored by society, is unable to fulfil his proper function of restoring 'the faith and moral, nature gave before' (*Essay on Man*, Ep. III, *l.* 286); his place is usurped by dunces who promote the inverted values of the anti-empire:[75]

> Lo, Ambrose Philips is preferred for wit!
> See under Ripley rise a new Whitehall,
> While Jones' and Boyle's united labours fall:
> While Wren with sorrow to the grave descends,
> Gay dies unpensioned with a hundred friends,
> Hibernian politics, O Swift! thy fate;
> And Pope's, ten years to comment and translate.
>   (Bk. III, *ll.* 326–32)

207

Pope thus abandons his hope for the unified society, the chain of order, the linking of monarch with his people, of subjects with each other, the whole expressed and maintained by the symbol of public works. Instead, the court, together with its traditional relation with the arts, has been overtaken by the commercial relationships of the city. Pope reflects bitterly that Walpole's commercialisation of literature has harmed it far more than Louis XIV's despotic use of the arts to serve the interests of his regime. After stating the sum spent by Walpole on propaganda, he goes on

> Which shows the benevolence of one minister to have expended, for the current dulness of ten years in Britain, double the sum which gained Louis XIV so much honour, in annual pensions to learned men all over Europe. In which, and in a much longer time, not a pension at court, nor preferment in the church or universities, of any consideration, was bestowed on any man distinguished for his learning separately from party-merit, or pamphlet-writing.
>
> (Bk. II, *l.* 314 n.)

Pope, like Dryden, felt acutely that art cannot flourish in a corrupt or disordered society. Given the fact of his alienation from the court tradition, Pope had to redefine his role as a poet, and it is in this connection that the example of Horace was so important to him. It was the independent, retired, apolitical Horace rather than Horace the admirer of Augustus that he adopted. One senses that by appealing to example Pope was both concealing and justifying a new and uncomfortable status for the poet. His feelings about his independence were necessarily ambivalent, since his political sympathies were to some extent paradoxically dissociated from his economic situation. It is clear from the social ideal of the *Essay on Man* and its inversion in *The Dunciad* that Pope looked back to a hierarchical, organic society, with mutually beneficial relationships between individuals; the rightful place of the poet would seem to be in a patronage relationship. But in spite of these sympathies Pope's career linked him with the commercial world of the dunces; he was independently wealthy from Homer, and proud of this and of the fact that he did not want or need court patronage. Pope was not connected with the Tory gentry view of life by interest but by inclination; he owed his freedom and his ability to define a new role for himself to the new commercial order of things that he deplored. By entering in the *Imitations of Horace* into the opportunities for self-sufficiency that it offered him, he left behind the animating mythology of the earlier poems.

Pope's Twickenham villa, although it appealed like many predecessors to Horace's Sabine farm as a model, in fact offered a new English version of the country idea. There appears to be in the *Imitations* an antithesis between commercial London values and traditional rural patriarchal values similar to that put forward in *To Bathurst* and *To Burlington*. In the *Epistle to Bolingbroke* the opposition to Pope's private doctrine of virtue and constancy is 'London's voice; "Get money, money still!"' (*Ep.* 1 i, *l.* 79). But the antithesis is not so much between two different social orders, as between one man and the whole idea of society. The hero of the *Imitations* is not a landed patriarch, one of Pope's aristocratic friends, a public model for society, but Pope himself. And Pope did not intend to use himself as a model of the old Tory order. The Twickenham villa itself indicates that an opposition of rural hierarchy to social disruption by commerce is impossible. Pope's attempt to assume a patriarchal landowner's role (an attempt made much more self-consciously by Bolingbroke at Dawley) seems to have been something of a joke to his friends. Robert Digby pointed out that Twickenham was hardly the country, and he ridiculed Pope's claims: 'How rural we are! at Twickenham.'[76] In fact Pope's suburban villa in the Thames valley was a reflection of the spread of London's affluence, as Defoe saw when he described this part of England in his *Tour*; he pointed out that the houses in the area were not ancient family seats but were mostly summer retreats of the gentry and citizens:

> In short all this variety, this beauty, this glorious show of wealth and plenty, is really a view of the luxuriant age which we live in, and of the overflowing riches of the citizens.[77]

Pope's idea of independence was necessarily different from the Tory country gentleman's, the independence idealised by Bolingbroke. But his leased villa was closer to the Horatian idea than the English patriarchal great house, Penshurst or Saxham, had been.

There was no real equivalent in Roman society to the English patriarchal landowner. The literary ideal was the peasant smallholder, the farmer of the *Georgics*, simple, selfsufficient, pious, patriarchal in the limited sense of controlling his own family; in Horace's day this class scarcely existed.[78] Horace specifically attacks the large estates, the *latifundia*, the growth of which had impoverished the peasants; as a philosophical solution, he offers Stoic acceptance and indifference to possession, particularly in the example of the dispossessed farmer Ofellus (*Sat.* II ii), or in the example of his own free enjoyment of wealth beyond his expectations but without desire for more (*Sat.* II vi).

The different economic conditions would seem to imply inevitable differences in attitude between Horace and Pope. In the early eighteenth century small landowners certainly suffered from the land tax, but large estates were consolidated and their perpetuity was ensured by the legal device of entail. The South Sea Bubble made evident the attractiveness and security of investment in land.[79] But that Pope fully absorbed Horace's attitudes to land tenure is made clear by his treatment of

Satire II ii, where two thirds of the way through he abandons the use of Horace's mouthpiece Ofellus (in his case his Yorkshire friend Hugh Bethel) and substitutes himself.

The parallel is not exact; anti-Catholic taxation and removal from Chiswick to Twickenham are not intended to equal the depredation of Ofellus's paternal estate. Both Pope and Horace liked to make themselves appear to be less comfortable than they probably were. The essential point of the identification is to emphasise Pope's strength as an individual, and the irrelevance of social pressures, whether the responsibility of inheritance or the nuisance of politics, to his capacity for self-support:

> Though double-taxed, how little have I lost?
> My life's amusements have been just the same,
> Before, and after standing armies came.
> My lands are sold, my father's house is gone;
> I'll hire another's, is not that my own...[80]   (*ll.* 152–6)

> What's property? dear Swift! you see it alter
> From you to me, from me to Peter Walter,
> Or, in a mortgage, prove a lawyer's share,
> Or, in a jointure, vanish from the heir,
> Or in pure equity (the case not clear)
> The Chancery takes your rents for twenty year:
> At best, it falls to some ungracious son
> Who cries, my father's damned, and all's my own.
>   (*ll.* 167–74)

> Let lands and houses have what lords they will,
> Let us be fixed, and our own masters still.   (*ll.* 179–80)

The same attitudes with regard to property are stated in *Epistle* II ii; Bathurst's agricultural improvements are laughed at:

> 'tis all a joke!
> Inexorable death shall level all,
> And trees, and stones, and farms, and farmer fall.
>   (*ll.* 261–3)

This is a striking departure from the idea of the useful landowner expressed in the *Epistle to Burlington*. Pope seems determined to dissociate himself from the hierarchical, gentry, Tory, landowning view of country life, to offer a new meaning, using Horace as a model though radically transforming him, to the ancient ideal of rural retirement.

To some extent Pope's cult of independence and the terms in which it is couched are to be attributed to the immediate political situation, to his friendship with members of the opposition and his exclusion from political rewards. There is a strong similarity between the most irritating and repetitious of Pope's pronouncements on this subject (in, for example, the Letter to the Publisher and the Testimonies prefixed to the 1729 *Dunciad*), and the attacks on the court and claims to private integrity made in the poems of Swift and Gay, both of whom, as Pope noted with superiority in Gay's case, were eager to find places for themselves.[81] His pride in praising those out of office, in associating with those 'who dare to love their country, and be poor',[82] lends some plausibility to this view. But Pope was well aware of the ironies and potential bathos inherent in this kind of self-aggrandisement. The witty 'Bounce to Fop: An Heroic Epistle from a Dog at Twickenham to a Dog at Court', while embodying his basic views also exposes them, if not to ridicule, at least to criticism, simply through the grotesque device of making a dog cultivate independence:

> While you, and every courtly Fop,
> Fawn on the devil for a chop,
> I've the humanity to hate
> A butcher, though he brings me meat;
> And let me tell you, have a nose,
> (Whatever stinking Fops suppose)
> That under cloth of gold or tissue,
> Can smell a plaster, or an issue.

> (VI, *p.* 367, *ll.* 25–32)

It seems that in the first four lines the joke is on Bounce, while the speaker of the rest is Pope.

However, Pope's idea of independence is a much more complicated thing than his political affiliations would sometimes make appear. Towards the end of his career he found himself commending those out of power not so much because of his friendship for Walpole's opponents (and in the *Epilogue to the Satires* II he was anxious to distribute praise to deserving members of the court), but because his interest now was in individual independent good men, in presenting private virtue rather than in upholding or shaping a public ethos. And in the *Imitations of Horace* this retreat from a public poetic role led him into the process of discovering himself.[83]

Pope's self-discovery was not achieved in private, but in the face of society; he understood himself by understanding society and his own public powerlessness, which did not deter him in the *Imitations* from achieving his strongest public voice. In three poems, the Epistles to Fortescue (*Sat.* II i, 1733), to Arbuthnot (1735), and the *Epilogue to the Satires* (1738), Pope set out to clarify his position and his relationship with the public. The history of that relationship meant that he was on the defensive. He was thrown back on his independence, on his new identification of himself, in the act of wrestling with his critics. He discovered himself in conflict, in the writing of satire. In the *Epistle to Arbuthnot* his forced isolation from society and from his critics enabled him to define the proper nature of his poetry:

> Not fortune's worshipper, nor fashion's fool,
> Not lucre's madman, nor ambition's tool,
> Not proud, nor servile, be one poet's praise
> That, if he pleased, he pleased by manly ways;
> That flattery, even to kings, he held a shame,
> And thought a lie in verse or prose the same:
> That not in fancy's maze he wandered long,
> But stooped to truth, and moralized his song:
> That not for fame, but virtue's better end,
> He stood the furious foe, the timid friend,
> The damning critic.... (*ll.* 334–44)

The interest shifts constantly from satire, the public criticism of society, to the satirist, the private individual, and the personal moral sources from which he draws his attacks. The transition between the two is evident in the *Epilogue to the Satires* II, which is ostensibly a defence of his right to make politically dangerous criticism:

> Ask you what provocation I have had?
> The strong antipathy of good to bad. (*ll.* 197–8)

> *Fr.* You're strangely proud.
>   *P.* So proud, I am no slave:
> So impudent, I own myself no knave:
> So odd, my country's ruin makes me grave.
> Yes, I am proud: I must be proud to see
> Men not afraid of God, afraid of me. (*ll.* 205–9)

The redefinition of the public function of his poetry, as truth, as impartial glass to expose society (*Sat.* II i, *ll.* 57–8) gives way to emphasis on finding himself and indifference to society:

> So slow the unprofitable moments roll,
> That lock up all the functions of my soul;
> That keep me from myself; and still delay
> Life's instant business to a future day: (*Ep.* I, i *ll.* 39–42)

> Late as it is, I put myself to school,
> And feel some comfort, not to be a fool. (*ll.* 47–8)

Although in leaving a public role for self-discovery Pope was following Horace (particularly in his turning from *Satires* and *Odes* to *Epistles*) it is in rejecting society that Pope is most untrue to his example. He recognised in the *Epilogue to the Satires* I the differences in technique and outlook;

the implication is that for Pope Horace was a tool to help him find himself, much as Lucilius was for Horace.[84] For Horace retreat from Rome to his Sabine farm was not ultimately an anti-social, selfish act. In the *Odes* particularly it is made evident that Horace's own way of life, even his style, are to be accepted as models for the proper conduct and development of Roman society.[85] In turn Horace models himself on those idealised ancient Roman values which were the basis of Augustus's moral reforms. There is a dynamic process at work. Horace discovers himself by retreat, by retiring from public life and responsibility; at the same time, he rediscovers the virtues and values which are essential to public life, he sees the ideal Roman society as a glorified ancient peasant community. There is thus no tension between Horace's ideals and the ideals with which Augustus was trying to reinvigorate Roman life, even though Horace only implements these ideals in his own person. He was certainly reluctant to assume an epic voice, to be another Virgil to Augustus; but he describes himself as not wholly in control of this reluctance, as being driven to praise Augustus by a force stronger than himself.[86] Temperamentally Horace is antagonistic to responsibility and political involvement, but his self-discovery through the means of private retreat is animated by a public myth.

In his appeal to truth and emphasis on self-revelation, Pope in the *Imitations* appeared to have abandoned myth. There is no evident connection, hardly even any hope for such a thing, between the life of the good man and the life of society.[87] The correspondence and inter-dependence of men and things stated in *Windsor Forest* and the *Essay on Man* give way to the hostility felt by the proud satirist towards the unhearing public. But it is possible to see Pope's new position as a distortion, a travesty of truth, disqualifying him from the part he wished to play in society. It seemed like this to W. J. Courthope, Pope's Victorian biographer, and also to Samuel Johnson.

Perhaps it was the many points of agreement and sympathy he felt that made Johnson so antagonistic to the Augustan satirists; the differences were that much more glaring. In his *Life of Pope* he was constantly critical of what he saw as the arrogant friendship of the satirists, and in Pope's case he concentrated on what he saw as dishonest (because disavowed) hankering after fame and the company of the great:

> Pope was, through his whole life, ambitious of splendid acquaintance .... Next to the pleasure of contemplating his possessions seems to be that of enumerating the men of high rank with whom he was acquainted.... He was sufficiently a fool to fame, and his fault was, that he pretended to neglect it.[88]

Pope's claim to independence seemed to Johnson selfish and inaccurate, and the motive behind his poetry seemed to be vanity rather than moral fervour. He did not think that the design of *The Dunciad* was really moral, and the *Epilogue to the Satires* seemed to him self-indulgent:

> He pleased himself with being important and formidable, and gratified sometimes his pride, and sometimes his resentment.[89]

Johnson's hostile reaction, his refusal to accept Pope's version of himself, is particularly interesting because the Pope of the *Imitations* seems much closer to Johnson himself, in attitudes, in the transmutation of Toryism (though not in technique), than to Swift or Bolingbroke.

In attacking Pope's self-portrayal Jonson seized on what seemed to him a falsification and a myth. Johnson's whole effort as a moralist can be seen as a shedding of myth, an uncompromising testing of what men live by; he rejected his own youthful belief in political remedies and attainable solutions. In *London* (published, like the *Epilogue to the Satires*, in 1738) a whole catalogue of opposition grievances and hopes is listed in brief: patriotic xenophobia is directed against Spain and the French, the excise bill and licensing act are attacked, and in contrast to contemporary degradation the touchstones for judgement are an idealised Elizabethan age and the rural retirement for which the speaker Thales leaves London. Johnson was later to be specifically critical of large ideal solutions, and of solutions which involved change in personal circumstances. He satirises Savage's hankering after rural retirement,[90] and in *Rasselas* every goal is found to be useless. Ultimately it is impossible to make 'a choice of life' and the answer (if it can be called an answer) is in acceptance and resignation. This does not mean that Johnson fell back on the kind of solution offered in the *Essay on Man* (which seemed to him to be characterised by 'penury of knowledge and vulgarity of sentiment'); he was severely critical of Soame Jenyns' vulgarisation of the social implications of a chain of being.[91] To both complacent universalised Toryism and Whig idealised abstractions, Johnson opposed the efforts of the individual to alleviate pain and misery; it is a plea for the extension of philanthropic benevolence.[92]

But Johnson's moral scepticism left him in a curious literary situation; he virtually stripped himself of a poetic persona. There is a striking difference between *London* and the poem that appeared ten years later, *The Vanity of Human Wishes*. The latter is much the best poem that Johnson ever wrote, but it is a poem that could only be written once. A series of mythologised historic figures, Wolsey, Laud, Charles XII, is used to undermine the ideas of fame, ambition, learning, or wealth as valid props or goals. Even the ideal of a benevolent old age is attacked. The negative drive of the poem leaves Johnson with scarcely anything to present in antithesis to his own uncompromising view of the world. He allows no supporting myth or means of consolation but an unrewarding religion; his final position is bleak and impersonal:

Pour forth thy fervours for a healthful mind,
Obedient passions, and a will resigned;
For love, which scarce collective man can fill;
For patience sovereign o'er transmuted ill;
For faith, that panting for a happier seat,
Counts death kind nature's signal of retreat:
These goods for man the laws of heaven ordain,
These goods he grants, who grants the power to gain;
With these celestial wisdom calms the mind,
And makes the happiness she does not find.[93]

By taking such a stand Johnson was making it almost impossible for himself to write poetry. The solution found by Pope – the creation of a new poetic self in the act of repudiating society – was seen by Johnson not as a literary device but as a moral perversion. Johnson left himself, as a basis for future living and writing, only the self-denying and pessimistic stoicised Christianity of *The Vanity of Human Wishes*. Pope had come to feel by the time of the *Imitations of Horace* and *The Dunciad* of 1743 that a cosmic Tory myth was an inadequate poetic weapon in a world which seemed less and less to fit that myth, and rather than fall back on an impersonal and admittedly unconsoling philosophy he took Montaigne's step of turning to himself, of making his self-discovery the subject of his book.

To see Pope's mythologising of his literary role, his moral self-aggrandisement (which plays an important part in the letters as well as in the later poems) as the result of defects of character and of private squabbles is to underestimate the serious literary and political problem facing him. Both Johnson and Courthope assumed that Pope illogically and dishonestly moved outwards from private resentment to public moral pronouncements. Courthope was conscious of Pope's deliberate poetic transformation of himself, his friends, and his enemies, but he regarded this process as a subterfuge to conceal Pope's true personal motives:

The qualities that he admired in idea, he believed himself to possess. On the other hand, those whom he personally hated he identified with all that was ignoble and vicious in the character of the age.[94]

It is fair to recognise, as Johnson and Courthope do, that this is to some extent an artificial process. For them this recognition involves condemnation, since they are determined to read the poems as transparent autobiographical documents. But Pope's movement from a large social myth of public order to a private mythologising of his own experience as a basis for poetic expression should be seen in terms of his new and unusual political and literary situation.

In place of the ordered, coherent society of *Windsor Forest* and the

Essay on Man, Pope in his last years saw the triumph of vice and dulness, the disintegrating world of the *Epilogue to the Satires* and *The Dunciad*. Such a deliberate depiction of the annihilation of organised society is as much an inaccurate and exaggerated interpretation of contemporary events, a poetic fiction, as Pope's heightened and idealised view of Queen Anne's England. Horace Walpole pointed this out when he bitterly criticised the Tory satirists (again on biographical grounds) for their 'lamentations on the ruin of England, in that era of its peace and prosperity, from wretches who thought their own want of power as a proof that their country was undone'.[95] To the next generation Robert Walpole's world seemed safe and stable. What is more interesting than Pope's rejection of a new economic and social order that operated smoothly by a system of values to which he was hostile is the political and literary solution he created from this negative stance. Throughout the *Imitations* one is conscious of the fact that the Tory complex of attitudes, the sense of place, of the land, of rootedness, of history, has come to matter less to Pope, to seem almost irrelevant in the face of the existing social situation, and that in its place he has substituted a more private and limited but nevertheless powerful sense of self and of friendship.

The Pope of the *Imitations* is 'To virtue only and her friends, a friend' (*Sat.* II i, *l.* 121). One editor has tried to avoid what seem to him (as perhaps to Johnson) the embarrassing implications of such a remark by interpreting 'virtue' in the sense of the opposition of landed to moneyed values, in other words as a class concept.[96] But while in the *Epistles to Several Persons* Pope is still making use of the Tory sense of the importance of the landed class and of a structured society, in the *Imitations*, where the individual has no ordained role, 'virtue' has a more private and specific meaning. In terms of the writing of poetry, it is the poetic self-reliance of the satirist who is unable to support the public ethos. In terms of Pope's understanding of the inadequacy of the Tory social myth to interpret and change existing society, 'virtue' is the benevolence of the few who act, not in concert with the chain of love of the *Essay on Man*, but in spite of the universal tendency to vice and chaos. Even in the *Essay on Man* the prospect of the mutual working of benevolence is undermined by Pope's sense of the smallness of the individual's sphere of action; his critical idea of fame differs radically from Ben Jonson's view of its public usefulness:

> What's fame? a fancied life in others' breath,
> A thing beyond us, even before our death.
> . . . .
> All that we feel of it begins and ends
> In the small circle of our foes or friends.
>
> (*Ep.* IV, *ll.* 237–8, 241–2)

This pessimistic shrinking of the social world Pope felt able to interpret or control explains to a large extent his obsession with the idea of friendship, expressed particularly in the letters. His interest in the idea of the few virtuous and politically insignificant individuals who effect good quietly among their friends, blameless Bethel, humble Allen,[97] the Man of Ross, can perhaps be attributed partly to the influence of Swift, who suggested in a letter to Pope that the existence of such individuals made unnecessary the schemes of the moral writer:

O, if the world had but a dozen Arbuthnots in it I would burn my *Travels*.[98]

Swift's creed (stated in the same letter), of hatred of nations and communities but love of individuals, led him to idolise his friendships, particularly with Bolingbroke and Pope. There are several references in his letters to the importance of friendship among men of genius and to the idea that he, Pope, and Bolingbroke constituted a peculiar triumvirate – a view that Pope repeated to Swift some years later.[99] Johnson was inevitably hostile to the deliberately exclusive and self-regarding tenor of these letters:

From the letters that pass between him [Swift] and Pope, it might be inferred that they, with Arbuthnot and Gay, had engrossed all the understanding and virtue of mankind.[100]

Swift's pessimism about the possibility of large-scale changes in the human condition or in human attitudes (which Gulliver voices to his cousin Sympson) leads him necessarily to rely on the individual men he knows and can believe in. It is interesting to note that Pope, at the time that he was fully engaged in his 'ethic scheme' and thus committed to the view of an intelligible and controllable social order, was nevertheless willing in his letters to Swift to restrict his role as a poet to the private sphere of friendship. Thus he described the principal aim of *The Dunciad* as the perpetuation of their friendship, and in reply to Swift's request that might be honoured in one of the moral essays, he stated that

the chief pleasure this work can give me is, that I can in it, with propriety, decency, and justice, insert the name and character of every friend I have, and every man that deserves to be loved or adorned.[101]

Pope's feeling that he had not in fact produced an adequate poetic monument to his friendship with Swift is perhaps responsible for his repeated attempts in the late 1730s to get Swift to allow the publication of their correspondence, as a kind of subsidiary memorial. The whole question of Pope's attitudes to his letters – his rewriting of them, his underhand attempts to have them published as though without his consent, his moral self-aggrandisement in them – has evoked the hostility of posterity. To some extent Pope may have seen himself as in the classical epistolary tradition; the letters of the famous Scriblerians were perhaps to evoke the letters of other great men, of Cicero to Atticus, or Seneca to Lucilius. But vanity or the desire for fame is much the least interesting aspect of Pope's epistolary theory. His letters were intended to be finished works like his poems. But his idea of their function as a monument, his repeated assertions in the last five years of his life that his letters are written for the purpose of asserting friendship and love,[102] do not imply that they are to have the wide social importance of, for example, Ben Jonson's epistolary verses. Pope's emphasis on the friendship, the benevolence, the mutual love of the few is an adjunct of his reluctant relinquishing of the idea of a society in which it is the public great men, the aristocrats, the Bathursts or the Burlingtons, who are the leaders, and his development of the idea that with the loss of this hierarchic society perhaps it is the private philanthropists, the Ralph Allens, even the Popes, who are most effective. Pope's most admired hero, Bolingbroke, was politically powerless, shut out from the sphere where he was meant to perform; Pope, in his self-created role at Twickenham, could feel more sure of himself as an individual than of the continuation of a society he had unsuccessfully tried to perpetuate in his writings.

Louis Bredvold has suggested that there is in the Tory satirists no trace of the 'new sensibility', the sentimentalism of the later eighteenth century; he distinguishes the Tories' toughmindedness from the tender-mindedness of Addison's spiritual descendants.[103] Pope's reaction to an uncongenial political situation puts these statements in some doubt. For the Tories in the 1730s, in the unrewarding era of Walpole, there were perhaps two ideological paths to follow. One was Bolingbroke's Toryism refurbished as patriotism, the idea of a national, unified, one-party government, embodying the country love of independence and antagonism to the growth of central government, and the Tory hostility of land to money. The alternative was the path apparently taken by Pope in the *Imitations*, where he relinquished a national myth of social order, and instead emphasised the power of the benevolent heart to defeat, though in a necessarily limited and private manner, the effects of Whig political and economic machinery. It may be argued that Pope's sympathies in the 1730s and early 1740s were thoroughly with the anti-Walpole opposition, that in the pessimism of *The Dunciad* and the patriotic hopes of *1740* he was sympathetic with both the disaffection and the solutions of the patriots.[104] But the evidence of the *Imitations of Horace* suggests otherwise. This is not to imply that Pope was necessarily conscious of a deliberate break with the Tory tradition; it was after all his mentor Bolingbroke who suggested the imitation of Horace as a defence of Pope's literary career.[105] But there are, it seems, two important departures in this group of poems. The first is Pope's literary isolation, his self-concern, his demand not to be kept from himself. The second is his sentimentalising of the individual benevolent man, of which his friends Bethel or Allen or he himself in his role at Twickenham are the paradigms. Pope's fierceness as a satirist should not be allowed to conceal this interest in sentimental benevolence. And this interest points to an increasing tendency in Tory feeling in the later eighteenth and the nineteenth centuries. By the mid-eighteenth century the Tory public rallying points of divine right, royal prerogative, the sanctity of a landed society, even the last hopeless creed of Jacobitism had fallen one by one in the face of the organised Whig society to which they were irrelevant. A reliance on benevolence, when there is seen to be no worthy public structure to direct behaviour, may be characteristic of pessimistic Tory toughmindedness, as well as of tenderminded Whig sentimentalising of the essential improvability of human nature (and Pope may have learned from Shaftesbury in the writing of the *Essay on Man*). The Tory Samuel Johnson, sceptical about government and the possibility of useful political change, put his faith in the charity of the individual. Pope's Man of Ross foreshadows Fielding's Squire Allworthy (modelled on Allen) or Dickens' powerful benevolent men, the Jarndyces or Boffins whose good nature is strong enough to counteract the effects of a corrupted, money-idolising society. The Tory social myth, the reverence for land and history, for the idea of an organic society, has its late-eighteenth century exponents in men like Smollett and Goldsmith, or in the politics of Burke; and it assumes a particular importance in the nineteenth century as a form of response to the effects of industrialism, in the work of men like Cobbett or Ruskin. But the historical, pre-industrial myths of the Tory Radicals were much further removed from the realities of political life than the Toryism of the late seventeenth and early eighteenth centuries. The sentimental individual fully developed in Dickens and explored by Pope is the result of recognition that a social myth is helpless to confront or avert a mechanical self-generating political system. Where large solutions are unavailable, the only answer is a limited one, in the idealisation not of the ordered society but of the benevolent heart. For the poet, for Pope in his last years, it involves an abandonment of a public role, of the voice of Horace or Jonson or Boileau or Dryden, and a turning back to the proud self.

Notes

NOTES TO CHAPTER 1

1 e.g. by E. M. W. Tillyard, *The Elizabethan World Picture* (London, 1943).
2 Richard Hooker, *Of the Laws of Ecclesiastical Polity* (London, 1965), I, 157, 185.
3 Edmund Spenser, *Works*, ed. Edwin Greenlaw *et al.* (Baltimore, 1932–4), I, 167. The influence on Spenser of humanist views of education and society is described by Fritz Caspari, *Humanism and the Social Order in Tudor England* (Chicago, 1954).
4 The fullest account of the split is by Perez Zagorin, *The Court and the Country: The Beginnings of the English Revolution* (London, 1969).
5 See G. R. Elton, *The Tudor Constitution* (Cambridge, 1965), *pp.* 451–6; J. P. Kenyon, *The Stuart Constitution* (Cambridge, 1966), *pp.* 492–7.
6 Some critical views of James's and Buckingham's extravagance are collected in *James I by his Contemporaries*, ed. Robert Ashton (London, 1969).
7 Lawrence Stone, *The Crisis of the Aristocracy, 1558–1641* (Oxford, 1965), *p.* 397. Proclamations against building in London are described by Norman G. Brett-James, *The Growth of Stuart London* (London, 1935). See also F. J. Fisher, 'The Development of London as a Centre of Conspicuous Consumption in the Sixteenth and Seventeenth Centuries', *Trans. Royal Hist. Soc.*, Fourth Series, XXX (1948), 37–50.
8 James I, *Political Works*, ed. C. H. McIlwain (Cambridge, Mass., 1918), *pp.* 343–4.
9 Fisher, *Trans. Royal Hist. Soc.*, Fourth Series, XXX (1948), *p.* 46.
10 Kenyon, *p.* 502.
11 *The Oxford Book of Seventeenth Century Verse*, ed. H. J. C. Grierson and G. Bullough (Oxford, 1958), no. 356.
12 H. R. Trevor-Roper has defined 'The General Crisis of the Seventeenth Century' (in *Crisis in Europe, 1560–1660*, ed. Trevor Aston), which resulted in revolutions in mid-century throughout Europe, in terms of the strain imposed by ever-expanding, wasteful, and parasitic courts, and the eventual refusal of the countries concerned to tolerate them any longer.
13 David Mathew, *The Jacobean Age* (London, 1938), *p.* 254.
14 See John Summerson, *Inigo Jones* (Harmondsworth, Middx., 1966), and Per Palme's detailed study of the banqueting house, *Triumph of Peace* (Stockholm, 1956).
15 Palme, *p.* 18.
16 Summerson, *p.* 134, suggests that this was very much a misconceived ambition: 'The new Whitehall would have been a grave and fitting backcloth for the bloodier revolution which it would most certainly have helped to precipitate.'
17 See Waller's poem, 'Upon his Majesty's Repairing of Paul's', in *Poems*, ed. G. Thorn Drury (London, n.d.), I, 16–18.

18 Palme, *p.* 23.

19 Stephen B. Baxter, *William III* (New York, 1966), *p.* 301.

20 See ch. 4, n. 19.

21 Roy Strong, *The English Icon* (London, 1969), *p.* 27, states that as the Dutch painters, Mytens, Van Dyck, and Rubens, became popular at court, 'neo-medievalism', the court style under Elizabeth, became the portrait art of the bourgeoisie and country gentry. C. V. Wedgwood, *Poetry and Politics under the Stuarts* (Cambridge, 1960), *pp.* 48, 53, points out the gap between the court idea of a virtuous and fruitful family at the centre of peaceful and prosperous kingdoms, and the existing national divisions and lack of effective government to cure them; perhaps too simplistically she sees the court poets who propagated this idea as ministering to Charles's self-deception.

22 Wedgwood, *p.* 172, is more critical of poets of Charles II's reign, who should have known better.

23 The fortunes of the gentry during the earlier part of the period have been the subject of a large amount of stimulating but inconclusive research and speculation in the last half-century. A bibliography of the gentry controversy, involving chiefly R. H. Tawney, H. R. Trevor-Roper, Lawrence Stone, and J. H. Hexter, is given in Lawrence Stone, *Social Change and Revolution in England, 1540–1640* (London, 1965). The tendency of this speculation has been to see the revolution of the seventeenth century not in political, constitutional, or religious terms, but in terms of social structure and mobility. Depending on which particular view seems promising, the revolution can be seen as a result of the gentry's rise at the expense of the aristocracy or the declining gentry's reaction to an over-burdened court from which they were excluded. Trevor-Roper's view, which is rigid and simple-minded to the extent that he refuses to acknowledge the influence of any other factors, seeing Catholic rebellions and the Puritan revolution alike as movements of reactionary protest, nevertheless is valuable in that it focuses on the attitudes of country gentry excluded from power and the social and psychological tension between court and country. See 'The Gentry, 1540–1640', *Ec. Hist. Rev. Supplement* I (1953); 'The Country House Radicals, 1590–1660', 'The Social Causes of the Great Rebellion', in *Historical Essays* (London, 1963).

24 Bonamy Dobrée, 'The Theme of Patriotism in the Poetry of the Early Eighteenth Century', *Proc. Brit. Acad.* xxxv (1949), *p.* 56.

25 For the relation of mercantilism to state power see Eli F. Hecksher, *Mercantilism*, trans. M. Shapiro (2 vols.; London, 1934).

26 Virgil, *Eclogues and Georgics*, ed. H. Rushton Fairclough (rev. ed.; London, 1960), *p.* 30, *l.* 31.

27 Horace, *Satires, Epistles, and Ars Poetica*, ed. H. Rushton Fairclough (Cambridge, Mass., 1966), p. 210, *l.* 1.

28 For the development of these attitudes see Steele Commager, *The Odes of Horace* (New Haven, 1962), ch. iv.

29 Thomas Carew, *The Poems*, ed. Rhodes Dunlap (Oxford, 1964), *p.* 77, *ll.* 96–100.

30 Andrew Marvell, *Poems*, ed. Hugh Macdonald (London, 1960), p. 91, *l.* 322.

31 The chief poems are discussed in G. R. Hibbard, 'The Country House Poem of the Seventeenth Century', *Essential Articles for the Study of Alexander Pope*, ed. Maynard Mack (Hamden, Conn., 1964).

32 Its development and divergent types have been fully documented by Maren-Sofie

Røstvig, *The Happy Man* (2 vols.; Oslo, 1954–8), but she does not really consider the relationship of this genre, which concentrates on the good life as lived by the individual, to poems concerned with images of the harmonious whole society, nor to the influence of political and social developments, though she gives some weight to the enforced retirement of royalist poets after the civil war. She is particularly interested in the religious and mystical possibilities of the genre. Some aspects of Restoration poems of country life are discussed by Rachel Trickett, *The Honest Muse* (Oxford, 1967), ch. v.

33 Abraham Cowley, 'The Dangers of an Honest Man in Much Company', *Essays, Plays, and Sundry Verses*, ed. A. R. Waller (Cambridge, 1906), *pp.* 446–7.

34 Thomas Fuller defined 'the true gentleman' as one without ambition for office but willing to serve if chosen: 'If the Commission of the Peace finds him out, he faithfully discharges it. I say, finds him out; for a public office is a guest which receives the best usage from them who never invited it.' *The Holy State and the Profane State*, ed. M. G. Walten (New York, 1938), II, 151.

35 *The Oxford Book of Eighteenth Century Verse*, ed. D. Nichol Smith (Oxford, 1963), *p.* 2. 'Genteel' here has its original meaning of 'belonging to or included among the gentry' (*OED*).

36 *Poems*, ed. John Buxton (London, 1958), *pp.* 33–4, *ll.* 55–7, 73–8.

37 T. B. Macaulay, *History of England from the Accession of James II* (London, 1957), I, ch. iii, 'England in 1685'.

NOTES TO CHAPTER 2

1 For a detailed account of satire at this time see Alvin Kernan, *The Cankered Muse* (New Haven, 1959). *Every Man out of his Humour, Cynthia's Revels*, and *Poetaster* are all described as comical satires in the 1616 folio. See *Ben Jonson*, ed. C. H. Herford and Percy and Evelyn Simpson (Oxford, 1925–52), IX, 396–7; hereafter cited as H & S. The poems are in VIII, and are identified by collection: *Ep.* (*Epigrams*), *For.* (*The Forest*), *Und.* (*The Underwood*), *U.V.* (*Ungathered Verse*).

2 *Und.* xxiii, *p.* 174.

3 It was also expedient; publication of the Apologetical Dialogue was prohibited. H & S, I, 29–30.

4 Geoffrey Walton, *Metaphysical to Augustan* (London, 1955), *pp.* 24–5.

5 *Conversations with Drummond*, H & S, I, 137.

6 The connection with Juvenal is important. In *Satire* I Juvenal criticises epic as irrelevant, and portrays himself as driven to write satire by what he sees around him. But no explicit moral scheme underlies this condemnation of contemporary society; indeed in *Satire* XIII he dissociates himself from the creeds of Cynics, Stoics and Epicureans. Where, as in *Satire* X, he asks what can be opposed to the way of the world, his answer is negative and personal: one should pray for a sound mind in a sound body, for a strong soul that can endure, that is free from fear, anger, and desire. Though disclaiming allegiance to Stoicism, Juvenal sets forward as the answer to the satirist's indignation the apathy of the Stoic sage.

7 Jonson's technique of making inverted social values into the real dramatic ones is discussed by E. B. Partridge, *The Broken Compass: A Study of the Major Comedies of Ben Jonson* (New York, 1958).

8 Léontine Zanta identifies three levels in the Stoic revival: philosophical, theological

(particularly Protestant), and humanist. She shows how some of the French humanists managed to separate practical morality both from the metaphysical principles of the classical Stoics and the theological dogma with which it conflicted (*La Renaissance du Stoicisme au XVIᵉ Siècle* [Paris, 1914], *pp.* 21–6, 87–8).

9 J. L. Saunders, *Justus Lipsius: The Philosophy of Renaissance Stoicism* (New York, 1955), *pp.* 111, 139–43. Lipsius' works of synthesis are *Manductio ad Stoicam Philosophiam* and *Physiologia Stoicorum* (1604).

10 *Heaven upon Earth and Characters of Vertues and Vices*, ed. Rudolf Kirk (New Brunswick, N.J., 1948), *pp.* 84, 29.

11 *Essais*, ed. Albert Thibaudet (Paris, 1950), *pp.* 682–3.

12 A useful bibliography of editions and translations of Stoic authors showing their popularity in the sixteenth and early seventeenth centuries is given in Rudolf Kirk's introduction to *Two Bookes of constancie written in Latine by Iustus Lipsius; Englished by Sir John Stradling* (New Brunswick, N.J., 1939).

13 There is a handful of poems expressing Christian humility: *For.* xv, *Und.* i, ii, iii.

14 C. B. Hilberry, 'Jonson's Ethics' (unpublished dissertation, Chicago, 1930), has examined in detail Jonson's relation to classical and humanist Stoicism without being aware of the discrepancy between his ethics and his poetics.

15 For an account of the changes in Stoic ideas see E. V. Arnold, *Roman Stoicism* (Cambridge, 1911).

16 I give no specific references for Seneca since his ideas are repeated throughout his work. The following summary is based on these texts: *Ad Lucilium Epistulae Morales*, with trans. by Richard M. Gummere (3 vols.; London, 1917–25); *Moral Essays*, with trans. by John W. Basore (3 vols.; London, 1928–35). Seneca did not always adhere to the prescriptions of his own school, which required the political involvement of the wise man. Some of his work does have a public purpose, for example *On Benefits* (drawn on by Jonson in 'An Epistle to Sir Edward Sackville' [*Und.* xiii]), and *On Mercy*, addressed to Nero. But Seneca's usual intention is to provide the individual with a system of aids to virtuous life. His idea of virtue is as follows. It can be attained by any man who follows nature, which means, since reason is natural and peculiar to man, being ruled by reason. Reason teaches one to distinguish immediate advantages and disadvantages from good and evil. Happiness is achieved only by the practice of virtue, which is its own reward; there is no inducement to the Stoic in the promise of present or future rewards. Externals are nothing to the wise man. However, the unequal distribution of material prosperity in the world has a purpose. Providence gives riches to the undeserving and misfortune to the good to show that fortune or misfortune are neither good nor evil. The wise man cannot call himself happy until he has been tested by Providence and can show that he is unaffected by misfortune. If his suffering is intolerable, he has the choice of ending his life. The wise man is independent from his circumstances, since they cannot affect his firmness. The emotions – fear, greed, grief, or joy – are not goods, since they involve reaction to external events and objects. But Seneca is careful to distinguish between slavery to and proper enjoyment of prosperity. It is the man who is unable to tell an advantage from the good who will be made perpetually unhappy by his pursuit of the wrong end. Seneca's ethics may be criticised on two main grounds: on the grounds chosen by Montaigne and Pascal, that Seneca overestimates the individual's capacity to achieve happiness without reference to anything outside himself; and on the grounds that he underestimates

224

the human capacity to alter circumstances. The early Stoa was founded on the assumption that political institutions, as well as the individual, could be perfected. But Seneca assumes that circumstances are immutable, and that the individual should ignore them. By his overambitious and naive attempt to account for and explain away the problem of evil, Seneca removes the possibility of confronting it usefully.

17 Epistles cxix, cx, cxv: H & S, XI, 254–6.

18 Jonson's difficulties and the directions he took can be further understood by comparing him with poets who shared his social position. Samuel Daniel seems to have found, like Jonson, a way of reconciling his personal ethics with the demands of his place in a hierarchical society (see his epistles, especially 'To the Lady Margaret Countess of Cumberland'). Michael Drayton, however, was frustrated in his attempt to create a useful public role for himself; unable to find his national audience he withdrew to celebration of a private group of friends (see the prefaces to and song xxi of *Polyolbion* and the elegies published in 1627).

19 Useful analyses of the poets' social and financial relations can be found in E. H. Miller, *The Professional Writer in Elizabethan England* (Cambridge, Mass., 1959); J. W. Saunders, 'The Social Situation of Seventeenth-Century Poetry' in *Metaphysical Poetry*, ed. D. J. Palmer and Malcolm Bradbury (London, 1970); Patricia Thomson, 'The Literature of Patronage, 1580–1630', *Essays in Criticism*, II (1952). Much of my material has been collected independently of these accounts.

20 Eleanor Rosenberg, *Leicester Patron of Letters* (New York, 1955) shows how successful a 'progressive' use of patronage, supporting the popularisation of learning, could be; but it was not the patronage that writers like Spenser and Drayton wanted. H. S. Bennett, taking all kinds of publication into consideration, agrees with Rosenberg that patronage was flourishing, but admits that professional men of letters were in difficulties. See *English Books and Readers 1558 to 1603* (Cambridge, 1965), *pp.* 31, 45, and *1603 to 1640* (Cambridge, 1970), *p.* 23.

21 Miller, *p.* 110.

22 Thomson, *Essays in Criticism*, II (1952), 273–4.

23 See e.g. *Und.* lxviii, lxxvii.

24 H & S, I, 31, 139.

25 John Danby in *Elizabethan and Jacobean Poets* (London, 1964) defines the poets' tones in relation to their social standing, their position on 'fortune's hill'; he attributes Jonson's confidence (*p.* 44) to the fact that he invaded the field of the 'greatest persons' after having conquered his own professional territory.

26 The role of a family like the Sidneys in both exemplifying virtue and renewing ancient traditions is discussed by Hugh Maclean, 'Ben Jonson's Poems: Notes on the Ordered Society', *Essays in English Literature from the Renaissance to the Victorian Age*, ed. Millar MacLure (Toronto, 1964), *pp.* 58–61. See also Walton, *pp.* 32–5, on the use of Philip Sidney as representative of civilisation and on the relation of such family groups to society at large.

27 *Life of Sir Philip Sidney*, ed. Nowell Smith (Oxford, 1907), *p.* 150.

28 Critics with strong views on this subject are L. C. Knights in *Drama and Society in the Age of Jonson* (London, 1962, 1st pub. 1937), and 'On the Social Background of Metaphysical Poetry', *Scrutiny*, XIII (1945), 37–52; Jeffrey Hart in 'Ben Jonson's Good Society', *Modern Age*, VII (1962/3), 61–8; G. R. Hibbard in 'The Country House Poem of the Seventeenth Century', *Journal of the Warburg and Courtauld*

Institutes, XIX (1956); P. M. Cubeta in 'A Jonsonian Ideal: "To Penshurst"', *PQ*, XLII (1963), 14–24; and Walton in *Metaphysical to Augustan*. Knights depicts the displacement of feudal society and values by new economic methods and a corresponding ethic; he warns against romanticising the old and vulgarly criticising the new order, perhaps because he tends to do it himself. Hart sees the threat to traditional values and hierarchy in a new individualism and frankly associates himself with the past; to him 'Penshurst' is partly a historical document, as it is to Walton and Hibbard, who in tracing images of society from Jonson to Pope see a decline in the quality of life in Pope's day and tend to overestimate the extent to which Jonson found his society congenial. To Cubeta 'Penshurst' is an idealisation in sharp contrast with empirical reality.

29 Quoted in F. B. Young, *Mary Sidney Countess of Pembroke* (London, 1912), *pp.* 155–6.

30 Sir Philip Sidney, *The Prose Works*, ed. Albert Feuillerat (Cambridge, 1962), I, 15.

31 *Ibid.*, *pp.* 185–6.

32 *Ibid.*, *p.* 187.

33 Danby suggests, *pp.* 155–6, that *Arcadia* is the product of a great house culture independent of the court, and that the Jacobean court by asserting itself usurped the function of the great house and upset the balance.

34 Greville, *p.* 16.

35 *Ibid.*, *pp.* 175–6, 183, 189. Elizabeth insisted on the maintenance of degree; she told Sidney that 'the gentleman's neglect of the nobility taught the peasant to insult upon both'. *Ibid.*, *p.* 68.

36 See especially 'Of Seditions and Troubles', 'Of Ambition', 'Of Nobility', 'Of Empire', 'Of the True Greatness of Kingdoms and Estates'.

37 The change in the fortunes of the aristocracy has been charted by Lawrence Stone, *The Crisis of the Aristocracy 1558–1641* (Oxford, 1965). Stone's thesis is aimed at finding new social and economic reasons for the civil war to supplement R. H. Tawney's view of the conflict between the old social order based on status and obligation and the new Puritan individualism (see especially *The Agrarian Problem in the Sixteenth Century* [New York, n.d., 1st pub. 1912] and 'The Rise of the Gentry 1558–1640', *Ec. Hist. Rev.* XI [1941], 1–38). Stone finds these reasons partly in the change in the status of the nobility, which in turn undermined the monarchy and made revolution feasible. It was necessary for the Tudors to limit the power of the nobility, and under Elizabeth contemporaries thought the right balance had been found; but by the early seventeenth century the process had gone too far, and the nobility were dangerously weakened (Stone, p. 13). Stone attributes their slump in prestige to many causes: the decline of their wealth relative to that of the gentry, the shrinking of their territorial possessions, the decay of their military power, the creation and sale of titles of honour by James, the aristocracy's change in attitude to their tenantry (as sources of profit rather than of service), their preference for living in town, the spread of education and the demand for an administrative elite of proven competence, regardless of rank, the influence of Puritan individualism and belief in a spiritual hierarchy, the exaltation of private conscience, and the growing psychological breach between court and country (*pp.* 748–9). Elizabeth's extreme parsimony (not only in her management of finances but in her reluctance to create peers) put the nobility under great strain and made corruption inevitable; James's lavish creation and sale of honours undermined their value and involved nobility and monarchy in a vicious inflationary spiral. An

increase in conspicuous consumption (such as the traditional country house hospitality that Jonson describes, maintenance of pomp in the royal service, attendance at court, or life in London) was necessary to justify status as it was being undermined (*pp*. 97, 120, 123, 185-6, 501). The decline in the military utility of the aristocracy and the opening of the ranks by James corresponded with an artificial revival of chivalry and an obsession with genealogy.

38 The 'speech' of the title is assumed by K. A. McEuen, *Classical Influence upon the Tribe of Ben* (Cedar Rapids, Iowa, 1939), *p*. 47, to be a translation of the Horatian *sermo* or satire. Jonson is also undoubtedly alluding (H & S, XI, 81-2) to the patriotic odes of Book III, such as *Ode* ii, which advocates military service, and *Ode* v, which celebrates the example of Regulus.

39 The Essex rebellion of 1601 is a classic example of the attempt to revive the military side of the retaining system. See G. R. Elton, *England under the Tudors* (London, 1963), *p*. 473.

40 See respectively Partridge, *Broken Compass*, and Knights, *Drama and Society*.

41 Knights, relying heavily on Tawney's thesis in *Religion and the Rise of Capitalism* of the rise of a middle class in the late sixteenth and early seventeenth centuries, sees Jonson as the inheritor of an anti-acquisitive tradition, of a medieval system of values in which status rather than class, public good rather than private profit are emphasised; he sees Jonson in the plays implicitly defending these against the monetary, individualistic values of the rising capitalist class (*Drama and Society*, passim). Knights's account of contemporary definitions of these opposed values is excellent, but he accepts them too easily as accurate; men living through a period of change surely tend to romanticise what it is that is being changed. Thus Knights sees 'To Penshurst' as embodying inherited values of hierarchy, liberality, and hospitality (*Scrutiny*, XIII [1945], 37-52), but he accepts the poem too readily as historical description. He rightly emphasises moralists' complaints about the decay of hospitality and the social irresponsibility of 'new men' (*Drama and Society*, *pp*. 105-17), without inquiring too closely into the reality behind these complaints.

42 Tawney describes how the old feudal lord assessed the value of land in terms of the number of tenants able to serve him, and how this kind of landlord–tenant relationship posed a military threat to the crown in the sixteenth century. It persisted longer in the north, where the nobility were more powerful and more dangerous; in the south the crown's destruction of feudalism meant that land came to be seen as a source of financial profit (*Agrarian Problem*, *pp*. 2, 188-92).

43 This is the view of Hart, *Modern Age*, VII (1962/3), 61.

44 The great era of housebuilding, 1580-1620, corresponds to the crisis in the nobility's status and was partly a result of the inflation of honours. Most of the great houses at the turn of the century were built by Elizabeth's and James's statesmen: Burghley and Theobalds by Burghley, Holdenby by Hatton, Hatfield by Salisbury, Audley End by Suffolk (Stone, *pp*. 452, 550-1; H. Avray Tipping, *Late Tudor and Early Stuart* [London, 1927], *pp*. xi, 305-53, Period III, vol. II of *English Homes*; John Summerson, *Architecture in Britain 1530-1830* [London, 1953], *pp*. 30, 38-41, 49).

45 Besides Hatfield he owned Cecil House in the Strand; Beaufort House, Chelsea; and Cranborne Manor in Dorset. He decided to rebuild Hatfield while his London house was still unfinished. 'To Penshurst' was written before 1612 (when Prince Henry died); Salisbury exchanged Theobalds for Hatfield with James in 1607, and died in 1612. Salisbury is praised in *Ep*. xliii, but Jonson's opinion of his hospitality

was given to Drummond (H & S, I, 141): 'being...demanded by my lord, why he was not glad My lord said he you promised I should dine with you, but I do not, for he had none of his meat, he esteemed only it his meat which was of his own dish'. See H & S, I, 57.

46 So ruinous was the honour of entertaining Elizabeth that some gentry left their houses and counties as a progress threatened (Stone, *p*. 453). The expansion of Theobalds put a great strain on Burghley, and was sneered at by contemporaries, but he protested that it was all on the Queen's behalf: 'Theobalds...was begun by me with a mean measure; but increased by occasion of her Majesty's often coming: whom to please, I never would omit to strain myself to more charges than building it. And yet not without some special direction of her Majesty' (from a letter of 1585). Each visit of the Queen cost him £2,000–£3,000. See J. Nichols, *The Progresses...of Queen Elizabeth* (London, 1788), I, 1566 *p*. 111, 1572 *p*. 15. The royal household might well exhaust the provisions of the surrounding countryside. In 1604 one of James's favourite dogs Jowler was kidnapped at Royston and returned to his master with this message round his neck: 'Good Mr. Jowler, we pray you speak to the King (for he hears you every day, and so doth he not us) that it will please his Majesty to go back to London, for else the country will be undone; all our provision is spent already, and we are not able to entertain him longer' (Nichols, *The Progresses...of King James I* [London, 1828], I, 465. See also D. H. Willson, *King James VI and I* (London, 1962), *pp*. 183–4.

47 These are taken from *Georgic* II.

48 Here Jonson borrows from Juvenal's *Satire* X.

49 To several poems Jonson owes debts of structure and phrasing; these include *Georgic* II (a comparison of the independent countryman's life with that of the town) and three epigrams of Martial: Book III, lviii (a eulogy of Faustinus' country house at Baiaie, compared with Bassus' house in the suburbs), Book I, xliv (on Licinianus' life in Spain, reviewing the pleasures of the seasons), and Book X, xxx (on Apollinaris' villa at Formiae, where the fish in the pond answer to their master).

50 Horace alludes to the craze for ostentatious building in *Odes*, II, xv.

51 One typical genre of Latin poetry, the complaint at grudging hospitality, is not used by Jonson. Its opposite type, the invitation to a simple meal, is the subject of a single poem, 'Inviting a friend to supper' (*Ep*. ci, *p*. 64), although Jonson translated one of Martial's poems on the subject of the simple life, Book X, xlvii (*Und.* xc, *p*. 295), and Horace's *Epode* II (*Und.* lxxxv, *p*. 289).

52 Some useful background studies are Paul Reyher, *Les Masques Anglais* (New York, 1964, 1st pub. 1909); E. K. Chambers, *The Elizabethan Stage* (Oxford, 1923), vol. I; Enid Welsford, *The Court Masque* (New York, 1962, 1st pub. 1927). Recent interpretative studies include E. W. Talbert, 'The Interpretation of Jonson's Courtly Spectacles', *PMLA*, LXI (1946), 454–73; Dolora Cunningham, 'The Jonsonian Masque as a Literary Form', *Ben Jonson: A Collection of Critical Essays*, ed. Jonas A. Barish (Englewood Cliffs, N. J., 1963); W. Todd Furniss, 'Ben Jonson's Masques', *Three Studies in the Renaissance* (New Haven, 1958); Stephen Orgel, *The Jonsonian Masque* (Cambridge, Mass., 1965), the best of these. J. C. Meagher, *Method and Meaning in Jonson's Masques* (Notre Dame, Ind., 1966), gives the most thorough account of the moral assumptions of the court masque (part of my analysis parallels his) without being critical enough of its conditions.

53 Herford and Simpson (I, 72-4) relate his interest in epic to his nine-year absence from drama from 1616.

54 Ruth Kelso, *The Doctrine of the English Gentleman in the Sixteenth Century* (Urbana, Ill., 1929), analyses the ethical components of the literature of humanist education and courtesy.

55 *Works*, I, 167-8.

56 In the *Nicomachean Ethics* a certain level of good fortune is necessary to happiness, which is realised not in the possession but the exercise of virtue; it is not a state of mind, but of action. Virtue is practised by choosing the middle path between two extremes, by following the rule of the mean. However, an individual is not required to have an abstract idea of the mean, nor can he be considered virtuous simply because he is disposed towards virtue. A man does not become virtuous by prior knowledge of the mean, but through habit (Book II, i, 4-5). The mean, which is the principle by which right action is decided, is what would be formulated by the sensible man, who is a norm rather than an ideal. Aristotle's list of moral virtues (Book II, vii, elaborated in Books III and IV) includes those of liberality, magnificence, magnanimity, and proper ambition. These virtues are all social, outward-looking, and appropriate to a particular class. Liberality differs from magnificence only in the sense that the magnificent man is wealthier than the liberal man, so that his gestures are necessarily more public. The extremes of which magnificence is the mean are vulgarity and paltriness: the display made by the magnificent man must be both adequate and appropriate to the occasion. Magnanimity (pride, or self-esteem) and proper ambition (the mean between too much and too little ambition) perhaps approximate more closely to Spenser's idea of magnificence. The magnanimous man is conspicuous through virtue; he has a right to honour, which is the greatest of external goods and his chief ambition. The extremes of this mean are vanity, the claim to honour beyond desert, and poor-spiritedness. Proper ambition stands in the same relation to magnanimity as liberality to magnificence: it is a necessary condition. The virtuous man who does not seek proper recognition from society damages himself not only in reputation but in his disposition to virtue.

57 H & S, XI, 260.

58 James I, *Political Works*, ed. C. H. McIlwain (Cambridge, Mass., 1918), Speech in Star Chamber, 1616, *p.* 333.

59 *Ibid.*, Speech to Lords and Commons, 1610, *p.* 307.

60 *Ibid.*, *pp.* 308-10. For James as a constitutional monarch see F. D. Wormuth, *The Royal Prerogative 1603-1649* (Ithaca, N.Y., 1939), *pp.* 90-3; Kenyon, *Stuart Constitution*, *p.* 8. However, W. H. Greenleaf, *Order, Empiricism, and Politics* (London, 1964), regards James as a serious theorist of absolutism.

61 *Political Works, Basilikon Doron*, *p.* 12.

62 *Ibid.*, *p.* 30.

63 *Ibid.*, Speech to Parliament, 1604, *p.* 272.

64 On the idealisation of Elizabeth see E. C. Wilson, *England's Eliza* (Cambridge, Mass., 1939), and Roy Strong, *Portraits of Queen Elizabeth I* (Oxford, 1963).

65 Samuel Daniel, *The Complete Works in Verse and Prose*, ed. A. Grosart (New York, 1963), III, 193-4, *ll.* 199-202.

66 The quarrel is examined in detail by D. J. Gordon, 'Poet and Architect: The Intellectual Setting of the Quarrel between Ben Jonson and Inigo Jones', *Journal of the Warburg Institute*, XII (1949), 152-78.

67 See Welsford, *p.* 272. Stephen Orgel in his introduction to the Yale Ben Jonson *Collected Masques* (New Haven, 1969) argues that Jonson came to regard the masque as a unified form with the machinery an integral part.

68 Nichols, *Progresses...of James I*, II, 72–4.

69 H & S, X, 703.

70 This wedding and Overbury's murder, according to Godfrey Davies, *The Early Stuarts, 1603–1660* (2nd ed.; Oxford, 1959), did more to bring the crown into disrepute than any act before Charles's attempt to arrest the five members in 1642.

71 i.e. Sir Christopher Hatton's Holdenby.

72 Orgel, *Jonsonian Masque*, *p.* 74.

73 Carew, *Poems*, *p.* 170, *ll.* 659–65. Note that Aristotle has here been turned inside out.

74 Bacon, *Essays* (London, 1962), p. 214.

75 'The virtue of princes is to masque as the fall of princes is to tragedy', Cunningham, 'Jonsonian Masque', *p.* 173.

76 The Tudor and Stuart development of the theory of the king's natural and politic bodies is traced in Ernst H. Kantorowicz, *The King's Two Bodies* (Princeton, 1957), *pp.* 7–23.

77 Orgel on the other hand (*Jonsonian Masque*, *pp.* 77, 81) considers that praise degenerates into gratuitous flattery if the monarch is not established as a figure worthy of praise within the masque; he criticises *Oberon, the Fairy Prince* on these grounds.

78 Furniss, *p.* 113.

79 See D. J. Gordon, '*Hymenaei*: Ben Jonson's Masque of Union', *Journal of the Warburg Institute*, VIII (1945), 107–45.

80 Walton, *p.* 44.

81 *The Poems of John Donne*, ed. Herbert Grierson (London, 1960), *p.* 383, *ll.* 11–12.

NOTES TO CHAPTER 3

1 As I am concerned exclusively with the development of the revolution in England, I am not taking into account the establishment of Puritan societies in New England.

2 Though an equally important (in terms of the future, more important) intellectual development of the English revolution was the growth of a wholly secular view of politics and society, exemplified by Hobbes, I do not propose to deal with it here, as it has little bearing on the poets whose work I am discussing.

3 The best account of this process is the chapter 'Church-outed by the prelates' in William Haller, *The Rise of Puritanism* (New York, 1938).

4 *The Reason of Church Government urged against Prelaty, The Works of John Milton*, ed. F. A. Patterson *et al.* (New York, 1931–40), III i, 242. Subsequent references for prose are to this edition, cited as Columbia; references for poetry are to *The Poems of John Milton*, ed. John Carey and Alastair Fowler (London, 1968), cited as *Poems*.

5 On Milton's early development J. H. Hanford's interpretation in 'The Youth of Milton', *John Milton: Poet and Humanist* (Cleveland, 1966), and *John Milton, Englishman* (London, 1950), seems more convincing than that of W. R. Parker, *Milton: A Biography*, 2 vols. (Oxford, 1968).

6 The content of Milton's studies has been investigated in detail by D. L. Clark, *John Milton at St Paul's School* (New York, 1948), and H. F. Fletcher, *The Intellectual Development of John Milton*, 2 vols. in progress (Urbana, 1956–61).

7 Fletcher, II, 549, dates this decision 1627 or 1628.

8 The period of Jonsonian influence is discussed by Parker, I, 91.

9 See Northrop Frye's comparison of the conservative artist who perfects inherited form with the revolutionary artist who explores the boundaries of art, *Five Essays on Milton's Epics* (London, 1966), *pp.* 94–7.

10 *Coelum Britannicum* is discussed above, ch. 2, *pp.* 61–2.

11 There is no evidence that he proposed for himself a life of celibacy. His attitude to chastity is discussed by E. M. W. Tillyard, *Milton* (London, 1968), Appendix C; Ernest Sirluck, 'Milton's Idle Right Hand', *JEGP*, LX (1961), *pp.* 749–85; and Parker, II, 800–1.

12 'Additur huic scelerisque vacans, et casta iuventus, / Et rigidi mores, et sine labe manus. / Qualis veste nitens sacra, et lustralibus undis / Surgis ad infensos augur iture deos. / . . .Diis etenim sacer est vates, divumque sacerdos, / Spirat et occultum pectus, et ora Iovem.' (*Poems, pp.* 116–17.)

13 In Prolusion VII there is a movement from retirement to social involvement. Douglas Bush points out that the poet of *Ad Patrem* is 'the scholar-artist of the elite' rather than the poet-priest, *A Variorum Commentary on the Poems of John Milton*, I (London, 1970), 236.

14 'Spiritus et rapidos qui circinat igneus orbes, / Nunc quoque sidereis intercinit ipse choreis / Immortale melos, et inerrabile carmen; / . . .Ergo ego iam doctae pars quamlibet ima catervae / Victrices hederas inter, laurosque sedebo, / Iamque nec obscurus populo miscebor inerti, / Vitabuntque oculos vestigia nostra profanos.' (*Poems, pp.* 150–2.)

15 *Of Education*, Columbia, IV, 290.

16 For the decline of the Arthurian legend in relation to parliamentary rediscovery of the Saxons see Roberta F. Brinkley, *Arthurian Legend in the Seventeenth Century* (Baltimore, 1932).

17 Michael Fixler, however, *Milton and the Kingdoms of God* (London, 1964), *pp.* 66–72, sees an apocalyptic element in Milton's conception of national epic. Although this argument seems farfetched, Fixler provides an extremely useful investigation of Milton's relation to millenarian thought and of his change in interest from an earthly to an inner kingdom.

18 In *The Doctrine and Discipline of Divorce* marriage is seen as a form of society, and happiness in marriage as the necessary basis for a useful Christian life. Milton speaks of 'the household estate, out of which must flourish forth the vigour and spirit of all public enterprises' (Columbia, III ii, 392). Similarly in *Paradise Lost* VIII Adam argues the need for the society of an equal: 'Of fellowship I speak / Such as I seek, fit to participate / All rational delight' (*ll.* 389–91). Marriage is the model for relationships between individuals, but Milton does not have a sense of wider social relationships between groups.

19 Cromwell's interest in religion rather than politics is analysed in different ways by R. S. Paul, *The Lord Protector* (London, 1955), and Maurice Ashley, *The Greatness of Oliver Cromwell* (London, 1957). His break with the sectaries and republicans is described at length by W. C. Abbott, *The Writings and Speeches of Oliver Cromwell* (Cambridge, Mass., 1937–47), vols. III and IV.

20 The development of Milton's ideas in relation to those of his contemporaries is very usefully set out in great detail in the introductions to the *Complete Prose Works of John Milton*, ed. Don M. Wolfe *et al.* (New Haven, 1953–), hereafter cited as Yale Milton. The most sympathetic account of Milton's idea of liberty is by Arthur Barker, *Milton and the Puritan Dilemma* (Toronto, 1942). Don M. Wolfe, *Milton in the Puritan Revolution* (New York, 1941), is more critical, as is Perez Zagorin, *A History of Political Thought in the English Revolution* (London, 1954), ch. ix. Zera S. Fink, *The Classical Republicans* (Evanston, 1945), argues rather unconvincingly for the coherence of Milton's political thought, considered apart from his religious interests, as a belief in the mixed state and the aristocracy of virtue.

21 As Hanford argues, *John Milton, Englishman*, p. 74.

22 In contrast M. M. Ross, *Milton's Royalism* (Ithaca, N.Y., 1943), sees a suppressed royalism as the basis of Milton's intellectual development.

23 This problem is defined and discussed at length by Haller, *Rise of Puritanism*.

24 Richard Baxter, *Autobiography*, ed. J. M. Lloyd Thomas (London, 1931), p. 84.

25 Claudius Salmasius, *Defensio Regia pro Carolo I*, Yale Milton, IV ii, 989.

26 Sir Robert Filmer, *Observations on Mr Milton against Salmasius*, in *Patriarcha and other Political Works*, ed. P. Laslett (Oxford, 1949), p. 252.

27 Milton also advised Cromwell to use the services of his early supporters (some of whom were now his opponents), to avoid a proliferation of lawmaking, and to improve education.

28 *Constitutional Documents of the Puritan Revolution*, ed. S. R. Gardiner, 3rd ed. (Oxford, 1906), p. 416.

29 There were two editions of *Ready and Easy Way*. In each case Milton's argument was rapidly overtaken by events. The first edition was addressed to the Rump, but before publication Monk restored the Presbyterian members, and it became the Long Parliament again. Milton added a paragraph addressed to this parliament, but already the decision had been made to call a new one. The second edition was addressed to the new Convention Parliament about to meet, and widely expected to recall Charles II. Parker, *Milton*, I, 543–56. Barbara Kiefer Lewalski gives an excellent and detailed account of Milton's political arguments in this period, seeing no inconsistency between his pragmatic shifts of allegiance and his underlying principles, in 'Milton: Political Beliefs and Polemical Methods, 1659–60', *PMLA*, LXXIV (1959), 191–202.

30 Anne Davidson Ferry, in *Milton's Epic Voice: The Narrator in Paradise Lost* (Cambridge, Mass., 1963), pp. 25–38, discusses the blind bard's loss and gain of sight as a paradigm of the experience of Adam and Eve and the reader of the poem; in each case what is gained in the fallen world is in some sense more precious than what is lost (p. 38).

31 As is argued respectively by Tillyard, *Milton*, p. 241, and Ross, p. 92.

32 See e.g. the morning hymn of Adam and Eve, *Paradise Lost*, V, *ll.* 153–208.

33 Christopher Hill, *God's Englishman: Oliver Cromwell and the English Revolution* (London, 1970), ch. ix, gives an interesting interpretation of the Puritan God as the principle of change.

34 Usually dated 1656–60; Parker, *Milton*, II, 1056.

35 *Paradise Lost* was written *c.* 1658–65; *ibid.*, II, 1065, I, 595; *Paradise Regained* and *Samson Agonistes* are usually assumed to have followed in that order. Parker, how-

ever, dates *Samson c.* 1647 (II, 910), and his dating is accepted by Carey and Fowler. His arguments, both stylistic and interpretative, do not seem convincing. He reads it as a pessimistic poem (II, 937), and associates it with the period in the late 1640s when Milton lost his faith in parliament and turned to the idea of coercive enlightened leadership. I do not think that the poem is pessimistic (the chorus must be regarded ironically if this is the case); the political ideas seem to belong to a later stage in Milton's thought. Samson cannot lead the Israelites: he can only provide an example and an opportunity.

36 William Haller, 'The Tragedy of God's Englishman', *Reason and the Imagination*, ed. J. A. Mazzeo (New York, 1962), *pp.* 208–11, compares the resilient mood of *Samson* with that of *Paradise Lost* and *Paradise Regained*; having risen above defeat, Milton returned to pamphleteering (in *Of True Religion*).

37 Columbia, XIV, 90–174.

38 See above, ch. 2, pp. 29–31.

39 Ephesians 6: 10–18.

40 The most extreme statement of the view that revolution made Marvell's balanced frame of mind impossible and ruined his poetry is by Patrick Crutwell, *The Shakespearian Moment* (London, 1954), *p.* 200.

41 These attempts have been made by George de F. Lord, 'From Contemplation to Action: Marvell's Poetical Career', *Andrew Marvell: A Collection of Critical Essays*, ed. Lord (Englewood Cliffs, N.J., 1968), and in his edition of Marvell's *Complete Poetry* (New York, 1968); and by John M. Wallace, *Destiny his Choice: The Loyalism of Andrew Marvell* (Cambridge, 1968), a brilliant elucidation of the political climate of Marvell's work, with some eccentric interpretations of certain poems.

42 As Harold E. Toliver does, *Marvell's Ironic Vision* (New Haven, 1965).

43 M. C. Bradbrook and M. G. Lloyd Thomas, *Andrew Marvell* (Cambridge, 1940), trace a 'conjectured progression' (*p.* 72) in Marvell's lyrics, and date the religious poems and 'The Garden' in the Eton period.

44 *The Poems of Andrew Marvell*, ed. Hugh Macdonald (London, 1952), *p.* 118. This text, cited as Macdonald, is the one used for all poems except the satires, for which I have used *Poems on Affairs of State*, vol. I, 1660–1678, ed. George de F. Lord (New Haven, 1963), cited as *POAS*; I have also referred to the 2nd edition of H. M. Margoliouth, 2 vols. (London, 1952), cited as Margoliouth.

45 Lord makes a similar point in comparing 'An Horatian Ode' with 'The Garden', 'From Contemplation to Action', *Marvell: Critical Essays*, *p.* 59.

46 A sympathetic account is by M. A. Gibb, *The Lord General* (London, 1938).

47 In my discussion of 'Appleton House' I am concerned with Marvell's manipulation of perspective; I do not attempt to analyse the poem as a whole. Detailed and interesting readings are given by D. C. Allen, *Image and Meaning* (Baltimore, 1960), ch. vii; Kitty W. Scoular, *Natural Magic* (Oxford, 1965), *pp.* 163–90; Wallace, ch. vi; J. B. Leishman, *The Art of Marvell's Poetry* (London, 1966), *pp.* 250–73. Røstvig, *The Happy Man*, I, 235, links Marvell with the work of More, Fane, and Benlowes. Her tracing of parallels is extremely useful, but her reading of the poems themselves is too heavy. She takes Marvell's use of allegory and nature mysticism far too seriously.

48 Wallace, *p.* 255, sees 'Appleton House' as the parting gesture of a man seeking active life.

49 Andrew Marvell, *Complete Works in Verse and Prose*, ed. A. B. Grosart (privately printed, 1873), III, 212–13. Subsequent references for prose are to this edition, cited as Grosart.

50 'I never had any, not the remotest relation to public matters, nor correspondence with the persons then predominant, until the year 1657, when indeed I entered into an employment, for which I was not altogether improper, and which I considered to be the most innocent and inoffensive toward his Majesty's affairs of any in that usurped and irregular government, to which all men were then exposed' (*Rehearsal Transposed* II, *Ibid.*, III, 322).

51 The relationship between the perspective of the 'Horatian Ode' and that of 'The First Anniversary' is discussed by J. A. Mazzeo, 'Cromwell as Davidic King', *Renaissance and Seventeenth-Century Studies* (New York, 1964).

52 Abbott, *Cromwell*, III, 583.

53 *The Diary of John Evelyn*, ed. E. S. de Beer (London, 1959), *p.* 394.

54 Paul, *p.* 300, describes the theory of Cromwell's rule as a kind of Divine Right of Vocation.

55 *Political Ballads of the Seventeenth and Eighteenth Centuries*, ed. W. W. Wilkins (London, 1860), I, 79.

56 In spite of the useful external evidence that he assembles, and though much of his commentary is perceptive, Wallace's contention that Marvell's object is to persuade Cromwell to accept the crown (*p.* 108) and the people to elect him king (*p.* 124) is unconvincing in terms of the poem itself. The 'Poem upon the Death of O.C.' is much more obviously monarchist.

57 An excellent account of the problems faced by panegyrists of Cromwell is given by Ruth Nevo, *The Dial of Virtue* (Princeton, 1963), ch. iii–v. She makes a detailed comparison of the attitudes of Cowley and Marvell. Waller's treatment of Cromwell is discussed by Warren L. Chernaik, *The Poetry of Limitation* (New Haven, 1968), *pp.* 153 ff.

58 As Zagorin points out, *Political Thought*, *p.* 116.

59 *Political Ballads*, I, 124.

60 'To follow Marvell's political career is to trace his allegiance to the providential constitution' (Wallace, *p.* 228). Donal Smith, 'The Political Beliefs of Andrew Marvell', *University of Toronto Quarterly*, XXXVI (1966/7), *pp.* 55–66, emphasises Marvell's pragmatic, trimming position. Caroline Robbins, however, *The Eighteenth-Century Commonwealthman* (Cambridge, Mass., 1959), *pp.* 53–4, sees Marvell as a contributor to 'real Whig', i.e. republican doctrine.

61 For a more detailed account of constitutional royalism in relation to Dryden see ch. 4, *pp.* 148–51.

62 K. H. D. Haley, *William of Orange and the English Opposition 1672–4* (Oxford, 1953), *p.* 58.

63 Margoliouth, II: March 21, 1670, *p.* 302; April 14, 1670, *p.* 303; *c.* January 24, 1671, *p.* 308.

64 Lord, 'From Contemplation to Action', *p.* 73.

65 Letter to Sir Edward Hartley, May 3 1673 (Margoliouth, II, 312).

66 The case for is argued by Lord, *POAS*, I, 21, 35, and against by Wallace, *p.* 154. The convention of the painter poem is discussed by Nevo, *pp.* 156 ff.

67 Grosart, III, 75.

68 Pierre Legouis, *Andrew Marvell: Poet, Puritan, Patriot* (Oxford, 1965), *p.* 199.

69 Grosart, IV, 282.

70 *Ibid.*, IV, 81.

71 The mock speech is printed by Bradbrook and Lloyd Thomas, *pp.* 125–7.

72 Legouis thinks that the verse satires show the prose to be not completely honest; he regards the pamphlets as expressing 'such dulcified opinions as would not frighten the electors' (*p.* 179). But this does not mean that the aim of the verse satires is different from that of the prose; both, by different means, are designed to preserve constitutional monarchy. I am assuming that Marvell is not the author of *Britannia and Raleigh*, in which Britannia claims that it is no longer possible 'the Stuart from the tyrant to divide' (*l.* 142). This is precisely what Marvell is trying to do. See *POAS*, I, 228–36.

73 J. G. A. Pocock, 'Machiavelli, Harrington, and English Political Ideologies in the Eighteenth Century', *William and Mary Quarterly*, XXII (1965), *p.* 564, points out the part played by *The Growth of Popery* in founding the eighteenth-century country ideology. Two essays on Marvell were published in *The Craftsman* in 1735 (Legouis, *p.* 228).

74 Marvell also criticised Dryden in 'On Mr Milton's *Paradise Lost*' (1674); Dryden retaliated in the preface to *Religio Laici* (1682, after Marvell's death). Margoliouth, I, 260–1.

75 As Lord does, introduction to *Marvell: Critical Essays, p.* 10.

NOTES TO CHAPTER 4

1 Attempts to characterise Dryden's position as a whole tend to simplify his variousness. Louis Bredvold, *The Intellectual Milieu of John Dryden* (Ann Arbor, Mich., 1962), while tracing the changes in Dryden's political and religious opinions, sees underlying consistency in his sceptical cast of mind. This account ignores the extent to which his writing was influenced by the real disorder in political events. Earl Miner, 'Dryden and the Issue of Human Progress', *PQ*, XL (1960), 128, and *Dryden's Poetry* (Bloomington, Ind., 1967), *pp.* xiii–xv, sees Dryden's virtues in his ambiguities. He suggests that Dryden's historical awareness and his combination of humanist and conservative with progressive and relativist attitudes account for the best in his poetry.

2 John Dryden, *Of Dramatic Poesy and other Critical Essays*, ed. George Watson (London, 1962), I, 44; cited as Watson. The following editions of Dryden's work are used: for poems, prefaces to poems, prologues, and epilogues, *The Poems of John Dryden*, ed. James Kinsley (4 vols.; Oxford, 1958), cited as Kinsley; for critical essays excluding some prefaces to poems, Watson; for plays, dedications, and miscellaneous prose, *The Works of John Dryden*, ed. Sir Walter Scott and George Saintsbury (18 vols., Edinburgh, 1882–93), cited as S–S; for letters, *The Letters of John Dryden*, ed. Charles E. Ward (Durham, N.C., 1942), cited as *Letters*. I have also consulted the California Dryden, *The Works of John Dryden*, ed. H. T. Swedenberg Jr *et al.* (Berkeley and Los Angeles, 1956–), which will supersede these editions with the exception of letters.

3 Kinsley, I, 452, *l.* 377.

4 *Ibid.*, I, 52, *l.* 5.

5 *Ibid.*, I, 102, *l.* 1143; 98, *ll.* 1051–2; 54, *ll.* 47–8.

235

6 The most detailed account of Dryden's poetic technique as the elaboration of a system of analogies is by Alan Roper, *Dryden's Poetic Kingdoms* (New York, 1965), on which I have partly relied.

7 'To John, Marquess of Normanby', Watson, II, 250.

8 Roper, *p.* 138.

9 'The Epilogue Spoken to the King...1681', Kinsley, I, 210, *l.* 5.

10 'Prologue, To the University of Oxon', *ibid.*, I, 369, *ll.* 16–19.

11 *Ibid., ll.* 40–1.

12 'The Prologue at Oxford', *ibid.*, I, 211, *l.* 23.

13 Prologue to *The Loyal Brother, ibid.*, I, 246.

14 *The Life of John Dryden*, ed. Bernard Kreissman (Lincoln, Neb., 1963), *p.* 382.

15 *Lives of the English Poets* (London, 1954), I, 219.

16 James Sutherland, *John Dryden: The Poet as Orator* (Glasgow, 1963), *p.* 23; James Kinsley, 'Dryden and the Art of Praise', *English Studies*, XXXIV (1953), 58, 63.

17 David Ogg, *England in the Reign of Charles II* (2nd ed.; London, 1956), II, 450.

18 'A Panegyric on the Author of Absalom and Achitophel', *POAS*, II, ed. Elias F. Mengel Jr. (1965), 504, *ll.* 90–8.

19 Propaganda of every kind played an important part in Louis' effort to transform radically the structure of French society, to create an efficient military state and to shift power from pluralist to central authority. This crisis needed to be covered by the mystique of kingship, to be justified symbolically. See John B. Wolf, *Louis XIV* (New York, 1968), *pp.* 368–9. Louis had to make the elements of society whose power he had displaced acquiesce in their relegation from real political to simply symbolical roles. His theory of kingship emphasised his *métier*, the exercise of real power, and *gloire*, which is not personal reputation but the wealth and strength of the country with which the king identifies himself. See Louis XIV, *Mémoires*, ed. Jean Longnon (Paris, 1923), *pp.* 69, 226. The increase of *gloire* had various functions: to enhance the king's image, to establish the superiority of the nation in the face of Europe, to conceal constitutional change, to satisfy the previous holders of power. Louis often understood *gloire* in military terms, but the arts played an important part in this process. See Anthony Blunt, *Art and Architecture in France, 1500–1700* (Harmondsworth, Middx., 1957), *pp.* 184–6. On the symbolic function of Versailles, by means of which Louis could both underline his own power and satisfy the old nobility for its loss of power, see Wolf, *p.* 362, and Louis Hautecoeur, *Louis XIV Roi-Soleil* (Paris, 1953), *pp.* 13, 24, 29, 40. Literature also played its part in the elaborate cult of royalty; Louis' pensions to men of letters were used by English writers up to the mid-eighteenth century as a yardstick against which to measure the feeble patronage of their own governments. The most interesting writer of political panegyric was Boileau; see especially *Discours au Roi, Epistles* I, IV, VIII.

20 *The Origins of Political Stability: England 1675–1725* (Boston, 1967), *pp.* 15–17.

21 Kenyon, *Stuart Constitution, p.* 374.

22 I have found the accounts of Charles as a ruler in Ogg, *Reign of Charles II*, and Maurice Ashley, *Charles II: The Man and the Statesman* (London, 1971) more convincing than Arthur Bryant's admiring portrait, *King Charles II* (rev. ed., London, 1955).

23 As Bredvold says, *p.* 135.

24 Boileau disclaimed an epic role for himself but in the conclusion of *L'Art Poétique* he was anxious to point the way for others.

25 Charles E. Ward, *The Life of John Dryden* (Chapel Hill, N.C., 1961), *pp.* 250, 331; dedication of *King Arthur* to Halifax, S-S, VIII, 130.

26 Ward, *p.* 212; Hugh Macdonald, *John Dryden: A Bibliography of Early Editions and of Drydeniana* (Oxford, 1939), *p.* 127; S-S, VII, 130.

27 S-S, II, 285.

28 Watson, I, 158, 163.

29 S-S, IV, 11, 12.

30 Thus Almanzor and Granada are restored to the Christian fold, and the conflicting claims of the usurping and deposed rulers in *The Spanish Friar* are reconciled by marriage.

31 George, Duke of Buckingham, *The Rehearsal*, Act IV, scene i.

32 Charles's influence on the development of the heroic play and its reflection of his absolutist tendencies are pointed out by James Sutherland, 'The Impact of Charles II on Restoration Literature', *Restoration and Eighteenth century Literature*, ed. Carroll Camden (Chicago, 1963), *p.* 260. The connection between the heroic play and the pindaric as an outlet for feelings otherwise repressed in Restoration literature has been made by Walton, *Metaphysical to Augustan, p.* 83.

33 Nevo argues that Restoration panegyric, which she describes as baroque heroic, in contrast to the historical consciousness underlying the attempt to define Cromwell's position, posited an ideal norm for society which did not need definition. Waller's *Instructions to a Painter* was particularly vulnerable because its abstract heroic descriptions were fixed in a particular historical context which was open to a quite different interpretation. Dryden's sense of audience made him abandon baroque heroic, and the development of mock-heroic destroyed the earlier form. (*Dial of Virtue, pp.* 137, 146, 158–9.) Unfortunately Nevo does not take her argument further than *Absalom and Achitophel*.

34 Ogg, *Charles II, p.* 459; *England in the Reigns of James II and William III* (Oxford, 1955), *p.* 144.

35 'Great writing does not persuade; it takes the reader out of himself. The startling and amazing is more powerful than the charming and persuasive, if it is indeed true that to be convinced is usually within our control whereas amazement is the result of an irresistible force beyond the control of any audience.' Longinus, *On Great Writing* (On the Sublime), trans. G. M. A. Grube (New York, 1957), *p.* 4.

36 Preface to *Pindaric Odes, Poems*, ed. A. R. Waller (Cambridge, 1905), *p.* 156.

37 Johnson, I, 256.

38 *Ibid.*, I, 244.

39 Dryden's poem on Cromwell's death, 'Heroic Stanzas' (1659), does not place Cromwell in the context of history. On the question of whether Dryden held office under the Protectorate see Ward, *p.* 17, and Appendix B, and California Dryden, I, 187.

40 *Poems*, ed. G. Thorn Drury (London, n.d.), II, 39, *ll.* 103–8.

41 See Charles I in answer to parliament's Nineteen Propositions of 1642 (Kenyon, *Stuart Constitution, pp.* 21–3), and Charles II in defence of his dissolution of the Oxford parliament of 1681 in *His Majesty's Declaration* (*The Letters, Speeches and Declarations of King Charles II*, ed. Arthur Bryant [London, 1968], pp. 319–22). Charles I's view of parliamentary interference with his office was stated more

strongly in *Eikon Basilike* (1649): 'For thus have they designed and proposed to me the new modelling of sovereignty and kingship, as without any reality of power or without any necessity of subjection and obedience, that the majesty of the kings of England might hereafter hang, like Mohammed's tomb, by a magnetic charm between the power and privileges of the two Houses in an airy imagination of regality' (ed. Philip A. Knachel [Ithaca, N.Y., 1966], *pp.* 47–8).

42 For the political tendencies of the legalistic middle party see J. H. Hexter, *The Reign of King Pym* (Cambridge, Mass., 1961).

43 This summary is based on M. A. Judson, *The Crisis of the Constitution* (New Brunswick, N.J., 1949), *pp.* 8, 52, 57, 377. The reapeated attempts in the seventeenth century to make the balance work are traced by Clayton Roberts, *The Growth of Responsible Government in Stuart England* (Cambridge, 1966).

44 Clarendon did not believe in divided sovereignty as defined and attacked by Hobbes (he disapproved of the king's answer to the Ninteeen Propositions): authority was not shared among the three estates, but the extent of the king's authority was limited by law. See B. H. G. Wormald, *Clarendon: Politics, Historiography, and Religion* (Cambridge, 1964), *pp.* 223–4.

45 Edward Hyde, Earl of Clarendon, *Selections from The History of the Rebellion and Civil Wars and the Life by Himself*, ed. G. Huehns (London, 1955), *p.* 31.

46 *Ibid.*, *p.* 2.

47 Sir John Denham, *The Poetical Works*, ed. T. H. Banks, Jr. (New Haven, 1928), *p.* 85, *ll.* 329–34.

48 Keith Feiling, *A History of the Tory Party, 1640–1714* (Oxford, 1959), *pp.* 38–40, argues that Clarendon's constitutional theory was out of date at the Restoration because it failed to recognise the struggle for sovereignty between king and parliament. However, Roberts, *Responsible Government*, *p.* 154, argues convincingly that the attempt to balance king and parliament after 1660 was not unworkable, even though it broke down by 1667. B. Behrens, 'The Whig Theory of the Constitution in the Reign of Charles II', *Cambridge Historical Journal*, VII (1941/43), *pp.* 42–71, gives a very unsympathetic account of Whig appeals to the balanced constitution during the Exclusion Crisis.

49 Feiling, *pp.* 164, 174.

50 Kenyon, *pp.* 7–9.

51 The development of the modern idea of sovereignty in opposition to medieval government by divided and limited rule was a logical reaction to the conflicts between the estates in several European countries in the late sixteenth and early seventeenth centuries. Bodin's theory of sovereignty in *Six Books of the Commonwealth* (1576) was evolved in relation to the danger to the monarchy of the conflict between Catholics and Huguenots. It seemed obvious to Hobbes that the view that power should be divided and that the sovereign should be subject to the civil law tended to the dissolution of the commonwealth; he rejected outright the idea of mixed monarchy and the historical rule of king in parliament. Limited sovereignty was a contradiction in terms; if power is limited, the limitation must necessarily proceed from a greater power. The civil wars need never have occurred if only men had understood the inevitable connection between subversive thought and anarchy, and obedience and peace. (*Leviathan*, ed. A. D. Lindsay [London, 1962], *pp.* 14, 173, 391; *Philosophical Rudiments concerning Government and Society*, ed. William Molesworth [Aalen, 1962], *pp.* 11, 88, 151; *Behemoth*, ed. William

Molesworth [New York, n.d.], *pp.* 71, 74.) Hobbes' theories were based on the wrong premisses both for the constitutional royalists who were unsympathetic to the idea of absolute sovereignty and for the later divine-right Tories. This was recognised by Filmer, who came into his own as the Tories' posthumous propagandist. To a view of sovereignty as uncompromising as that of Hobbes (Filmer thought that monarchy should be absolute and that the idea of tyranny was meaningless) he added the sanction of religion, history, and custom. Absolutism was supported and made acceptable by the accompanying theories of patriarchalism and divine right. (See especially *Patriarcha* and *Observations upon Aristotle's Politics* in *Patriarcha and other Political Works*, ed. Peter Laslett [Oxford, 1949].) Bossuet, the spokesman for a type of absolutism that Filmer could only imagine, added some important refinements to the question of the relationship of absolute monarchy to divine right. *Politique Tirée des Propres Paroles de l'Écriture Sainte*, designed for the instruction of Louis XIV, includes both logical deductions of the nature of sovereignty after the manner of Hobbes and moral prescriptions for the king's divine function reminiscent of James I. For Bossuet royal authority is sacred, paternal, absolute, and reasonable; he distinguishes between absolute and arbitrary government. Under arbitrary government there is no law outside the prince's will; absolute government is under God and respects the country's fundamental laws. Bossuet is concerned with the ideal relations that should exist between the prince who is the true viceregent of God and his people. The prince should use his power for the public good, should be mild and merciful, and should fear God. (*Politique*, ed. Jacques Le Brun [Geneva, 1967], *pp.* 64, 70–88, 112, 231, 291–3.)

52 Macaulay, *History of England*, II, 177, describes how this practical disaster, rather than intellectual rebuttal, put an end to the combination of divine right and absolutism: 'The system of Filmer might have survived the attacks of Locke: but it never recovered from the death blow given by James.' Feiling, *p.* 203, points out the impossible ideological position of the Tories under James II; their political theory could not be reconciled with their constitutional sense nor with their religious convictions.

53 On the motives for Dryden's conversion, which I do not propose to deal with, see Donald R. Benson, 'Theology and Politics in Dryden's Conversion', *Studies in English Literature*, IV (1964), 393–412, and Philip Harth, *Contexts of Dryden's Thought* (Chicago, 1968). Harth, *pp.* 227–8, criticises Benson's thesis that Dryden's conversion was politically motivated and implied a wish for enforced public agreement on religious questions, since Dryden knew that Catholics in England would always be a minority.

54 See Earl Miner's comments on Dryden's preference for the rationalist over the voluntarist view of God in *The Hind and the Panther*, California Dryden, III, 338.

55 John Locke, *Two Treatises of Government*, ed. Peter Laslett (rev. ed.; New York, 1965), *p.* 413.

56 George Savile, Marquess of Halifax, *The Complete Works*, ed. Walter Raleigh (Oxford, 1912), *p.* 207.

57 F. C. Turner, *James II* (London, 1948), *pp.* 105, 160.

58 *POAS*, III, 123–4, *ll.* 373–7, 382–6.

59 This conflict echoes the barrage of remonstrance and declaration which passed between king and parliament shortly before the outbreak of civil war, and which is epitomised by the statements of Strafford and Pym at the former's trial in 1641. Strafford's view of the constitution was that 'the prerogative of the crown and the

propriety of the subject have such mutual relations that this took protection from that, that foundation and nourishment from this; and as on the lute, if anything be too high or too low wound up you have lost the harmony, so here the excess of a prerogative is oppression, of a pretended liberty in the subject disorder and anarchy'. Pym's reply hardly differed: 'The prerogative [is] a cover and defence to the liberty of the people, and the people by their liberty are entitled to be a foundation to the prerogative; but...if the prerogative of the king overwhelm the liberty of the people it will be turned into tyranny; if liberty undermine the prerogative, it will grow into anarchy' (Kenyon, *Stuart Constitution*, pp. 212, 214).

60 *POAS*, II, ed. Elias F. Mengel Jr. (1965), 389, *ll*. 224–7.

61 Kenyon, *p*. 387; J. R. Jones, *The First Whigs* (London, 1961), *pp*. 10–12.

62 Ward, *p*. 148.

63 See John Dryden, *His Majesties Declaration Defended*, intro. by Godfrey Davies (Los Angeles, 1950), *pp*. iii–iv; Godfrey Davies, 'The Conclusion of Dryden's *Absalom and Achitophel*', *Essential Articles for the Study of John Dryden*, ed. H. T. Swedenberg, Jr. (Hamden, Conn., 1966), *pp*. 212, 219, 221. Dryden's authorship of the *Declaration Defended* is argued by Roswell G. Ham in 'Dryden as Historiographer-Royal', *Essential Articles for Dryden*. The relevant passage from Charles's *Declaration* is as follows: 'Let not the restless malice of ill men who are labouring to poison our people, some out of fondness for their old beloved Commonwealth principles, and some out of anger at their being disappointed in the particular designs they had for the accomplishment of their own ambition and greatness, persuade any of our good subjects that we intend to lay aside the use of parliaments. For we do still declare that no irregularities in parliament shall ever make us out of love with parliaments; which we look upon as the best method for healing the distempers of the kingdom, and the only means to preserve the monarchy in that due credit and respect which it ought to have both at home and abroad... And who cannot but remember that religion, liberty and property were all lost and gone when the monarchy was shaken off; and could never be revived till that was restored' (*Letters of Charles II*, *pp*. 321–2). On Charles's insincerity see K. H. D. Haley, *The First Earl of Shaftesbury* (Oxford, 1968), *pp*. 633–40.

64 *Declaration Defended*, *pp*. 3, 4, 11, 16.

65 *Ibid.*, *p*. 19.

66 Ralph B. Long, in 'Dryden's Importance as a Spokesman of the Tories', *Univ. of Texas Studies in English* (1941), *pp*. 81, 83, 92, argues that the influence of *Absalom and Achitophel* has been overestimated by Ogg, and that the poems were read by already convinced Tories. But what matters is not what effects the poems can be traced as having had, but the audience Dryden intended to reach.

67 A Tory satire of 1681, *The Parliament Dissolved at Oxford*, opens with Charles's speech from the throne: 'Under 500 kings three kingdoms groan' (*POAS*, II, 411).

68 Miner argues in *Dryden's Poetry*, *p*. 176, in opposition to my view, that Dryden's principles in *The History of the League* are harshly presented but constitute a fair statement of his beliefs; he does not take into account the extent to which these beliefs were constantly in process of modification.

69 *POAS*, III, ed. Schless, *pp*. xxxii–xxxiii. The use of Trimmer as a pejorative term has been traced by Donald R. Benson, 'Halifax and the Trimmers', *HLQ*, XXVII (1963–4), 115–34. He argues that Halifax was not identified with the Trimmers and that there was no Trimmer party.

70 Halifax, *Works*, *p*. 103.

71 *Ibid.*, *pp*. 76, 90, 96.

72 *Political Thoughts and Reflections, ibid.*, *pp*. 211–13.

73 H. C. Foxcroft, *A Character of the Trimmer* (Cambridge, 1946), *p*. 119. Instead of the exclusion of James from the succession, Halifax suggested the limitation of his power, a policy as unwelcome to the Whigs as to the heir. Though it got no support from the Shaftesbury Whigs and aroused no enthusiasm among moderate Tories, the policy of limitation had some advantages. Some form of curtailment of the Duke of York's ability to fulfil his ambitions was certainly desirable; as Jones puts it (*First Whigs*, *p*. 217), the Revolution of 1688 justified the Exclusionists. There were three reasons why Halifax supported the policy of limitation: the passing of the Exclusion Bill would have involved a bloody civil war, not the bloodless revolution that occurred when James had alienated the country; limitation had Charles's support; Halifax opposed the claim of Monmouth to the succession and supported that of William of Orange (Foxcroft, *pp*. 71, 110–11). Shaftesbury's great error, which split the Whigs (and alienated Halifax), was to set up Monmouth as the movement's focus and the potential heir to the throne (Feiling, *p*. 179; Jones, *pp*. 78, 87).

74 Foxcroft, *pp*. 152, 184.

75 Macaulay, I, 304.

76 As Bernard N. Schilling does in *Dryden and the Conservative Myth* (New Haven, 1961).

77 Jones, *pp*. 9–18.

78 This point is made by Arthur W. Hoffman, *John Dryden's Imagery* (Gainesville, Fla., 1962), *p*. 88.

79 Charles's absolutist ambitions and the nature of the Grand Design are discussed in detail by Sir John Pollock in *The Popish Plot* (London, 1903), *pp*. 24–30. See also Ogg, *Charles II*, ch. ix.

80 The extent of Dryden's dramatic satire is indicated by John R. Moore in 'Political Allusions in Dryden's Later Plays', *PMLA*, LXXIII (1958), *pp*. 36–42.

81 For the possible meanings of this expression see Alan Roper, 'Dryden's Secular Masque', *MLQ*, XXIII (1962), 29–40.

82 e.g. Bredvold, *p*. 148; Miner, *Dryden's Poetry*, *p*. 136. Roper, *Poetic Kingdoms*, *p*. 132, sees the relations of parliament and king in the poem as a fall from Dryden's earlier-held Stuart absolutism.

83 An excellent volume which analyses the changes in politics and society after 1688 is Geoffrey Holmes (ed.), *Britain after the Glorious Revolution* (London, 1969).

84 The process of party realignment is described by Feiling, *pp*. 288 ff., and Plumb, *pp*. 129 ff.

85 As Hoffman suggests, *pp*. 131–2.

86 See above, *pp*. 120.

87 Reuben A. Brower in 'Dryden and the "Invention" of Pope', *Restoration and Eighteenth Century Literature*, discusses ways in which Dryden anticipated Pope in his later years, including his professionalism and his feeling for the countryside, but he does not examine the influence of their parallel political situations.

88 Some of the following ideas are explored by Jay Arnold Levine, 'John Dryden's Epistle to John Driden', *JEGP*, LXIII (1964), 450–74.

89 Merritt Hughes, for example, argues that Dryden's belief was that the correct political position was an independent attitude guided by respect for law. Of *Absalom and Achitophel* he writes, 'if Dryden was David's partisan, he was so because it happened that the laws, in letter and in spirit, were on David's side' ('Dryden as Statist', *PQ*, VI [1927], 350).

90 Kinsley, IV, 2071; Ward, *p.* 323.

NOTES TO CHAPTER 5

1 *Epilogue to the Satires* II, *Twickenham Edition of the Poems of Alexander Pope*, ed. John Butt *et al.* (London, 1939–69), IV, 325, *l.* 222; hereafter cited as *TE*.

2 *Epistle to Dr Arbuthnot, TE*, IV, 120, *l.* 339.

3 The scheme from the 1744 edition is printed in *TE*, III ii, xvii–xix.

4 As F. W. Bateson suggests, *ibid.*, *p.* xvi.

5 See Joseph Spence, *Observations, Anecdotes, and Characters of Books and Men*, ed. James M. Osborn (Oxford, 1966), I, 153.

6 *TE*, III ii, xix.

7 Spence, I, 229.

8 Thomas R. Edwards Jr. in *This Dark Estate: A Reading of Pope* (Berkeley, Calif., 1963) traces Pope's gradual abandonment of the Augustan synthesis and his turning to privacy and a 'grotesque mode' in his later poems. Although I agree with much of his analysis, my study is concerned with Pope's changing sense of the possibilities of his political role.

9 *The Correspondence of Alexander Pope*, ed. George Sherburn (Oxford, 1956), I, 194, 220, 238, 241, 245; hereafter cited as *Correspondence*.

10 George Sherburn, *The Early Career of Alexander Pope* (Oxford, 1934), *pp.* 67, 101.

11 J. R. Moore, '*Windsor Forest* and William III', *Essential Articles for Pope*, *p.* 233; Earl R. Wasserman, *The Subtler Language* (Baltimore, 1959), *p.* 160.

12 For a detailed reading of this theme in the poem see Wasserman, ch. iv.

13 *TE*, I, 193, *l.* 414.

14 The rigidity of Pope's opposition to the reigns of William and Anne prevented him from seeing that the Treaty of Utrecht of 1713 fulfilled the objects of the Grand Alliance of 1701 by finally achieving the partition of the Spanish empire. Bolingbroke, the negotiator of the peace, saw himself as the heir to William's policy. See G. M. Trevelyan, *England under Queen Anne*, vol. I: *Blenheim* (London, 1930), *p.* 146; vol. III: *The Peace and the Protestant Succession* (London, 1934), *p.* 88; also G. C. Gibbs, 'The Revolution in Foreign Policy', *Britain after the Glorious Revolution*, *p.* 62.

15 Joseph Addison, *Works*, ed. Richard Hurd (London, 1811), I, 43.

16 The consequences of such a problem for the future of the philosophical poem are discussed by Basil Willey in *The Seventeenth Century Background* (London, 1934), ch. xii.

17 Willey's phrase in *The Eighteenth Century Background* (London, 1940), ch. iii.

18 The classic history of the eighteenth-century development of ideas of harmony is Arthur O. Lovejoy, *The Great Chain of Being* (Cambridge, Mass., 1936). Maynard Mack (for whom the poem is by no means a failure) studies the *Essay on Man* in relation to classical-Christian views of order: 'Poets from Sophocles to Eliot have generally been disinclined to accept as final the fragmentations of man and

universe that usually present themselves when one has got behind the poetic and religious pictures – one of the virtues of such pictures, as they might define it, being precisely to keep these fragments ordered into wholes' (*TE*, III i, lxix). The problem is that in the writing of the satires Pope did not see any way of circumventing fragmentation, of ordering the political world into a whole.

19 *TE*, III i, 8.

20 *TE*, III ii, 188. Arguments for Pope's authorship of *A Master Key*, obviously written in answer to attacks on *Burlington*, are stated on *pp.* 175-6.

21 John Lord Hervey, *Memoirs*, ed. Romney Sedgwick (abridged ed.; London, 1952), *p.* 236.

22 *TE*, IV, 191.

23 Spence, I, 246.

24 *Correspondence*, I, 462.

25 Sherburn, *pp.* 297-301.

26 *Correspondence*, I, 454.

27 The best accounts of early eighteenth-century party politics are J. H. Plumb, *The Origins of Political Stability* (Boston, 1967), and Geoffrey Holmes, *British Politics in the Age of Anne* (London, 1967). These refute the attempt by Robert Walcott in *English Politics in the Early Eighteenth Century* (Cambridge, Mass., 1956) to apply to this period Lewis Namier's demonstration that after 1750 party designations ceased to have any real meaning and that they were irrelevant to the structure of political life. (See in general *The Structure of Politics at the Accession of George III*, 2nd ed. [London, 1957]; *England in the Age of the American Revolution*, 2nd ed. [London, 1963]; 'Monarchy and the Party System' and 'Country Gentlemen in Parliament, 1750-1784', *Personalities and Powers* [London, 1955].) An excellent anthology illustrating party conflict is G. S. Holmes and W. A. Speck, eds., *The Divided Society* (London, 1967).

28 Holmes, *British Politics*, *p.* 59; Walcott, *p.* 74.

29 Plumb, *pp.* 133-5; Walcott, *p.* 87.

30 Plumb, *p.* 168; Namier, *Personalities and Powers*, *pp.* 33, 62, 65.

31 Holmes, *British Politics*, *pp.* 47, 64, 467.

32 Swift's basic political ideas are repeated throughout his writings. I have found the following works most relevant (references are to *The Prose Works of Jonathan Swift*, ed. Herbert Davis, 14 vols. [Oxford, 1957-68]): *The Examiner* (vol. III), especially Nos. 21, 31, 34, 35, 44; *The Conduct of the Allies* (vol. VI); *Some Advice to the October Club* (vol. VI); *Some Free Thoughts upon the Present State of Affairs* (vol. VIII); *Gulliver's Travels* (vol. XI), especially Bk. II. A useful summary of Swift's attitudes on church and state is W. A. Speck, 'From Principles to Practice: Swift and Party Politics', *The World of Jonathan Swift*, ed. Brian Vickers (Oxford, 1968).

33 Trevelyan, I, 292; Holmes, *British Politics*, *p.* 160. See W. R. Ward, *The English Land Tax in the Eighteenth Century* (London, 1953).

34 Swift, *Works*, III, 169, 119.

35 *Ibid.*, XI, 119-120.

36 For Swift's treatment of Marlborough see especially *The Examiner*, No. 16. Pope's suppressed character of Marlborough, originally an addition to the *Essay on Man*, is printed in *TE*, VI, 358-9.

37 *The History of John Bull*, ed. Herman Teerink (Amsterdam, 1925), *p.* 144.

38 *Ibid.*, *p.* 161.

39 Irvin Ehrenpreis, *Swift: The Man, his Works, and the Age*, vol. 1 (Cambridge, Mass., 1962), *p.* 16, suggests that Swift's enduring sense that land was the only real wealth should be related to his early experience of social instability in Ireland.

40 There was an inevitable ambivalence in Tory attitudes to trade. On the one hand there was the extreme xenophobia of the landed squires, such as those who made up the October Club, and of Swift in his more honest moments. On the other hand the Tories contained an important business element. Mandeville indirectly pointed out the ambiguity of the Tory position. The poverty inflicted on the minor gentry by war taxation and their hatred of the new financiers and the funds led them to sentimentalise a more simple, patriarchal past. At the same time their natural wish to enrich themselves involved a glorification of commercial enterprise. Mandeville saw the incompatibility of these views; it was illogical, though understandable, to try both to profit from the new world and to reject it. In the preface to *The Fable of the Bees* (1714) he wrote: 'The main design of the fable...is to show the impossibility of enjoying all the most elegant comforts of life that are to be met with in an industrious, wealthy and powerful nation, and at the same time be blessed with all the virtue and innocence that can be wished for in a golden age' (ed. F. B. Kaye [Oxford, 1957], I, 6). Nor were the Whigs a one-class party, but drew their support from all sections of the community, not simply from aristocrats, financiers, and dissenters, as Swift tried to suggest (Holmes, *British Politics*, *pp.* 164–9). It is more accurate to see an alliance of land and trade against high finance. Speck defines the moneyed interest as 'those elements in society who were involved in the new machinery of public credit which was created after the Revolution along with the setting up of the Bank of England in 1694' ('Conflict in Society', *Britain after the Glorious Revolution*, *p.* 135). Merchants and small traders were as antagonistic to the finance brokers as were the landed gentry. As is pointed out by Isaac Kramnick, *Bolingbroke and his Circle* (Cambridge, Mass., 1968), *pp.* 42–54, this community of interests continued after the war and is exemplified by the joint opposition of Bolingbroke and Sir John Barnard (Lord Mayor of London 1737–8) to Walpole. Nevertheless Holmes concludes (*British Politics*, *p.* 170) that the class distinction between the parties was justified. Swift was generally correct in his analysis of the social consequences of the land tax and the national debt. The small squires suffered a great deal by the tax, while the institution of the debt opened a new field of investment to merchants and tended to make the cleavage between these groups greater: after 1690 the mercantile and financial classes became a more coherent group whose interests centred mainly in London. See H. J. Habakkuk, 'English Landownership, 1680–1740', *Ec. Hist. Rev.*, x (1939–40), 12–13, 17. The important class that Swift left out of his black and white picture was the amphibious aristocracy, the wealthy landowners who were not greatly affected by the land tax as they drew their income from a variety of sources (Habakkuk, *pp.* 10–11; G. E. Mingay, *English Landed Society in the Eighteenth Century* [London, 1963], *pp.* 11, 82, 107). Walpole's government placed this class at the heart of political life; by the 1750s the Tory aristocracy had been absorbed by the court Whigs, and the Tory fear of the first decade of the century, that their collapse as a party would mean the collapse of the power of the landed interest, was proved ludicrous (Plumb, *pp.* 168, 187; Holmes, *British Politics*, *pp.* 182, 405).

41 Joseph Addison *et al.*, *The Spectator*, ed. Donald F. Bond (Oxford, 1965), I, No. 108, *p.* 446.

42 *Ibid.*, No. 69, *p.* 296.

43 *Ibid.*, IV, No. 549, *p.* 467.

44 *A Tour through England and Wales*, ed. G. D. H. Cole (London, 1928), I, 337.

45 Feiling, *The Tory Party, 1640–1714*, *p.* 482; *The Second Tory Party, 1714–1832* (London, 1959), *p.* 2.

46 Henry St John, Viscount Bolingbroke, *Works* (Philadelphia, 1841), I, 115. Kramnick, *Bolingbroke*, gives a useful account of his views as the politics of nostalgia for a gentry-dominated, prefinance-capitalist society.

47 A representative of this ideal among Pope's acquaintance is to be found in the description of Robert Digby at Sherborne in *Correspondence*, II, 239.

48 Vanbrugh, who is a minor villain of the *Epistle to Burlington* and of poems by Swift (see 'Vanbrug's House' and 'The History of Vanbrug's House' in *Poems*, ed. Harold Williams [Oxford, 1958], I, 78, 86), was the man mainly responsible for the tradition of enormous baroque palaces against which Burlington set himself. For detail of Vanbrugh's works and his architectural principles, see H. Avray Tipping and Christopher Hussey, *The Work of Sir John Vanbrugh and his School, 1699–1736* (London, 1928), Period IV, vol. II of *English Homes*. His most famous works are Castle Howard, begun in 1699 for Lord Carlisle, and Blenheim, the nation's reward to Marlborough, begun in 1705. Vanbrugh imported the Versailles manner to England; he conceived of a house as a monument. In building Castle Howard, he destroyed the original house, Henderskelfe Castle, together with the surrounding parish church and villagers' homes; the patriarchal conflicted with the monumental mode (*ibid.*, *pp.* xx, 39). During the building of Blenheim, he was in constant conflict with the Duchess of Marlborough, who really wanted a comfortable home to live in; Vanbrugh defended himself in a letter of 1710: 'I found it the opinion of all people and of all parties I conversed with, that although the building was to be calculated for, and adapted to, a private habitation, yet it ought at the same time, to be considered as both a royal and a national monument, and care taken in the design, and the execution, that it might have the qualities proper to such a monument, viz. beauty, magnificence, and duration' (*ibid.*, *p.* 66). The most famous great houses to continue the Vanbrugh tradition were the Duke of Chandos's Cannons, Sir Richard Child's Wanstead, and Sir Robert Walpole's Houghton. For Cannons, see C. H. Collins Baker and Muriel I. Baker, *The Life and Circumstances of James Brydges First Duke of Chandos* (Oxford, 1949); for Wanstead, see John Summerson, 'The Classical Country House in Eighteenth-Century England', *Journal of the Royal Society of Arts* (1959), *pp.* 550–1; for Houghton, see Tipping, *Early Georgian, 1714–1760*, Period V, vol. I of *English Homes*, *pp.* 67–108. (Although Chandos was certainly not Timon, Pope would have been pleased at the fate of Cannons, which was pulled down in the late 1740s; Chandos himself much preferred his Elizabethan house Shaw Hall, which he used for retirement, to his expensive modern palace. See Baker, *pp.* 375, 442.) The later date of these houses means that some of them have Palladian elements (Campbell, Burlington's protégé, was responsible for Wanstead and originally for Houghton), since by 1710 the baroque style was losing ground to the Palladian (Summerson, *Journal of Royal Soc. of Arts* [1959], *pp.* 549–50, 560).

49 For the view that Timon was intended as a satire of Walpole, and that there was

245   9-2

a conspiracy to divert ridicule from Walpole by identifying Chandos as Timon, see Kathleen Mahaffey, 'Timon's villa: Walpole's Houghton', *Texas Studies in Literature and Language*, IX (1967), *pp*. 193–222, and Maynard Mack, *The Garden and the City: Retirement and Politics in the Later Poetry of Pope* (Toronto, 1969), *pp*. 123–6, and Appendix F.

50 Summerson, *Journal of the Royal Soc. of Arts* (1959), *pp*. 544, 567.

51 *Ibid.*, *p*. 552; Christopher Hussey, *English Country Houses: Early Georgian, 1715–1760* (rev. ed. London, 1965), *p*. 22. The public buildings for which Burlington was responsible are discussed in Fiske Kimball, 'Burlington Architectus', *Journal of the Royal Institute of British Architects*, XXXIV (1927), *pp*. 675–93.

52 A reversal of Vitruvius' theory of the perfection and harmony of the human body, on which architectural principles should be based. See Rudolf Wittkower, *Architectural Principles in the Age of Humanism* (New York, 1965), *pp*. 14, 101.

53 'To My Ingenious and Worthy Friend W[illiam] L[owndes]' and 'A Panegyrical Epistle to Mr Thomas Snow' in John Gay, *Poetical Works*, ed. G. C. Faber (London, 1926), *pp*. 174, 177. See also Swift, 'The Run upon the Bankers' and 'The Bubble' in *Poems*, I, 238, 250.

54 Mandeville, I, 37. The difference between Pope's and Mandeville's ethics is outlined in Paul J. Alpers, 'Pope's To Bathurst and the Mandevillian State', *Essential Articles for Pope*.

55 Mandeville, I, 103, 119, 136.

56 *Correspondence*, III, 290.

57 The best and most thorough account of Pope in this period is Maynard Mack, *The Garden and the City*. My work on Pope was completed before the publication of this book in 1969. The most useful parts are chapters i and ii, on Pope's creation of his villa and grotto at Twickenham as 'an act of the mythopoeic imagination' (*p*. 9), and chapters iv and v, on the political background of Pope's satires and his use of insinuation and innuendo. A briefer and less satisfactory account of Pope's place in the anti-Walpole opposition is given by Robert W. Rogers, *The Major Satires of Alexander Pope* (Urbana, Ill., 1955).

58 As he is designated by Kramnick, *p*. 217. Mack, *Garden and City*, *pp*. 190, 193, also refers to Pope as opposition spokesman. This may have been how some of his admirers and the government regarded him, but it was not how he regarded himself.

59 Spence, I, 121.

60 Pope, *Correspondence*, III, 163.

61 Bolingbroke, *Works*, I, 167 ff.

62 Plumb, *p*. 171.

63 Bolingbroke, I, 26.

64 Feiling, *Second Tory Party*, *p*. 29. The opposition saw Walpole's excise scheme as a dangerous opportunity for an extension of the powers of central government. Walpole's propaganda appealed unsuccessfully to the landed gentry's hatred of the land tax (which the excise was intended to replace), as in 'The Countryman's Answer to the Ballad called "Britannia Excised"' (1733): 'Lords of manors and yeomen, / Freeholders and gem'men, / Drink a health to King George, your friend: / 'Tis his gracious intent, / With his good Parliament, / To bring the Land-tax to an end' (Wilkins, *Political Ballads*, II, 243).

65 Bolingbroke, I, 168.

66 *Ibid.*, I, 87.

67 For the tradition of neo-Harringtonianism, the idealisation of the independent man of property, see J. G. A. Pocock, 'Machiavelli, Harrington, and English Political Ideologies in the Eighteenth Century', *William and Mary Quarterly*, 3rd series, XXII (1965), 549–83.

68 *The Idea of a Patriot King,* ed. Sydney W. Jackman (New York, 1965), *pp.* 38, 42, 45.

69 Kramnick, *p.* 168.

70 *TE*, IV, 337, *l.* 98.

71 For Pope's antagonism to those members of the opposition (especially Pulteney) whom he regarded as using patriotism as a stepping stone to office, see his letters to Lyttleton, 1 Nov. 1738, and Marchmont, 22 June 1740 (*Correspondence*, IV, 142–4, 248–51).

72 *Liberty, The Complete Poetical Works of James Thomson*, ed. J. Logie Robertson (London, 1963), Part V, *ll.* 121–3.

73 On Pope's relations with Allen see Benjamin Boyce, *The Benevolent Man: A Life of Ralph Allen of Bath* (Cambridge, Mass., 1967).

74 References are to the four-book *Dunciad* of 1743, *TE*, V, B, in which the potential chaos of the 1729 version is realised.

75 Pope's use of the idea of the translation of empire has been demonstrated by Aubrey L. Williams in *Pope's Dunciad: A Study of Its Meaning* (London, 1955). The Goddess Dulness' prayer as she crowns Cibber (Bk. I, *ll.* 311–16) should be compared with the envoys concluding the painter poems of the 1660s (see *pp.* 118–21), in which the function of the poet is to unite king and people: 'O! when shall rise a monarch all our own, / And I, a nursing-mother, rock the throne, / 'Twixt prince and people close the curtain draw, / Shade him from light, and cover him from law; / Fatten the courtier, starve the learned band, / And suckle armies, and dry-nurse the land: / 'Till senates nod to lullabies divine, / And all be sleep, as at an ode of thine.'

76 Pope, *Correspondence*, II, 305.

77 Defoe, I, 168.

78 Such a man was likely to be a tenant not a freeholder; the middlesized farms like Horace's own were likely to be held by rewarded veterans, and to have passed through several hands. The large estates, the *latifundia*, were owned by wealthy absentee landlords and were farmed by slaves. The civil wars, and the habit of commanders of paying off their followers with requisitioned estates, meant that there must have been a sense of insecurity in the tenure of property. See M. Rostovtzeff, *The Social and Economic History of the Roman Empire* (2nd ed. rev.; Oxford, 1957), I, 13, 18, 23, 59; J. F. D'Alton, *Horace and his Age* (New York, 1962), *pp.* 149, 151, 159.

79 Habakkuk, *Ec. Hist. Rev.*, X (1939/40), 7, 12.

80 Pope's father sold his house at Binfield in 1716 probably to avoid anti-Catholic taxation; Pope leased his villa at Twickenham from Thomas Vernon in 1718 after his father's death (Sherburn, *pp.* 159, 215, 217).

81 See 'A Libel on D- D- and a certain great Lord', 'To Mr Gay', and 'On Poetry; A Rhapsody' in Swift, *Poems*, II, 480, 530, 640; 'An Epistle to a Lady', 'Epistle to Paul Methuen', and *Fables* (2nd Series) in Gay, *Poetical Works*, *pp.* 147, 161, 275 ff. Pope remarked that Gay got nothing by trying not to offend the great (Spence, I, 106).

82 'Verses on a Grotto', *TE*, VI, 382.
83 Pope's use of the example of Oldham in this respect, especially his *Upon a Printer* and *Letter from the Country to a Friend in Town*, is discussed by Rachel Trickett, *The Honest Muse* (Oxford, 1967), *pp.* 94–104.
84 Eduard Fraenkel, *Horace* (Oxford, 1959), *p.* 152.
85 e.g. *Odes*, I, xxxviii, II, xvi, xviii, III, vi, xvi.
86 Horace resists the idea of writing praise of Augustus in *Odes*, II, xii, and IV, ii; he is driven involuntarily in III, xxv.
87 The difference in the social attitudes of Pope and Horace is brought out by G. K. Hunter, 'The "Romanticism" of Pope's Horace', *Essential Articles for Pope*.
88 Johnson, *Lives*, II, 147, 205, 208.
89 *Ibid.*, II, 194.
90 *Ibid.*, II, 125.
91 *Ibid.*, II, 226. Johnson reviewed Soame Jenyns' *A Free Inquiry into the Nature and Origin of Evil* in the *Literary Magazine*, 1757.
92 Johnson's view of Whiggery has been defined by James L. Clifford in *Young Sam Johnson* (New York, 1955), *p.* 106: 'Whiggery to Johnson meant an easy optimism, a bland acceptance of fashion, a willingness to experiment and tamper without absolute certainty of improvement, a sophistical use of theory instead of a realistic approach to the ills of mankind.' Donald J. Greene in *The Politics of Samuel Johnson* (New Haven, 1960), *pp.* 51–3, has pointed out Johnson's leaning towards Evangelicalism, and its connection with social reform and political conservatism.
93 *Poems*, ed. E. L. McAdam Jr. with George Milne, vol. VI of *The Yale Edition of the Works of Samuel Johnson* (New Haven, 1964), *pp.* 108–9, *ll.* 359–68.
94 *The Life of Alexander Pope*, vol. V of *The Works of Alexander Pope*, ed. Whitwell Elwin and William John Courthope (London, 1889), *p.* 275. With this view should be compared Mack's description (*Garden and City*, *p.* 232) of Pope's retreat at Twickenham as 'a true country of the mind'.
95 Quoted by Kramnick, *p.* 205.
96 F. W. Bateson, *TE*, III ii, xli.
97 *TE*, III i, 140; IV, 308.
98 Pope, *Correspondence*, II, 326.
99 *Ibid.*, II, 199, 497; III, 276; IV, 64.
100 *Lives*, II, 272.
101 *Correspondence*, III, 349. On Pope's villa as a memorial to his friends, furnished with their portraits, see Mack, *Garden and City*, *p.* 31.
102 *Correspondence*, e.g. IV, 193.
103 'The Gloom of the Tory Satirists', *Pope and his Contemporaries*, ed. James L. Clifford and Louis A. Landa (New York, 1949), *pp.* 15, 18.
104 Kramnick, *pp.* 218–19.
105 Spence, I, 143.

Bibliography

This bibliography does not aim at completeness. I have included both works cited in the notes, and works which I have found generally useful. Where I owe a debt for a specific interpretation, this is indicated in the notes. For ease of reference the bibliography is divided by subject, as follows:

A Texts by and criticism of the main poets.
B Other primary sources.
C Secondary works.

A JONSON

TEXTS

Jonson, Ben. *Ben Jonson*, ed. C. H. Herford and Percy and Evelyn Simpson. 11 vols. Oxford, 1925–52.
—— *Complete Masques*, ed. Stephen Orgel. (The Yale Ben Jonson.) New Haven, 1969.

CRITICISM

Barish, Jonas A. ed. *Ben Jonson: A Collection of Critical Essays*. Englewood Cliffs, N.J., 1963.
Cubeta, P. M. 'A Jonsonian Ideal: "To Penshurst",' *PQ*, XLII (1963), 14–24.
Furniss, W. Todd. 'Ben Jonson's Masques', *Three Studies in the Renaissance: Sidney, Jonson, Milton*. New Haven, 1958.
Gordon, D. J. '*Hymenaei*: Ben Jonson's Masque of Union', *Journal of the Warburg Institute*, VIII (1945), 107–45.
—— 'Poet and Architect: The Intellectual Setting of the Quarrel between Ben Jonson and Inigo Jones', *Journal of the Warburg Institute*, XII (1949), 152–78.
Hart, Jeffrey. 'Ben Jonson's Good Society', *Modern Age*, VII (1962/3), 61–8.
Hilberry, Clarence B. 'Jonson's Ethics in Relation to Stoic and Humanistic Ethical Thought', unpublished dissertation, Chicago, 1930.
Meagher, John C. *Method and Meaning in Jonson's Masques*. Notre Dame, Ind., 1966.
Orgel, Stephen. *The Jonsonian Masque*. Cambridge, Mass., 1965.
Partridge, Edward B. *The Broken Compass: A Study of the Major Comedies of Ben Jonson*. New York, 1958.
Talbert, E. W. 'The Interpretation of Jonson's Courtly Spectacles', *PMLA*, LXI (1946), 454–73.
Trimpi, Wesley. *Ben Jonson's Poems: A Study of the Plain Style*. Stanford, 1962.

MILTON

TEXTS

Milton, John. *Complete Prose Works*, ed. Don M. Wolfe *et al*. In progress. New Haven, 1953– .
—— *The Poems*, ed. John Carey and Alastair Fowler. London, 1968.
—— *The Works*, ed. Frank Allen Patterson *et al*. 20 vols. New York, 1931–40.

CRITICISM

Barker, Arthur. *Milton and the Puritan Dilemma, 1641–1660*. Toronto, 1942.
Clark, Donald Lemen. *John Milton at St Paul's School*. New York, 1948.
Ferry, Anne Davidson. *Milton's Epic Voice*. Cambridge, Mass., 1963.
Fixler, Michael. *Milton and the Kingdoms of God*. London, 1964.
Fletcher, Harris Francis. *The Intellectual Development of John Milton*. 2 vols. In progress. Urbana, Illinois, 1956–61.
Frye, Northrop. *Five Essays on Milton's Epics*. London, 1966.
Haller, William. 'The Tragedy of God's Englishman', *Reason and the Imagination*, ed. J. A. Mazzeo. New York, 1962.
Hanford, James Holly. *John Milton, Englishman*. London, 1950.
—— *John Milton: Poet and Humanist*. Cleveland, 1966.
Lewalski, Barbara Kiefer. 'Milton: Political Beliefs and Polemical Methods, 1659–60', *PMLA*, LXXIV (1959), 191–202.
Parker, William Riley. *Milton: A Biography*. 2 vols. Oxford, 1968.
Ross, Malcolm Mackenzie. *Milton's Royalism*. Ithaca, N.Y., 1943.
Sirluck, Ernest. 'Milton's Idle Right Hand', *JEGP*, LX (1961), 749–85.
Tillyard, E. M. W. *Milton*. Rev. ed. Harmondsworth, Middx., 1968. 1st pub. 1930.
A Variorum Commentary on the Poems of John Milton. Vol. I: Douglas Bush, *The Latin and Greek Poems;* J. E. Shaw and A. Bartlett Giamatti, *The Italian Poems*. London, 1970.
Wolfe, Don M. *Milton in the Puritan Revolution*. New York, 1941.

MARVELL

TEXTS

Marvell, Andrew. *Complete Works in Verse and Prose*, ed. A. B. Grosart. 4 vols. Privately printed, 1873.
—— *Complete Poetry*, ed. George de F. Lord. New York, 1968.
—— *Poems*, ed. Hugh Macdonald. London, 1960.
—— *Poems and Letters*, ed. H. M. Margoliouth. 2nd ed. Oxford. 1952.

CRITICISM

Bradbrook, M. C., and Lloyd Thomas, M. G. *Andrew Marvell*. Cambridge, 1961. 1st pub. 1940.
Legouis, Pierre. *Andrew Marvell: Poet, Puritan, Patriot*. 2nd English ed. Oxford 1968. 1st pub. in French 1928.
Leishman, J. B. *The Art of Marvell's Poetry*. London, 1966.
Lord, George de F., ed. *Andrew Marvell: A Collection of Critical Essays*. Englewood Cliffs, N.J., 1968.
Mazzeo, J. A. 'Cromwell as Machiavellian Prince in Marvell's "An Horatian Ode"'; 'Cromwell as Davidic King', *Renaissance and Seventeenth Century Studies*. New York, 1964.

Smith, Donal. 'The Political Beliefs of Andrew Marvell', *UTQ*, XXXVI (1966/7), 55–66.
Toliver, Harold E. *Marvell's Ironic Vision*. New Haven, 1965.
Wallace, John M. *Destiny his Choice: The Loyalism of Andrew Marvell*. Cambridge, 1968.

DRYDEN

TEXTS

Dryden, John. *Of Dramatic Poesy and Other Critical Essays*, ed. George Watson, 2 vols. London, 1962.
—— *The Letters of John Dryden*, ed. Charles E. Ward. Durham, N.C., 1942.
—— *His Majesties Declaration Defended*, ed. Godfrey Davies. Los Angeles, 1950.
—— *The Poems of John Dryden*, ed. James Kinsley. 4 vols. Oxford, 1958.
—— *The Works of John Dryden*, ed. Sir Walter Scott, rev. by George Saintsbury. 18 vols. Edinburgh, 1882–93.
—— *The Works of John Dryden*, ed. H. T. Swedenberg Jr. *et al*. In progress. Berkeley and Los Angeles, 1956– .

CRITICISM

Benson, Donald R. 'Theology and Politics in Dryden's Conversion', *Studies in English Literature*, IV (1964), 393–412.
Bredvold, Louis I. *The Intellectual Milieu of John Dryden*. Ann Arbor, Mich., 1962. 1st pub. 1934.
Harth, Philip. *Contexts of Dryden's Thought*. Chicago, 1968.
Hoffman, Arthur W. *John Dryden's Imagery*. Gainesville. Fla., 1962.
Hughes, Merritt Y. 'Dryden as a Statist', *PQ*, VI (1927), 335–50.
Kinsley, James. 'Dryden and the Art of Praise', *English Studies*, XXXIV (1953), 57–64.
Levine, Jay Arnold. 'John Dryden's Epistle to John Driden', *JEGP*, LXIII (1964), 450–74.
Long, Ralph Bernard. 'Dryden's Importance as a Spokesman of the Tories', *Univ. of Texas Studies in English* (1941), 79–99.
Macdonald, Hugh. *John Dryden: A Bibliography of Early Editions and of Drydeniana*. Oxford, 1939.
Miner, Earl. 'Dryden and the Issue of Human Progress', *PQ*, XL (1961), 120–9.
—— *Dryden's Poetry*. Bloomington, Ind., 1967.
Moore, John Robert. 'Political Allusions in Dryden's Later Plays', *PMLA*, LXXIII (1958), 36–42.
Roper, Alan. *Dryden's Poetic Kingdoms*. New York, 1965.
—— 'Dryden's Secular Masque', *MLQ*, XXIII (1962), 29–40.
Schilling, Bernard N. *Dryden and the Conservative Myth*. New Haven, 1961.
Scott, Sir Walter. *The Life of John Dryden*, ed. Bernard Kreissman. Lincoln, Neb., 1963.
Sutherland, James. *John Dryden: The Poet as Orator*. Glasgow, 1963.
Swedenberg, H. T., Jr., ed. *Essential Articles for the Study of John Dryden*. Hamden, Conn., 1966.
Ward, Charles E. *The Life of John Dryden*. Chapel Hill, N.C., 1961.

TEXTS

Pope, Alexander. *The Correspondence*, ed. George Sherburn. 5 vols. Oxford, 1956.
—— *The Twickenham Edition of the Poems of Alexander Pope*, ed. John Butt *et al.*
11 vols. New Haven, 1939–69.

CRITICISM

Brower, Reuben A. *Alexander Pope: The Poetry of Allusion*. Oxford, 1963. 1st pub.
1959.
Courthope, William John. *The Life of Alexander Pope*. Vol. v of *The Works of Alexander
Pope*, ed. Whitwell Elwin and W. J. Courthope. London, 1889.
Edwards, Thomas R., Jr. *This Dark Estate: A Reading of Pope*. Berkeley and Los
Angeles, 1963.
Mack, Maynard. *The Garden and the City: Retirement and Politics in the Later Poetry of
Pope, 1731–1743*. Toronto, 1969.
Mack, Maynard, ed. *Essential Articles for the Study of Alexander Pope*. Hamden, Conn.,
1964.
Mahaffey, Kathleen. 'Timon's Villa: Walpole's Houghton', *Texas Studies in Literature
and Language*, IX (1967), 193–222.
Rogers, Robert W. *The Major Satires of Alexander Pope*. Urbana, Ill., 1955.
Sherburn, George. *The Early Career of Alexander Pope*. Oxford, 1934.
Williams, Aubrey L. *Pope's Dunciad: A Study of its Meaning*. London, 1955.

B OTHER PRIMARY SOURCES

Abbott, Wilbur Cortez, ed. *The Writings and Speeches of Oliver Cromwell*. 4 vols.
Cambridge, Mass., 1937–47.
Addison, Joseph. *The Spectator*, ed. Donald F. Bond. 5 vols. Oxford, 1965.
—— *Works*, ed. Richard Hurd. 6 vols. London, 1811.
Arbuthnot, John. *The History of John Bull*. ed. Herman Teerink. Amsterdam, 1925.
Aristotle. *The Nicomachean Ethics*, with trans. by H. Rackham. Cambridge, Mass., 1962.
Ashton, Robert, ed. *James I by his Contemporaries*. London, 1969.
Bacon, Francis. *Essays*. London, 1962.
Baxter, Richard. *Autobiography*, ed. J. M. Lloyd Thomas. London, 1931.
Bodin, Jean. *Six Books of the Commonwealth*, trans. M. J. Tooley. Oxford, 1955.
Boileau. *Oeuvres*, ed. Georges Mongrédien. Paris, 1961.
Bolingbroke, Henry St John, Viscount. *The Idea of a Patriot King*, ed. Sydney W.
Jackman. New York, 1965.
—— *Works*. 4 vols. Philadelphia. 1841.
Bossuet, Jacques-Bénigne. *Politique Tirée des Propres Paroles de l'Ecriture Sainte*, ed.
Jacques Le Brun. Geneva, 1967.
Buckingham, George, Duke of. *The Rehearsal*, ed. Cedric Gale. Great Neck, N.Y., 1960.
Carew, Thomas. *The Poems, with his Masque Coelum Britannicum*, ed. Rhodes Dunlap.
Oxford, 1964. 1st pub. 1949.
Charles II. *The Letters, Speeches, and Declarations*, ed. Arthur Bryant. London, 1968.
1st pub. 1935.
Clarendon, Edward Hyde, Earl of. *Selections from the History of the Rebellion and Civil
Wars and The Life by Himself*, ed. G. Huehns. London, 1955.
Cotton, Charles. *Poems*, ed. John Buxton. London, 1958.

Cowley, Abraham. *Essays, Plays, and Sundry Verses*, ed. A. R. Waller. Cambridge, 1906.

—— *Poems*, ed. A. R. Waller. Cambridge, 1905.

Daniel, Samuel. *The Complete Works in Verse and Prose*, ed. Alexander Grosart. 5 vols. New York, 1963. 1st pub. 1885.

Defoe, Daniel. *A Tour Through England and Wales*, ed. G. D. H. Cole. 2 vols. London, 1928.

Denham, Sir John. *The Poetical Works*, ed. Theodore H. Banks, Jr. New Haven, 1928.

Donne, John. *The Poems*, ed. Herbert Grierson. London, 1960.

Drayton, Michael. *Works*, ed. J. W. Hebel, Bernard Newdigate and Kathleen Tillotson. 5 vols. Oxford, 1961. 1st pub. 1931–41.

Eikon Basilike, ed. Philip A. Knachel. Ithaca, N.Y., 1966.

Evelyn, John. *The Diary*, ed. E. S. de Beer. London, 1959.

Filmer, Sir Robert. *Patriarcha and Other Political Works*, ed. Peter Laslett. Oxford, 1949.

Fuller, Thomas. *The Holy State and the Profane State*, ed. Maximilian Graff Walten. 2 vols. New York, 1938.

Gardiner, Samuel Rawson, ed. *The Constitutional Documents of the Puritan Revolution.* 3rd ed. rev. Oxford, 1906.

Gay, John. *Poetical Works.* ed. G. C. Faber. London, 1926.

Greville, Sir Fulke. *Life of Sir Philip Sidney*, ed. Nowell Smith. Oxford, 1907.

Halifax, George Savile, Marquess of. *The Complete Works*, ed. Walter Raleigh. Oxford, 1912.

Hall, Joseph. *Heaven upon Earth and Characters of Vertues and Vices*, ed. Rudolf Kirk. New Brunswick, N.J., 1948.

Hervey, John Lord. *Memoirs*, ed. Romney Sedgwick. Abridged ed. London, 1952.

Hobbes, Thomas. *Behemoth*, ed. William Molesworth. New York, n.d.

—— *Leviathan*, ed. A. D. Lindsay. London, 1962.

—— *Philosophical Rudiments concerning Government and Society.* Vol. II of *The English Works of Thomas Hobbes of Malmesbury*, ed. William Molesworth. Aalen, 1962.

Hooker, Richard. *Of the Laws of Ecclesiastical Polity.* 2 vols. London, 1965.

Horace. *The Odes and Epodes*, with trans. by C. E. Bennett. London, 1925.

—— *Satires, Epistles, and Ars Poetica*, with trans. by H. Rushton Fairclough. Cambridge, Mass., 1966.

James I. *The Political Works*, ed. C. H. McIlwain. Cambridge, Mass., 1918.

Johnson, Samuel. *Lives of the English Poets.* 2 vols. London, 1954.

—— *Poems*, ed. E. L. McAdam Jr. with George Milne. Vol. VI of *The Yale Edition of the Works of Samuel Johnson.* New Haven, 1964.

Juvenal and Persius. With trans. by G. G. Ramsay. Rev. ed. Cambridge, Mass., 1950.

Lipsius. *Two Bookes of Constancie written in Latin by Iustus Lipsius; Englished by Sir John Stradling*, ed. Rudolf Kirk. New Brunswick, N.J., 1939.

Locke, John. *Two Treatises of Government*, ed. Peter Laslett. Rev. ed. New York, 1965.

Longinus. *On Great Writing* (On the Sublime). Trans. by G. M. A. Grube. New York, 1957.

Louis XIV. *Mémoires*, ed. Jean Longnon. Paris, 1923.

Mandeville, Bernard. *The Fable of the Bees*, ed. F. B. Kaye. 2 vols. Oxford, 1957.

Montaigne, Michel de. *Essais*, ed. Albert Thibaudet. Paris, 1950.

Nichols, John, ed. *The Progresses, and Public Processions, of Queen Elizabeth.* 2 vols. London, 1788.

—— *The Progresses, Processions, and Magnificent Festivities of King James the First.* 4 vols. London, 1828.

The Oxford Book of Seventeenth Century Verse, ed. Herbert Grierson and G. Bullough. Oxford, 1958. 1st pub. 1934.

The Oxford Book of Eighteenth Century Verse, ed. David Nichol Smith. Oxford, 1963. 1st pub. 1926.

Poems on Affairs of State: Augustan Satirical Verse, 1660–1714, ed. George de F. Lord *et al.* In progress. New Haven, 1963– .

Seneca. *Ad Lucilium Epistulae Morales*, with trans. by Richard M. Gummere. 3 vols. London, 1917–25.

—— *Moral Essays*, with trans. by John W. Basore. 3 vols. London, 1928–35.

Sidney, Sir Philip. *The Prose Works*, ed. Albert Feuillerat. 4 vols. Cambridge, 1962. 1st pub. 1912.

Spence, Joseph. *Observations, Anecdotes, and Characters of Books and Men*, ed. James M. Osborn. 2 vols. Oxford, 1966.

Spenser, Edmund. *Works*, ed. Edwin Greenlaw *et al.* 9 vols. Baltimore, 1932–34.

Swift, Jonathan. *Poems*, ed. Harold Williams. 3 vols. 2nd ed. Oxford, 1958.

—— *Prose Works*, ed. Herbert Davis. 14 vols. Oxford, 1957–68.

Thomson, James. *The Complete Poetical Works*, ed. J. Logie Robertson. London, 1963.

Waller, Edmund. *The Poems*, ed. G. Thorn Drury, 2 vols. London, n.d.

Wilkins, W. Walker, ed. *Political Ballads of the Seventeenth and Eighteenth Centuries*. 2 vols. London, 1860.

C SECONDARY WORKS

Arnold, E. V. *Roman Stoicism*. Cambridge, 1911.

Ashley, Maurice. *Charles II: The Man and the Statesman*. London, 1971.

—— *The Greatness of Oliver Cromwell*. London, 1957.

Baker, C. H. Collins, and Baker, Muriel I. *The Life and Circumstances of James Brydges First Duke of Chandos*. Oxford, 1949.

Baxter, Stephen B. *William III and the Defence of European Liberty, 1650–1702*. New York, 1966.

Behrens, B. 'The Whig Theory of the Constitution in the Reign of Charles II', *Cambridge Historical Journal*, VII (1941/3), 42–71.

Bennett, H. S. *English Books and Readers 1558 to 1603*. Cambridge, 1965.

—— *English Books and Readers 1603 to 1640*. Cambridge, 1970.

Benson, Donald R. 'Halifax and the Trimmers', *Huntington Library Quarterly*, XXVII (1963/4), 115–34.

Blunt, Anthony. *Art and Architecture in France 1500 to 1700*. Harmondsworth, 1957.

Boyce, Benjamin. *The Benevolent Man: A Life of Ralph Allen of Bath*. Cambridge, Mass., 1967.

Brett-James, Norman G. *The Growth of Stuart London*. London, 1935.

Brinkley, Roberta Florence. *Arthurian Legend in the Seventeenth Century*. Baltimore, 1932.

Bryant, Arthur. *King Charles II*. Rev. ed. London, 1955.

Caspari, Fritz. *Humanism and the Social Order in Tudor England*. Chicago, 1954.

Chambers, E. K. *The Elizabethan Stage*. 4 vols. Oxford, 1923.

Chernaik, Warren L. *The Poetry of Limitation*. New Haven, 1968.

Clifford, James L. *Young Sam Johnson*. New York, 1955.

Commager, Steele. *The Odes of Horace*. New Haven, 1962.

Crisis in Europe, 1560–1660, ed. Trevor Aston. New York, 1965.

Cruttwell, Patrick. *The Shakespearean Moment and its Place in the Poetry of the Seventeenth Century*. London, 1954.

D'Alton, J. F. *Horace and his Age*. New York, 1962. 1st pub. 1917.

Danby, John F. *Elizabethan and Jacobean Poets*. London, 1964. 1st pub. 1952 as *Poets on Fortune's Hill*.

Davies, Godfrey, *The Early Stuarts, 1603–1660*. 2nd ed. Oxford, 1959.

—— *The Restoration of Charles II, 1658–1660*. San Marino, Calif., 1955.

Dobrée, Bonamy. 'The Theme of Patriotism in the Poetry of the Early Eighteenth Century', *Proceedings of the British Academy*, xxxv (1949), 49–65.

Ehrenpreis, Irvin. *Swift: The Man, his Works, and the Age*. 2 vols. In progress. Cambridge, Mass., 1962–7.

Elton, G. R. *England under the Tudors*. London, 1963. 1st pub. 1955.

—— *The Tudor Constitution: Documents and Commentary*. Cambridge, 1965. 1st pub. 1960.

Essays in English Literature from the Renaissance to the Victorian Age, ed. Millar MacLure and F. W. Watt. Toronto, 1964.

Feiling, Keith. *A History of the Tory Party, 1640–1714*. Oxford, 1959. 1st pub. 1924.

—— *The Second Tory Party, 1714–1832*. London, 1959. 1st pub. 1938.

Fink, Zera S. *The Classical Republicans: An Essay in the Recovery of a Pattern of Thought in Seventeenth-Century England*. Evanston, Ill., 1945.

Fisher, F. J. 'The Development of London as a Centre of Conspicuous Consumption in the Sixteenth and Seventeenth Centuries', *Transactions of the Royal Historical Society*, Fourth Series, xxx (1948), 37–50.

Foxcroft, H. C. *A Character of the Trimmer: Being a Short Life of the First Marquis of Halifax*. Cambridge, 1946.

Fraenkel, Eduard. *Horace*. Oxford, 1959.

Gibb. M. A. *The Lord General: A Life of Thomas Fairfax*. London, 1938.

Greene, Donald J. *The Politics of Samuel Johnson*. New Haven, 1960.

Greenleaf, W. H. *Order, Empiricism and Politics: Two Traditions of English Political Thought 1500–1700*. Oxford, 1964.

Habakkuk, H. J. 'English Landownership, 1680–1740', *Economic History Review*, x (1939/40), 2–17.

Haley, K. H. D. *The First Earl of Shaftesbury*. Oxford, 1968.

—— *William of Orange and the English Opposition, 1672–4*. Oxford, 1953.

Haller, William. *The Rise of Puritanism*. New York, 1957. 1st pub. 1938.

Hautecoeur, Louis. *Louis XIV, Roi-Soleil*. Paris, 1953.

Heckscher, Eli F. *Mercantilism*, trans. Mendel Shapiro. 2 vols. London, 1934.

Hexter, J. H. *Reappraisals in History*. London, 1967. 1st pub. 1961.

—— *The Reign of King Pym*. Cambridge, Mass., 1961. 1st pub. 1941.

Hill, Christopher. *God's Englishman: Oliver Cromwell and the English Revolution*. London, 1970.

Holmes, Geoffrey. *British Politics in the Age of Anne*. London, 1967.

Holmes, Geoffrey, ed. *Britain after the Glorious Revolution, 1689–1714*. London, 1969.

Holmes, Geoffrey, and Speck, W. A. *The Divided Society: Party Conflict in England, 1694–1716*. London, 1967.

Hussey, Christopher. *English Country Houses: Early Georgian, 1715–1760*. Rev. ed. London, 1965.

Jones, J. R. *The First Whigs: The Politics of the Exclusion Crisis, 1678–1683*. London, 1961.

Judson, Margaret Atwood. *The Crisis of the Constitution: An Essay in Constitutional and Political Thought in England 1603–1645*. New Brunswick, N.J., 1949.

Kantorowicz, Ernst H. *The King's Two Bodies: A Study in Mediaeval Political Theology*. Princeton, N.J., 1957.

Kelso, Ruth. *The Doctrine of the English Gentleman in the Sixteenth Century*. Urbana, Ill., 1929.

Kenyon, J. P. *The Stuart Constitution 1603–1688: Documents and Commentary*. Cambridge, 1966.

Kernan, Alvin. *The Cankered Muse: Satire of the English Renaissance*. New Haven, 1959.

Kimball, Fiske. 'Burlington Architectus', *Journal of the Royal Institute of British Architects*, 3rd Series, XXXIV (1927), 675–93.

Knights, L. C. *Drama and Society in the Age of Jonson*. London, 1962. 1st pub. 1937.

—— 'On the Social Background of Metaphysical Poetry', *Scrutiny*, XIII (1945), 37–52.

Kramnick, Isaac. *Bolingbroke and his Circle: The Politics of Nostalgia in the Age of Walpole*. Cambridge, Mass., 1968.

Lovejoy, Arthur O. *The Great Chain of Being*. New York, 1960. 1st pub. 1936.

Macaulay, Thomas Babington. *History of England from the Accession of James II*. 4 vols. London, 1957. 1st pub. 1848–61.

McEuen, Kathryn Anderson. *Classical Influence upon the Tribe of Ben*. Cedar Rapids, Iowa, 1939.

Mathew, David. *The Jacobean Age*. London, 1938.

Metaphysical Poetry, ed. Malcolm Bradbury and D. J. Palmer. London, 1970.

Miller, E. H. *The Professional Writer in Elizabethan England*. Cambridge, Mass., 1959.

Mingay, G. E. *English Landed Society in the Eighteenth Century*. London, 1963.

Namier, Lewis. *England in the Age of the American Revolution*. 2nd ed. London, 1963.

—— *Personalities and Powers*. London, 1955.

—— *The Structure of Politics at the Accession of George III*. 2nd ed. London, 1957.

Nevo, Ruth. *The Dial of Virtue: A Study of Poems on Affairs of State in the Seventeenth Century*. Princeton, N.J., 1963.

Ogg, David. *England in the Reign of Charles II*. 2 vols. 2nd ed. London, 1956.

—— *England in the Reigns of James II and William III*. Oxford, 1955.

Palme, Per. *Triumph of Peace: A Study of the Whitehall Banqueting House*. Stockholm, 1956.

Paul, Robert S. *The Lord Protector: Religion and Politics in the Life of Oliver Cromwell*. London, 1955.

Plumb, J. H. *The Origins of Political Stability: England, 1675–1725*. Boston, 1967.

Pocock, J. G. A. 'Machiavelli, Harrington, and English Political Ideologies in the Eighteenth Century'. *William and Mary Quarterly*, 3rd Series, XXII (1965), 549–83.

Pollock, John. *The Popish Plot*. London, 1903.

Restoration and Eighteenth-Century Literature, ed. Carroll Camden. Chicago, Ill., 1963.

Reyher, Paul. *Les Masques Anglais*. New York, 1964. 1st pub. 1909.

Roberts, Clayton. *The Growth of Responsible Government in Stuart England*. Cambridge, 1966.

Robbins, Caroline. *The Eighteenth-Century Commonwealthman*. Cambridge, Mass., 1959.

Rosenberg, Eleanor. *Leicester, Patron of Letters*. New York, 1955.

Rostovtzeff, M. *The Social and Economic History of the Roman Empire*. 2 vols. 2nd ed. rev. by P. M. Fraser. Oxford, 1957.

Røstvig, Maren-Sofie. *The Happy Man: Studies in the Metamorphoses of a Classical Ideal.* 2 vols. Oslo, 1954–8.

Saunders, Jason Lewis. *Justus Lipsius: The Philosophy of Renaissance Stoicism.* New York, 1955.

Scoular, Kitty W. *Natural Magic: Studies in the Presentation of Nature in English Poetry from Spenser to Marvell.* Oxford, 1965.

Stone, Lawrence. *The Crisis of the Aristocracy, 1558–1641.* Oxford, 1965.

—— *Social Change and Revolution in England 1540–1640.* London, 1965.

Strong, Roy. *The English Icon: Elizabethan and Jacobean Portraiture.* London, 1969.

—— *Portraits of Queen Elizabeth I.* Oxford, 1963.

Summerson, John. *Architecture in Britain, 1530 to 1830.* London, 1953.

—— 'The Classical Country House in Eighteenth-Century England', *Journal of the Royal Society of Arts* (1959), 539–87.

—— *Inigo Jones.* Harmondsworth, Middx., 1966.

Tawney, R. H. *The Agrarian Problem in the Sixteenth Century.* New York, n.d. 1st pub. 1912.

—— *Religion and the Rise of Capitalism.* Harmondsworth, Middx., 1938. 1st pub. 1926.

—— 'The Rise of the Gentry 1558–1640', *Economic History Review*, XI (1941), 1–38.

Thomson, Patricia. 'The Literature of Patronage, 1580–1630', *Essays in Criticism*, II (1952), 267–84.

Tillyard, E. M. W. *The Elizabethan World Picture.* London, 1956. 1st pub. 1943.

Tipping, H. Avray. *English Homes.* Period III, vol. II: *Late Tudor and Early Stuart.* London, 1927. Period IV, vol. II: *The Work of Sir John Vanbrugh and his School,* with Christopher Hussey. London, 1928. Period V, vol. I: *Early Georgian.* London, 1921.

Trevelyan, G. M. *England under Queen Anne.* 3 vols. London, 1930–4.

Trevor-Roper, H. R. *The Gentry, 1540–1640. Economic History Review* Supplement I (1953).

—— *Historical Essays.* London, 1963. 1st pub. 1957.

Trickett, Rachel. *The Honest Muse: A Study in Augustan Verse.* Oxford, 1967.

Turner, F. C. *James II,* London, 1948.

Vickers, Brian, ed. *The World of Jonathan Swift.* Oxford, 1968.

Walcott, Robert, Jr. *English Politics in the Early Eighteenth Century.* Cambridge, Mass., 1956.

Walton, Geoffrey. *Metaphysical to Augustan.* London, 1955.

Ward, W. R. *The English Land Tax in the Eighteenth Century.* London, 1953.

Wasserman, Earl R. *The Subtler Language: Critical Readings of Neoclassic and Romantic Poems.* Baltimore, 1959.

Wedgwood, C. V. *Poetry and Politics under the Stuarts.* Cambridge, 1960.

Welsford, Enid. *The Court Masque.* New York, 1962. 1st pub. 1927.

Willey, Basil. *The Seventeenth Century Background.* London, 1934.

—— *The Eighteenth Century Background.* London, 1940.

Willson, David Harris. *King James VI and I.* London, 1962. 1st pub. 1956.

Wilson, Elkin Calhoun. *England's Eliza.* Cambridge, Mass., 1939.

Wittkower, Rudolf. *Architectural Principles in the Age of Humanism.* New York, 1965. 1st pub. 1949.

Wolf, John B. *Louis XIV.* New York, 1968.

Wormald, B. H. G. *Clarendon: Politics, Historiography and Religion, 1640–1660.* Cambridge, 1964. 1st pub. 1951.

Wormuth, Francis D. *The Royal Prerogative, 1603–1649*. Ithaca, N.Y., 1939.
Young, Frances Berkeley. *Mary Sidney Countess of Pembroke*. London, 1912.
Zagorin, Perez. *The Court and the Country: The Beginning of the English Revolution*. London, 1969.
—— *A History of Political Thought in the English Revolution*. London, 1954.
Zanta, Léontine. *La Renaissance du Stoicisme au XVIe Siècle*. Paris, 1914.

Chronology

This chronology lists for the convenience of the reader most of the works and significant historical events discussed in the book, and the main events in the lives of the five authors. It is not a complete record of their works. The following abbreviations are used: J: Jonson; JM: Milton; AM: Marvell; D: Dryden; P: Pope.

Private Events	Writings, Performances, and Publications	Public Events
1572 J born.		
1588 ? J leaves Westminster School.		
1593	Hooker: *Ecclesiastical Polity* I–IV pub. Sidney: *Arcadia* pub.	
1596	Spenser: *Faerie Queene* pub.	
1597 (*c.*) J actor and playwright for Henslowe.		
1598	J: *Every Man in his Humour* acted. James VI: *True Law of Free Monarchies* pub.	
1599 Death of Spenser.	J: *Every Man out of his Humour* acted. James VI: *Basilikon Doron* pub.	
1601	J: *Cynthia's Revels*, *Poetaster* acted.	
1602 (*c.*) J lives with Lord Aubigny for 5 years.		
1603	J: Ent. at Althorpe, *Sejanus* acted. Daniel: *Certain Epistles* pub.	Death of Elizabeth, accession of James I.
1604	J: King's coronation ent., *Penates* acted. Daniel: *Vision of Twelve Goddesses*.	

Private Events	Writings, etc.	Public Events
1605 J imprisoned over *Eastward Ho*; though Catholic gives information on plot.	J: *Masque of Blackness, Volpone* acted.	Gunpowder Plot.
1606 J friendship with Sidney family and Lucy Harrington during these years.	J: *Hymenaei*, for marriage of Essex and Frances Howard; ent. of King of Denmark at Theobalds.	
1608 JM born.	J: *Masque of Beauty, Haddington* acted.	
1609	J: *Masque of Queens* acted.	
1610	J: *Prince Henry's Barriers, The Alchemist* acted. Daniel: *Tethys' Festival.* Greville: *Life of Sidney* written? (pub. 1652).	
1611	J: *Oberon, Love Freed from Ignorance, Catiline* acted.	
1612 J in France with Raleigh's son (to 1613).	J: *Love Restored* acted. Drayton: *Polyolbion* pub. (II 1622).	Death of Prince Henry.
1613	J: *Irish Masque & Challenge at Tilt* (Dec–Jan 1614) for marriage of Somerset and Frances Howard.	Marriage of Elizabeth to Elector Palatine.
1614	J: *Bartholomew Fair* acted.	
1615 JM at St Paul's?	J: *Golden Age Restored* acted.	
1616 Death of Shakespeare. J writes no plays for 9 years; yearly pension of 100 marks from James.	J: *Mercury Vindicated, The Devil is an Ass, Christmas* acted; folio *Works* pub. James I: *Works* pub.	
1617 J working on epic?	J: *Vision of Delight, Lovers made Men* acted.	
1618 J's journey to Scotland, visit to Drummond.	J: *Pleasure Reconciled to Virtue, For the Honour of Wales* acted.	Beginning of Thirty Years' War on continent.
1619 J made Oxford M.A.		
1620	J: *News from the New World, Pan's Anniversary* acted.	Strong anti-Spanish feeling. Voyage of Mayflower to New England.
1621 AM born.	J: *Gypsies Metamorphosed* acted.	Parliament impeaches monopolists and Bacon.
1622	J: *Masque of Augurs* acted.	Inigo Jones' Banqueting House completed.

Private Events	Writings, etc.	Public Events
1623 J loses many mss in fire.	J: *Time Vindicated* acted; *Execration upon Vulcan* written.	Charles and Buckingham in Spain to arrange marriage.
1624	J: *Neptune's Triumph* (for Charles' return) written; *Masque of Owls* acted.	Buckingham now anti-Spain.
1625 J loses favour at new reign. JM at Cambridge.	J: *The Fortunate Isles* acted.	Death of James I. Accession of Charles I and marriage to Henrietta Maria.
1626 J returns to drama.	J: *Staple of News* acted.	
1627	Drayton: *Elegies* pub.	
1628 J paralysed. JM prolusions delivered *c.* 1628–32.		Petition of Right. Murder of Buckingham. Laud Bishop of London.
1629 Controversy over reception of *New Inn*. JM takes B.A.	J: *The New Inn* acted. JM: *Elegy* VI to Diodati, *Nativity Ode* written.	Charles I rules without parliament to 1640.
1630 Charles increases J's pension.	JM: *Arcades* acted?	Much emigration to New England.
1631 J's quarrel with Inigo Jones. D born.	J: *Love's Triumph through Callipolis, Chloridia* (J's last court masque) acted. JM: *L'Allegro* and *Il Penseroso* (?), sonnet VII written.	Laud plans to rebuild St Paul's.
1632 JM takes M.A. and retires to father's house.	J: *The Magnetic Lady* acted. JM: 'Letter to a friend', *Ad Patrem* written?	
1633 AM at Cambridge.	J: *Tale of a Tub* (attacks Jones), Ent. at Welbeck acted.	Laud Archbishop of Canterbury.
1634 End of J's public career.	J: *Love's Welcome at Bolsover* acted. Carew: *Coelum Brittanicum* acted. JM: *Comus* acted.	
1635		Ship money levied.
1637 Death of J.	JM: *Comus* pub., *Lycidas* written.	
1638 JM's journey to France, Italy, and Switzerland, till mid 1639.	*Jonsonus Virbius* pub. on death of J. *Lycidas* pub. in *Justa Edouardo King Naufrago*.	
1639 AM takes M.A. JM thinking about epic.	JM: *Mansus*(?), *Epitaphium Damonis* written.	First Bishops' War.

Private Events	Writings, etc.	Public Events
1640 JM tutoring in London, thinking about tragedy, studying history and doctrine.	J: 2nd folio *Works* pub., ed. Kenelm Digby. Carew: *Poems* pub.	Second Bishops' War. Beginning of Long Parliament. Impeachment of Strafford and Laud.
1641 AM leaves Cambridge.	JM: *Of Reformation, Of Prelatical Episcopacy, Animadversions* pub.	Episcopal controversy. Effective end of bishops' power.
1642 JM's 1st marriage. AM probably travelling in Holland, France, Italy, Spain, till *c.* 1648.	JM: *Reason of Church Government, Apology for Smectymnuus* pub. Denham: *Cooper's Hill* pub.	Charles I leaves London; 1st Civil War begins. Theatres closed.
1643	JM: *Doctrine and Discipline of Divorce* pub.	Order for licensing press. Westminster Assembly meets.
1644 JM's divorce books attacked.	JM: *Of Education, Judgement of Martin Bucer, Areopagitica* pub.	Toleration controversy.
1645	JM: *Tetrachordon, Colasterion* pub.	Laud executed.
1646 D at Westminster School. Hyde begins writing history.	JM: *Poems 1645* pub.; Sonnet 'On the New Forcers of Conscience' written?	End of 1st Civil War.
1648 AM back from abroad?	JM: Sonnet to Fairfax, *Character of Long Parliament* written? (pub. 1681).	2nd Civil War. Royalists and Scots defeated. Pride's Purge.
1649 JM appointed Secretary for Foreign Tongues to Council of State.	JM: *Tenure of Kings and Magistrates, Eikonoklastes* (answer to *Eikon Basilike*) pub. Lovelace: *Lucasta* pub. (with poem by AM); *Lachrymae Musarum* (contributions by AM and D). Salmasius' *Defensio Regia* in England.	Execution of Charles I. Government by Council and Rump. Cromwell in Ireland (to 1650).
1650 D at Cambridge.	AM: 'Horatian Ode' written.	Resignation of Fairfax. Charles II recognized in Scotland; Cromwell defeats Scots.
1651 AM tutor to Mary Fairfax. JM licensing *Mercurius Politicus*.	JM: *Defensio pro Populo Anglicano* pub. Hobbes: *Leviathan* pub.	Charles II crowned in Scotland but defeated at Worcester; escapes to France.
1652 JM totally blind; death of 1st wife.	Filmer: *Observations* (attacks JM). JM: Sonnets to	Committee considering state church. Disagreement between army

Private Events	Writings, etc.	Public Events
	Cromwell, 'When I consider' written. AM: *Appleton House* and *Upon the Hill and Grove* prob. written during these years. Du Moulin: *Regii Sanguinis Clamor* pub.	leaders and parliament. Dutch war.
1653 AM leaves Fairfaxes; JM writes to Bradshaw on his behalf. AM tutor to Dutton, Cromwell's ward.		Cromwell dissolves Rump. Military rule. Barebones Parliament. Cromwell Protector under Instrument of Government.
1654 D takes B.A.	JM: *Defensio Secunda* pub. AM: *1st Anniversary* written.	1st Protectorate Parliament.
1655 JM working on *Christian Doctrine* (late 1650s).	JM: sonnets to C. Skinner written? AM: *1st Anniversary* pub. Waller: *Panegyric to my Lord Protector* pub.	Rule of major-generals. Fifth monarchist agitation.
1656 JM's 2nd marriage.	Cowley: *Poems* (including odes) pub.	2nd Protectorate Parliament (to 1658). Cromwell asked to take crown by parliament; refuses because of army pressure. Protectorate reconstituted; creation of upper house.
1657 AM assistant secretary with JM.		
1658 JM begins *Paradise Lost* about now; 2nd wife dies. JM, AM (and D?) in Cromwell's funeral procession. (D possibly held minor office under Protectorate.)	AM: *Death of OC* written.	Death of Cromwell; succeeded by son Richard.
1659 AM M.P. for Hull (till 1678).	Waller, D, Sprat: *Three Poems upon the Death of Oliver* pub. JM: *Treatise of Civil Power, Considerations touching Hirelings* pub.	Richard abdicates. Army and Rump rule. Uncertainty about future of government.
1660 JM loses position, money; goes into hiding; regicide books burned; not excluded from Act of Indemnity; arrested and	JM: *Ready and Easy Way* (2 editions) pub. D: *Astraea Redux* pub. Waller: *To the King* pub.	Monk restores excluded members of Long Parliament. Declaration of Breda. Convention Parliament votes Charles

263

Private Events	Writings, etc.	Public Events
released. AM protests on his behalf in Commons.		II's Restoration. Act of Indemnity. Reopening of theatres.
1661		Cavalier Parliament (to 1679). Coronation of Charles II.
1662		Act of Uniformity. Charles marries Catherine of Braganza. Royal Society chartered.
1663 JM's 3rd marriage. AM on diplomatic work in Russia, Sweden, Denmark (to 1664). D elected member of Royal Society; marries; begins to write for stage.	D: *To Dr. Charleton* pub.	
1664	D and Howard: *The Indian Queen* (1st heroic rhyming play) acted.	
1665 JM moves to Bucks because of plague; D to Wilts. Thos. Ellwood reads complete mss of *Paradise Lost*.	D: *Indian Emperor* acted. Waller: *Instructions to a Painter* pub.	Second Dutch War. Naval battle at Lowestoft. Plague. Theatres closed (till Nov. 1666).
1666	AM (?): *Second Advice to a Painter, Third Advice to a Painter* pub.	Fire of London.
1667 Death of Cowley. Swift born.	JM: *Paradise Lost* pub. D: *Annus Mirabilis* pub. AM: *Last Instructions to a Painter* written.	Dutch in the Medway. End of Second Dutch War. Clarendon goes into exile.
1668 D Poet Laureate (salary £200 p.a., never paid in full); contracted to Theatre Royal.	D: *An Essay of Dramatic Poesy* pub. Cowley: *Works* (*Essays* 1st pub.).	Triple Alliance (England, Holland, Sweden). Building of Versailles begins.
1669	D: *Tyrannic Love* acted.	
1670 D Historiographer Royal.	JM: *History of Britain* pub. (written 1640s). D: *Conquest of Granada* I acted; *Tyrannic Love* pub., ded. to Monmouth.	Secret Treaty of Dover. The Cabal.
1671	JM: *Paradise Regained* and *Samson Agonistes* pub. AM: *Further Advice to a Painter* written.	

Private Events	Writings, etc.	Public Events
	D: *Conquest of Granada* II acted.	
	Buckingham: *The Rehearsal* acted.	
1672 Theatre Royal (in which D shareholder) burned; D thinking of epic.	AM: *Rehearsal Transprosed* pub. D: *Conquest of Granada* pub., ded. to Duke of York, with *Of Heroic Plays*.	Stop of Exchequer. Declaration of Indulgence. Third Dutch War. Shaftesbury Chancellor.
1673 ?D visits JM, intending to turn *Paradise Lost* into opera.	JM: *Of True Religion* pub. AM: *Rehearsal Transprosed* II pub. (defends JM).	Declaration of Indulgence withdrawn. Test Act. Duke of York resigns offices. Country party forming. Shaftesbury in opposition.
1674 Death of JM. ?AM acting as Dutch agent.	JM: 2nd ed. *Paradise Lost* pub. (with poem by AM). ?Ayloffe: *Britannia and Raleigh* written (or 1675).	End of Third Dutch War. Buckingham joins opposition.
1675	D: *Aureng-Zebe* acted.	
1676 Rochester's satire on D circulating.	D: *Aureng-Zebe* pub., ded. to Mulgrave. AM: *Mr Smirke* pub.	
1677 D no longer contemplating epic? Salary (in theory) increased to £300.	AM: *The Growth of Popery* pub. D: *The State of Innocence* pub. (based on *Paradise Lost*), with *Apology for Heroic Poetry*.	
1678 Death of AM. D ends relation with Theatre Royal.	D: *All for Love* pub., ded. to Danby.	Popish Plot. Danby impeached.
1679 Tonson becomes D's publisher.	D: *Troilus and Cressida* pub., ded. to Sunderland. Bossuet: *Politique* begun.	Danby in Tower. End of Cavalier Parliament. 1st Exclusion Parliament (dissolved July). 2nd Exclusion Parliament (to 1681).
1680	D: *Spanish Friar* acted; Prologue to Tate's *Loyal General* pub. Filmer: *Patriarcha* pub.	Duke of York indicted by Shaftesbury. 2nd Exclusion Bill defeated in Lords. Monmouth's progress in west.
1681	D: Epilogue at Oxford, *His Majesty's Declaration Defended* (June), *Absalom and Achitophel* (Nov.) pub.	Shaftesbury proposes Monmouth as heir. Oxford Parliament (last of Charles' reign) dis-

265

Private Events	Writings, etc.	Public Events
	JM: *Character of Long Parliament* pub. (written late 1640s). AM: *Miscellaneous Poems* pub. (mainly lyrics). L'Estrange: *Observator*.	solved (March). Charles' Declaration (April). Anti-Whig reaction. Shaftesbury in Tower (July); treason charge thrown out (Nov.).
1682 Several Whig attacks on D. Two theatre companies join.	D: Prologue to Banks' *Unhappy Favourite*, Prologue to Southerne's *Loyal Brother*, *The Medal*, *MacFlecknoe*, *Absalom and Achitophel* II (with Tate), *Religio Laici* pub.; (with Lee) *Duke of Guise* acted. Settle: *Absalom Senior* pub.	Medal struck in Shaftesbury's honour by Whigs. Shaftesbury flees to Holland.
1683 D pleads for salary to be paid.	D: *Vindication of the Duke of Guise* pub.	Death of Shaftesbury. Rye House Plot. 'The Stuart revenge.'
1684	D: trans. of Maimbourg's *History of the League*, with Postscript, pub.; *To the Earl of Roscommon* pub.	
1685 D converted to Catholicism.	D: *Threnodia Augustalis* pub.; *Albion and Albanius* acted.	Death of Charles II, accession of James II. Monmouth rebellion. Halifax dismissed.
1686 Part of arrears on D's salary under Charles paid; salary under James paid regularly.		Catholics widely appointed to office.
1687	D: *The Hind and the Panther* pub.	
1688 P born.	D: *Britannia Rediviva* pub. Halifax: *The Character of a Trimmer* pub. (circulated in ms 1684–5).	Declaration of Indulgence. Birth of James the Old Pretender. Landing of William of Orange. Flight of James II.
1689 D non-juror, loses posts of laureate and historiographer, returns to drama. Shadwell laureate.	D: *Don Sebastian* acted. Cotton: *Poems on Several Occasions* pub.	Convention Parliament. William and Mary accept crown. Toleration Act relieves Protestants of persecution; restrictions on Catholics. War of League of Augsburg.
1690	D: *Amphitryon* pub. Locke: *Two Treatises of*	William III defeats James II in Ireland.

Private Events	Writings, etc.	Public Events
	Government pub. (written 1679–83).	
1691 D beginning to con- centrate on translation.	D (and Purcell): *King Arthur* perf. and pub., ded. to Halifax.	
1692 Tate laureate on death of Shadwell; Rymer historiographer.	D: *Eleonora* pub.; *Cleomenes* acted in spite of inter- ference by Queen Mary.	
1693 Beginning of D's plan to translate Virgil.	D: trans. of *Juvenal* (with others) and *Persius*, with *Discourse concerning Satire*.	
1694 D abandons stage and makes living as trans- lator.	D: *To Mr Congreve, Love Triumphant* (his last play) pub.	Bank of England founded. Death of Queen Mary.
1695		End of licensing.
1697	D: trans. of *Virgil* pub.; *Aeneid* ded. to Normanby.	Treaty of Ryswick; peace with France.
1698 Collier and Milbourne attack D.	JM: *Prose Works* ed. Toland.	
1700 Death of D. P's family move to Binfield about now. P's education mostly private. Begin- ning of his ill health.	D: *Fables* pub., with *To my Honoured Kinsman*; *The Secular Masque* pub. Pomfret: *The Choice* pub.	
1701	D: *Collected Poems* and *Plays* pub. Addison: *Letter from Italy* written.	Grand Alliance against France. Death of James II. Old Pretender recog- nized by Louis XIV. Act of Settlement.
1702	Clarendon: *History of the Rebellion* pub. (to 1704; begun 1646).	Death of William III, accession of Anne. Tory government. Beginning of War of Spanish Suc- cession.
1704	Swift: *Tale of a Tub* pub.	Battle of Blenheim. Harley and St John in government.
1705 P begins to know Lon- don literary men, old friends of D, e.g. Wycherley, Congreve.		Building of Blenheim palace begins.
1706 Tonson seeks to publish P's *Pastorals*.		
1708		Harley and St John resign. Whigs dominate government.

Private Events	Writings, etc.	Public Events
1709 Sam. Johnson born.	P: *Pastorals* pub.	
1710	Swift: *The Examiner* (to 1711).	Trial of Sacheverell. Fall of Whigs; Tory triumph.
1711 P friendship with Steele and Addison (to 1713); contributes to *Spectator*.	P: *Essay on Criticism* pub. Swift: *Conduct of the Allies* pub. Addison (and others): *Spectator* (to 1712).	Marlborough dismissed. Land Qualification Act.
1712 P friendship with Gay, Swift, Arbuthnot, Parnell (Scriblerus Club); also with Oxford and Bolingbroke.	Arbuthnot: *John Bull* pub. Swift: *Advice to the October Club* pub.	
1713 P contributes to Steele's *Guardian*. P's proposals to translate *Iliad*.	P: *Windsor Forest* pub. Addison: *Cato* acted (Prologue by P).	Treaty of Utrecht; end of War of Spanish Succession.
1714 Scriblerus Club ceases to meet.	P: *Rape of the Lock* (enlarged version) pub. Mandeville: *Fable of the Bees* pub. (II 1729).	Death of Anne, accession of George I. Fall of Tories, Whigs in office.
1715 Hostility between P and Addison's circle.	P: trans. of *Iliad*, vol. I, pub.	Oxford in Tower, Bolingbroke joins Pretender. Jacobite rebellion.
1716 P family sell Binfield house (?to avoid anti-Catholic taxation), move to Chiswick (near Burlington).	P: *Iliad* II.	
1717 Death of P's father. Dennis attacks P's Homer.	P: *Iliad* III, 1st vol. of *Collected Works* pub. Bolingbroke: *Letter to Sir William Wyndham* written. Gay, Arbuthnot, P: *Three Hours after Marriage* acted.	Walpole in opposition.
1718 P and mother move to Twickenham; life to 1723 relatively peaceful. In next 10 years P spends much time on garden.	P: *Iliad* IV.	
1719 Death of Addison.		
1720	P: *Iliad* V & VI.	South Sea Bubble. Walpole in power.
1721 P begins work on edition of Shakespeare.	P: *Epistle to Oxford* pub.	
1723 P testifies for Atterbury at trial; begins trans. of	P's edition of *Works* of Sheffield, Duke of Bucking-	Bishop Atterbury (Jacobite) tried for treason

Odyssey (half of trans. by Broome and Fenton).	hamshire (Jacobite) pub. and temporarily suppressed.	and exiled.
1724	Defoe: *Tour through Great Britain* I pub. (II 1726).	
1725 P begins work on *Dunciad*.	P's edition of Shakespeare pub.; trans. of *Odyssey* I–III pub.	Bolingbroke's return from exile (barred from office); settles at Dawley, Uxbridge; becomes leader of opposition to to Walpole.
1726 Swift visits P. ?P's friendship with Spence begins.	P: *Odyssey* IV–V. Swift: *Gulliver's Travels* pub. Theobald: *Shakespeare Restored* pub., criticises P. Bolingbroke (and others): *The Craftsman* (to 1750).	
1727 Swift visits P again.	P–Swift *Miscellanies* pub. (several vols. to 1735). Gay: *Fables* pub. (2nd series 1738).	Death of George I, accession of George II. Walpole confirmed in office.
1728 Spence collects materials for life of P.	P: Three-book *Dunciad* pub. Gay: *Beggar's Opera* acted.	
1729	P: *Dunciad Variorum* pub.	
1730 P planning ethic scheme; Spence's notes. Cibber laureate.		
1731	P: *Epistle to Burlington* pub.	
1732 Death of Gay.		
1733 Death of P's mother.	P: *Epistle to Bathurst*, 1st *Imitation of Horace* (*Sat.* II i), *Essay on Man* I–III pub. Bolingbroke: *Dissertation upon Parties* pub. in *Craftsman* (to 1734). Swift: *On Poetry* pub.	Walpole's excise scheme defeated.
1734 P does no further work on ethic scheme.	P: *Epistle to Cobham*, *Essay on Man* IV, *Imitation of Horace* (*Sat.* II ii). pub.	Opposition fail to obtain repeal of Septennial Act.
1735 Death of Arbuthnot.	P: *Epistle to Dr Arbuthnot*, *Of the Characters of Women* pub. Curll's ed. of P's *Letters*. Thomson: *Liberty* pub. (to 1736).	Bolingbroke leaves England again. Frederick Prince of Wales becomes centre of opposition and 'boy patriots'.
1736 P's friendship with Allen.	P: *Bounce to Fop* pub. Bolingbroke: *Letter on the Spirit of Patriotism* written (pub. 1749).	

Private Events	Writings, etc.	Public Events
1737	P: *Imitations of Horace* (*Ep.* II ii, II i), *Letters* (P's ed.) pub. M. Green: *The Spleen* pub.	
1738	P: *Imitations of Horace* (*Ep.* I vi, I i), *Epilogue to the Satires* pub. Gay: *Fables* (2nd series) pub. Johnson: *London* pub. Bolingbroke: *Idea of a Patriot King* written (or 1739; pub. 1749).	Bolingbroke back in England (and in 1742 and 1743).
1739 P receives ms of *Patriot King* about now.	Swift: *Verses on the Death of Dr Swift* pub.	War with Spain.
1740 P's friendship with Warburton begins.	P: *1740* written. Thomson: *Alfred* acted.	
1742	P: *New Dunciad* (Bk IV) pub.	Fall of Walpole. Some old patriots join Newcastle administration.
1743 P working with Warburton on edition of works, thinking about epic on Brutus.	P: revised *Dunciad* in IV books pub. (Cibber hero instead of Theobald).	
1744 Death of P.	P: *Epistles to Several Persons* pub. privately with ethic scheme described.	
1745 Death of Swift.		
1749	Johnson: *Vanity of Human Wishes* pub.	
1751 Death of Bolingbroke.		

Index

273

279